C 1

Heath, Jennifer.

The scimitar and the
veil.

DATE			

DISCARDED

The Scimitar and the Veil
Extraordinary Women of Islam

Also by Jennifer Heath
(not published by HiddenSpring)

THE ECHOING GREEN:
THE GARDEN IN MYTH AND MEMORY

ON THE EDGE OF DREAM:
THE WOMEN OF CELTIC MYTH AND LEGEND

BLACK VELVET:
THE ART WE LOVE TO HATE

A HOUSE WHITE WITH SORROW:
A BALLAD FOR AFGHANISTAN

The Scimitar and the Veil
Extraordinary Women of Islam

Jennifer Heath

HiddenSpring

Jacket design by Amy C. King

Jacket image: Ladies Preparing a Picnic in the Country. Miniature from Amir Husrau Dihlavi, Hamsa, Iran, c. 1575. Bodleian Library, Oxford, MS. Elliott 189, f. 192 r.

Text design by Lynn Else

Library of Congress Cataloging-in-Publication Data

Heath, Jennifer.
   The scimitar and the veil : extraordinary women of Islam / Jennifer Heath.
      p. cm.
   Includes bibliographical references.
   ISBN 1-58768-020-3 (alk. paper)
   1. Muslim women—Biography. I. Title.
   BP73.H43 2003
   297′.092′2—dc22

                                                                  2003023780

Published by
HiddenSpring
an imprint of Paulist Press
997 Macarthur Boulevard
Mahwah, New Jersey 07430

www.hiddenspringbooks.com

Printed and bound in the United States of America

For

Marda Kirn
Ghada Elturk
Shireen Malik
Nadia Leggett Abouraya
and
Sabrina Omar
and

in loving memory of
Herbert, Mort, and Glenn Leggett,
men who were unafraid to marry
extraordinary women and
rear strong ones

Contents

CONTENTS

Foreword

I came of age in Afghanistan with Muslim girls of similar thoughts and ambitions in the 1960s. We were all tethered one way and another to the strictures of our societies. There were rules and protocol to which I was expected to adhere as the child of a diplomat, and these seemed as restrictive as the social conventions to which my chums were bound. We were all children of privilege. Class in any culture has everything to do with degrees of freedom and opportunities, regardless of gender.

My friends and I laughed, played, dreamed, learned the latest songs, practiced the latest dance steps, shared our innocent secrets, gossiped and talked through long, happy nights about our grand plans for the future. Looking back, I realize that the vibrant pictures we painted of our goals had little to do with weddings and babies, and everything to do with the glamorous professional lives we would lead when we were finally, *finally* adults. Living in a so-called Third World country (a term I actually prefer to *developing nation*, which ignores centuries of deeply refined culture, that is, if either expression must be used at all), we were profoundly affected by our surroundings, inspired toward reform, and most of us were bent on work that would in some way be of service. It was stimulating, exciting, motivating, and not something I found with American girls when we visited my grandmother in the States. For many years after we left Afghanistan, particularly when I wound up living and working in the United States, I was chronically homesick, unremittingly lost.

When the Soviets invaded Afghanistan in 1979, my beloved friends were forced to disperse around the world. A few did not survive the twenty-three-year war. Those who made it to safety continued as best they could in foreign lands to follow their callings as physicians, nurses, teachers, engineers, architects, lawyers, social workers, journalists, artists. Some are doing heroic work in refugee camps among the millions of Afghans who were forced to flee the Soviets, then the civil war, then the Taliban. Others risked their lives inside the country during the Taliban era, educating girls in secret. So far as I know, none of my friends were actual combatants during the long, continuous wars in Afghanistan, but many Afghan women did carry guns and used them.

All of us eventually married and had children. In fact, this was expected of me as an American woman—with an Irish mother— exactly as it was of my friends, for whom marriage and family life are part and parcel of being Muslim, and Afghan. All of us are now middle-aged; some of us are grandmothers.

I chose to be a writer, and among other things produced a novel drawing on my experiences in Afghanistan. Because I feel so comfortable in Muslim countries, I've traveled widely in Central Asia, India, and especially the Near and Middle East. My experiences do not make me an expert on Islam or Muslim women. But they did inspire a vision, long held, to make a meaningful study of the remarkable histories of women of the Islamic world. I had at last the opportunity to realize this vision a year before the tragedy of September 11, 2001, and believe it is now more urgent than ever. We must learn to know the peoples we erroneously proclaim our enemies and whom we too quickly label as utterly oppressive of women. Indeed, there are astonishingly conservative elements in Islam, and we are all aware of the terrible repression of women by the Taliban, *madrassa*-trained fanatics, who are an aberration and living testaments to the fact that war steals souls and engenders unspeakable inhumanity. Yet, as I wish to make clear, women's freedoms have ranged hugely within Islamic cultures and throughout Islamic history.

"The study of the Muslim world by the West has never been a neutral or scholarly exercise," Rana Kabbani writes in *Imperial Fictions: Europe's Myths of the Orient*. "Muslim women have a long, uphill battle...to wrest Islam from those who would make it an anti-women creed. They have legal, social and psychological problems to solve within what are often rigidly traditional societies. But it is a battle not peculiar to Muslim women alone....[Others]...have to wage the same war....Fundamentalism is a spectre that is stalking the globe, but Islam is not its synonym."

I am no scholar, although I wish I were. When I was a girl dreaming with my friends in Afghanistan, academia never occurred to me, and the years brought me instead to journalism and the arts. However, in this book, I've given scholarship my best shot. While writing this book, I often felt as if I were cheating, presenting abridgments of the exhaustive work conducted by real scholars, past and present. I abide by the words of the twelfth-century Persian poet and mystic, Farid al-Din Attar, who advised in his *Conference of the Birds*, "Do not do as you have always done. Do not act as you have always acted."

The research for this book seemed endless and yet was an eternal joy. Joy for the sheer giddy satisfaction of becoming acquainted with Muslim women of the past, privileged or poor, educated or non-literate, righteous or errant. Endless, because I will never get to the "bottom," never fully reach or even identify a destination or anything resembling absolute truth or come to any conclusions about what Islam is, who Muslims are, women or men. That, I believe, is how it should be.

The fundamental traditions of Judaism, Christianity, and Islam—the three Abrahamic religions—are patriarchal. Readers may be surprised to learn then that in principle Islam is the least unjust to women and in fact, unlike the Old and New Testaments, declares their rights in the holy book, the Qur'an. Seen in historical context, Muhammad ibn Abdallah, the Prophet of Islam, was, as it were, a feminist. He liberated Arab women, who were therefore attracted in droves to his mission. The Qur'an is unique among Abrahamic holy books in that it is directed to both men and women.

Sadly, many Westerners have a notion that Muslims are somehow automatons, marching along in blinkered, bovine formation. Nothing is further from reality. Muslim intellectuals, scholars, mystics, feminists, and ordinary folk deliberate, discuss, argue, and ponder questions of spirituality, law, current events, and everyday life with the same kind of energy and enthusiasm we customarily attribute to

Talmudic thinkers. That Islam has been exploited by Muslims themselves for sundry political reasons, whether to oppress women or battle an enemy, is no surprise. Such has been and continues to be the fate of all religions, one of whose unfortunate common denominators is apparently that at the moment of an enlightened leader's passing, wrongheaded extremists immediately arise, doubtless motivated in part—at first—to preserve what was begun—as *they* wish to interpret it or are capable of interpreting it. The exploitation, of course, is not limited to Muslims using Islam as a means to whatever end. The West has distorted Islam and Islamic cultures, cruelly, ignorantly, arrogantly for centuries on innumerable levels to further its own assorted agendas.

Islam is monotheistic, but it is *not* a monoculture. Unfortunately, it is usually presented as such in the West. In Eurocentric discourses, which bristle with stereotypes, Muslim women have not had a fighting chance. They are almost invariably portrayed as pitiable, shrouded creatures, the essence of oppression, the oblique Other. Women with no history, no self-determination, women who are merely ghosts awaiting resurrection into flesh by the superior forces of the West. In this book, I want to disabuse readers of such notions.

Recent tomes by Western women about Islamic women have frequently continued to be exploitive, coming at the questions of veiling and seclusion from culturally narrow points of view. Such approaches ignore immense and vital differences, dissimilarities in ways of thinking and being. The fixation by many Westerners on veiling is a sexual enthrallment—to reveal, expose, and lay naked that which is hidden and mysterious. The West loves mysteries, but cannot seem to do well with them, preferring that all things be uncovered, swabbed, and anesthetized in preparation for analytical surgery, in the name of, self-defined, and too commonly destructive, "progress."

Western women are too often provoked by the veil and determined that the *unveiling* of Muslim women will be the solution to all ills. But Moroccan feminist and sociologist Fatima Mernissi repeatedly notes in her work that Muslim women's strength, independence, and talents are born and nurtured within the private female space they inhabit, and the power they have within the family. It is that vigor and point of view which Muslim women bring to public life. Western women find this difficult to digest, for we have, as Elizabeth Warnock Fernea writes in her book, *In Search of Islamic Feminism*, been "brainwashed from childhood into believing that the only important acts are those that men perform and that women must replicate those acts if they are to gain power or agency. This leads us…to downgrade any activities and evidences of agency that take place outside the public, i.e., male orbit. In doing so, we are buying into the old public/private split."

Karen Armstrong points out in *Muhammad: A Biography of the Prophet* that "Western feminists who denounce Islam for its misogyny should perhaps reflect that the Christian tradition has also been extremely negative to women….The Western view of women and relations between the sexes is confused. We preach equality and liberation, but…exploit and degrade women in advertising, pornography and much popular entertainment in a way that Muslims find alien and offensive."

Many Muslim feminists put it more strongly, insisting that it is up to Westerners to support rather than impose. Western women, they contend, exercise a kind of feminist colonialism that, while well-intentioned is not necessarily appropriate. Coming from different social and political circumstances, they exhibit little understanding of cultural disparities and diversities in "female perspectives," and especially how women in Islam may wish to fight for and find their freedom and fulfillment as believing Muslims, devoted to their religion and the principles of that religion, which call for parity and simultaneously acknowledge and honor the physical differences and differing roles of men and women.

I have no interest in titillating readers or prescribing behavior. I have tried to cross cultural borders gently. Whether or not I've succeeded, I have written this book with love.

This book is two in one. It's a somewhat unconventional work of fact-based essays followed by stylized portraits of select Muslim

women from the beginning of Islam in the seventh century of the
Common Era through the nineteenth century. To do more than touch
occasionally on the twentieth and twenty-first centuries is another conversation entirely and requires an entirely different approach. Muslim
women, and women in Muslim nations, plow on with remarkable
achievements in the traditions of their foremothers and on behalf of
their sisters and their countries. A biographical encyclopedia of modern women of the Islamic world would extend to multiple volumes.
But it would be worth the effort, for everywhere Muslim women are
physicians, teachers, and politicians, poets, novelists, journalists, crit-
ics, and scholars. They are farmers, social workers, and artists of all disciplines, philanthropists, philosophers, and religious thinkers. They
are peacemakers, tackling poverty, education, women and children's
health, human rights, and nonviolence globally. As feminists, or simply as ordinary human beings, they offer shining examples to the world
and are quite possibly on the cutting edge, worldwide, of feminist
thought and feminine creativity in every aspect of life. We might do
well to look to them as models for the future.

It's my hope that the technique I've used here will delight,
enlighten, and even make unfamiliar history easier to digest. Let me
stress again that this book is entirely factual, as the facts are presented
by scholars and historians. So, although they may sometimes sound
like it, the portraits in this book are *not* fiction. Some are brief for
lack of detailed histories and biographies. The women who helped
establish Islam in the seventh century C.E. are the subjects of much
pious literature, folklore, and legend, enabling me to create fuller,
more quixotic pictures of them than of many later women. In my
portrayals of Islam's first female believers, I've incorporated myths,
for as with stories of all religious inceptions, these are the ones that
stand out, that help shape and stabilize people's beliefs. Mythologies
and legends, too, are "facts" to the people who tell them and depend
on them for spiritual content and ballast.

I remained true to facts as I unearthed them. However, I did
take the liberty of imagining how the women portrayed in this book
might have felt in a given situation, that is, how anyone might
respond to, say, the death of a child, the heart overtaken by love, the

gut wrenched by jealousy or revenge, authority given or snatched away. I have—*very* lightly—filled out, with atmosphere and color, the tales and histories as they already exist. I wanted to humanize and enliven what might otherwise be parched recitations of events, deeds, and dates. I tried to find the kernel around which the fruit of the story could swell and ripen. For instance, it is documented that the Abbasid queen Khayzuran as a young slave girl was a dreamer, and that the man who first owned her was an interpreter of dreams and predicted her success. This dreaminess became the core around which I built her biography. And so it went with various others, as you will read.

I also found and used many phrases from the texts that are completely charming: thus, for example, I repeat that Muhammad's father and uncles are said to have had "noses so large that the nose drinks before the lips." In cultures that do not see large noses as ugly, this and other such turns of speech are statements describing nobility and beauty.

And while I hope not to offend anyone anywhere, I doubtless will offend somebody somewhere. Facts, by their very nature, are not offensive, though some people may try to make them so and others may be so fearful as to want a whitewash or omission. But the truth, while it may be provocative, cannot be abusive, because it is, quite flatly, the truth.

While I am opinionated, have made an occasional deduction, or have come up with a theory of my own here or there, I have tried not to presume too much (and have probably not been as original in my ideas as I would like). I echo my friend, the theater director Betsy Tobin (with whom I collaborated on a project to bring to the stage legends of the Islamic world): "I understand that prayer rugs have always included at least one mistake by the weavers, as Allah alone made things without error. I find this comforting [for in working with this material] there would be more than one mistake and most would not be intentional."

My sources ranged from Swahili lore to Persian pageant plays to Muslim feminist writings to the explorations and translations of

Western scholars of Islam. The bibliography will give readers myriad resources for further information. In researching this book, I discovered contemporary Muslim theorists, philosophers, historians, and feminists, and am dazzled by their work: Mernissi, Kabbani, Nabia Abbott, Sayyed Hossein Nasr, Fadwa E. Guindi, Meyda Yegenoglu, Mohja Khaf, Leila Ahmed, Sherifa Zuhur are just a few to whom I am profoundly indebted. Contemporary Western scholars are less prone than their predecessors toward prejudice. Armstrong, Margaret Smith, Annemarie Schimmel, María Rosa Menocal, Leslie P. Peirce, Frederick Denny, John Renard have produced marvelous studies on which I've relied heavily.

I've broken this book into categories—saints, concubines, rulers, tradeswomen, warriors, poets, and so on—but found that they forever overlap, like the verses of a Turkish *gazel*, a poetic form that revolves in a lovely, continuous, unbroken circle. In each section of this book, I have expanded somewhat on specific beliefs, practices, and history of Islam, as they become relevant to the subject matter. For example, details about slavery appear in Chapter Five, "Rebels and Concubines." Particulars about, say, harems and marriage, appear in Chapter Seven, "Rulers, Regents, Queen Mothers, and Philanthropists," while a discussion of that great bugaboo, *jihad*, takes place in Chapter Four, "Warriors and Amazons." The first three chapters of this book deal most closely with the life of the Prophet Muhammad, the founding of Islam, and its spiritual doctrines.

The binding thread is Islam. "This world," the Prophet said, "is the seedbed for the next." As is repeatedly touched upon throughout this book, and specified in Chapter Two, "Scholars of the *Hadith*," there is no separation between, as it were, "church and state," for God is believed to have created it all. Islam holds that God's laws govern human behavior. Nevertheless, they are subject to much debate and interpretation and there are sundry sects and schools of jurisprudence, some more orthodox than others

Yet Islam is as varied as each individual, for although the community, the *umma*, is indispensable, it is each individual who must ultimately make her way alone toward Allah: God, who has no gender, but is transcendent, beyond all comparisons and yet is a personal God, "as near as the vein in one's neck."

There are nearly two billion Muslims worldwide and Islam is estimated to be the fastest-growing religion in North America and Europe. As I went along, I found it was wisest to restrict my geographical scope. I limited my focus mostly to Arabia, Persia, Turkey, Central Asia, India, and North Africa, for these are the richest and most available sources. Regrettably, therefore, I have given short shrift to the women of sub-Saharan Africa and Southeast Asia. I chose the women portrayed in this book because to me they are the most extraordinary. I chose some for idiosyncratic reasons, usually my own preferences for personalities, achievements, accessibility, or simply that it happened to be Tuesday. Some, even when I disliked them (and there are one or two I had to make myself deal with), were included as women whose contributions were vital, although I wouldn't care to take tea with them. In the end, I was obliged to remove a few favorite portraits, to sum them up in the prefaces to each section or leave them out altogether, lest this book grow into a volume the size of a small end table. Thus, a caveat: this book is incomplete. Perhaps it will draw readers to seek out more on their own.

Another caveat: I struggled with how to present certain passages in the Qur'an that have long been subjects of argument over the "woman question." One of these is the Quranic verse that begins (in some translations), "Women are your tillage...." At last, I decided not to examine it, for scholars, Islamists, and Muslim feminists range wildly in their analyses from claims that the statement is about the sex act to assertions that it is about ownership of women by men and on and on. There is plenty written about this and other controversial Quranic passages; I do not need to throw my hat in the ring. Indeed, with my limitations it seemed inappropriate to do so. Some of the books listed in the bibliography tackle these aspects of Islam, along with the disagreements.

My lack of more than the tiniest smattering of Arabic and Persian has been a stumbling block, so I have had to rely on translations into English and sometimes French and Spanish. My husband, poet Jack Collom, occasionally clarified German texts. He also helped me modernize stifling Victorian—and earlier—English translations of women's verse and the word-for-word translations from the Arabic kindly provided by my Egyptian friend Sahar Warraq.

I have looked to several translations of the Qur'an, noted in the bibliography, but frequently simplified the language, replacing *thee* and *thou* with *you* and *yours*, rearranging archaic sentence structures, which to our ears sound contrived and convoluted.

In this book, you will occasionally find discrepancies in spellings such as Mohammed/Muhammad or Moslem/Muslim. The former are old-fashioned and appear in quotes from writers before the 1980s. I have played a little fast and loose with spellings myself, in order to help readers discern between characters with the same name. For instance, because she is a primary character whom I wanted to be recognizable, I use the antiquated spelling for Asmaa bint Abu Bakr, but for others with the same name, I use its simpler modern form, Asma. I have tried to make things easier for readers by eschewing many orthographic peculiarities, including relentless mystifying apostrophes and accent marks. My apologies to any who find this irksome.

It may be difficult at first to keep track of the cast of characters and I considered outlining them, then realized that this would probably add to readers' confusion, but that patience—and I hope, pleasure—would more likely yield clarity.

Surnames are a modern invention. Arab women used *bint*, meaning "daughter of" (Aisha bint Abu Bakr) and men used *ibn*, meaning "son of" (Abdallah ibn Abu Bakr). The word *banu*, sometimes *bani*, simply means "tribe of," "house of," or "clan." At the back of this book, there is a glossary of terms that may be helpful, as well as a chronology that may also aid in keeping track of dynasties and empires. I have also added a brief explanation of Islam's Five Pillars for those who may be reading about Islam for the first time or who want a refresher.

Because the Islamic year is based on a lunar calendar, translating the years of the Common Era into those of the Anno Hegira can be exceedingly tricky, requiring mathematics that are beyond me. Thus I took the easiest, if somewhat inaccurate way out. The Islamic calendar begins in 622 C.E., so I merely subtracted 622 years from those of the solar Common Era. In this book, therefore, the year 1776 C.E. would be 1154 A.H. I've both lost and gained time.

Occasionally, when Western pundits want to make a point about Islam, they refer emphatically to "Allah," as if this were the name or title of some occult or alien deity. In fact, Allah is simply the Arabic word for God, the same God worshiped by Jews and Christians. I have alternated the words *God* and *Allah* in order to make the point and maintain it.

In Arabic, the word for veiling—whether of a woman or man, whether it is the *kiswah*, the cloth that covers the Ka'aba, the sacred house of God in Mecca, or the veil between humans and God—is *hijab*, literally, "curtain." All Islam is, in a sense, hidden by the *hijab*, never completely exposed, veils layered like golden sheets of mica. This is spiritual Mystery, not secrecy, not cultish concealment, but the enigma of that which is holy, the sanctuary or *haram*.

Hijab might also describe the obscuring mist that separates the Muslim and non-Muslim worlds or, indeed, all cultures.

As I researched this book, I grew ever fonder of the Prophet Muhammad, as if he were hanging around the house, helping with the laundry and washing the dishes (which he did in his own house-hold), darning his socks (indeed, he mended his own clothes and shoes), grinning and teasing, caring for the animals—not as parables, but as pets or precious livestock—playing wholeheartedly with the kids, showing off the new babies, arguing with his wives, or giving practical advice, such as the counsel he offered a Bedouin who asked whether, trusting in God's protection, he should let his camel wan-der loose. "First tether it," Muhammad said, "then trust in God."

Every woman in this book has become an old, dear companion. I have come to identify with each, perhaps especially those I dislike. On some levels, those became, of course, the most lucid. In the hours of thinking and writing about the women portrayed in this book, I discovered in every one some little thing we share or some small familiarity.

The lives and accomplishments of Islamic women have been largely overlooked. Until quite recently, historians have satisfied themselves commenting on the *hijab*, polygamy and the harem, slavery and concubinage. Although this is changing among scholars, for the general Western public, informed mostly by mainstream media, the image of the Muslim woman is too frequently still that of a despised, servile class, smothered in scorn and strangled by indignities, the property of fathers, husbands, and brothers, with no souls of their own. In this book, I hope to show that the truth is so much more complex than that image.

While many Muslim women resist *hijab*, others who continue to wear the veil may do so for many complicated—and valid—reasons. They may choose *hijab* on religious grounds. They may be following ancient custom. Whatever the case, the veil is not a burial shroud. Behind it there has always been dynamic life.

Behind the veil: the scimitar.

Introduction

The supremacy of God is the first principle of Islam; God's absolute oneness is proclaimed again and again in the Qur'an, the holy book:

> *Say: He is God the One and Only,*
> *God the Eternal, the Absolute:*
> *He does not beget nor is He begotten,*
> *And there is none like unto Him.*[1]

The word *Islam* means surrender, submission to the will of God. *Muslim*, from the same Arabic root, means one who submits to God. It is wrong to call members of Islam Mohammedans, for the religion's Prophet Muhammad is not worshiped as Christians worship Christ.

Polytheism and idolatry, the veneration of saints or divine consorts or sons, is the unforgivable sin of *shirk*. The use of imagery in worship, dwelling on human symbols of the Divine, is forbidden. Idolatry diverts the mind from God. Nor is the religion itself to be the focus for Muslims. Rather, Muslims are enjoined to concentrate only on God, who is all-merciful, all-compassionate. God is never referred to as "Father" or "Mother." The masculine pronoun is no more than a convenience (as, for example, English speakers say "mankind" to refer to human beings). God has no physical form. Rather, God is the whole universe. In Arabic, the language of the Qur'an, there is no distinction between genders when referring to God. Allah is neither "He" nor "She," rather the demonstrative, genderless article *who* may come closest. Because of the difficulties of translation, "He" is used throughout this book. In Islam, there are ninety-nine names for God, none of which, in Arabic, is feminine or masculine.

Islam is the third of the Abrahamic religions. It is the completion, according to Muhammad, of Judaism and Christianity. Muhammad is in the tradition of Moses and Jesus in conveying the word of God. His aim was not to create a new religion but to rectify and complete his predecessors' message and bring it to the pagan peoples of Arabia. The word of God is the call for social justice.

Westerners are not used to relating to their prophets as human. The life of the historic Jesus is, as Michael Wolfe puts it, "a postmodern invention,"[2] largely conjecture, whereas each move the Prophet Muhammad made—particularly after 622 C.E., when the community migrated to Medina—was carefully recorded. Among other things, Islam was born relatively recently. Fewer obfuscating centuries have passed.

Muhammad never claimed to have phenomenal qualities, or that he was divine. He wished to be only what he knew he was, a mediator, a servant.

Say: I am only a mortal, like you.
To me it has been revealed that your God is One God;
so go straight to Him.[3]

The Qur'an reminds us repeatedly of Muhammad's simple humanity, and constantly admonishes Muslims that only God can guide humankind. Although God revealed His word and will through Muhammad and the holy book, the Qur'an, Muhammad insisted he was merely a man, not to be worshiped, never to be called upon to intercede between human beings and God.

Believers of all creeds have an inevitable need to make their leaders superhuman (the veneration of saints and the need for intercession seem to be human nature, too). Extravagant claims of the Prophet Muhammad's singularity have naturally developed: he was so pure that flies avoided him, so luminous he did not cast a shadow, and so on. Yet the *Hadith* (or narratives, collections of the Prophet's sayings and deeds) and the biographies belie these wondrous latter-day fables and bring Muhammad—and therefore Islam—into focus with candid discussions on everything from food to table manners, sexual relations, brushing the teeth, or cleansing the genitals.

Muhammad is known to have been profoundly compassionate and forgiving. Perhaps for that very reason, he was, it is said, "not a man to trifle with." It is told that he didn't often laugh, but he had an enchanting smile and a good sense of humor. He liked to tell jokes and he was something of a tease. Once a crone asked him whether old women would also go to Paradise. "No," Muhammad answered, poker-faced.

The poor old woman was stricken and grief passed over her face.

"All will be transformed in Paradise," the Prophet continued, "where there is only one youthful age for all." She must have been greatly relieved.

Once when he frowned at a blind visitor who interrupted him, a Revelation came admonishing him for his impatience, and this Divine reproach is said to have taught Muhammad to offer a friendly word to everyone, to show largesse and grant the requests that he could. He was a remarkable spiritual leader, brilliant politician, and champion of social justice, who believed that people have an absolute responsibility to create equitable societies. To that end, he spoke against racism, for the just treatment of women and the poor and the manumission of slaves.

The centuries before the arrival of Islam are known as the *jahiliyah*, the Time of Ignorance. Muhammad was born in the sixth Christian century in Mecca—or Makkah, as it would be more accurately spelled to duplicate Arabic pronunciation—located in the Hijaz, the area along Arabia's west coast, bordering the Red Sea. It was an urban community, an axis of commerce for the caravan trade, linked to the hubs of existing civilization, to which tribes came from far and wide for a great annual fair and pilgrimage. Mecca then as now was a religious center, the city of the Ka'aba, a shrine dedicated to various gods and goddesses and filled with images, including those of Mary and Jesus, or Isa in Arabic. It was surrounded by 360 idols, thought to be tribal totems. The circling of the Ka'aba, called *tawwaf,* is a ritual that originated in pagan times. A Black Stone *(al-hajar al-aswad),* a meteorite—therefore representative of that which is Heaven-sent and beyond earthly mortality—sits at one corner of the Ka'aba. The Ka'aba's four corners are the four cardinal directions and the structure, thought to be situated at the world's core, unites Heaven and Earth.

Although pre-Islamic Arabs worshiped goddesses, women's place in society was, by all accounts massively grim. The principles of compassion and pacifism we have pasted onto societies with female deities can be wishful thinking and historically inaccurate, though useful and hopeful for establishing ideals by which the feminine might gain its equal place in today's world. And it was not only pre-Islamic Arabs who exercised a double standard. The ancient Greeks, for example, despite their highly populated pantheon of goddesses, were terrific misogynists; neither were women well treated in ancient Egypt, where Isis was adored.

To ancient Arabians, the word *Allah* meant simply, "the god." His three "daughters" were the goddesses al-Uzza ("the mighty one," who represented the planet Venus and was most important to the Meccans), Manat (Fortune, "she who settles fates" and who was a household deity), and al-Lat (which means "the goddess"). Al-Lat represented the Sun and her cult was widespread, although the center of her worship was the town of Taif near Mecca. Al-Lat is mentioned by Herodotus, in old Arabian inscriptions, and by pre-Islamic poets as the Great Mother, who, under various names was venerated all over the ancient world. In Taif—where, as we'll see, Muhammad tried to rally support but was rebuffed and humiliated—al-Lat was called al-Raba, "Sovereign," the title also given to Ishtar (Belit) and Astarte (Baalat).

Some scholars have put forth that, as he began his mission, Muhammad, desperate and distressed by the Meccans' growing hatred of him, tried to make a place for the three goddesses. Thus came the so-called Satanic Verses of the Qur'an, whereby al-Lat, al-Uzza, and Manat are named as interceding angels. It worked. The Meccans joined him. That is, until the angel Jibril, Gabriel, upbraided the Prophet for putting words in God's mouth. (For this

6

reason, it would be considered heresy by Muslims to call Allah "She" in English.)

The pre-Islamic pilgrims who visited Mecca brought rich profits to the city. The Meccans perceived that Islam, with its insistence on one God, threatened this economic system. But Muhammad stayed as true to Arabian customs as possible in the building of his new society and religion. His aim was not to destroy, but to remedy.

The Ka'aba, a cubicle made of granite, fifty feet high, is said to have been built by Abraham, or Ibrahim, the common ancestor of Jews, Christians, and Muslims, and his son Ismai'l, Ishmael, by the slave woman Hagar. According to Islam, although Ibrahim and Ismai'l created the shrine to the One God, it was subsequently polluted by polytheism.

When he was about fifteen, Muhammad became engaged in trade and probably accompanied caravans through Arabia and into Syria. During these travels, he would have had ample opportunity to meet people who influenced his religious thought: Jews, who dominated commercial life in the town of Yathrib (later Medina), Christians from Syria and Persia, Zoroastrians, and a sect of monotheists called *hanif*, who rejected polytheism, but were neither Jewish nor Christian.

The Revelations came upon an already deeply devout Muhammad in 610 C.E., when he was forty years old. His religious concerns combined with his profound disquiet about the corruption of the religious establishment in Mecca and issues of social justice such as women's property rights, infanticide, the treatment of the poor, orphans, and slaves.

He often spent the night in meditation and prayer in the mountains near the city. It was while he slept in a cave in Mount Hira that a holy spirit, the archangel Gabriel, or Jibril, appeared to him and ordered Muhammad to proclaim his faith in Allah, and in His word.

Jibril continued to bring Muhammad the word of God, piece by piece, verse by verse, across twenty-two years. With each Revelation, Muhammad lapsed into a state of spiritual communion, and when it was over, he delivered the Quranic Revelations orally to his followers, who committed them to memory and wrote them on palm leaves, flat stones, the shoulder blades of camels, or scraps of parchment. These fragments were assembled and organized into a book in the twenty-ninth Islamic year, 651 C.E., nineteen years after the Prophet's death, during the reign of the third Rightly Guided caliph Uthman ibn Affan.

The Qur'an is divided into 114 chapters, called *Surah*, which vary in length from as few as three to as many as 300 verses, or *aya*. The holy book is not an account of Muhammad's life. It is held to be literally the word of God, the will of God as revealed in Arabic for all Muslims. It is immutable and infallible, believed to be a transcript of parts of another, more formidable book preserved in Heaven, where all that has ever happened and all that ever will happen is recorded.

> *This is the Book, without doubt,*
> *a guidance to the Godfearing*
> *who believe in the Unseen, and perform the prayer,*
> *and expend what We have provided them;*
> *who believe in what has been sent down to you*
> *and what has been sent down before you,*
> *and have faith in the Hereafter;*
> *those who are guided by their Lord,*
> *they will prosper.*[4]

The Revelations transmitted to Muhammad while he was still in Mecca are short and deal with religious topics, whereas later *Surah*, revealed in Medina, are longer and speak to specific legal, social, or political situations, as the Muslim *umma*, or community, established itself.

Read with an unbiased mind and heart, the Qur'an is easily understood as one of the world's great sacred books. It is intensely venerated and often committed entirely to memory. Those who haven't memorized the complete book can still recite large parts of it. It offers passages for every occasion, public and private. It imparts meaningful consolation and comfort. Some never leave home without it. It is a talisman against disease or disaster. It must be treated with the utmost respect, never carried below the waist, never piled under other books. Smoking or drinking while reading or listening to it is forbidden.

The Qur'an, Muhammad told the detractors who demanded a marvel as proof of his prophethood, was his only miracle and confirmed his place among prophets.

Distinctions between social roles of men and women and their anatomical differences are made in the Qur'an, but nothing indicates that they are not of the same essential nature nor equal in the eyes of God.

Too much value seems to have been placed on Quranic passages that appear to suggest that men are superior to women. In acknowledging the dissimilarities between the genders, the Qur'an also recognizes that men and women function as individuals. But as Amina Wadud-Muhsin writes in *Qur'an and Woman*, "there is no detailed prescription set on how to function, culturally. Such a specification would be an imposition that would reduce the Qur'an from a universal text to a culturally specific text—a claim that many have erroneously made. What the Qur'an proposes is transcendental in time and space."

Islam is not some pale imitation of Judaism or Christianity. The Torah and Qur'an share many characters and incidents. The Qur'an calls Adam, Noah, Lot, and others (including Jesus from the New Testament) prophets. The stories of Jacob, Joseph, Moses, Solomon, the queen of Sheba, David, Goliath, Saul, Job, Jonah, and Joshua all appear basically the same in the Qur'an as in the Old Testament, but some details differ. For Muslims, it is Ismai'l, not Isaac, whom Ibrahim offered to sacrifice to God.

In addition to the Qur'an, the holy word of God, Islam is based, as we will see, on the *Hadith*. There are Five Pillars of Islam, five specific actions a Muslim must perform to stay on the right path: *Shahada*, testimony; *Salat*, prayer; *Zakat*, almsgiving; *Sawm*, fasting; and *Hajj*, pilgrimage.

When men from Yathrib made their pilgrimage to Mecca, met Muhammad, surrendered to Islam, and returned home to convert others, they invited the Prophet to bring his flock to their city, which was torn apart by violent rivalries between two Arab tribes and their Jewish supporters. Muhammad was to mediate between the warring factions. In return, the Muslims would have a safe haven away from Mecca. He sent 200 to Yathrib—soon renamed al-Madinah, Medina, City of the Prophet—in small groups to avoid suspicion.

It was here in 622 C.E. that Muslim history officially began and world history was changed. The year of the flight, the *hijra* (from the Arabic word for migration), begins the Muslim calendar, Anno Hegira, or A.H.

In Medina, Muhammad was transformed from the leader of a persecuted minority to a player on the Arabian scene. As he became the principal authority in this vital town, his influence spread. The Revelations now became the basis for government and social reforms with detailed instructions on legal and social matters such as marriage, divorce, dietary restrictions, taxes, and conduct in war. In Medina, the Prophet created a revolutionary charter—a constitution—binding all Muslims and thereby formalizing the community, the *umma*. Until then, Arabs had owed allegiance solely to family and tribe. And under the charter, Jews and Christians of Medina shared the same rights and privileges, as "a community along with the Muslims," the *dhimma*, or "protected minority." They were allowed to keep their own religions, although they were required to pay a special tax, equivalent to the *zakat*, or almsgiving, required of Muslims. Only pagans were forced to choose between Islam and the sword, a pattern that continued throughout Muslim conquests and settlements.

The Jews of Medina, however, rejected Muhammad's claim of prophethood and were suspected of political treachery. Rivalries flared between the Arab tribes of Medina and the Muslims. There was hunger, there were economic and social problems as the centuries-old symbiosis between nomadic and urban life changed. Muhammad's political gifts were tried, tested, and perfected.

He wanted to convert the Meccans and cleanse the Ka'aba of polytheism. To that end, understanding that it was the only means to accomplishing his goal and surviving, he began a series of raids, *ghazus,* on caravans flowing in and out of Mecca. Raids were not uncommon, and not only did banditry put food on the tables of the impoverished *umma,* but they shook the political authority of Mecca's ruling Quraysh tribe and the city's economic power.

In 2 A.H./624 C.E. at a watering place called Badr, Muhammad himself led a force of 300 believers against a Quraysh caravan defended by a thousand (some say 3000) Meccans.

In this first of the Muslim victories that changed the face of Arabia, the Muslims lost fourteen men, the Meccans seventy. The decisive factor in the victory is said to have been a handful of pebbles, which the Prophet tossed toward the Meccans, saying, "Not you cast when you cast, but God cast." That Allah flung fortune in favor of the Muslims offered undeniable proof that Muhammad's hand was guided by God's hand and that He would never fail to help His servants.

More attacks on Meccan caravans followed. In the Battle of Uhud, in 3 A.H./625 C.E., the outnumbered Muslims were forced to retreat and the Prophet was wounded.

Battles continued until the Quraysh of Mecca finally signed a treaty with Muhammad, which allowed the Muslims to attend the pilgrimage to the Ka'aba in exchange for a ten-year truce. Two years later, in 8 A.H./630 C.E., the Quraysh broke the truce by attacking a tribe under Muhammad's protection. Muhammad marched on Mecca at the head of 10,000 men and women, defeated the demoralized defenders with little loss of life, and entered the city as conqueror.

Muhammad returned to Medina, where he remained for two years. In the spring of 10 A.H./632 C.E., shortly before his death, he went back to Mecca for the Farewell Pilgrimage. His conduct became the model for all future pilgrims. He returned to Medina and on June 8 died in the arms of his favorite wife, Aisha bint Abu Bakr.

He left no heir. He named no successor. The struggle for leadership that ensued determined much of the future history of Islam, whose unity was soon broken. In the generation after Muhammad's death, the Muslim world divided into two major groups, the Sunna and the Shi'a. The split, as we'll see, was political more than reli-gious, with the followers of Muhammad's son-in-law Ali ibn Abu Talib—who eventually became the fourth Rightly Guided caliph—forming the Shi'at of Ali, "the party of Ali."

Sunnis comprise approximately 90 percent of Muslims world-wide and adhere to the practices and beliefs outlined in much of this book. There are variations among the Sunni, the most extreme being the Wahhabis, who follow the eighteenth-century teachings of Muhammad ibn Abd al-Wahhab. During the Ottoman Empire, the sect fell into a period of temporary decline, but reemerged in force in the twentieth century under Ibn Saud, founder of Saudi Arabia. Wahhabi conservative doctrine governs that state today.

Shi'ites comprise about 10 percent of the Muslim faith and are divided into many different sects. They form the majority in Iran and Yemen and are important minorities in Iraq, Syria, Lebanon, eastern Arabia, and parts of India. Whereas Sunnis believe in the consensus of the Islamic community through which God reveals His will, thus empowering the community to elect the caliph, Shi'ites restrict eli-gibility for the caliphate to descendants of Ali and his wife, Muhammad's daughter Fatima.

Other variations in Islam include the Sufis, the Marabouts (a North African cult of local saints), and the Black Muslim movement founded in the United States in the twentieth century.

1

In the Beginning: Women of the Prophetate

"Paradise lies at the feet of the mothers."

*I*t's often said that two-thirds of the religion of Islam was handed down by women and one-third was shaped by women.

"Of worldly things," the Prophet said, "women and fragrance are made dear to me and the comfort of my eyes is made in prayer."

Muhammad ibn Abdallah was born to a widowed mother, tended by a slave woman, and fostered by a Bedouin woman. His marriage to Khadija bint Khuwaylid was long, fruitful, and faithful, yielding unwavering support for him and his mission. She was the first to convert to Islam. He had four adored daughters, women fought by his side for Islam, he relied on one of his later wives, Umm Salamah, for sage military and political advice, he experienced Revelations in the presence of his favorite wife Aisha bint Abu Bakr, he counted women among his closest friends and companions. Certainly the Bedouin women with whom he lived as a child presented a model of freedom not known by settled Arab women.

It is no exaggeration to say that the community of Muslims worldwide originated with women.

Infanticide was prevalent among the pre-Islamic Arabs, just as it was among the Greeks, Romans, and early Christians. It was a method of population control, and newborn girls were the victims, buried alive at birth. Girls were thought to cost more than they brought in. Among other things, Muhammad's condemnation of infanticide was a primary factor in drawing women to the faith.

Slaves, as with Christianity, were also among Islam's original believers, women and men for whom Muhammad's message of emancipation and justice naturally resonated. It is through a slave woman that Islam traces its Abrahamic lineage. The prophet Ibrahim is the common ancestor of Judaism, Christianity, and Islam, who made Jews and Muslims half brothers through his sons Isaac

(Isaq) by his wife Sarah, and Ismai'l, by his Egyptian servant, Hagar (considered by Muslims to have been Ibrahim's legitimate wife).

Sarah's jealousy of Hagar, who bore Ibrahim's first son while Sarah was still childless, forced the old patriarch to cast Hagar and Ismai'l into the wilderness, where he abandoned them in the valley of Mecca. Hagar ran frantically between the dry hills of Safa and Marwah seeking water for her boy, begging God's help. The archangel Jibril opened the well of Zamzam to them and they survived. Later, Ibrahim visited them and together, it is said, they built the Ka'aba, a shrine to the One God. To this day, Muslim pilgrims drink from the sacred well of Zamzam and run seven times around Safa and Marwah in imitation of and tribute to Hagar's struggle and the blessings she received and gave.

The biblical account of Abraham's life is not based on historical records, but preserved by oral traditions. According to Arab tradition, it was Ismai'l, rather than Isaq, who was Ibrahim's intended sacrifice. Pilgrims to Mecca gather pebbles to throw stones at three pillars symbolizing the devil, who tried to tempt the patriarch away from his determination to give his son up to God. By throwing the stones, pilgrims are consciously casting away the evil in their souls.

Ibrahim proved his faith, Ismai'l was spared, and a ram was sacrificed in his place. The annual pilgrimage, the *hajj*, the Fifth Pillar of Islam, ends with the commemorative Feast of the Sacrifice, *Id al-adha*. God promised Ibrahim that Ismai'l would be the father of great nations. In Mecca, pilgrims pay homage at the grave of his mother, for Hagar is Islam's locus.

Muhammad's grandfather, Abd al-Muttalib, was keeper of the well of Zamzam. His task was to apportion water from the underground spring to pre-Islamic pilgrims visiting Mecca and supervise the feeding of them. In desert lands, to be in charge of water would be a vocation of great distinction. A dream-revelation is attributed to Abd al-Muttalib, in which he rediscovered Zamzam after it had been lost.

Islam does not conceive of original sin as passed on by a woman. A few popular Muslim legends have absorbed the biblical condemnation of Eve as a temptress, responsible for humankind's fall from grace, but in fact the Qur'an doesn't mention her role. Women are no more corrupt than men, no more liable for the world's evils. There is no demonizing of women in the Muslim holy book; they are not catalysts for sin or the cause of men's bad behavior.

The only woman actually named in the Qur'an is Mary (Miriam), a true handmaiden of God and the mother of Jesus (Isa), who is considered the last prophet before Muhammad:

> And mention Miriam in the Book when she withdrew
> from her people to an eastern place,
> and she veiled herself apart from them.
> We sent unto her Our Spirit who presented himself
> to her as a man without fault.
> "I take refuge in the All-Merciful from you!" she said.
> But he said, "I am only a messenger come from
> your Lord to give you a boy most pure...."
>
> And the birth pangs surprised her by the trunk of a palm tree.
> "Would I have died," she cried, "and become a thing forgotten!"
> But the one that was below called to her.
> "Do not sorrow. See how your Lord has set below you a rivulet.
> Shake the palm trunk,
> and fresh, ripe dates will come tumbling onto you.
> Eat and drink and be comforted."[1]

Thus Isa was conceived by the breath of an angel, a Spirit, and brought forth under a palm tree, which his mother grasped for ballast during her birth pangs. The dates that rained down on her and the stream at her feet would seem to be a sign of assurance, abundance, and nurturance for all humanity, as well as for Miriam and her newborn. In Islam, Isa is not considered the Son of God, but a prophet like Muhammad, God's servant, an "evident Warner," assigned by God to awaken hearts.

Isa's and Miriam's images were the only ones within the Ka'aba that the Prophet did not destroy when he took Mecca. Despite absolute dictates against idolatry, this sparing of the iconography describes the respect Muhammad held for Christians—as he admired Jews—as fellow monotheists, Abrahamists, and People of the Book.

His reverence for Miriam again speaks clearly to Muhammad's veneration of women, his need of the friendship of women, which begins with the love he had for his own mother and for those who mothered and sustained him after she died. "Paradise," he said, "lies at the feet of the mothers."

Muhammad was born to Amina bint Wabh in 570 C.E., four months after his father, Abdallah ibn Abd al-Muttalib, died on a trading journey. Their clan, the Hashim, were noble but poor relations among Mecca's powerful ruling Quraysh, who had, generations before, established residency around the Ka'aba in the town of Mecca and prospered there as merchants and traders. That almost nothing is known about Amina only fuels the marvelous lore about Muhammad's birth. In the narratives, Amina weeps a good deal—as well she might, having been left widowed and pregnant with nothing but five camels and a slave named Barakah. This emphasis in the stories on Amina's crying and sorrow may relate to the profuse lamentations made later by female ascetics, saints, and mystics.

The legends present Amina with one foot on Earth and the other in Heaven. She makes practical decisions and yet, like Mary, Amina is a vessel containing the future; she is a lantern from whom light emanates to illuminate the world. The heavenly light that radiates from her womb offers Amina a kind of clairvoyance: her vision of the palaces of Syria signifies the momentous centuries ahead and her child's exalted role. This is the guiding light for generations to come, similar in many ways to the Christian story of the star hovering over the infant Jesus. A luminous aura is a universal characteristic of a spiritual liberator.

Although the historical math doesn't quite add up, some claim that the year of Muhammad's birth was the Year of the Elephant, when a Yemeni king came to conquer Mecca and crush the Ka'aba with his terrifying army of Abyssinian mammoths. This tale, where birds pelt the invaders and their pachyderms with stones, each stone landing a killing blow, is among hundreds of miraculous stories that surround or accompany Muhammad's birth and youth. While miracles and myths are relatively unusual in Islam, the birth of a religious leader—Moses, Jesus, the Buddha, and more—naturally prompts wondrous legends and important mystical occurrences. Scholars, however, have speculated that as the enemy marched with their elephants through Arabia, frightening and easily defeating all opposition, they contracted smallpox and were forced to withdraw, dying along the roads, faces pocked as if they'd been caught in a hail of pebbles. Whether by pestilence or armed birds, God sent a miracle to save His house, the Ka'aba, from violation. For each appearance of a spiritual guide, there must be events that presage the coming and circumstances that illustrate the need. And Amina, confident of God's grace and the future, which will be her son, refuses to flee from Mecca.

In some versions of Muhammad's birth, the infant falls from the womb to the ground, spotless, circumcised, with his navel cord already cut. He takes a handful of earth and gazes into Heaven. Unlike the magi who appeared before the baby Jesus with gifts of frankincense, gold, and myrrh, the angels (*malaika*) visit Amina with necessities for health, comfort, and worship: water, a basin and towel, a blanket, and swaddling. The baby's first bath sets the Muslim ritual of ablution before prayer, but the blanket and swaddling give material relief to a woman whose poverty is palpable. There is always this twofold element in the lore about Muhammad's birth and youth: always sound, sensible threads woven into the wonderment. It is a spiritual aesthetic evident throughout Islam, right into its magnificent architecture and arts.

In all religious traditions, angels are intermediaries and messengers of God (or the many gods). In Islam's mystical Sufi system, they are The Spirit, Divine Beauty, and Divine Command, the eternal light given to all prophets.

"According to the Prophet Muhammad," Peter Lamborn Wilson writes, "[angels] are sent by God to earth to search out those places where individuals or groups are engaged in remembering or invoking the Deity. They listen with joy, hovering over the roofs of these humans who are fulfilling the task for which they were created:

to know God, Who loves to be known. Then they fly back to the Divine Throne and repeat what they have heard (though God already knows it better than they) and are entrusted with blessings to bestow on earth."[2]

As well as angels, there are *djinn* — often misinterpreted in the West as Disneyfied "genies." Djinn are invisible beings, similar to humans. But while humans are made of clay, djinn are made of fire. Some are morally upright characters, beautiful and committed to religion; others are hideous demons who bedevil and frighten with evil and wicked acts. Their origins are in pre-Islamic mythology and they lived on, as if to represent humanity's shadow, good and bad. "Angels are born out of light," Muhammad said, "and djinn are born out of the spark of fire."

In these earliest mythico-histories of Muhammad's beginnings and the women who helped him develop physically, spiritually, and intellectually, angels are not just glorifiers of God, not simply mediators, not only the heralds of God's Divine word and desire, not deus ex machina or merely proof of the Messenger of Allah's appointment, but the veins along which the stories of Islam's origins travel.

The Mecca of Muhammad's childhood was bustling and busy with traders and pilgrims. Parents considered it essential to send their children to be fostered among the Bedouins, the traditional people of the desert, for fosterage forged alliances and reminded Meccans of their forefathers, before the Quraysh settled around the Ka'aba and became the new urban rich. In the highly populated, fetid city, newborns died with horrifying frequency. Sending them to the desert helped ensure their health and survival.

Enter Halima, Muhammad's Bedouin foster mother, who in some cases is said to have taken him free of charge, and in all cases was blessed every hour by the child's presence. In cultures where fosterage was common, foster parents (and foster siblings) were counted high in a person's life, loyalty, and extended lineage. Halima served as a witness to the child's Divine initiation, when "strangers" — doubtless angels — removed Muhammad's heart to wash and weigh it. That the boy was living in the wilderness, among the purer clans of nomads, has, of course, collective significance. In all traditions, the wilderness is the place of revelations, epiphanies, purification, and ecstatic experience, where the seer is closest to Nature and therefore to the Divine. This initiation during his childhood prepared Muhammad for the primary mystical experience of his life, the Night Journey, when he traveled to the throne of God.

His mother died when Muhammad was six. His grandfather, Abd al-Muttalib, who'd had, in yet another oracular dream, a vision of the boy's singularity, took him in. It is sometimes implied that Abd al-Muttalib, favored his grandson even over his own sons, several of whom, including his uncle Hamza, were Muhammad's age and later became his followers. One son, Abu Lahab ibn Abd al-Muttalib, became Muhammad's enemy. Abu Lahab was from an earlier generation of Abd al-Muttalib's children, which included Muhammad's father Abdallah, as well as his uncle Abu Talib, his great protector.

Loved as he was by his grandfather, Muhammad must nevertheless have been profoundly aware of his status as an orphan. Throughout his life, he advocated on behalf of orphans, and in the Qur'an there are at least seven admonitions to care for them, to treat them with justice, and to deal honestly with their property.

> *It is not piety that you turn your faces*
> *to the East and to the West.*
> *True piety is this:*
> *To believe in God, and the Last Day,*
> *the angels, the Book and the Prophets,*
> *to give of one's substance, however cherished,*
> *to kin and orphans, to the needy, to travelers and beggars,*
> *and to ransom the slave.*[3]

A slave woman, Barakah, looked after Muhammad from the moment of his birth, and after Amina's death, he called Barakah "Mother." She was a continual presence in his life. That her name means "power of blessing," *baraqa*, and that she was present at the Prophet's birth, brings to mind the Irish Saint Bridget, who is sometimes called "the midwife of Christ." The *baraqa* is spiritual power, the Divine presence that transforms, the grace that makes the spiritual journey possible.

When Abd al-Muttalib died a few years after Amina, Muhammad came under the care of his uncle Abu Talib, now head of the Hashim, who, although he never became a Muslim, sheltered Muhammad through thick and thin. Across the years, there were plenty of both. At fifteen, Muhammad began traveling with Abu Talib on trading journeys. Some say he was an agent for the wealthy Meccan widow Khadija bint Khuwaylid, who noticed him as a reliable employee and set her heart on him. But less prosaic sagas have Khadija wishing for true and tender love in a harsh, irreligious, and materialistic era. She has prescient dreams and the angels give her signs that Muhammad, a stranger to her, is the one.

In pre-Islamic Arabia, women were not allowed access to the bride-price, but Muhammad changed that, ensuring women's inheritances and property rights and assuring that the *mahar*—the bride-price—was her own to be used as she pleased and that it would be returned to her in the event of divorce or her husband's death. This is made law in the Qur'an.

Khadija was a rare independent woman in a world where marriage was made by purchase, capture, or contract. Arabs and Jews—and doubtless others—were passing women around like trophies from one hand to another. Women became possessions of their husbands, objects to be used and discarded at men's will. Pre-Islamic women and slaves were chattel, with no legal rights. Men could take as many wives as they wanted and there are claims that promiscuity was rampant.[4]

Sources differ as to what life was like for women, particularly in urban areas like Mecca, but all agree, it was probably no picnic. By ancient custom, descent was calculated through the female line and property was officially inherited by women. Yet they had no power over it and were usually denied their inheritances. Divorce was unconstrained, as were conjugal violence and sexual abuse of slaves. Quranic laws improved the lot of women immeasurably, returning their property and their rights over it. Islam was far ahead of its time in ascribing to women equal value as men. As we'll see, Islam provides for women to choose their husbands—family pressures notwithstanding—and to accept or reject their proposals.

Somehow Khadija managed to design her own life. She was obviously generous and resolute, deserving of the adulation given to her in the traditions. She was a patrician public figure who made her own choices. Whether through celestial guidance, helpful heavenly hints, or her own thoughtful perceptions, she chose Muhammad to wed and loved him all the days of her life, as he loved her.

Muhammad was fifteen years younger than Khadija. He might not have succeeded without her support and advice at the start. Even when his own faith faltered, hers in him was unwavering. They had six or seven children (two or three boys, who died in infancy, and four daughters). After she died, Muhammad missed Khadija, his spiritual counselor, for the rest of his life. His later wife, Aisha, was often jealous of her memory and Muhammad's abiding adoration of her.

Indeed, Aisha once tartly informed the Prophet that Khadija was nothing but a "toothless old woman whom Allah has replaced with a better," referring, of course, to herself. But Muhammad quickly rebuked his young wife, saying, "No, God has not replaced her with a better. She believed in me when I was rejected. When they called me a liar, she proclaimed me truthful. When I was poor, she shared her wealth with me and"—the unkindest cut of all—"Allah granted me her children though He withheld those of other women."

Khadija is thought by some scholars to have been *hanif*, that is, neither Christian nor Jew but nonetheless monotheist. It is well documented that she and Muhammad first confided his Revelations to Khadija's *hanif* uncle, Waraqah.

Muhammad's reaction to the first Revelation in 610 C.E., when he was forty, was abject fear and the trepidation that he had become what he despised: a *kahin*, a street oracle. These were soothsayers, who used rhymed prose to communicate their predictions. Or perhaps he had become *majnun*, a mad poet, for the words that Jibril brought Muhammad were truly poetic. It was Khadija who understood that this was not divination, oracular utterance, or possession. It was she who realized immediately that the insight given to her husband would change the world.

There are no descriptions of Khadija's physical looks, and apparently few of Muhammad's other wives and female friends, or indeed his male Companions. But Muhammad himself has been frequently described, often as having had otherworldly beauty. In most religious lore, it is imperative that those chosen to be the messengers of the Divine be radiant and charismatic, towering, spellbinding.[5] Muhammad seems to have in fact been a fine-looking man, whose countenance was gentle and kindly. Nevertheless, pious, romantic accounts render him as resplendently handsome, with only seventeen white hairs in his beard, who exuded such light and sweet fragrance that animals fell at his feet and trees bowed before him and that he was free of all defects and without sin (this was not his own perception; he prayed for forgiveness, he said, a hundred times a day).

His cousin and son-in-law, Ali ibn Abu Talib, described Muhammad like this:

> *Muhammad was middle-sized, did not have lank or crisp hair, was not fat, had a white circular face, wide black eyes and long eyelashes. He walked as though he went down a declivity. He had the "seal of prophecy"* between his shoulder blades (a fleshy, bruise-colored protuberance the size of a pigeon's egg)....*He had thick, curly hair [which] reached beyond the lobe of his ear. His complexion was bright and luminous. Muhammad had a wide forehead and fine, long, arched eyebrows, which did not meet* (despite persistent legends that they were "connected like the two arches of a bow"). *Between his eyebrows there was a vein, which distended when he was angry. His nose was hooked; he was thick-bearded, had smooth cheeks, a strong mouth and his teeth were set apart. He had thin hair on his chest. His neck was like the neck of an ivory statue, with the purity of silver. Muhammad was proportionate...firm-gripped, even of belly and chest, broad-chested and broad-shouldered.*[6]

24

Asmaa bint Abu Bakr, the oldest daughter of the Prophet's closest Companion, Abu Bakr—who became the first successor, *khalif* or Rightly Guided caliph, after Muhammad's death[7]—is admired for her vital, if modest, role in the history of Islam. Clever and brave, she helped to hide the Prophet and Abu Bakr in a cave, then aided in their escape from Mecca. She performed no flashy, illustrious deeds. But her steady devotion and courage illustrate the valor of Muslim women at the founding of the religion. The small actions told of her in the Traditions constitute a moral example for later generations to follow.

Asmaa is a transitional figure who carries the story of Islam's early period from the deaths of Muhammad's greatest supporters, Khadija and Abu Talib, through his ultimate mystical experience, the Night Journey, then out of persecution in Mecca into authority in Medina: the *hijra*, when Muslims found a home.

Muhammad's Night Journey, *Isra*, and Ascension, *Mi'raj*, is the Muslim prototype for spiritual quest, when in a single night, God summoned the Prophet to travel from Mecca to Jerusalem, then into Heaven and back to Mecca. The *Isra* and *Mi'raj* confirmed Muhammad's prophethood and established Jerusalem as one of the three holy cities of Islam, along with Mecca and Medina.

> *Glory be to him, who carried His servant by night*
> *from the Sacred Mosque to the Farthest Mosque*
> *whose precincts We have blessed,*
> *that We may show him some of Our signs.*
> *He is the All-hearing, the All-seeing.*[8]

Outsiders and opponents have labeled the *Isra* and *Mi'raj* merely dream, merely delusion. But spiritual experiences worldwide confirm that such mystical travels are genuine and that they are, as Seyyed Hossein Nasr writes in *Ideals and Realities of Islam*, accomplished mentally, spiritually, and physically, implying "that the journey symbolizes the integration of [Muhammad's] whole being."

Legends have naturally flourished around the Night Journey. There is an exquisite tale that as he made his way into the Divine presence, up the ladder of light through the seven stages of Heaven, drops of Muhammad's sweat fell to the ground and from them the first fragrant rose materialized.

The women chosen for the portraits in this chapter are pivotal to the development of Islam, and they are also, in a sense, archetypes. Taken all together, they seem to represent Everywoman, each whole, yet each a part of a whole, each with characteristics possessed in various measure at various times by all women: mother, nurturer, lover, wife, sister, creator, dependent, self-sufficient, intellectual, intuitive, mystic, militant, and more.

Hind bint Utba, wife of the leader of the Meccan opposition to Muhammad, Abu Sufyan, has been stereotyped by the pious as a one-dimensional poster-girl for female evil.[9] Worldwide, morality tales are meant to teach girls to become obedient women, and Muslims are no exceptions with stories that illustrate good versus bad behavior.[10] In the religious lore, too, Hind is a model for sheer nastiness. The histories, however, convey a very definite sense that the Prophet himself did not perceive Hind as unusually fiendish. In her time, women took part in battles. Moreover, Hind is a grieving mother, and for that—though he condemned her to be executed for causing his uncle's death, unless she converted—Muhammad quite likely sympathized with her.

(After a battle against a Jewish tribe, a woman presented a poisoned lamb to Muhammad as revenge for the deaths of her husband, father, and uncle. The plot was discovered, but the Prophet pardoned her. He advocated forgiveness, but again, he must also have pitied the woman her losses.)

Although not everyone in Medina was willing to bow to his authority when he arrived, Muhammad was given an enthusiastic welcome. Back in Mecca, the Muslims' exodus meant sons and daughters had abandoned the fold; the old tribal hierarchies were suddenly undermined. Indeed, Ramlah, or Umm Habiba, the daughter of Abu Sufyan, was an early convert and migrated to Abyssinia with her Muslim husband, during a first attempt to escape persecution. She was widowed and later married the Prophet.

Nothing restrained Hind's amazing spirit and vigor. She became in some minds forever fixed as Islam's Salomé, its Jezebel. She was one of the last Meccans to hold out against Muhammad (she was nothing if not intrepid) and one of the last to surrender to Islam. Ironically, it was her line, the Umayyads, which dominated Islam during a dynasty that lasted for a hundred years out of Syria and then for centuries more in Spain.

By the time the small, victimized band of Muslims got to Medina, they realized that they were a force, actually making history. No longer hounded or hiding their faith, they were now a real community with an abode and a future. Whereas little was recorded before the *hijra*, in Medina every nuance was documented, every word and deed of the Prophet, every detail of every incident. Tales of angelic visitations and miraculous events gave way to straightforward historical records—although those sometimes bent toward gossip and innuendo, as well as historians' own prejudices and points of view.

This is not to say miracles end or that the angels desert humankind. But as time marches on, their appearances are less spectacular, less frequent, often attached to the emergence of saints or central figures of piety, such as Fatima, Muhammad's youngest, dearest, and last surviving daughter. Fatima's special connection to heavenly matters and her mythical status give proof to the Shi'a belief that she, her husband Ali ibn Abu Talib, and their two sons Hassan and Husayn are the only rightful successors to Muhammad—the People of the House,[11] Muhammad's direct descendants. (On some occasions in Shi'a doctrine, Ali is more eminent than the Prophet himself.) The Prophet, Fatima, Ali, Hassan, and Husayn form the *panjtan*, the Five People, or the *ahl al-kisa*, the People of the Cloak, for Muhammad took his daughter and son-in-law under his robe, or under his wing, as we'll see in the story of Fatima.

The Fatimids—a dynasty that began in North Africa in 287 A.H./909 C.E. and claimed the caliphate, then ruled Egypt and Syria until 549 A.H./1171 C.E.—took their name from Fatima. Their founder, Ubayd Allah al-Mahdi, claimed he was her descendant. As scholar and feminist Fatima Mernissi notes in *The Forgotten Queens of Islam*, for all that the Fatimids asserted their power through the lineage of a nearly divine woman, they were adamant in barring women from power.

In legends, folklore, and pageant plays, Fatima is confronted by the Angel of Death, Azrail, first when he visits to take her father Muhammad, and five months later when he comes to fetch Fatima herself. In these myths, he appears on Earth in more or less mundane form, but in Heaven, Lamborn Wilson tells us, Azrail

> is veiled before the creatures of God with a million veils. His immensity is vaster than the Heavens, and the East and West are between his hands like a dish on which all things have been set, or like a man who has been put between his hands that he might eat him, and he eats of him what he wishes; and thus the Angel of Death turns the world this way and that, just as men turn their money in their hands. He sits on a throne in the sixth Heaven. He has four faces, one before him, one on his head, one behind him and one beneath his feet. He has four wings, and his body is covered with innumerable eyes. When one of these eyes closes, a creature dies.[12]

Especially in Shi'a tradition, Fatima is festooned with wonders and miracles and almost deified by some Shi'ite branches. Like her father, she is said to have been born bathed in light; she was a virgin, she never menstruated, and her sons, Hassan and Husayn, were born through her left thigh. Like Mary, Fatima will intercede in Paradise for those who weep for her son.

It is said of her that in Paradise, Fatima sits on a throne, her head crowned, rings in her ears and a drawn sword at her girdle. The crown is her father, Muhammad the Prophet. The earrings are her sons. The sword is her husband, Ali. The throne is the Seat of Dominion, the resting place of God Most High. Fatima is ornamented with a million varicolored shimmering lights, which illuminate the whole of Paradise. She is the first vision the soul sees upon entering Paradise.

At the end of time, she will, with rigid retribution, ensure that justice prevails.

Not long after Khadija's death in 619 C.E. — and primarily after the migration to Medina in 622 — Muhammad embarked on a series of remarriages, of which Aisha bint Abu Bakr was the second after Sawdah bint Zamah, a plump, thirtysomething widow, who cared for his children and the household that was falling into disarray.

Aisha was nine years old at the time of her marriage to the Prophet. The union formed a kinship link to Aisha's father, Abu Bakr, Muhammad's closest Companion. Child brides were not unusual.[13] The marriage was not consummated until she reached puberty.

Muhammad was very much of a father figure to Aisha, yet their deep mutual love was far more complex than that of paternal affection and daughterly adoration. That Aisha became the Prophet's favorite, his Best Beloved, speaks to her strong personality, her wit and talents (she was a poet, a skilled astronomer, and more). She is said to have grown into a lovely woman; she was forthright and extremely bright, qualities in women that appealed to Muhammad, whose second favorite was Umm Salamah, a twenty-nine-year-old widow and sister of a leading member of the powerful Makhzum clan of Mecca. Although his wives took turns accompanying Muhammad on his campaigns, it was Umm Salamah he preferred to bring, for she had a strategist's mind and offered important advice.

Like Aisha, Umm Salamah had a jealous streak. Before marrying Muhammad, she informed him that she was not at all sure she could stand life in a harem as one among many. She managed. Marriage to the Prophet was, after all, highly valued. And since every wife had her own apartment built onto the new mosque at Medina, there was some privacy. Muhammad stayed with each of his wives in turn and was scrupulous about the schedule. Unlike many men, he genuinely enjoyed women's company, and he seemed to need their affection, as may be natural to one who has lost his mother at an early age.

Aisha was not chosen for her seductive charms, as was a later wife, Zaynab, a beauty whom Muhammad had accidentally seen undressed. He arranged for her to marry his adopted son Zayd, but

Zaynab, knowing the Prophet had feelings for her and not wishing to be married to a former slave, seems to have made life enough of a turmoil for Zayd that he offered to divorce her, and after a suitable period, Muhammad married her. Zaynab, too, came from a family of note, whose connection by marriage to the Prophet was beneficial to them and to his mission to unite Muslims.

Hafsa bint Umar, the young woman Muhammad married immediately after Aisha, was unattractive to him. She was the daughter of his Companion Umar ibn al-Khattab, and while she could be loving and jovial, she apparently also possessed her father's bad temper and cranky disposition. The marriage, however, created another vital family alliance, which would seal the "tribe" of Muslims.

Whereas Sawdah was an "old" woman, Hafsa gave Aisha an ally more or less close to her own age. When she died, Sawdah, whom the two younger ones ribbed incessantly with practical jokes, left Aisha her quarters. No doubt Aisha was grateful for many reasons, not least because as we'll see, with three graves populating her own quarters, she must have felt crowded.

Hafsa and Aisha were best friends all their lives. Fatima and Aisha were adversaries. One can imagine that Muhammad's favorite daughter would not welcome a favorite wife ten years her junior, a little girl who was married to her father before Fatima herself was wed. It's impossible, of course, to know from this cultural and chronological vantage point how Fatima really felt. But historians agree that there was no love lost between her and Aisha, although specific confrontations between the two women seem not to be discussed and there are few anecdotes in which the two are even in the same room.

The first political parties in Islam began with factions among Muhammad's wives. The lack of a named heir to the Prophet only exacerbated the divisions. Umm Salamah allied herself with Fatima and Ali. Umm Habiba, the daughter of Abu Sufyan, was of the Umayyad clan, in support of Uthman ibn Affan. Uthman had been married to Muhammad's daughter Ruqqayah, until her death. He was an early convert to Islam and with his great wealth, had helped support the Prophet financially.

30

Aisha and Hafsa supported their fathers, Abu Bakr and Umar, who became the first of the four Rightly Guided caliphs, or Successors. Uthman was the third. The disagreements in the *umma* about the chain of command came to a head with the murder of Uthman in 656 C.E. and Aisha's attempts to remedy the dissension among Muslims. Her activism culminated at the Battle of the Camel, where she fought Ali, in the belief that he had instigated or had some part in Uthman's death.

Ali became the fourth Rightly Guided caliph and went on to fight Hind bint Utba's son, Mu'awiya. After a member of Kharijite sect assassinated Ali in 39 A.H./661 C.E., Mu'awiya became the fifth caliph (though not "Rightly Guided"—a title reserved for the "Four Friends," Abu Bakr, Umar, Uthman, and Ali, contemporaries and Companions of the Prophet). Mu'awiya established the Umayyad Dynasty and took the Muslim capital out of Arabia to Damascus.

During the Prophet's lifetime and beyond, despite jealousies and competition within the harem, there were also affection and camaraderie and hours of immense enjoyment, gossip, fun, and activity between the "sisters," as his wives called themselves. As Mothers of the Believers, after Muhammad's death, his wives periodically came together to confer about the direction of the *umma*, the turns that politics were taking. Occasionally, they acted together as one decidedly authoritative voice. Yet their differences also reflected the schisms within the Muslim community, and it appears that as time went on and the divisions widened, many of Muhammad's widows grew increasingly estranged.

Across the centuries, some Westerners have labeled Muhammad "lustful," a "seducer," a "lecher." This prurient interest in the Prophet's sexual prowess has been lurid and misguided, often depicting the Prophet as having waited until his first wife was dead to give rein to his nether impulses. Sadly, this colonialist picture of the Prophet as immoral or decadent extended into an acutely harmful concept that Muslims are licentious and promiscuous, an idea aggravated by accounts of European travelers looking at Muslim societies through culturally alien lenses.[14]

31

In all three Abrahamic religions, there is no sexual duality in God and all three call on their followers to "go forth and multiply." Islam acknowledges the real and God-given human desires, does not hold to celibacy, and believes that marriage, the union between feminine and masculine, is God's will.

"To marry is my *sunna* (custom)," Muhammad said. And: "There is no monkery in Islam." Polygamy was the norm in pre-Islamic Arabia, as elsewhere in tribal societies. Yet there were no limitations and no laws to protect women. The Qur'an tried to correct these injustices by limiting to four the number of wives a man could have. But he may not have even that number if he cannot treat them all equitably. This rule is not about a man's financial wherewithal, but about whether he can love them each unvaryingly and treat them accordingly. Many contemporary Muslim feminists, female and male, believe the endgame was to eliminate polygamy altogether, for the trick—as the Prophet was well aware—is that most people find it impossible to act toward everyone with equal justice. Today, polygamy is practiced only very rarely among Muslims.

There are also strong admonitions in the Qur'an to "marry the spouseless," to take as wives the widows and the orphans, that is, those with no providers, no fathers or grown sons to feed, clothe, and house them. The wars between Muslims and Meccans left many females alone and helpless. To take them as wives was to give them support and roofs over their heads. To marry them would also have saved them from dependence on the Quraysh, whereby they risked punishment for being Muslim and would have been forced to revert to the old ways where they had no legal status.

Why then did Muhammad have more wives than the four proscribed by the Qur'an? When he died, he had nine (and some say it may have been eleven or twelve, although some might have been concubines). In *Muhammad: A Biography of the Prophet*, Karen Armstrong proposes that as an increasingly powerful Arab *sayyid*, it may have been expected of Muhammad that he have many wives to emphasize his status. Marrying these women—all of whom, except Aisha, were widows—helped keep the new Muslims together and shaped kinships with important tribal groups (such as his marriage to

Safiyyah bint Huayy, from a Jewish tribe). Through these women and their children, family ties radiated farther and farther into the world, bringing others closer to the *umma*.

"The multiple marriages of the Prophet," Nasr writes, "far from pointing to his weakness towards 'the flesh,' symbolize his patriarchal nature and his function, not as a saint who withdraws from the world, but as one who sanctifies the very life of the world by living in it."[15] Muhammad's wives never diverted him from God.

He did his best to treat each one with equal justice and was an example to his flock of honorable behavior toward women. There was, however, an incident in which he threatened to divorce every one of them and moved into cramped quarters to be separated from them for a month. It was not their jealousies and tiffs that drove him out, but their escalating hunger for comfort and luxury, as wives of the leader of a progressively prosperous community. Regardless of how much the *ghazus*—the raids—and his growing standing throughout the region brought affluence and wealth, Muhammad lived frugally. He hated extravagance. He had only one set of clothes made of the coarse cloth worn by ordinary folk, and sometimes there was not enough to eat in his household, for when he received gifts of his share of the booty, he gave it away to the poor. His Companions, particularly Umar ibn al-Khattab, exhorted him to dress to match his position, but he would not. The poor, he told his people, would make their way to Paradise before the rich, a statement that mirrors those of Jesus.

That his own wives proposed to violate the duties of Muslims to create an egalitarian society was too much. He gave them the choice to shape up and live a righteous Islamic life or leave with an amicable divorce.

> *It is possible that if he divorces you,*
> *his Lord will give him wives better than you,*
> *women who have surrendered, believing,*
> *penitent and devout, given to fasting.*[16]

All his wives agreed to his terms and Muhammad returned home.

That the Prophet had no children with all those wives other than Khadija has also led to unpleasant speculations about his health and habits. But it may simply have been that, although he spent time with each in her turn, he rarely had sexual congress with them, except to do his husbandly duty and preserve their honors, since most of his marriages were alliances for political or charitable reasons. All but Aisha had children from previous marriages. Aisha may not have conceived for the very reason that she was so young, widowed when she was barely eighteen. That Muhammad was in his fifties when he began taking new wives after Khadija's death may well have been a factor, too, although a few years before he died he had a son, who died in infancy, by Maryam, a Coptic Christian from Egypt, given to him as a concubine.

Poor Aisha longed for a *kunya* like the other wives, such as Umm Salamah, "Mother of Salamah," or Umm Habiba, "Mother of Habiba." A *kunya* is an Arabic honorific whereby women and men, rather than using their given names are called *Umm* or *Abu*— "mother of," "father of"—followed by the name of the eldest child. It seemed to Aisha that within the harem, only she would be destined forever to be merely Aisha (though she took pride in having been the only virgin). As a consolation, Muhammad designated her Umm Abdallah, "Mother of Abdallah," her nephew, her sister Asmaa's son. That Abdallah was the first Muslim child to be born in Medina was a mark of high distinction for Aisha, having as much to do with the birth of the community as with the birth of an actual child. Throughout her life, Aisha loved Abdallah more than anyone, she said, except Muhammad. They were indeed close, though there was a brief period during the battles over succession that she and Abdallah argued. After some breathing space, they were happily reconciled and he led the prayer for the dead at her funeral.

Cultural changes throughout the ages affected the lives of Muslim women, but early Islam allowed them to realize and satisfy

their capabilities and talents. Aisha's life illustrates this as no other.
While she may have failed in her quest to bring peace, order, and
justice back to a community at odds with itself, and while she felt
acute guilt about that failure for the rest of her life, still she was
able to move freely and be heard as she attempted to implement
her husband's vision, to fulfill her potential, as well as what she saw
as her duty.

Islam is not, as many in the West imagine, a faith designed to
stifle and devastate women, in spite of the subjugation that began
soon after the Prophet's death or attempts made even before by such
as Umar ibn al-Khattab, the second Rightly Guided caliph, to keep
women locked up, out of public life. Umar is frequently quoted as
saying, "Take refuge in God from the evils caused by women and
beware [even] of the most pious of them." *Hadith*, or sayings of the
Prophet, which seem to indicate that Muhammad thought little of
women, are quoted as well as proof that the repression of women is
acceptable, in fact, desirable, in Islam. But these are frequently
taken out of context and belie Muhammad's true admiration for
women and his determination to reform the laws and customs that
oppressed them.

From the standpoint of the Qur'an, the subjugation appears to
begin with the Verses of the Curtain, which cause extreme confusion
among Muslims and Westerners alike about women's place in Islam
and issues of seclusion, the veil, and the harem. In fact, the curtain
was meant to discourage petitioners from constantly approaching the
Prophet's wives and to spare them harassment. Muhammad's wives
were to stay behind a curtain to speak to outsiders and to wear mantles on their heads, not full facial coverings. There were those in
Medina, called "The Hypocrites," who remained dangerous enemies
of the Muslims and resented Muhammad's authority.

O Prophet, say to the wives and daughters
and the believing women, that they draw their veils close to them
so that it is likelier they will be known, and not hurt.[17]

Yet the Qur'an allowed that

There is no fault in the Prophet's wives touching their fathers,
their sons, their brothers, their brothers' sons,
their sisters' sons, their women
and what their right hands own.[18]

That the *hijab*—the curtain or veiling—reflected the high rank of the Mothers of the Faithful seems to have caused envy among other women, who took to the veil and the curtain as a symbol of distinction and respect. As is common among many societies, certain kinds of headdresses distinguished not only tribes among the pre-Islamic Arabs, but the freeborn from slaves, rich from poor. These often decorative head cloths—which among the traditional Bedouin people can be ornamented with coins and other items describing a family's wealth and status—were not veils, per se, and did not necessarily hide the face. Headgear protected against the driving desert sun.

All Muslims are enjoined to dress and act moderately. Men and women alike must exercise Quranic principles of self-constraint. "The Qur'an acknowledges the virtue of modesty and demonstrates it through the prevailing practices," Amina Wadud-Muhsin writes in *Qur'an and Woman*. "The principle of modesty is important—not the veiling and seclusion which were manifestations particular to that context....All believing women deserve the utmost respect and protection of their modesty—however it is observed in various societies."

From Umar, suppression escalated, such that an Islamic theologian of the eleventh century C.E. echoed attitudes of other men, claiming, "all the trials, misfortunes and woes which befall men come from women."

Not all Muslim men were in favor of the suppression of women. "Whosoever knows the worth of women and the mystery reposing in them will not refrain from loving them," Spanish-Arab mystic Ibn al-Arabi (523 A.H./1145 C.E. to 618 A.H./1240 C.E.) said.

"Indeed, love for them is part of the perfection of a man knowing God for it is a legacy of the Prophet and a Divine love."

And Ibn Rashd, the great Spanish-Arab philosopher known as Averroës (504 A.H./1126 C.E. to 576 A.H./1198 C.E.), wrote, perhaps also addressing Jews and Christians, "In our states...the ability of women is not known, because they are taken only for procreation. They are therefore placed at the service of their husbands and relegated to the business of childrearing and breastfeeding. Because women are considered unfit for any of the human virtues, it often happens that they resemble plants. That they are a burden to the men in these states is one of the reasons for the poverty of these states."

Across centuries and despite oppressive measures, there were always vociferous women of strong personality, skills, and talents, who played assertive roles in the history and cultural life of Islamic countries. It begins at the beginning with the women of the Prophetate.

Barakah

Barakah was a slave from Abyssinia (today's Ethiopia and Eritrea), in the Meccan household of the Prophet Muhammad's father, Abdallah. Like most Abyssinians, she may originally have been a Coptic Christian. She attended Muhammad's birth and outlived him. She was Muhammad's surrogate mother and one of the first of his devoted followers. Her dates are unknown.

In the household of Abdallah, Barakah is the only servant. Among the Arabs there are no more prominent and stately men than the ten sons of Abd al-Muttalib. Their noses are so large that the nose drinks before the lips. Abdallah is the youngest son and none is more handsome or dear to Abd al-Muttalib. When Abdallah marries Amina bint Wabh, Barakah cares for the young woman and they become as family.

Two weeks after the wedding, Abdallah's father, Abd al-Muttalib, clan chief of the Hashim, comes to the door. He speaks to his son in hushed tones. The young man's voice rises in protest. The next morning, Abdallah leaves his bride with Barakah and departs with a trading caravan for Syria.

Amina weeps. "O Barakah, how can my husband go while traces of the wedding henna are still on my hands?"

"The son may not disobey the father," Barakah answers and leads Amina to her bed to rest. Amina refuses to eat and will see and speak to no one but Barakah, although she receives her father-in-law,

38

old Abd al-Muttalib, hoping for news of Abdallah. Barakah sleeps on a mat at the foot of Amina's bed.

Amina remains in bed for weeks. One afternoon, she calls for Barakah.

"I have had a strange dream," she says.

"Something good, I hope," Barakah replies.

"Lights flooded from my belly, rising like the dawn. Brighter and brighter until they lit the mountains. They illuminated the hills and all the valleys around Mecca. What can it mean?"

"Are you pregnant, my lady?"

"I feel no discomfort."

"You will give birth to a blessed child, who will bring goodness," Barakah tells Amina.

This news does not cheer her. The baby grows inside her, but Abdallah is still in Syria and she has no word of him. Barakah sits with her and tells her stories—"There was and there was not...a mighty monarch...a mischievous monkey...a greedy merchant"—and Amina is delighted. Yet as quickly as she laughs, she slips back into melancholy.

An angel visits Amina in a dream. The lights soaring out of her womb are so intense she can see the Syrian castles of Bostra. She is marveling at them, wondering if Abdallah is awed by them, too, when the angel speaks:

You carry in your womb the Lord of this people. When he is born, say aloud, "I place this child beneath the protection of the One, from the evil of every envier." And name your son Muhammad, the Praised One.

The days pass, slowly, too slowly, while they await Abdallah's return. One day, Abd al-Muttalib arrives, hurried, breathless, still without news of his son, but with urgent orders to Amina that she must flee immediately to the mountains.

Abraha of the Yemen is closing in on the prosperous city. Meccans are evacuating. Abraha brings Abyssinian elephants to destroy the Ka'aba and steal away the sacred Black Stone that fell from Heaven long ago like a plunging sunray and which now links Earth and Sky. With their behemoth flat feet Abraha's beasts will kick to splinters the 360 tribal totems that surround the shrine and grind to gravel the square granite building. With their mighty trunks, Abraha's elephants will crush the images of the tribal gods and the three daughters of Allah housed near that place of pilgrimage: al-Lat the Sovereign, al-Uzza the Mighty One, and Manat goddess of Fate.

"I cannot leave," Amina tells Abd al-Muttalib. "I am weak with child and weaker still with yearning for Abdallah."

Her father-in-law insists. They will die at the hands of Abraha and then what will Abdallah find on his return? Then it will be his turn to grieve.

"Abraha will never enter Mecca nor raze the Ka'aba," Amina says. "It is protected by Allah. It cannot be harmed."

Abd al-Muttalib orders her, then pleads with her, and at last realizes that his daughter-in-law is immovable, that she has no fear. Abd al-Muttalib sees no choice but to allow Amina the fate she chooses. May al-Lat and Manat watch over her. He scurries home to pack up his own brood and escape.

If her mistress is unafraid, neither will Barakah allow herself to be fearful.

And lo, Abraha's elephants refuse to attack the City of the Future Prophet. The animals stand fast. No prodding, beating, or shouting can force them through the city gates. Behind them, flocks of birds drop stones from their beaks onto the heads of Abraha's cavalry. They gallop away in retreat.

> *Have you not considered how your Lord dealt with the*
> *men of the elephant?*
> *Did He not send their schemes astray?*
> *He sent flocks of birds against them,*
> *Hurling against them stones of baked clay,*
> *and he made them devoured like green blades.*[19]

Amina has no interest in wars or victories. As the Meccans return from the mountains, she stares at the street through her screened window, hoping that each young man who passes will be Abdallah. He will turn the corner and burst in the door. The reunion will be pure joy, it will be bliss, the marriage will truly begin and when he hears that she is with child, he will praise Allah and the daughters of Allah and then praise her.

Amina moans and mutters and calls for Abdallah in her sleep. Barakah awakens when the groans turn to shrieks. She slips into Amina's bed, holds her, tries to comfort her, and failing that comforts the baby by patting Amina's growing belly. Barakah's hand warms from the heat escaping from within that womb.

She slides from the bed while Amina sleeps on. Preparing the morning meal, Barakah peers out the screened window at an approaching caravan. Families tumble into the street to welcome home their trading sons and brothers and fathers. Barakah opens the door quietly so as not to waken her mistress and runs to Abd al-Muttalib's house.

But this is only the first leg of the caravan that departed for Syria so many months ago. Abdallah is not yet among them. Very soon, Abd al-Muttalib assures Barakah, the rest will return.

More hopeful now, Barakah returns to Amina, who heaves herself belly first from the bed. Barakah offers bread and goat's milk—just a little for the baby's sake, she urges. Amina nibbles and collapses onto the sheepskin mattress. Barakah does not mention the caravan.

Again Barakah goes to the house of Abd al-Muttalib. She goes for gifts of dates, grain, milk, and meat to sustain her mistress and herself. She is there when Abdallah's brother Harith arrives from Yathrib. News had come to Abd al-Muttalib that Abdallah was ill. He had told no one, least of all Amina. Instead he sent his son Harith to collect his brother. Now Harith announces that he was too late. Abdallah is dead.

Abd al-Muttalib beats his chest. The women of the household wail.

Barakah bolts onto the street, running along the alleys, crying and keening. She trips and stumbles, careens into walls and donkeys and strangers.

41

At Amina's door Barakah pauses to collect herself. She presses her hands on her chest to stop her heart's flailing. She wipes the tears from her face. She strides purposefully into Amina's bedroom and gently tells her mistress the painful news.

Amina rolls her eyes heavenward, as if she'd known all along, as if she had been mourning all along for Abdallah's death. And then she faints. She hovers between life and death, aware only of the vibrant light within her.

It is a hot August day when the birth pangs come upon Amina. And although the heat could melt rocks, Amina does not sweat in her labor, for the wings of angels shelter and fan her. The baby slides into the world, aglow like a tiny lantern.

Barakah is the first to hold the newborn infant in her arms.

Amina caresses her son's sweet small face, she runs her finger along the trace of arched eyebrows, she smooths the wet, curly down on his head and intones, "I place this child beneath the protection of the One, from the evil of every envier. I name him Muhammad, 'the Praised One.'"

The heavens are resplendent. The sheltering angels leave a new mattress and a clean, soft coverlet so that Amina can rest in comfort.

Barakah hands the baby to Abd al-Muttalib, who waits on the doorstep. He carries the infant to the Ka'aba, and makes the *tawwaf*, circling the shrine seven times, rejoicing and offering prayers of thanksgiving for this gift to his clan. A *kahin* has prophesied that one day one of his descendants will rule the world. This child is surely the one, for Abd al-Muttalib has had a dream in which a luminous tree grew from his grandson's back. It ascended into heaven and its branches stretched east and west. "I have seen the *sakina*," Abd al-Muttalib tells Amina. "The glory of God coming forth and his Peace from your son."

Indeed, the infant bears a mark between his shoulder blades. Some whisper that this is a seal of prophecy.

He takes his grandson to his house, where his young wife, Amina's cousin Halah, awaits the birth of her own son, the boy who will be Hamza. Abd al-Muttalib shows the beautiful child

Muhammad to all his family. One by one, down to the youngest, they kiss the newborn in greeting.

Barakah guards Amina, who sleeps soundly now, her son nestled against her heart. The slave girl is nodding off, squatting on the floor, her back against the wall, when a form appears. Barakah is neither startled nor afraid. The shape shimmers and gleams like an ember and when it has departed, Barakah finds a warm blanket, a pitcher of water, a basin, and a towel beside Amina's bed. Barakah drops the blanket softly over mother and baby. At the day's first light, *falaq al-subh*, when the sun breaks through the darkness, she and Amina bathe the infant Muhammad and dedicate him to God.

It is customary for children of city families to send their infants to the *badiyah*, to the desert's clear air. No matter how poor—and Amina is poor, for Abdallah did not live long enough to make his fortune—families of the Quraysh send their children to learn the arts and way of life of the Bedouin.

Amina chooses a woman called Halima to take the baby Muhammad. The foster mother is also poor. She has barely any milk, yet when she puts the infant Muhammad to nurse, her milk flows and flows, thick and nutritious. She nurses Muhammad on one breast. He refuses to take the other, but leaves it for Halima's birth son. The babies are plump and satisfied. Even Halima's dried out flock begins to give milk again, so much the family now has cheese and yogurt in profusion.

"Your boy," Halima tells Amina, "is a blessed creature indeed."

"Great things are in store for my son," Amina agrees.

Amina asks to have her little one back. But Halima begs to keep him just a while longer. He is thriving in the desert, she reminds Amina, see how the badiyah agrees with him, how sturdy he is and how he walks with straight, strong legs. Halima brings Muhammad to visit his mother and Barakah often. If not for Barakah, Amina would be unbearably lonely. Yet Halima persuades her to let Muhammad stay, for with his presence her family prospers.

43

Muhammad and his foster brothers toddle off to play behind the tents, while Halima cooks. The foster brothers scream. Halima drops her vessels and runs to them. There is Muhammad, only three, lying as if dead. Two strangers in white seized him, the other boys cry. They cut him open from chest to gut. They took his heart from his body. They took a shining black stone, shaped like a teardrop, from his heart and then they washed it with snow. They lifted him onto a pair of scales. They declared the child was heavier than all the Arabs put together. They kissed him on the forehead and one of the strangers said gently: "O beloved of God, you will never be frightened and if you knew what good has been prepared for you, you would be very happy."

Halima sends her sons to find their father. The child who has brought such success to their family has had a stroke, she says. They cannot keep him any longer, they must return him to his mother before there is more damage. Perhaps it is the intensity of the goodness Muhammad provides that has opened and emptied him.

Amina languishes again. Weeping and weeping. She hates this separation from her son. They tell her it is right, it is customary. It is good for the child. Leave him with the Bedouin.

She is overjoyed when Halima arrives and this time hands the child over for good. Halima tells Amina of Muhammad's wound. She calms Halima and reassures her. This is an exceptional child, she reminds Halima.

"A great future has been foretold for my son," Amina says.

Halima weeps and embraces Muhammad as she departs. She tells her husband, "Here is a child who will change the world."

Barakah, too, has missed Muhammad. She welcomed the happy company of the child from that first moment she held him, when she herself washed him and swaddled him and rubbed her cheek against his and smelled his fragrance of musk.

She tells him stories: "There was and there was not…a mighty monarch…a mischievous monkey….a greedy merchant…." She plays and laughs with him. He brings laughter at last into the house, laughter and love to sad Amina.

Barakah takes the child to visit daily with his grandfather and his uncles Hamza and Abbas. Hamza is three weeks younger than Muhammad and Abbas younger still. And dear to all three boys is Hamza's and Abbas' little sister, Muhammad's aunt Safiyya. All their lives, Hamza and Safiyya and Muhammad will be inseparable.

Amina must at last reconnect with Abdallah. The years she has missed him, yearned for the life they might have lived, must be put to rest.

When Muhammad is six, his mother determines to visit the grave of Abdallah in Yathrib. Barakah begs Amina to change her mind. It will only rekindle the pain. But Amina is stubborn. There is never any gain in arguing with her. They join a northbound caravan, traveling on camels for ten days. Muhammad rides in the *hawdaj* snuggled in Barakah's robe. In Yathrib, the boy plays with his cousins and learns to swim and fly kites. Barakah stays close by his side while Amina visits her husband's grave each day for many weeks.

They are riding in the *hawdaj*, returning at last to Mecca, when Amina complains of illness. Barakah touches her lips. They burn with fever. Amina cannot hold her eyes open. Her cheeks ache. Her tongue swells. At al-Abwa, Barakah brings her mistress down from the camel and lays her on the ground. She cradles Amina, rocks her and sings to her. Muhammad grasps Amina's hand, his eyes wide with confusion.

Night descends. It battens down the sky like the black, dense flap of a tent so even the desert stars are shut out. Amina opens her eyes and looks at her son. He is enveloped in a golden aura, like an egg, the same texture of light that soared from her belly when she carried him.

"I am dying, Barakah," she says in a voice thick as a syrup of dates. "I will be gone within the hour. I commend my son Muhammad to your care. Be a mother to him. Never abandon him."

The little boy sets up a howl and throws himself at his mother. He clings to her neck to bind her to him. She kisses him, sighs, and is gone. All his life, Muhammad will be afflicted by grinding pain

45

when those he loves depart, though he will come to know that they await him in Paradise.

Barakah's heart shatters. She wails. She sobs as she digs Amina's grave with her own hands.

She does not want to leave the grave, to forsake Amina in the desert. Nevertheless, she mounts the camel with Muhammad and returns to Mecca. She tells tales to distract the frightened little boy. "There was and there was not...."

She takes the child to Abd al-Muttalib and stays with him for two years, until that beloved grandfather passes on as well. Then Barakah takes the boy to the house of his kind uncle Abu Talib and looks after him there until he is grown.

He calls her Umma, Mother, "The mother after my own mother. The mother who will never abandon me."

Khadija bint Khuwaylid

*Khadija was born in 555 C.E., a member of Mecca's lead-
ing Quraysh family, the daughter of Khuwaylid ibn Asad
and Fatima bint Za'idah. She was widowed twice before
marrying Muhammad, and had two sons. Khadija was a
businesswoman, who increased her already considerable
fortune by fitting out caravans to engage in trade. It is generally related that Khadija was forty and Muhammad
twenty-five when they married, but some authorities believe
they were thirty-three and eighteen. Khadija died in 619
C.E., before the* hijra, *the Flight to Medina. She is known
as "the Pure One" and "the Great."*

No sooner does Khadija's second husband die than she is beset with
proposals of marriage from one merchant after another. Princely
clans of the Quraysh send their emissaries offering profitable unions.
But Khadija does not desire more profit. Greed is god in Mecca.
What she seeks is not found in the worship of money. If she marries
again, she will marry for love and no other reason.

Her dreams are vivid with yearning for companionship. To
have and to be a helpmeet. To love and encourage. To share all that
she owns with an open and willing heart. When she has a moment
away from the clamor of business, she meditates on her balcony,
avoiding her suitors, musing, reflecting on the past, contemplating
what could be. At last she calls forth a monk.

She has, she tells the old Christian, dreamed of a full moon
falling in her lap and shining across the world.

The sage glares long and hard at his hands. When he finally clears his throat and speaks, his voice is so low, Khadija must lean forward to hear him.

"You will marry a man about to receive God's Revelations, but to be sure you recognize him, you must watch carefully for signs."

Khadija leans in a little closer.

"Though the sun beats mercilessly on others, this man always walks in the shade," the monk says. "He will have pure white eyeballs and jet-black pupils. His eyebrows are connected like the two arches of a bow. The scent of musk surrounds him and lingers behind him. This is the fragrance of Divine knowledge."

Khadija's mind, shrewd in business and therefore the ways of the world, snatches the words of the sage and stores them carefully. Her future is contained in them.

"You will have twenty-five years of happy marriage with this man," the sage adds as he departs.

The heat is unbearable. Khadija sits under an awning on the flat roof of her three-storied house, hoping for a fresh breeze. Since the monk has been to see her, she's less lonely, more hopeful, yet still somehow suspended, merely waiting.

She fans herself and watches caravans leaving and entering the city, bound for Syria and the Yemen, Abyssinia, Yathrib, and Jerusalem. The long camel processions jingle and jangle with bells on their saddles; the goods they carry clank and clatter. Braided colors of bridles undulate on waves of dazzling sunlight and shimmering dust motes. Rich caravans pass and then a modest train, which Khadija knows to be that of the Banu Hashim, whose fortunes have greatly waned since the death of their patriarch, Abd al-Muttalib.

His son Abu Talib leads the procession. They suffer in the midday sun, but one young man, lean and handsome, rides in the shade no matter which way he turns. A trick of clouds? Khadija squints to make out the shape. The cloud is an angel, whose wide wings are spread over the young man's head. She alone, it seems, can see the angel. The young man's fellow travelers and the other women watching from roofs and balconies are unaware of its presence.

48

The caravan moves out of sight. Khadija drops back under her awning, dizzy, holding her head in her hands. Is this the sign Allah has sent as the sage promised?

That afternoon, Khadija calls for her friend and neighbor, Atika. Cautiously, casually, she asks Atika about the caravan that passed by at noon that day. Atika nibbles dates and settles into the conversation.

Yes, indeed, the caravan belongs to her relative Abu Talib, who has been traveling with his orphaned nephew Muhammad ibn Abdallah. They are upright folk of excellent family, but poor. Although Abu Talib is searching high and low for a bride for his nephew, Atika says, no suitable candidate has appeared.

"Abu Talib loves his nephew like a son, but his lowly position makes it difficult to find the right match," she tells Khadija. "Why, Muhammad even asked for his cousin, Fakhita—they grew up together—but Abu Talib decided this was not advantageous and made Fakhita a much more prosperous match with the Makhzum clan. That boy has many abilities, but he is, after all, a penniless orphan."

Khadija nods, taking in the family gossip. She is a business-woman. She knows when to be subtle and sly and when to be blunt. Here is her moment.

"Might I be a suitable candidate for marriage to Muhammad ibn Abdallah?"

The date Atika is aiming at her mouth drops from her hand. Muhammad is fifteen years younger than Khadija! Khadija is experienced. A widow—twice! A mother. She has all the money in the world. What would she want with a young man of no means?

Khadija persists. "I would like to meet him," she says. "Here in my own house. I would like you to convey this message to Abu Talib."

She does not add that she believes it is God's design that she should marry Muhammad. There are some things a clever woman keeps to herself.

Atika arrives, breathless and thrilled, at Abu Talib's house. She flings Khadija's proposal at him. Abu Talib is first taken aback and then delighted.

The scent of musk precedes him as Muhammad ibn Abdallah enters Khadija's room. His hair and beard are curly. His face has the hungry look of an ascetic, and his expression is luminous. His eyebrows meet like the two arches of a bow. Black pupils penetrate pure white eyeballs.

She is always in control, always aloof in order to observe, then make the best decision. But suddenly, Khadija feels lost and sick with a buoyant sickness that must be love.

He gives her his full attention. Throughout his life, he will give each person and each task his entire awareness. For this—and for his honesty and decisiveness—he is known in Mecca as al-Amin, the Reliable One. It is a name given him one day when he arrived at Ka'aba to make the *tawwaf* and found men repairing the shrine, but arguing over who would have the honor of replacing the last stone. Muhammad suggested that they transport it on a cloth, each taking a corner. For this, they named him al-Amin, the Trustworthy, and gave him the privilege of setting the stone. It is a story that further reassures Khadija.

She finds her voice. She tells Muhammad ibn Abdallah that she wishes to marry him and that she expects no *mahar* from him. "I have no need of money."

"It is the custom among Arabs to pay the bride-price," he replies, "and I do not wish to change it."

"I will advance you the money. You can pay me later when you are in better circumstances."

No. He insists he must earn his own bride-wealth as the patriarch Jacob had earned his by working for seven years. He smiles at her. For all that she is older, she is nonetheless attractive. She has grace and nobility and a face that is calm and welcoming and wise. She is in no way haughty, as a woman of her wealth might be, but her stance reveals independence, a quality he likes in women. Although he is not usually one to ascribe motives, he had wondered why a woman of such status would want him. Standing before her, it becomes clear that here is a woman with a restless spirit, reaching for something higher and purer than is possible in Meccan society. It's the same for him: he is frustrated by the ignorance and acquisi-

WOMEN OF THE PROPHETATE

tiveness of the Quraysh and the other clans, yet he knows no solution, has no handle with which to grasp another way of thinking.

Khadija smiles sadly back at Muhammad. She hasn't time to
wait. Not if they are to have twenty-five years of happy marriage. She
does not argue or try harder to persuade him to take her loan of the
bride-price. Love is not about bargaining in the bazaar. He leaves
with the matter unsettled.

The scent of the perfume of Paradise lingers. She is more certain than ever that Muhammad is the one the monk described. And
with that certainty comes the faith that he will be back soon.

Barakah wakes abruptly in the night. Is the house on fire? She
sprints toward Muhammad's room and the golden flames. She can
never forget the marvels that attended him even before he was
born. Yet since Amina's death and then Abd al-Muttalib's, since
they went to live with Abu Talib, those signs of greatness seem to
have diminished. A child needs to play and learn in the ordinary
ways of children. Abu Talib made sure that Muhammad was
trained with his uncles in archery, wrestling, and swordsmanship.
He did well, though Hamza, the uncle born just weeks after
Muhammad, truly excelled. Muhammad was taught the skills of
merchants so prized by Meccans. At this, too, he was adroit, but
Abbas, younger still than Hamza, took to accounting as a bird to
air. And Abu Talib instructed the three boys to pray at the Ka'aba,
and although once he sacrificed a white sheep to al-Uzza the
Mighty One, daughter of Allah, for some reason Muhammad
refused to direct his devotion to any but Allah. Barakah watched
the boy circle the house that Ibrahim built and caught glimpses of
the holy aura that had surrounded him as a child.

A hot orange glow streams from the open door. Barakah is ready
with a jar of water to put out the flames, and she is about to hurl it,
when the figure of an angel holding a basket takes shape within the
blaze. He lays the basket beside the young man's sleeping head and
says aloud that it is the will of Allah that he should marry Khadija.

"Give her this as a wedding present," the angel orders
Muhammad.

Barakah slips back to her bed. This marriage will nourish Muhammad and restore the brilliance that has been buried these years. When the sun rises, she hurries to pour him at least a cup of milk and honey before he careens out the door. "Thank you, Umma," he shouts, and runs along the winding streets to Khadija's three-storied house.

Khadija is half asleep. Muhammad, grinning, presents her with the little basket. She scoops rubies, emeralds, sapphires through her fingers. Each stone is worth a fortune. A *mahar* for a queen.

On their wedding day, they agree: this *mahar* from God must go to the poor.

"Which poor, my dear?" Khadija asks, and Muhammad chooses that the basket of gems go to the orphans, for he himself is an orphan.

Her gift to him is a slave boy, Zayd ibn Harith.

Muhammad's hands are cool as ice and soft as silk.

"Ya Umma," Muhammad calls to Barakah one day. "Now I am a married man, what would you think if someone asked to marry you?"

Barakah glances at him skeptically and returns to her task. "I shall never leave you," she says. "Does a mother abandon her son?"

Muhammad smiles and kisses her head.

"Barakah," Khadija turns the serving woman toward her. "You have sacrificed your youth for Muhammad. Now he wants to pay back some of his obligations to you."

Barakah lowers her eyes. "Whom shall I marry?" she murmurs. This is unimaginable. She has no sense of her self beyond her duties and the love she bears for Muhammad, no sense of her own beauty.

"Ubayd ibn Zayd from the Khazrajd tribe of Yathrib has come to us seeking your hand. Don't refuse, Barakah. He has seen you at your chores and in the street and market. For Muhammad's sake and mine, say yes. You should be married before old age overtakes you. You should have a household and children of your own."

Khadija gives Barakah a sumptuous wedding and afterward Barakah goes with Ubayd ibn Zayd to Yathrib. Her heart aches for Muhammad and for familiar places. But it is not long before she bears a son she calls Ayman.

Khadija settles into deep contentment. Her husband takes her caravans to trade throughout the region. When he returns, they lie awake at night talking not much of business, but of all he's ascertained on his journeys. He has met Zoroastrians from Persia, Hindus from India, Christians, and Jews. The holy books of Jews and Christians—words bestowed by God and preserved in supple lines on parchment—intrigue him. He cannot read or write.

He is devout. He performs the *tawwaf*, trotting around the Ka'aba every day that he is home. Khadija joins him. He is admired by the Meccans, who nevertheless disapprove of the way he seems to pray to himself as he circles the great granite structure, ignoring the totems, paying no tribute to the idols within. And he despises the *kahin*, who hang about the Ka'aba and on whom so many Meccans rely. These soothsayers who call themselves prophets fall into trances, babble auguries for the finding of lost camels or fortunes to appear around the corner. They chant, cover themselves with their cloaks, drooling drivel and gibberish.

"They are worthless," Muhammad tells Khadija and anyone else who will listen. "Their prophecies are senseless. They cause more harm than good and only keep souls tied to their earthly corruptions."

The Meccans are incredulous, too, that with Khadija's wealth, the family lives so frugally. Muhammad gives large sums to orphans and the poor. It is wrong, he tells Khadija, to hoard riches. We are not in this life to deprive others. He will not own more than one set of clothing at a time. He loathes luxury.

Khadija enjoys puzzling out the labyrinth of business, but she too has little interest in money. In *zakat*, the giving of alms, she discovers joy and relief from unnecessary burdens. Her husband's way of life provides more concentration on the family, on affection. To live lavishly distracts from the satisfactions of daily life, the simplicities that lead the heart to the Divine.

And she is busy with babies. They delight her and they break her heart, for of the six, both her newborn sons, her little Qasim and Abdallah, have died.

Khadija and Muhammad spend hours with their daughters, Zaynab, Ruqayyah, Umm Kulthum, and Fatima. He brings young

Zayd into the fold, as if the slave boy were one of his own. He does not hold with slavery. "Let them wear what we wear and let them eat what we eat," he says.

He is enchanted by children. His girls tug at his robes and lead him about like a pet. They climb all over him demanding hugs and kisses he readily furnishes. He joins them in their games. Khadija laughs as he crawls about the courtyard playing at wolves and sheep or sits on the floor dressing their dolls with them.

How can people bury alive their unwanted infant daughters? He holds his girls, ferociously, protectively, to his breast. The thought of killing such small, sweet innocents repels him.

He surely mourns and misses his boys. Yet it seems to Khadija that Allah has filled the hole in Muhammad's heart left by their deaths. Muhammad frees Zayd and adopts him. Abu Talib's fortunes have fallen farther, so Muhammad takes in his uncle's youngest son, Ali.

Each year, the whole family makes a spiritual retreat to Mount Hira, to a cave, where they spend a month in prayer and almsgiving.

Where her household had seemed barren, even during her earlier marriages—and her first sons who are grown and gone—now her home is full of noise and love, no longer subjugated by concerns of trade and property.

At certain moments, out of the corner of her eye, Khadija sees the angel, whose outstretched wings sheltered Muhammad from the sun, hovering at his right shoulder. Yet it does not take the appearance of angels to tell her that her husband is exceptional. *You will marry a man about to receive God's Revelations,* the old Christian told her. She perceives it in all Muhammad's actions. She nightly places her hand on the seal of prophecy, the mark between his shoulder blades. He tells her of incandescent dreams overflowing with expectation and promise, like water from the spring of Zamzam. They are like Hagar and Ismai'l, stranded in the desert—though this desert is the ever more hollow world of the Meccans and their neglect of God. As it did for Hagar and Ismai'l, the blessed waters will pour forth for Khadija and Muhammad.

His radiant dreams come more frequently. He becomes more and more pensive as he reaches his fortieth year. He takes to the caves of Mount Hira often and alone, praying, making ablutions to Allah.

It is a dazzling morning in the month called Ramadan. The sun explodes into the sky. Khadija stands in her courtyard, shielding her eyes, fascinated by this blast of light, when Muhammad bursts through the gate and staggers toward her, arms wide, reaching desperately for her.

"Cover me! Cover me!" he cries. He trembles and his teeth chatter.

She steps into his arms and steadies him. She guides him into the house and flings a blanket over his head and back. Wild sobs: "What has happened? What have I become? O Khadija, I have become a *kahin!*"

"No, no, my dear. All is well. All is well," she chants until at last the shuddering and quaking stop.

"I was comfortable in cavernous sleep," he tells her, "when I felt the breath being forced from my body. I thought surely my heart had stopped, my lungs had collapsed.

"I opened my eyes and it was an angel embracing me, pressing me until I could bear it no longer. He held a length of silk brocade on which words were written.

"'Read!' the angel shouted. But I protested: 'I am *ummi*. I do not know how to read.'

"Again he enveloped me and again commanded me: '*Iqra!* Recite!' but again I protested, 'I am not a *kahin*. I cannot recite.'

"His embrace tightened until I was choking. I thought I had reached the end.

> *Recite: In the Name of your Lord who created all that exists*
> *and created humankind from a blood-clot.*
> *Recite: And your Lord is all-Generous,*
> *who taught humankind what you knew not.*

"The angel shook me, and squeezed me again.

*Humankind is insolent, for you think you are self-sufficient.
Surely, unto your Lord is the Returning...*[20]

"Something is happening to me, Khadija. Am I *majnun*, possessed by djinn? Am I mad?"

She lifts his chin firmly and looks straight into his eyes. "God does not act cruelly. You know that God is not capricious. Allah will never disgrace you, my dear. You have tried to live as He would want. You are kind to kith and kin, you give to the poor and forlorn and bear their burdens. You strive to restore the high moral qualities our people have lost. You honor your guests and go to the assistance of those in distress. Do not think that you are suddenly deranged, Muhammad. What has happened is far beyond the lunatic ecstasies of the *kahin* or the bewitchment by djinn of poets."

Muhammad is not convinced. She washes his tired, sweat-stained face, his hands and feet. She tries to feed him, but he will not eat. He is dazed and repeats again and again that he would rather be dead than insane.

He shuts his eyes and sees Jibril, saffron hair ablaze illuminating his thousand green wings that stretch from east to west. His yellow feet, his necklace of rubies, his pearl teeth and words inscribed between his eyes, "There is no god but God, and Muhammad is the Prophet of God." He does not believe it. He is no prophet. He has gone mad.

There must be some way to reassure him. It is as the monk said: her husband is receiving God's Revelations. How else would Divine manifestation appear but through an angel wringing the life from him in order to reach into his soul? Would the body not become insensible when the soul is awakening?

That evening, Khadija takes Muhammad to her cousin Waraqah ibn Nautal, the *hanif*. He knows the scriptures, he can write the Hebrew letters, though in his old age, his eyesight fails him.

Perhaps Waraqah can comfort Muhammad, perhaps he can explain or advise.

Waraqah listens carefully. They have barely finished telling him the story, when Waraqah lifts his arms to the heavens and exclaims, "Holy! Holy! If you have spoken truth to me, O Khadija, there has come to him the Messenger who came to Moses and lo, he is the prophet of his people. I wish I were young and could live to the time when your people will turn you out."

Terror freezes Muhammad's face, the black pupils gleaming like polished onyx. "They will drive me out?"

"All who have had this experience have been met with hostility. Has there ever been a prophet who was not treated dishonorably by his own? If I could be alive when this time comes, I would support you with all my strength."

Muhammad takes his supper on a cold day and perspires as if it were high noon in high summer. Khadija catches him as he swoons.

He repairs the camel bridles and the clanging of bells in his ears deafens him. He hangs his head between his knees.

The Revelations arrive at ordinary moments on ordinary days unannounced. He tells Khadija of the back-breaking agony, the heaviness and grief that overcome him. Each time, he says, it is as if his soul were being torn away.

Khadija the businesswoman knows to keep these Revelations a secret. She, Muhammad, and Waraqah pray together in private and tell no one of the angel Jibril's visitations.

Then suddenly, silence. Day after day, Muhammad complains of dryness in his spirit, as if his soul had desiccated and were blowing away. Day after day, nothing, no word. And with every day of God's silence, Muhammad prays harder in his cave on Mount Hira, sometimes wishing he could throw himself off the mountain into oblivion.

Two years pass. He tells Khadija he must have been deluded. Allah did not send the angel, he merely imagined it. This was only an illness that has passed. A sickness of mind like that of the *kahin*. It was real, Khadija tells him. It was *baraqa*, the power of blessing bestowed upon you. Wait, pray without anxiety, and God will return.

And then he is shaken head to toe as never before. The Earth quakes, a thunderous voice resounds and echoes.

> *By the white forenoon*
> *and the brooding night!*
> *Your Lord has neither forsaken you nor hates you…*
> *Did He not find you an orphan, and shelter you?*
> *Did He not find you erring, and guide you?*
> *Did He not find you needy, and suffice you?*
>
> *As for the orphan, do not oppress him,*
> *and as for beggar, scold him not;*
> *and as for your Lord's blessing, declare it.*[21]

The one, unique God, all-merciful, all-compassionate, orders Muhammad to call his fellows to absolute faith, to spread a message of joy and justice and charity and rebirth, to Islam, the surrender.

Her household are witnesses as Khadija delivers the words: *Ashadu anna la ilaha illa llahu.* She is the first Muslim, smiling before her husband: "I testify that there is no God but God."

Their daughters are next, Zaynab, Ruqayyah, Umm Kulthum, and Fatima. Zaynab the eldest is newly wed to her cousin Abu al-As ibn Rabi, who refuses to convert. "Divorce her!" his family insists, but Abu al-As loves Zaynab as he loves life itself and will not repudiate her though he will not follow her into Islam. No matter, Khadija tells Muhammad, for Allah smiles on those who love totally and truly, and Abu al-As will come through when he is ready.

Then Ali, Zayd, and Barakah, whose husband has died and who has returned to Muhammad with her son Ayman. Muhammad's friend Abu Bakr and his wife, Umm Ruman, surrender without hesitation, and anoint their newborn daughter Aisha. Abu Bakr's son and daughter, Abdallah and Asmaa, enter the fold. Abu Bakr's son

Abd al-Ka'aba is vehemently opposed. So is Asmaa's mother, divorced from Abu Bakr and unwilling to withdraw her loyalty from the Daughters of Allah, al-Lat the Sovereign, al-Uzza the Mighty One, and Manat goddess of Fate.

Muhammad and Khadija proceed cautiously. The mission begins in earnest and in secret.

In secret, yet the believers come quickly: women, for in this gospel there is freedom. God wills they are no longer mere property. God wills that they may possess their own dowries and bride-wealth, that they may inherit, that they may be witnesses against those who have done wrong and for those wrongly accused. God wills that their infant daughters may not be ripped from their breasts and interred wailing for mother's milk, while the mothers sob alone and carry on as if no grief had been done to them.

> *Say: Come, I will recite what your Lord has forbidden you:*
> *that you associate not anything with Him,*
> *and to be good to your parents,*
> *and not slay your children because of poverty.*
> *We will provide for you and them,*
> *that you commit no indecency outward or inward,*
> *and that you slay not the soul God has forbidden, except by right.*[22]

Slaves. "I am a slave-prophet," Muhammad says, "and not a king-prophet like Da'ud or Suleyman. I eat as a slave eats and sit as a slave sits, for I am a slave of God."

The sons of the Quraysh.

"O Prophet of God, we love you," they tell Muhammad.

"Be ready for poverty," he warns.

"We seek more than this life of our fathers. We seek virtue. Tell us, Muhammad, what is virtue?"

"Ask your heart for a decision. Virtue is when the soul feels peace and the heart feels peace, but sin is what creates restlessness in the soul and rumbles in the bosom."

The proud young men learn to make the *salat*, bowing and touching their foreheads to the ground. Their rich fathers are disgusted by such humility. They kick and beat their sons for praying like slaves on their knees at the Ka'aba. The growing band of Muslims meet each morning and evening outside the city to prostrate themselves before God in peace.

"I have come," Muhammad says, "to perfect the noble habits." Those who claim nobility eye him blankly. Are not "noble habits" those they already practice: pride, flamboyance, the amassing of wealth?

The Meccans mock Muhammad. The Quraysh laugh at him and ridicule his mission. Each one who becomes a Muslim is a stone in Quraysh hearts. Rarely have they observed such determination to enter the heart of Allah alone, one god among many. Who but Jews would turn their backs on idols? Surely, the Meccans will be punished by Allah and his daughters.

> *Call not upon another god with God,*
> *lest you be one of those who are chastised.*
> *And warn your clan, your nearest kin.*
> *Lower your wing to those who follow you...* [23]

Here and there and slowly, Muhammad begins to preach in public. Khadija fears for him, even as she encourages him.

Some of the unbelieving Quraysh point at Muhammad and muse aloud: "There is the orphan of the clan of al-Muttalib who speaks things from Heaven."

But others taunt: "Perform us a miracle or two!" and snigger behind their beards.

"I am only a servant to whom revelation has come," he replies. "That in itself is a miracle."

Families split. Khadija's cousins quarrel with their fathers. Her brother despises the new religion and the more so because his son becomes a Muslim. Her favorite nephew Hakim ibn Hizam will not convert, though he loves his aunt and visits her frequently. She is aging and tired, unable to withstand for long the excitement—anxiety as well as joy—that's descended upon their lives like an avalanche.

Muhammad tells her he too sometimes feels that the task of openly calling the Quraysh and all their clans to Islam is beyond his strength. Khadija prepares a modest meal to which forty leading men of Muhammad's Hashim clan are invited.

Ali, son of Abu Talib, serves the meager repast, the simple foods Muhammad likes best: foreleg of lamb, milk and dates, melon and squash. This meal is the first statement of Muhammad's message to his kin: revoke ostentation; let there be diffidence toward the plight of the poor and reserve in all things. When the meal is set before them, Muhammad prays, "O Lord, keep me hungry one day and satiated one day. When I am hungry, I pray to you and I am full, I sing your praise."

The guests are insulted by such scanty, inhospitable fare. Their round bellies are still growling when young Ali removes the last of the meal and Muhammad begins to speak of Islam and of the Revelations.

His uncle Abu Lahab wipes his beard, scowls, stands, and stomps out of the house. The rest of the clansmen follow.

Again, Khadija prepares a meal and again the men of Hashim come. Again, Muhammad expounds upon the meaning of Islam and now he begs them to surrender.

"Sons of my beloved grandfather Abd al-Muttalib, I know of no Arab who has come to his people with a nobler message than mine. I have brought you the best of this world and the next. Allah has ordered me to call you to Him. Which of you will cooperate with me in this venture?"

Not even Hamza and Abbas, the uncles with whom Muhammad grew up, respond. Ali shifts from toe to toe, swaying with impatience until he can stand it no longer.

"I, though the youngest, pledged my help to the Prophet of God!" Ali shouts at his father and uncles and brothers. "Muhammad laid his hand on the back of my neck and said, 'This is my brother. Listen to him and obey him.'"

"What is this?" the guests turn to Abu Talib, laughing. "Muhammad has ordered you to listen to your son and obey him!"

Khadija hears all from her bed. She sighs and turns her mind to pray that this failure to bring Muhammad's clansmen to understanding will not last long and that the clans of the Quraysh will follow peacefully into the fold of Muslims.

But as he preaches, they turn their backs, for Muhammad tells them of a Last Judgment, when wealth and influence on Earth will be of no help before Allah's authority. God will demand a reckoning of honesty and justice and generosity to the poor and vulnerable.

> Upon the day when Heaven will be as molten copper
> and the mountains will be as plucked wool tufts,
> no loyal friend will question loyal friend...
> The sinner will wish that he might ransom himself
> from the chastisement of that day
> even by his sons, his companion wife, his brother,
> his kin who sheltered him
> and whosoever is in the earth, all together,
> so that then it might deliver him.[24]

Khadija studies the raised purple veins on her hands. She examines a lock of hair and can no longer count the strands of gray. Nothing in her life makes her feel old and unwanted, and yet age is coming upon her swiftly, and soon, death. She is not afraid, for will she not meet Muhammad again in the Garden of Eternity, which is

> ...promised to the god-fearing,
> and is their recompense and homecoming.
> Therein they shall have what they will, dwelling forever;
> it is a promise binding upon the Lord.[25]

The Quraysh call Muhammad an atheist and an enemy. Young Umar ibn al-Khattab is Islam's most vehement foe and demands violent reprisals. A delegation marches to Abu Talib's house. As chief of Muhammad ibn Abdallah's clan, they say, Abu Talib must renounce his nephew. "He has cursed our gods, insulted our religion, mocked our way of life, and accused our forefathers of error in worship. You stop him yourself or else give up protection of him so that we may kill him."

Abu Talib will not join the Muslims, nor does he care for Muhammad's denunciation of the old religion. Yet he loves his nephew. And no responsible clan chief will disown a kinsman.

Muhammad continues to preach and Meccans continue to join him.

The Quraysh approach Abu Talib a second time. "We will fight the two of you until one side perishes," they threaten.

"Spare me and yourself," Abu Talib begs Muhammad. "Don't put a greater burden on me than I can bear."

Tears blind Muhammad's jet-black eyes. "I am ready to die, Uncle. I will not abandon this course until God has made it victorious or I have perished."

He yearns for Khadija's comfort. He weeps bitterly as he leaves his uncle's house. But Abu Talib calls him back: "Go and say what you please, Nephew. I will never give you up."

Khadija receives an envoy from Muhammad's uncle Abu Lahab, whose sons are betrothed to her daughters, Ruqayyah and Umm Kulthum. With this latest refusal by Muhammad to mend his ways, Abu Lahab withdraws the marriage proposal. His sons repudiate Khadija's daughters.

When he hears the news, Uthman ibn Affan, of the House of Umayya, elegant, wealthy, and handsome, devout in his belief, asks for Ruqayyah's hand, for he has long admired her beauty and grace. Khadija nods her approval. To gaze upon these two is to rejoice. "God is beautiful," Muhammad says. "And He loves beauty."

Abu Talib—who will not forsake the old religion and will not desert his nephew—writes passionate poems condemning the clans that had been his allies. Some draw closer to him. Others unite with the opposition. More families divide. Abu Bakr buys, then frees, seven slaves whose masters brutalize them for following Muhammad. Muslim sons are imprisoned by their unbelieving fathers, deprived of food and water. Muhammad sends a delegation to the Negus of Abyssinia, seeking asylum for as many of the Muslims as wish to escape the persecution. Khadija bids a tearful farewell to her daughter Ruqayyah and Uthman. In Abyssinia, they can practice Islam freely.

The Meccans impose trade sanctions against the Hashim. Abu Talib's miserable fortunes worsen. Khadija's wealth diminishes.

Still the Muslim community grows. The Qur'an, the word of God, penetrates hearts and minds as no poetry in this land of poets can. Even sworn enemies of Islam, when they stop to listen, are touched swiftly and utterly by the power of the verses.

Muhammad visits the Ka'aba. Quraysh surround him and pull his robe. They will rid themselves of him despite Abu Talib's protection. Abu Bakr pleads with them to leave off: "Would you kill a man for saying 'Allah is my Lord'?"

Mighty Hamza, the strongest man in Mecca, surrenders, as much in anger at this treatment of his nephew and childhood companion, as in devotion.

Abu al-Hakam, chief of the Quraysh, rises to the forefront of Muhammad's foes. His viciousness inspires the Muslims to rename him Abu Jahl, Father of Ignorance. Abu Jahl imposes a boycott on the households of the Hashim and persuades the clans to sign a treaty. The Hashim may not intermarry or trade with the Meccans. No one may sell them food. The Hashim—those who have become Muslims, as well as the unbelievers—move for safety onto the street of Abu Talib, for his protection is a promise that none may be murdered.

Abu Bakr and Muslims of other clans secretly dispatch supplies by camels loaded with goods. They point the beasts into the ghetto and someone inside catches the loose bridles, unloads them, and sends them back where their owners wait.

Nevertheless, wood and food are scarce. Khadija languishes, aging, often hungry. Muhammad comforts her as she rests. Her breathing is labored and she is weak.

Her favorite nephew Hakim is rounding a corner onto her street, when Abu Jahl seizes him and grabs the bag of flour Hakim is carrying to Khadija. What treason is this that Hakim, not even a Muslim, would bring aid to Mecca's enemies? Hakim lunges for the bag, but Abu Jahl clings to it, yelling abuse. Hakim has broken the ban. What punishment should be meted to such a traitor?

A stranger steps forward.

"How dare you stop a man from taking food to his aunt?" he demands. He steps between the men and tries to pull Abu Jahl away from Hakim. "What matter about your treaties if a man desires to help an old woman who is his kin?"

Abu Jahl will not let go of the flour bag. The stranger reaches into his cloak and pulls out a camel's jaw. He rears back and clouts Abu Jahl, who falls to the ground. Hakim snatches the flour bag, thanks the man, and rushes to Khadija.

Muhammad curses the cruel and faithless clan: "O Quraysh, I bring you slaughter!"

Umar ibn al-Khattab, passionate worshiper of the gods of his father, has had enough. He marches to Muhammad's house, sword in hand. It is time to kill this usurper of the goddesses. He does not know his sister and her husband have become Muslims. He does not know that Khabbab ibn al-Aratt the blacksmith has become a Muslim. He strides along the streets toward Muhammad's house, grinding his teeth, swinging his sword. A man accosts him, a relative.

"Go home, Umar," the man says. "See what is going on in your own home." Umar does not know that this man, too, is a Muslim.

He is alarmed at his clansman's tone. He turns and runs to his own house. There is murmuring, a sound that grows into chanting the closer he gets. He bursts in the door. His sister, her husband, and the blacksmith are reciting the Qur'an.

"What is this claptrap you're spouting?" Umar yells and smacks his sister with his fist, knocking her to the ground. The blood spurts onto the floor. For a moment Umar feels shame. He picks up the palm leaf on which are written the words

We have not revealed the Qur'an to you that
you may be unsuccessful.
No, it is a reminder to those who fear,
a Revelation from Him Who created the Earth
and the high Heavens.
The beneficent God is all-powerful.
His are the Heavens and the Earth and what
is between them and beneath the ground.
He knows all secrets and what is yet hidden.
Allah—there is no god but He. His are the very best names.[26]

Umar ibn al-Khattab can read. He is a rare man among the Quraysh. His eyes pass over and over the *Surah*. His face softens. He sits, marveling. "How fine and noble is this speech. How beautiful these words."

He cannot control his impulses. He picks up his swords and rushes out the door. He dashes down the streets and along the alleys and bursts into Muhammad's house. He strides toward the Prophet, who stands and grabs Umar's cloak.

"What has brought you here?" he demands, holding Umar at bay.

"O Muhammad," Umar sobs. "I have come to believe in God and His Messenger and what he has brought from God."

And Muhammad gives praise.

As adamant as Umar was against the Muslims, now he is the most adamant among them, the fiercest fighter for the faith. He is called al-Faruq, "he who distinguishes truth from falsehood."

When at last the ban is lifted, Khadija rejoices with her husband that times of less suffering for Muslims may now be here. Ruqayyah and Uthman return from Abyssinia, hopeful that now they can settle at home near Khadija and Muhammad.

Two years of hardship have taken a toll. Khadija is bent and withered, light as feathers. Muhammad carries her to the roof of their old home and settles her on the couch where once she watched the caravans. Here she spied the angel shading her future husband, the angel she still sees residing close beside him.

Her daughters and her beloved husband sit around her bed. She holds their hands and smiles. All her treasures are here. And behind them stand her adopted son Zayd, Muhammad's cousin Ali, Barakah, and her son Ayman.

Khadija has lived a life of happiness beyond her wildest expectations. She chose Muhammad and was loved by him as few women are by their husbands. Together they made their way to God and he has become God's Messenger.

She turns her head toward him. He presses his cheek to hers.

"I am summoned to the Abode of Peace," she whispers. The angel wraps his wings around her. With her last breath she inhales her husband's musk, the Divine fragrance.

Her flesh has grown cold before Muhammad lifts his cheek from hers. He cannot stop the tears.

He buries her with his own hands.

The Muslims crowd around him, chanting as he lowers her shrouded body into the grave:

Khadija, Khadija, great and pure.
Dearer to us than our own mother...

Asmaa bint Abu Bakr

The daughter of one of the Prophet Muhammad's closest Companions, Abu Bakr, Asmaa was an early convert to Islam. She was half sister to the Prophet's wife Aisha and renowned for her generosity, courage, and wisdom. She was closely involved with the beginnings of Islam, a participant and witness to its birth and growth. An action during the Prophet's flight to Medina earned Asmaa the soubriquet, "She of the two girdles." Her dates are unknown.

Abu Bakr wraps his arm around the Prophet's shoulder's. Khadija's death has left Muhammad hollow and unable to contain his tears, except to comfort in turn his daughters.

Then Abu Talib, who has protected the Messenger all these years, dies, too.

It is, Asmaa thinks, a Year of Sorrow.

Abu Bakr's esteem and influence have plunged among the Quraysh, even as they have risen among the believers. Why, Asmaa wonders, do the Meccans fear her father? He is soft-spoken, studious, fine-featured, never a threat.

He has, with quiet determination and passion, drawn many to the heart of God's Oneness.

Night falls and Asmaa waits with her stepmother, Umm Ruman, for Abu Bakr's return. His supper is cold, the house is eerily empty. Umm Ruman wrings her hands and fusses at little tasks until at last she falls asleep, clutching her youngest, Aisha.

Asmaa sits up until nearly dawn. Before the sun rises, she walks through the city and out the gates onto the highway.

She has trudged a mile or so, when she catches sight of a large bundle by the side of the road. She runs toward it. Abu Bakr and his cousin Talha are bound hand and foot and roped together. She removes a knife from her girdle and saws at the ropes.

At home, fed and rested, Abu Bakr consults the Prophet, who is himself suffering constant small persecutions by the Quraysh. Since Abu Talib's death, Abu Lahab has taken over as Hashim clan chief and Muhammad's protector, but he bestows only indifference.

For safety's sake, they decide that Abu Bakr must join the Muslims remaining in Abyssinia. By the end of the day, Abu Bakr has hidden his wealth, bid farewell to his wife and children, and, still dazed from the beating and binding on the highway, departs. Asmaa stands at the door, rocking her sister Aisha on her hip. Aisha waves happily, for surely their father will return soon with gifts. He looks, Asmaa thinks, like a hermit, shabby and so bruised he is barely able to balance on the swaying camel as he proceeds along the streets toward the gates of Mecca.

Neither Asmaa nor Umm Ruman thought to remind him that the family needs money to survive. Neither remembered to ask whether they might join him in Abyssinia.

Children, chirping like birds, call Aisha's name and she skips off to play. It was not long ago that Asmaa, too, frolicked in the streets. She misses the freedom and yet she does not. She enjoys the responsibility the family, especially her preoccupied stepmother, places on her. She was always serious, a much different child from Aisha, who is merry and uninhibited.

Turning back to the house, she considers how to make supplies last until…who knows when? God provides. All will be well. Of this she's sure.

Umar ibn al-Khattab, blustering and bad tempered, weeps when looking at the Prophet's miserable household.

"Why do you cry?" Asmaa asks, expecting no answer from this man who thinks of women as less valuable than his camels.

But to Asmaa's surprise, Umar answers her. "I cannot bear that Khosroes and Caesar lived in luxury, while the Prophet of God is near starvation."

The Prophet smiles at Umar. "They have this world and we have the next one," he says. "My poverty is my pride."

Then so be it, says Asmaa. So it will be for her, as well.

The door flies open. Abu Bakr's blind father enters, clinging to the arm of his slave and whipping his cane wildly. Abu Quhafah refuses to surrender to Islam and he's infuriated that his son has left the city and his family. Abu Quhafah's cane, like a separate animal, hunts for Asmaa. She is dependable, practical, and keen. She is as devout as her dreamy father, who has given himself entirely to Allah and the Prophet, but God planted Asmaa's wide feet squarely on the ground.

Swift and quiet as a mouse, she scoops pebbles from the court-yard and tosses them into a niche where money is usually kept. She throws a cloth over the heap, then turns to greet her grandfather.

His cane whacks the floor with a loud ring. "Asmaa!" His beard vibrates when he shouts. Aisha giggles and scampers from the room.

"They say my son has abandoned you and left you bereft of money!"

Abu Quhafah straightens his bent back, a sign not so much of anger as of pride.

"What business is this? Are you to starve? Wear rags? This is shame upon our family! Others will say—and rightly—that my son did not provide for you or shelter you. Is this how you Muslims behave?" He rails on and on.

Asmaa snatches her grandfather's bony hand flailing in midair and leads him to the niche. She places his hand on the cloth that covers the pile of pebbles.

"Feel these, Grandfather. My father left us much money. We have plenty. Don't fret any longer."

The old blind man is fooled. Asmaa offers him tea and dates, the last in the larder. He carps about the new religion, then shifts into the usual litany of complaints about his son. "You are of marriageable age, and pretty. Yet Abu Bakr has taken no pains to arrange the proper alliances for you. O Asmaa, I despair!"

She has no reply. If her father has considered this detail, he has not mentioned it. Surely he's waiting until the right husband appears—and that husband must be Muslim.

Abu Quhafah leaves, barking promises of help along with curses upon his son for his wistful ways.

Asmaa sighs and sits to ponder how indeed they will care for themselves with only pebbles for money.

She has not long to worry. Two days later, Abu Bakr staggers into the house with Muhammad by his side. Umm Ruman rushes to him. Asmaa follows, smiling. She knew God would send him back to them soon. Umm Ruman washes and rubs Abu Bakr's feet as he tells of meeting a Bedouin chief on the road.

"He questioned me and I told him how my people ill-treated me and drove me out. 'All I seek,' I explained, 'is to travel the Earth, worshiping God.'

"The chief—an ally of the Quraysh no less—could not understand it. 'Why have they done this?' he asked. 'You are as an ornament to your clan, a help in misfortune, a doer of right, ever fulfilling the needs of others. Return!' he ordered me. 'You are hereby under my protection.'"

Abu Bakr flops onto the couch exhausted and Umm Ruman places a cold cloth on his forehead. Muhammad is still as stone, lost in thought. He is always much absorbed in thought, silent for long periods. He has never spoken without cause, and though he's known much sorrow, he honors each of God's signs of grace and tries not to find blame. Yet with each of his daily visits, Asmaa perceives his growing loneliness, a dishevelment of spirit that was contained and maintained by Khadija. It is as if, since her passing, he is unraveling.

Aisha scurries in from the street, and seeing the Prophet, squeals with delight. She hops across the floor and into his lap. He laughs, alive and present again. Children cheer and restore him. And no wonder she loves him: when he finds little Aisha in tears, he rebukes her parents for reprimanding her too severely. Abu Bakr is a stern, forgetful father; Muhammad is lenient and attentive.

"There was one condition," Abu Bakr continues. "The chieftain gave me his protection, but made me promise to pray in my own house, not in public, and to keep my faith to myself."

Abu Bakr builds a mosque in his house.

Outside, the hounding of Muslims by Quraysh continues unabated. Someone throws offal into Muhammad's cooking pot. Another tosses a bloody sheep's uterus across his back while he prays. "It is your time to depart," Abu Bakr tells Muhammad. They agree that the Prophet will go to Taif, to the guardians of the temple of the goddess al-Lat, and ask for help.

Asmaa thinks of her own mother, Qutaylah, long divorced from Abu Bakr. Since the rest of the family surrendered, Asmaa rarely sees her mother, who will not embrace the faith and takes regular pilgrimages to lush, green Taif to offer prayers to al-Lat. She has begged her mother to convert, but Qutaylah is adamant. Nothing can turn her from these Daughters of Allah to whom she attributes all things. Asmaa begged and then stopped seeing her mother altogether.

Muhammad rides to Taif and is rejected.

The next year, Asmaa calls the Time of Journeys and Dreams.

Muhammad loves to visit the Ka'aba at night and sometimes sleeps at the shrine.

A foot spurs his hip and he sits upright, sees nothing and falls back to sleep again. A second kick and then a third until he is fully awake. The angel Jibril raises the Prophet and leads him to a white beast of burden. Jibril orders Muhammad to mount winged Buraq and with the archangel by their side, Muhammad on Buraq speeds to Jerusalem. He is met by a company of prophets. Ibrahim, Musa, Isa, Haroun, Yusuf and more, gather behind Muhammad to pray at the rock where Ibrahim offered to sacrifice Ismai'l. Two vessels are brought before him, one of wine, one of milk. He chooses the milk and Jibril says, "O Muhammad, you have been guided onto the primordial path and wine is forbidden you."

The archangel leads Muhammad riding Buraq out of this life beyond space and time and form. The prophets reappear, not in human dimension, but as celestial beings. He sees the people of Paradise. If a woman of Paradise appeared to the people of Earth, she would fill the space between Heaven and Earth with light and fragrance.

Muhammad marvels at the gardens of Heaven, saying, "A piece of Paradise the size of a bow is better than all beneath the sun."

Muhammad sees all with the eye of the Spirit. He comprehends his spiritual nature to be older than Earth, older than the Beginning.

And Muhammad riding Buraq led by Jibril comes to the Lote Tree of the Uttermost End, rooted in the Throne, the end of the knowledge of every knower and beyond it is the Mystery hidden to any but God alone.

Here at the summit of the universe Jibril burns with splendor. Divine Light descends upon the Tree and enshrouds it and all else all around and the eye of the Prophet beholds it all without wavering. He does not turn aside. He is not afraid. He takes refuge in the light of God's Countenance.

And he receives the command for his people of fifty prayers a day. And he receives the Revelation that will be the creed:

The Messenger believes
and the faithful believe
in what has been revealed to him from his Lord.
Each one believes in God and His angels
and His books and His messengers:
we make no distinction between any
of His messengers.
And they say:
we hear and we obey;
grant us, O Lord, forgiveness;
unto You is the ultimate becoming.[27]

And Muhammad riding Buraq led by Jibril descend through the
seven Heavens as they ascended until they pass the Prophet Musa,
whom the Jews call Moses. What a good friend he was to Muslims!

"How many prayers have been laid upon you?" Musa asks.

"Fifty," the Prophet replies.

"Your people are weak," Moses tells him. "Return to the Lord and
ask him to lighten the load for you and your people."

So Muhammad returns, but when he passes Musa, the ancient
asks how many prayers and says forty are too many. Muhammad
appeals to God and ten more are struck. Again he passes Musa; again
Musa sends him back, again and again until finally all but five prayers
have been taken away. Unto those who perform the five in good faith
and in trust of God's bounty will be given the meed of fifty prayers.

God charges no soul save to its capacity.[28]

And Muhammad riding Buraq led by Jibril touches down on the
Rock at Jerusalem, then flies to Mecca. It is still night when they reach
the Ka'aba.

Men shove Asmaa and Umm Ruman aside and crush into Abu
Bakr's mosque.

"What do you think now of your friend?"

"Every child knows it takes a month to travel from Mecca to
Syria!"

"He stands at the Ka'aba and tells us he has gone to Jerusalem in
a night and prayed there and returned to Mecca on the same night!"

"What do you think now of your friend's lies and exaggerations?"

"If Muhammad says it, it is true," Abu Bakr replies. "And where's
the wonder of it? Tidings come to him from Heaven in any hour of day
or night."

The Prophet names Abu Bakr "as-Siddiq," "the great witness of
truth."

In June, the Prophet goes to the valley of Mina, to the camps of
pilgrims, who come from far and wide to visit the Ka'aba and cele-

brate in the marketplace at Mecca. Muhammad declares his message to all who will listen. Six men from Yathrib listen carefully to him and when he has finished, they tell him how their city and the tribes are divided by enmities. The tribes are familiar with the oneness of God, for they have lived for generations among the Jews of Yathrib.

"Come to Yathrib," the pilgrims beg Muhammad, "for God will unite us through you. We will summon the tribes to accept your new religion and if God gathers them about you, then no man will be mightier than you."

And Muhammad dreams of a man carrying someone wrapped in silk. This is your wife, uncover her, he says. Beneath the silk is Aisha.

When he awakes, Muhammad says to himself, "If this be from God, it will come to pass."

And Muhammad dreams of an angel carrying a bundle of silk. Beneath the silk is Aisha.

"If this be from God, it will come to pass."

He tells no one and waits for a third sign.

The Time of Journeys and Visions, Asmaa thinks, will change all their lives forever. Like her father, she is a skillful interpreter of dreams.

His friend Khawlah has helped Muhammad with his household since Khadija's death. With Barakah, who is widowed and busy with her own son, Khawlah cares for the Prophet's yet unmarried daughters, Umm Kulthum and Fatima, whose devotion to Muhammad has earned her the name Umm Abi-ha, the mother of her father.

"You must take another wife," Khawlah tells Muhammad.

"Whom should I marry?" he asks. He cannot absorb the notion of any wife but Khadija.

"You must marry either Aisha bint Abu Bakr or Sawdah bint Zamah. But since Aisha is only six years old and cannot care for your household, take Sawdah, who is widowed and alone."

Here is the third sign. He tells Khawlah he will take both if she will arrange the marriages.

To the proposal, plump, stolid Sawdah answers, "I am at your service, O Messenger of God."

But Aisha is promised to another and Abu Bakr must break the arrangement. This is not difficult, for the family to whom she is pledged are suspicious of the Muslims.

Asmaa and Umm Ruman are present at the betrothal ceremony. Aisha plays outdoors with her friends. When the ceremony is complete, Umm Ruman retrieves Aisha. "You may no longer play in the road," Umm Ruman says. "Bring your friends to the house, but do not play in the road."

"Why must I do this?" Aisha asks Asmaa.

"You are betrothed to the Messenger of God," Asmaa says, and Aisha claps her hands happily. She loves this man who has visited daily ever since she can remember, who calls her Humaira, "little reddish girl." Asmaa watches Aisha shouting and skipping and laughing in the courtyard with her friends, her life unchanged though she will marry the Prophet. Asmaa considers what God's plan may be for her. She is older, but has no prospects.

Weddings inspire weddings. Muhammad gathers his Companions. "Should one of you wish to marry a woman from the people of Paradise, let him marry Barakah."

Barakah is no longer attractive. Her age is beginning to show. The Companions remain silent. All but Zayd ibn Harith, Muhammad's adopted son, the boy who was once his slave.

"Messenger of Allah, I will gladly marry Umm Ayman. She is better than any woman with grace, youth, and beauty."

Soon Zayd and Barakah are blessed with a son, whom they call Usamah. Asmaa holds the newborn, the Prophet's first grandchild. Few can release the baby from his adoring grandfather's arms. Muhammad spends hours hugging and kissing the little one. "O tiny Usamah," Asmaa coos. "You are the beloved son of the beloved."

The time for *hijra*, for Flight, has come.

God sends the six pilgrims from Yathrib to Muhammad's door.

Sawdah lets them in and disappears. They consult in whispers with the Prophet.

As soon as they have gone, Muhammad calls forth Abu Bakr and others of his Companions.

"I have been shown the place of your emigration: I saw a well-watered land, rich in date palms, between two tracts of black stones."

The migration to Yathrib begins: Muhammad's uncle Hamza and his son will build homes before bringing their wives from Mecca; Uthman takes Muhammad's daughter Ruqayyah; for safety's sake his daughter Zaynab leaves her husband al-Asad, who will not embrace Islam. It is a sad parting. Cousins, brothers and sisters, mothers and fathers siphon slowly out of Mecca, day by day, away from their oppressors to the city they call al-Medina, City of the Prophet.

The Quraysh try to stop them. Again, sons are imprisoned. Abu Jahl, Father of Ignorance, sends a messenger to his brother Ayyash to say that their mother has sworn not to comb her hair or take shelter from the sun until she sets eyes on him again.

Umar takes Ayyash aside: "They want nothing more than to seduce you from your religion. By Allah, if lice troubled your mother, she would use her comb; and if the heat of Mecca oppresses her, she will take shelter." Ayyash insists he must relieve his mother of her oath and rides away with Abu Jahl, who leaps on him and ties him hand and foot and takes him back home as a prisoner.

"See, people of Mecca," Abu Jahl points triumphantly at his trussed brother. "Do with your fools as we have done with this fool of ours."

And though some are forced to renounce the faith, the Revelation comes to Muhammad:

> *O My slaves who have acted unwisely against yourselves,*
> *despair not of God's mercy.*
> *Verily God forgives sins in their entirety.*
> *He is the All-Forgiving, the All-Merciful.*[29]

Each day that Asmaa strolls to the market she passes more and more empty houses. The market is quiet. There are few friends to visit. This city which was so prosperous is becoming forlorn and threadbare.

The other Companions are gone, but Abu Bakr cannot get the Prophet's permission to leave.

"Don't hasten away, Abu Bakr. Wait for me."

Abu Bakr chafes, unusually impatient, until one day the Prophet gives orders for two of his camels to be fed on gum acacia leaves to prepare them for their journey.

"God has allowed me to leave the city and to emigrate," he tells Abu Bakr.

"With me?"

"With you."

Men conspire to kill Muhammad. They lie in wait outside his house. The voices of Sawdah, Umm Kulthum, Fatima, and Barakah stop them as they climb the wall. They will ever be dishonored among Arabs if they violate the privacy of women.

In deepest night, Muhammad and Abu Bakr slip through a window onto two saddled camels. Asmaa's brother Abdallah follows to bring home the camels while a shepherd brings his flock to cover their tracks as they gallop to the caves of Mount Thawr, in the direction of the Yemen, away from Yathrib.

Beyond the precincts of the city, Muhammad halts his camel and turns. "Of all God's Earth," he says, "Mecca is the dearest place to me and the dearest unto God."

Alarms sound. Men scurry here and there seeking Muhammad. They burst into Abu Bakr's house and tear it apart. Asmaa, Aisha, and Umm Ruman huddle in a corner, terrified. Abu Jahl gathers search parties, trackers who can locate a scorpion in sifting sand. He offers a reward of a hundred camels to anyone who can find Muhammad and Abu Bakr and return them to Mecca. They ride fast out of the city to the northern outskirts, and failing that, they follow every route, every road, every path, every trail that leads to Yathrib.

The next night, Abdallah returns to the caves with Asmaa bearing food. Asmaa has never been so far from home in the wilderness. The dark is petrifying. She holds her breath against ghosts or strange night creatures, wolves or lions or bats or flesh-eating birds with red eyes. With each stone that rolls and every tree that groans in the wind, she shudders and prays.

Late in the afternoon of the third day, the silence of their mountain sanctuary is broken by the cooing and flutter of rock doves. Then a low buzz and Muhammad and Abu Bakr realize that men's voices are approaching. No one is expected until nightfall. The voices grow louder, closer.

"Don't worry, my friend," Muhammad lays a steady hand on Abu Bakr's quaking shoulder. "We are not just two, but three, for God is with us."

Steps draw near and stop at the mouth of the cave. "There's no point in searching this one!" a voice says. The others murmur agreement. Hunched in the depths of the cave, Muhammad and Abu Bakr hear the footsteps retreating back the way they came.

The Prophet and Abu Bakr sneak to the cave entrance. An acacia tree the height of a man covers the entrance. A spider has woven her web across the gap between the tree and the cave wall. Muhammad and Abu Bakr peer through the web and there in the hollow of a boulder, where one might step to enter the cave, a rock dove has made a nesting place and sits upon her eggs, while her mate perches on a ledge above.

At the expected hour, in the deepest night, Asmaa climbs the trails and paths bearing food. She has carefully noted each marker, every stone and shrub along the slope, and counted each step it takes to reach the cave. But there is no cave. Nothing is where it is supposed to be. She is sure she made every right move. She looks up and down. Panic squeezes her throat. Should she try to make her way down and start again? What if she gets lost? What if she is lost?

A figure materializes from behind a huge spider's web. Asmaa stifles a scream. The specter is her father.

Abdallah waits below with camels. Asmaa, Abu Bakr, and Muhammad descend the mountain. Asmaa has brought a bag of provisions for their journey, but forgotten to bring a rope. She unravels the band of cloth from her waist, divides it into two lengths and uses one to tie the food and water bags securely to her father's saddle. She of the two girdles.

Abdallah, Abu Bakr, and Muhammad ride off under starlight toward Yathrib. Asmaa turns home to Mecca. Once again, she and her stepmother and half sisters and brother will fend for themselves until word comes for them to join the Muslims.

In Medina, the Messenger is welcomed and beset with offers of hospitality from this family and that family, from this party and that party. Muhammad smiles and nods thanks to them all, then says he will let his camel choose, for she will decide without bias.

Barakah, too, has been left in Mecca with her sons. Muhammad has told her to stay until she and Ali return to their owners all the goods that have been in Muhammad's safekeeping. He is still known in Mecca as al-Amin, the Reliable One. They trust him even as they hate him.

She longs for Muhammad. The old feelings of barrenness—as when he was a little boy fostered with Bedouins or when she left Mecca as a bride the first time—are unbearable. Ali ibn Abu Talib awaits word from Muhammad to pack up the women of his household. Muhammad will send for them when dwellings have been built in Yathrib, the place they now call Medina.

Barakah wraps the baby Usamah tightly to her. She straps provisions on Ayman's small back and hangs water sacks from each of their shoulders. Few notice this former slave, this poor Abyssinian woman and her brats leaving Mecca.

Barakah and Ayman trek into the desert, heads bent against the wind. The infant is safe on her back under bundles of blankets. Barakah ties Ayman to her against the blinding sand, lest she lose him in the storms. They scramble and trudge up and down mountains. The sun beats down mercilessly on them, yet Barakah persists until at last she arrives in Medina footsore and swollen. At first no one recognizes her and Ayman for the sand and dust that stain their faces.

"O Umm Ayman! O Umm!" the Prophet exclaims, running to greet her. "O my brave mother, for you there is a place in Paradise!" He wipes her face and eyes, massages her feet, and rubs her shoulders. Zayd bathes the baby and Ayman with tenderness and joy.

Asmaa clings to her faith. It is, she's sure, absolute, despite little worms of worry and doubt. She prays hard. Family by family, the community of Muslims that sustains her has left Mecca. The *hijra* has taken place for almost everyone else. Months drag on with no word for the family to join Abu Bakr in Medina. Patience, patience, Asmaa reminds herself, but the wait taxes the fortitude and serenity with which God has blessed her.

Umm Ruman, too, is sad. She is a woman of exquisite beauty, whom the Prophet has likened to *huris* of Paradise. Aisha has inherited her mother's glorious features, though not her angelic temperament and sweet, vague hold on everyday life. The nine-year-old sulks and balks at doing her chores. She misses her father. Even more, she misses Muhammad.

Ali ibn Abu Talib appears at the door. Asmaa's brother Abdallah is on his way from Medina to fetch Asmaa, Aisha, and Umm Ruman. Ali is readying the women of Muhammad's household to go, too. He cannot resist a chuckle. "There will be a surprise for you, Asmaa, when we get there."

Tedious as the journey is, for Asmaa it is as if they are flying on the back of winged Buraq. When they alight there will be fellow Muslims. There will be friends. There will be her father and the Prophet. There will be new things to see, new people to meet, a new world to build. There will be elation and pleasure in prayer together. There will be liberation from the hatred in Mecca and the divisiveness of the Quraysh.

The Prophet stands just inside the gate, his arms open wide in welcome as the caravan enters the city of Yathrib. Medina! It is an oasis. Aisha shrieks and claps her hands. Muhammad helps the girl from the *hawdaj* and hugs her, then moves to the next camel and respectfully brings Sawdah down. He takes his wife to her new house in the new mosque.

Abu Bakr helps Umm Ruman from her *hawdaj*, then Asmaa.

"It is," he says, swinging his daughter to the ground, "time for you to marry."

This is the surprise that awaited her.

Asmaa takes Zubayr ibn al-Awwan as her husband in the first wedding of Muslims in Medina. He is a poor man, but cousin to the Prophet, and the marriage brings Abu Bakr's family into the Prophet's.

Life is difficult in Medina for all the Muslims. There are weeks when they live on dates and water. Zubayr owns nothing but a horse. They toil in fields. Asmaa learns to groom and water and fodder Zubayr's mare. She grinds grain and carries it on her head from Zubayr's plot. This is work she has never known but to which she applies herself as if born to it. They have little — and Zubayr less than many — but Asmaa is generous and will hold on to nothing if another needs it. She tries to bake, but does not do it well. The women of Medina bake for her in small repayment for her constant kindnesses.

Yet she cannot extend her generosity to her mother. Word has reached Qutaylah that Asmaa is with child. Qutaylah stands at her daughter's door, still a woman of al-Lat, offering gifts of raisins, nuts, and butter.

Asmaa will not let her in. To do so would be to compromise her honor and her faith. Qutaylah begs. Asmaa's heart hurts. She sends a boy for the Prophet.

The Revelation arrives:

God does not forbid you from dealing kindly and justly
with those who have not fought you or driven you out of your homes.
Surely God loves the just.[30]

Asmaa's son, Abdallah, is the first child born to the Muslim community in Medina. Her mother is by her side throughout her lying in.

Hind bint Utba

Hind bint Utba was the wife of Muhammad's final Meccan opponent, Abu Sufyan, who took over the leadership of Quraysh from Abu Jahl. Having lost members of her family in the Muslim-Meccan wars, she was vehemently opposed to Islam and exacted a brutal revenge. Eventually, like her husband, she converted. She was the mother of Mu'awiya, the fifth caliph, founder of the Umayyad Dynasty. Her dates are unknown.

Hind plays with her youngest son Mu'awiya. Bellowing rises from the streets of Mecca into her open window. She leaves the baby and rushes to see what is happening. No one is safe these days with the Muslims raiding out of Yathrib—their Medina! As if they could change the name of a city as arrogantly as they have declared the rightful gods false! Some say Muhammad ibn Abdallah decided on the *ghazu* because his followers are poor and hungry; they raid for they have nothing but the dates of Yathrib to harvest. Well, what did they expect?

"Step aside! Let me see!" Hind shouts out the window at the crowd. Cowed by the wife of Abu Sufyan, hereditary chief of the Banu Umayya, several step aside. Men are already running toward their houses, calling for mares, camels, and slaves.

A messenger is at the center of the throng, panting and sweating. He calls up to Hind: "Your husband heard of a Muslim raid near Badr and sent me to get reinforcements." The horse whose bridle he clutches looks winded enough to drop dead on the spot.

She is about to send water and food to the messenger, when her father and brother and two sons stride into the room buckling their swords and armor. All men of Mecca are hurrying to help Abu Sufyan's caravan returning from Syria. Even Muhammad's uncle Abbas and Khadija's beloved nephew, Hakim, ride out to meet the Muslim raiders. Muhammad's uncle Abu Lahab, head of the Hashim clan, believes his nephew to be an imposter. He is old and waits anxiously in Mecca.

Hind shuts the window against rising clouds of dust as a thousand march out of Mecca to the wells of Badr by the Red Sea.

At the head of the throng, women carry the idols of al-Lat the Sovereign and al-Uzza, crying, "Strength is ours, you have no strength!" The victorious goddesses will show Muhammad and his followers that they are not merely "names" invested by the forefathers of the Quraysh.

"It is now a blood feud," Hind tells her little Mu'awiya. She spins her gauzy skirt around his head. The infant laughs.

"They killed during the sacred month of the Rajab, when fighting is forbidden. Now they will be killed." She twirls the baby round and round the room. "It is a blood feud and we will win."

In two nights' time, the men who went out with such bravado heave themselves back to Mecca, bedraggled and defeated. Slung across the backs of their own mares are Hind's father and brother and her two older sons.

There is no loathing like that which Hind holds in her heart for the household of Muhammad.

When her husband asks for the comfort a wife gives a man who has fought valiantly, Hind snarls: "Do we bear and nurture sons only for you to kill them in battle?"

She goes from warrior to weary warrior. "Who killed them? Who exactly put the death wounds on my father, my brother, my sons? Whose sword was it that ran them through?"

Hamza. Mighty Hamza ibn Abd al-Muttalib, the younger uncle of Muhammad, flew fearlessly though the throngs and with each blow took a man down. His blade never missed its mark.

"I will eat his liver," Hind vows.

"There will be reprisal," Abu Sufyan reassures Hind. "As soon as men are recovered. As soon as we have gathered force."

Abu Jahl, Father of Ignorance, also died at Badr. Abu Sufyan is now *sayyid* in Mecca. He forbids weeping and lamenting. He vows he will take no pleasure until he has paid the Muslims back in their own coin.

Hind broods. She mourns and mopes, her spirit is heavy and hopeless. She cannot eat or sleep. She sees her boys as phantoms around the trays of meat at mealtimes. She sees them in their empty beds. She sees her father as she saw him when she was very small, looming and large and imperious. She tries to cry despite Abu Sufyan's command, but her eyes are dry.

"I will give you your freedom and your weight in gold and silver," Hind promises Wahshi. The Abyssinian slave is renowned for his skills with the javelin.

Muhammad's uncle Abu Lahab visits Abu Sufyan. He is anxious for news of Badr. Every detail. "Believe me," Abu Sufyan tells the old man, "it was an effortless surrender. We seemed to be at their command, submitting our necks for slaughter and our hands for being taken prisoners. And I do not blame the Quraysh! None of us could stand against their onslaught."

Abu Lahab wails with grief, cursing the Muslims. He never gave true protection to his nephew, not as Abu Talib had. He would have let Muhammad ibn Abdallah die and now look! Now he's winning.

Abu Lahab's slave sits beside him. Abu Lahab suspects the slave of having sympathy toward Islam—as all slaves seem to have. In his anger, Abu Lahab slaps the slave across the face. A visitor, Umm Fadhl, cannot bear such unprovoked cruelty. She smacks Abu Lahab on his head.

He returns home, bitter and humiliated. He dies within the week.

The *ghazus* continue. The Muslims capture Abu al-As ibn al-Rabi, the Prophet's son-in-law. He escapes to visit his wife Zaynab.

85

Their separation since the Flight has been painful, but Abu al-As refused to embrace Islam.

Zaynab announces she has given her husband sanctuary. Muhammad supports her right to do so but tells her not to sleep with him. He returns Abu al-As's merchandise and sends him back to Mecca to distribute it to its owners. When he has accomplished this task, Abu al-As leaves Mecca, returns to Zaynab, and submits to Islam.

It is tales like this that make Hind sick.

Women on both sides join the troops in battle to fight, to nurse the fallen, and encourage the fighters. Hind and a bevy of high-born women join this new expedition. Their *hawdaj* are filled with drums and tambourines and cymbals. They sing and play riding behind a white camel whose ornate litter holds the resplendent figure of Hubal, supreme clan deity of the Banu Umayya, traveling all the way from the Ka'aba to visit the battlefield. This is more than a blood feud, more than a fight of retaliation. With Hubal, Abu Sufyan has declared this a war between gods.

Three thousand strong march to Medina. The Prophet has gathered 700 and ordered them to prepare for battle. The mountain of Uhud is at their rear. Abu Sufyan's forces face Uhud with Medina behind them. The lines are drawn. Hind and her women wait silently as Talha ibn Abu Talha advances, bearing the Meccan standard and challenging the Muslims to single combat.

Hind squats atop her camel and surveys the Muslim ranks. Hamza is at the front of the line. Mighty Hamza, squat, powerful legs fixed like tree stumps to the ground, watches as Talha moves forward with the challenge.

It is not Hamza who springs to meet Talha, but doughty young Ali ibn Abu Talib, whose swift, double-edged sword slashes across Talha's shoulders. Talha's eyes stare uncomprehending at Ali while his head, as if not yet convinced it has been separated from his body, rolls languidly to the ground.

From within the ranks, the voice of Muhammad the Messenger bounces off the peak of Mount Uhud. "*Allahu Akbar!* God is Great!" and the Muslims echo his words.

Talha's brother leaps before Ali and snatches the banner. Ali dispatches him instantly. Another comes forward and another and another, until nine Meccans are skewered on the double-edged sword of Ali. Panic quivers through the Meccan ranks. Ali presses on foot into the cavalry. Hamza is not far behind, hacking through the dense enemy.

Hind shakes her long hair from its fastenings and the women follow suit. Her tongue trills against her lips. The women raise an ululation, shrieking, beating their tambourines. "Advance!" The squadron of women cheer their men on.

> Advance and we shall embrace you!
> Advance and we shall spread soft carpets beneath you!
> Retreat and we will leave you!
> Leave you and come to you no more!

The Meccan troops charge into the Muslim formation. The Muslims, that pathetic band of 700 infantry against Abu Sufyan's 3000 mounted, hold their own, fighting in tight formation.

> Go forward!
> The Daughters of al-Lat,
> the Daughters of the Morning Star
> cannot abide cowards!
> Are you afraid? Are you children?
> Go forward!

The Meccan women scream and dance around Hubal, who gazes blankly at the clash and clamor and bloody sand. The Muslims seem invincible.

Wahshi appears. He helps Hind back into her *hawdaj*. The camel rises to its full height. The next time Hind sees Wahshi, the slave is behind a rock, waiting. Hind thinks she has never witnessed such calm and patience.

Hamza fells a Meccan and suddenly the space around him is clear. In that half minute, Wahshi stands, takes aim, and hurls the javelin straight into Hamza's groin. He does not stagger. He does not cry out. He drops to the ground. He bleeds and bleeds and dies.

Hind howls for a driver to bring her camel to its knees. She scrambles out of the *hawdaj* and onto the ground, pushing the hair out of her eyes and clasping a knife.

In the clutch and heat of battle, none of the Muslims have yet noticed that Hamza is down. But they realize the Meccans are confused, about to be routed. Someone in the Muslim ranks cries to his fellows that this is the opportunity for plunder. The formation that was so tight unravels quickly as men disperse here and there seeking booty. Khalid of Mecca attacks, surging forward with his cavalry. Muhammad raises his arms to stop the Muslims and regroup them. Two teeth are knocked out of the Messenger of God's jaw. His standard-bearer, Mus'ab, is killed as he steps in front of the Prophet to protect him.

"He is dead!" the triumphant Meccans holler to one another and bring their horses to halt.

Muhammad is carried to a grove. His eyes open and he shakes his head. Fatima hurries to her father. Ali brings water in his shield. Fatima washes the blood from Muhammad's head. The Muslims are overjoyed that the Prophet is alive. The Meccans are overjoyed that they have killed the Messenger. It is their victory, but not a great one. Twenty-two Meccans are dead. Sixty-five Muslims have ascended to Paradise.

Hind walks gingerly through the bodies strewn across the sand. She is followed by a Quraysh warrior.

She points at Hamza. "Here he is."

The warrior splits Hamza's leather armor and then his belly. He reaches into mighty Hamza's gut and extracts the liver.

Hind tears a morsel of the organ with her teeth and chews.

She cannot swallow. She spits it out and throws Hamza's liver into the dirt. She grinds it with her foot. She unsheathes her knife. She chops off his nose and ears and genitals.

"Come, women! Come adorn yourselves with plunder, with the jewels of the enemy." She digs into Hamza's corpse. She wraps his steaming entrails, heart, kidneys, and spleen around her ankles, wrists, and throat. The other women do the same with other Muslim dead. They depart the field sporting grisly pendants, anklets, bracelets, and collars, their arms and legs and faces dripping and smeared with blood and bowels.

The Bedouin allies are disgusted. "Your women have polluted our cause," they tell Abu Sufyan.

When Muhammad finds his uncle's torn, maimed body, belly ripped and liver missing, eyes gone, and nose and ears lopped off, he says, "Were it not that his family would be miserable and that it might become a custom after me, I would leave him as he is, that his body might find its way into the bellies of beasts and the crops of birds. If God grants me victory of Quraysh in the future, I will mutilate a third of their men."

Yet it comes to pass that Allah sends Muhammad these words:

> If you punish, then punish as you have been punished.
> If you endure patiently that is better for the patient.
> Endure patiently. Your endurance is only in God.
> Grieve not for them, and be not in distress at what they plot.[31]

Thus there is pardon and patience and the command to all Muslims against mutilation.

Abu Sufyan enjoys the victory, yet it was half-measured and the Muslims continue their *ghazus*, raiding as they please. He will now take 10,000 men and put an end to this once and for all. He will enter Medina and set the Muslims aside for good.

With men from other settlements, with Bedouins and Jews and Quraysh, Abu Sufyan marches again toward Medina. The Muslims have dug ditches outside the city. Now, indeed, they are invincible. Abu Sufyan's army cannot gain purchase against this weird new form of warfare. Scimitars and swords can find no targets. Arrows defy gravity as the Muslims crouch in their trenches. Only eight are killed on both sides. Abu Sufyan returns home frustrated.

"I cannot, will not, attest to Muhammad ibn Abdallah's claim to prophethood," Abu Sufyan tells the Quraysh leaders. "Yet our gods are showing themselves useless against him. What do they want? They fight us, yet I have seen all their armies bowing toward our city and the Ka'aba. What of these prostrations toward Mecca in their morning prayers? Is there not some attachment, something so strong it will draw them to triumph?

"In truth," Abu Sufyan tells the Quraysh, "though it is anathema, I fear we may have to give in."

Hind sneers at him.

How often can a man be thwarted? Abu Sufyan is not alone in losing a child to Islam. Haven't all the clans of the Quraysh had someone surrender? His own daughter, Umm Habiba, left Mecca a decade ago to accompany her Muslim husband to Abyssinia.

How often can a man be humiliated? Word comes to Abu Sufyan that Umm Habiba has been widowed and returned with her daughter—not to Mecca, but to Medina to marry this so-called Messenger! Himself!

At this news, Hind's wrath is reborn tenfold. Not a jar or vessel in the house is left unbroken. Little Mu'awiya toddles for cover.

When Abu Sufyan and the other Meccan chiefs agree to a treaty, Hind abandons his bed. There will be an armistice for ten years, a truce, and in exchange for no attacks, the Muslims will be allowed to make the pilgrimage to the Ka'aba.

Does Hind quietly goad the Quraysh who attack a Muslim tribe? None will ever know. So much for the treaty that lasted only two years.

"We can soon expect a visit from Abu Sufyan," Muhammad tells the worshipers gathered at the Medina mosque. "He is beset with doubts. He knows this feud is pointless."

Indeed, Abu Sufyan arrives and knocks upon the door of his daughter's apartment. Ramlah will not allow him to so much as sit upon her rugs. Standing, he begs her to use her influence with the Messenger. "Impress upon him that we Meccans were not responsible for the killings and the breaking of the treaty."

Abu Sufyan visits Ali ibn Abu Talib for advice. "Ask the Prophet if he will agree to honor you as protector of any Meccans who want to surrender," Ali says. "Do so, and you will preserve your honor and your lives."

All the way home, Abu Sufyan contemplates Ali's advice and thinks of what words he can use to prepare the Quraysh for the inevitable.

The Messenger prepares in great secrecy for a final onslaught. It is 10 Ramadan, when Muhammad sets out at the head of an army of 10,000. No one knows where they are going. Likely Mecca, but perhaps Taif, the city of al-Lat.

In Mecca, Muhammad's uncle Abbas pleads with the Quraysh: "Alas, if the Prophet enters the city by force, it will be our end forever." That night, he sets out to join Muhammad and overtakes Abu Sufyan who is already on his way.

"Abu Sufyan, are you ready to submit to the One God?" Muhammad asks.

"There is no God but Allah," Abu Sufyan says. "This is easy to proclaim. Al-Lat, Hubal, and the rest have been useless to us. But whether you are His prophet, I still am not convinced."

Abu Sufyan hastens back to Mecca. He stands upon the roof of his house and summons his people.

"O Quraysh, Muhammad comes with a force you cannot resist! Should anyone wish to surrender, I will protect you and Muhammad will honor my protection. Take refuge in my house or stay locked in your own houses when the 10,000 Muslims arrive."

Hind stands behind him. She snatches his whiskers and wrenches his head around.

"People of Mecca!" she cries. "Kill this fat, greasy bladder of lard! What a rotten protector of his people!"

"Quraysh, do not listen!" Abu Sufyan struggles to loosen his wife's grip. "You are defeated. The time for Hind's defiance is over. The time for our resistance has passed. I have seen an army we will not be able to withstand!"

The Meccans retreat to barricade their homes, awaiting the unavoidable.

There are a few who try to fight. From the safety of her house, where Abu Sufyan has demanded she must stay with their children, Hind urges them on. They are quickly defeated. Hind weeps at last. She hugs young Mu'awiya to her. He, at least, will not be sacrificed to battle.

Muhammad enters the city with 10,000 Muslims behind him. There is no opposition. His red tent is pitched near the Ka'aba. One by one, the Meccans come to surrender. Ali and Fatima want vengeance against the last Quraysh rebels, but Muhammad wants no bloody reprisals. Nor are there demands that any Meccan accept Islam. "It is time for reconciliation, my children," he tells Ali and Fatima.

He sleeps and when he wakes he makes ablutions and offers prayer. He mounts his camel and makes the *tawwaf*, riding seven times round the Ka'aba. With each circle, he touches the Black Stone and calls, "Allahu Akbar! God is Great!" The Muslims answer the call: "Allahu Akbar." The city of Mecca joins them: "Allahu Akbar!"

And now they watch as the Messenger of God smashes each of the idols surrounding the shrine.

> *The truth has come.*
> *Falsehood has vanished.*
> *Surely falsehood is certain to vanish.*[32]

He orders the pagan deities whose images decorate the Ka'aba interior to be demolished. All but the frescoes of Isa and his mother Miriam. Then he enters to pray.

He stands in the door of the house that Hagar and Ibrahim built for God and speaks to those unbelievers gathered around him.

"O Quraysh, God has taken from you the haughtiness of paganism and its veneration of ancestors."

> *Man springs from Adam, and Adam sprang from dust.*
> *O mankind, We have created you*
> *male and female, and appointed you*
> *races and tribes, that you may know one another.*
> *Surely the noblest among you in the sight of God*
> *is the most God-fearing of you.*
> *God is All-knowing, All-wise.*[33]

All but ten are granted amnesty. Hind is one, for these ten have spread evil words about Islam or injured the Prophet's own family. Yet he declares that any who ask forgiveness will be spared.

The Prophet is flanked by Abu Bakr and Umar as the Quraysh come one by one in a line to swear fealty.

She has covered her face with a black veil. She stands before Muhammad silent, summoning the courage to be humble.

"You are Hind bint Utba?" the Prophet asks.

"I am," she replies. "Forgive me and God will forgive you."

"Do you forgo adultery and theft?" Muhammad asks. "Do you swear not to kill your own children?"

Hind pulls her shoulders back and glares into the Prophet's eyes. "I brought them up when they were little, but you killed them on the day of Badr when they were grown. You are the one to know about them!

"There was not a house on Earth, O Messenger of Allah, that I wanted to destroy more than yours. Now I have entered your house and surrendered. You cannot proceed against me, for I am a professing Muslim."

He smiles at her. "You are welcome, Hind bint Utba. You are free."

In two years' time, the Prophet returns to Mecca to make his Farewell Pilgrimage. His wives and Companions accompany him. At the gates of Mecca, he cries, "Here I am at your service, O God!"

A Final Revelation comes upon him in Mecca and God's word is this:

Today I have perfected your religion.
I have completed My blessing upon you,
And I have approved Islam for your religion.[34]

And when he has finished the rites to the One God in the place that housed the many, he makes his final sermon on Mount Arafat. Be just, he tells his people. Remember the straight path, the creed of Ibrahim, a man of pure faith. Be at peace with one another. Treat women kindly....

The Prophet then goes home to die.

Abu Sufyan who fought on behalf of Hubal and the goddesses, now fights to annihilate them. He will lead an army to Syria and Hind will accompany him, singing and chanting to encourage the *mujahidin*, the warriors for Islam. Her son Mu'awiya grows in her shadow and can lay claim to her belligerence. She stands behind him when he becomes the governor of Damascus.

Fatima bint Muhammad

Fatima was born in 604 C.E., the Prophet's fourth, youngest, and last surviving daughter, his favorite for they were especially close. Her mother Khadija died when Fatima was a child. She is revered as a saint, especially in Shi'a tradition. She died in Medina in 11 A.H./633 C.E., five months after Muhammad, some say of a broken heart over the loss of her father. She is called "the Luminous and Radiant."

There is a hollow knock on the door of Aisha's apartment. The Prophet's wives have all retired to their own apartments. Old Barakah snores on a mat on the floor. His Companions have dispersed to pray.

Fatima pulls her veil across her face and pads on bare feet across the cool clay floor to unlatch the wooden portal.

A stranger looks down at her. He is tall. His large eyes burn through her and his face is so lean and stern she trembles. He speaks the Arabic of noblemen and kings. His voice seems to come from the sky, although his mouth is moving.

"I am here to see Muhammad ibn Abdallah. I have urgent business."

Fatima slams the door in the stranger's face and runs to her father.

The Messenger of God lies on Aisha's bed, burning with fever, his head on the lap of his young wife. Aisha looks disapprovingly at Fatima rushing into the room.

There is little love lost between them. Forgiveness is difficult. Ali once supported those who accused Aisha of infidelity and Fatima was once the envoy of her father's other wives, protesting Aisha's favored position. "Little daughter," Muhammad said, "You must also love what is pleasing to me."

But so well aware are the other wives of their husband's attachment to Aisha, it is they who suggest that in his illness he stay with her though it is not her turn.

"Father," Fatima gasps. "There is a man at the door. He speaks like a nobleman, but I think he must come from a faraway country, for he is very rude to disturb you so late at night. He frightened me. I would not let him in."

Her father smiles. She is his favorite daughter and the only one he has left. She is the one he would not let marry until she was eighteen, the one whose husband he would not allow to have other wives, saying, "Fatima is a part of me and what harms her, harms me."

Eyes gleaming, the Messenger struggles to sit up. Aisha, slight as she is, supports him upright with her arms.

"My daughter, the stranger who knocks on the door is neither man woman, but a slave of God. God sent this stranger to me as a friend. Some fear him like a scourge, though he never does a wicked thing. He is not stopped by doors nor held by walls. No bolts can shut him out...or in. Go, my daughter, bring him."

To Fatima's surprise, the stranger is still there. She ushers him in and he walks quietly, as if on air, into the room where Muhammad lies. The Messenger opens his arms to the dark figure. "Welcome, my brother."

Barakah has awoken and crawled into a corner. Fatima huddles with her in the shadows.

Azrail, Angel of Death, speaks solemnly.

"Prophet of God! It has pleased our Master to call you to Heaven. He—praised be His name—told me to respect your wishes and withdraw if you are not ready for me. You are the only one of his creatures to whom He has ever commanded me to grant respite."

Muhammad glances dotingly at his favorite daughter and at Barakah hovering in the corner. He caresses the hand of his favorite wife to comfort her. Aisha is unafraid of the angel, unafraid of death, yet she is filled with anguish, knowing she will soon lose this man she has loved since she was a baby.

"I am grateful to you and to my Lord for his generosity," Muhammad says. "If he would kindly grant me three hours so that I can settle the affairs of my community, then I shall rest in peace."

Azrail nods and Fatima, still trembling, steps toward the door to see him out. But the Angel of Death has evaporated like steam.

Now, Muhammad directs Fatima to fetch his Companion Abdur-Rahman ibn Auf and to bring her husband Ali ibn Abu Talib.

Her own apartment is next to Aisha's. Once there was a door between them, but after Ali supported her accusers, bricks replaced the door.

The night is hot, her husband is asleep on the roof. Fatima hurries up the stone steps, remembering how, when he had asked for her hand, she had not known how to answer. Both were so shy as to be almost mute. And they had been as brother and sister from childhood, when Ali came to live with Muhammad and Khadija.

"Ali is mentioning you," her father said. He repeated it several times, but Fatima remained silent, so Muhammad spoke out and gave permission. He deemed this man the best choice, though others had asked for her, among them Aisha's father Abu Bakr.

Ali had little with which to pay the bride-price. His reluctance to marry was in part his poverty. It shamed him to be so poor. In that unwillingness, Muhammad saw his own when Khadija proposed to him. He advised Ali to sell his shield. Uthman ibn Affan, husband of Fatima's sister Ruqayyah, bought it gladly, then handed it back to Ali as a wedding gift. Ali offered the 480 dirhams as *mahar*, but Muhammad would not take it.

"Invest two-thirds of it in scent and a third in land and cotton," he advised. "Now, what dowry will you give my daughter?"

Ali shook his head. He had nothing left.

"Where is the coat of chain mail I gave you?"

Ali grinned. He'd forgotten all about it.

"Give it to her," Muhammad said, and so Fatima was married for an iron coat of chain mail.

She reaches the roof and the bed. She leans over Ali and shakes him awake. "Hurry! My father calls for you."

Ali leaps up at once and rushes away. Fatima sits on the bed. Ali bought scent and land and cotton with the 480 dirhams, as her father advised, but he spared some to give her a wonderful wedding feast, better than any wedding there had yet been in the community of believers.

Her father gave her a palm-leaf bed, a ram skin, a pillow of leather, a small leather vessel tooled and painted in lovely designs, and a water skin. She was his treasure, he said, and with these things, she would have comfort.

The marriage contract was signed; the singing women sprinkled soft sand on the floor and escorted her into the bridal room to wait for Ali to join her on the palm-leaf bed and the ram skin. As her bridegroom entered the room, she saw her father behind him, as if he, too, would enter the bridal bower. But Muhammad stopped at the doorway and stood under the lintel. He called for water and washed his hands. He beckoned Ali and sprinkled water on the young man's barrel chest and between his wide shoulders. Then he called for Fatima. She was so nervous, she tripped on her garment. As her father anointed her, he whispered, "I waited until I could give you to the finest of my family." Then he embraced them and covered them with his robe.

At Aisha's apartment, Ali and Abdur-Rahman help the Messenger to his feet and support him as he walks to the mosque. When the believers fled from Mecca, they built this mosque in Medina, the first mosque, and the Prophet wishes to visit it one last time. He enters and Abu Bakr, who is leading prayers, interrupts the service, ready to hand back leadership to Muhammad. Muhammad faces the congregation. He asks if anyone in the mosque has anything against him. All deny it. Then, with gradual, painful steps, Ali and Abdur-Rahman help Muhammad home.

Fatima waits with Aisha. They are silent, neither looking at each other, each caught in her own thoughts. When Aisha speaks, Fatima jumps, startled out of her reveries.

"What were the secrets he told you that made you weep and then laugh in the same moment that day?"

It was a question Aisha had asked before, but Fatima refused to tell. Now she sighs, a sad, resigned sigh. "When I walked into the room that day my father was with you, he asked me to sit at his right hand. First he whispered to me that the angel Jibril had come to him twice. Once a year, as you know, since the first Revelation, Jibril came to my father and together they recited the Qur'an. But this year, Jibril came twice.

"'I think my end is near,' he told me. 'I will be waiting for you with your mother and all your sisters and brothers.' That is when I wept. But then he said, 'Are you not content to be the mistress of the women of this community and the best of women in the world?' and that is when I laughed."

Aisha can barely stifle her jealousy. It ripples through her like an angry djinn. Jealousy is her curse, the thing that plagues her most. She has been jealous of Muhammad's other wives and jealous of his children. But none of those compare to the jealousy she feels for Khadija. She shudders thinking of the day she lashed out at Muhammad's fond memories of that "toothless old woman of the Quraysh!"

Fatima knows of Aisha's harsh words about her mother. These are resentments that burn, even in one as devout and diffident as Fatima.

Aisha is younger than Fatima and beautiful, whereas beauty has eluded Fatima. Her sister Ruqayyah's gift was beauty. Perhaps Fatima looks too much like her father, a handsome man, but such strong features and the brows connected like the two arches of a bow do not make a comely woman.

"I have not seen any one of God's creations resemble the Messenger of God more in conversation and manner than Fatima, may God be pleased with her," Aisha says. "When the Prophet sees her approaching, he welcomes her, stands up and kisses her, takes her by the hand, and sits her down in the place where he was sitting."

Fatima is timid, yet when she is roused to speech, it flows as if the angels themselves moved her tongue. Hers is the gift of devotion.

99

Is Aisha not the best of women in the world? Before she can reply or react to defend her hurt feelings, to cut Fatima down to size, Ali and Abdur-Rahman return from the mosque bearing the Messenger. They lay him in his bed and Aisha slips her lap under his head. She holds him upright, one hand flat against the seal between his shoulder blades. He rests his head on her chest.

He calls to Fatima. The grief encases her like a death-cloth and chokes her. She kneels at his feet. He touches her head. "I bid you goodbye, my dearest daughter," he says. A sob untangles from the knot in her throat. "Don't cry, my Fatima. Six moons from now you join me in Paradise."

He is luminous, the light pours from him, like water flowing into the spring of Zamzam under the full moon, or like the *falaq al-subh*, the sudden dawn. He tries, though his arms are weak, to pass his hands over his face. He has prayed for forgiveness in this way all his life, every day, many times a day.

He bids the others farewell. The Companions and wives and followers who have squeezed into Aisha's apartment hold back their crying, listening for last words. Listening for the naming of a successor. The three hours have passed. Azrail has returned. With the grace of a midwife guiding an infant from the room, the Angel of Death releases the soul of the Prophet from his body.

Aisha slips out from under his body and rests his head on a pillow. She joins the others in weeping.

They bury Muhammad under Aisha's floor.

It is Fatima, in a voice gurgling with tears, who delivers her father's funeral speech.

She reminds the followers that the Prophet spoke against loud lamentations and beating of breasts and smiting of cheeks to mourn the dead, but that when Ruqayyah died and he sat with her beside the grave, he daubed at her tears with his cloak and comforted her: "Weep. What comes from the heart and from the eye, that is from God and His mercy. But what comes from the hand and from the tongue, that is from Satan."

100

She has the ability to stir emotions, move people to tears, fill hearts with praise and gratitude to God for His grace and inestimable bounties.

"My son, my son," Barakah sobs softly. "I can live without you on Earth, knowing we will soon be together in Paradise. But what will life be without your Revelations from God?"

Fatima's grief is great and she is lonely, though she has her sons Hassan and Husayn and her daughters Zaynab and Umm Kulthum, named for her dear sisters. And she has Ali. She thinks how he once said that God created sexual desire in ten parts, and then gave nine parts to women. She laughs aloud. He is like Umar ibn al-Khattab and unsympathetic to women, sometimes even mean. Ali ibn Abu Talib was reared by her father. How did he come to have such contempt for women?

But Ali is a good husband after all. He, who was harsh to her in the beginning, until her father overheard.

They were arguing, loud and bitter, passionately at war. Muhammad, unexpected, entered the room. They stopped their bickering, shocked as the Messenger lay down on the bed. He motioned Fatima to come lie beside him, then Ali to lie down on the other side.

Fatima wraps her arms around her body recalling how her father took Ali's hand and placed it on his own navel. Next he placed her hand on his navel and there they lay, the peace from Muhammad's body traveling through their hands into their hearts until at last those hands grasped each other and the love between them was kindled. How long had it taken? How long had they lain there, the three of them?

When her father left the house that day, someone asked why he had entered looking so sad, and was leaving so joyfully.

"What would prevent me from being happy, when I have made peace between the two I love most?" he replied.

And when her children were born, he was ecstatic. What pleasure he took as they crawled over his back while he made prostrations in the mosque.

101

Her arms are wrapped around her body, yet that body feels like liquid. It is as if she has no more root in this Earth. Her father's dying words come back to her—"six moons," "six moons"—and it has been six moons.

She summons Ali and asks him to buy barley and black cloth. When he returns, she places the barley on the millstone and begins to turn the granite wheel against the slab. Barakah protests.

"I will do it, granddaughter. You must rest."

"You ground the grain yesterday, Umm Ayman," Fatima says. "Today I want to speak to the millstone myself."

She turns the wheel, round and round. The sensation of her body returns. "You are the companion of my soul," she tells the millstone. "You are the friend of my afflicted heart, turned by the constant pouring of my blood."

But the exertion soon makes her weak. She stops. Barakah rushes to her and guides her as she tries to stand. She is faint. Amid the ringing in her ears, she hears voices of angels like birdsong.

"Tell me," she murmurs, "is my father the Prophet there?"

A voice, that of the stranger on the night of her father's death, replies. "Yes, he is there. And when I left him, he was weeping."

"Why is my father weeping? Has he been wronged?"

"He weeps because he sees that you are suffering."

"Did he not tell you when he will receive me up there in Paradise?"

"Yes, he said to me, 'Tell her that tomorrow my Fatima will be with me here in Paradise!'"

"O Azrail," Fatima says aloud, "thank my father for his love and care, thank you for comforting me."

With that she rises from her slump and goes to her grinding with renewed energy. When she has finished, she bakes the barley cakes that are offered to condolence visitors. Then with the black cloth Ali has brought her, she sews clothes for her two sons. When the clothes are ready, she calls for her elder daughter Zaynab to sit with her in the courtyard.

Fatima washes her daughter's hair and combs it, leaving tears on the long, black tresses. "This is the last time I can care for this beloved head on this earth," she murmurs. "Tomorrow I shall no longer be here. One sad day, stones will be thrown at this precious head."

Ali enters the courtyard. He gasps at his wife, who is flushed as if she were on fire. He lays his hand on her forehead, then snatches it away. "Fatima! You have fever! What can I get you? How can I give you relief?"

"I would have the juice of pomegranates," Fatima answers, kissing her daughter's head and lying back, exhausted. The comb slips from her hand.

"I will find pomegranates if I have to search all Arabia," Ali promises. She is the worthy companion of his life. He calls her the peacemaker of his troubled mind.

The Prophet said that the juice of the pomegranate washes away all envy and hatred. Ali finds only one in the whole city of Medina. Simeon the Jewish merchant has all but sold out of pomegranates and he makes the last a gift to Ali.

Ali races through alleys, scurries through the narrow gaps between houses, and nearly falls over a blind beggar burning with fever. He is begging not for alms but for a cure.

"I have a cure for your fever," Ali says and hands the blind man the only pomegranate left in the city, the one meant for Fatima.

And as he does so, the angel Jibril descends into Fatima's courtyard, where she sits with Zaynab, talking quietly. Her younger daughter, Umm Kulthum, plays quietly in a corner, happy in her baby games. Jibril carries a basketful of pomegranates from the orchards of Paradise, freshly picked by the angels. Jibril tears one open and hands it to Fatima. One bite and she feels better, but the splendor of that mound of shining red fruit makes her yearn for Paradise.

She stands and takes Zaynab's hand. She leads Zaynab to her own room, where she keeps her treasures.

"I want you to have these precious things," she says, and opens the first box. Two rubies shimmer on a cloth.

"Here are the teeth which an unbeliever's stone, viciously thrown, knocked out of my father's mouth during the Battle of Uhud. You see, they are freshly bleeding. Keep them as your finest jewels."

Zaynab nods. Fatima brings out a second box. "Here is a signet ring, which once belonged to King Sulayman. The signet is composed of the four divine stones which an angel gave Sulayman and with it the power to rule the four kingdoms of created beings: humans, animals, djinn, and *shayytan*.

"Tell no one this secret, except your brothers Hassan and Husayn. Remember: never can one use this power against God."

Zaynab gives her word. Fatima brings out a third box containing a bottle.

"In this bottle you can see what looks like soil, but it is really ambergris from the floor of Paradise. It was brought to us by the angel Jibril. This dust from Heaven will turn red at the very moment of your brother Husayn's death."

Zaynab can bear it no longer. She bursts into tears. Through her sobs she again pledges to her mother that she will look after the three family treasures and always keep them in a safe place.

"Now prepare me a bath," Fatima says, and when Zaynab has washed her, Fatima tells the girl where she keeps the shroud she has prepared for wearing in the grave and where she keeps the bottle of camphor which is to be used for the ceremony of ablution before her internment.

It is time to lie down on her palm-leaf bed and the ram skin her father gave Fatima on her wedding day. She sleeps through the night, with Barakah curled on the end of her bed. She wakes to her last dawn with Ali by her side. He holds her hand and wets it with his tears. Husayn and Hassan embrace their mother, while she reminds them of the black clothes she has made them to wear when she is gone. Zaynab holds Umm Kulthum on her hip, the grief gripping her belly. Fatima reminds her of the barley cakes to offer friends when they come for condolences.

"Do not wail over my body," she tells her family. "I do not wish to be disturbed or upset."

She closes her eyes. "Make my soul a ransom to save the sweet beloved souls of my husband and children," she prays.

Her breath is short, her speech labored. "I have lived twenty-eight years. I go at last to see my father."

> *Say: My worship and my sacrifice,*
> *My living and my dying are for God,*
> *Lord of the worlds.*[35]

Aisha bint Abu Bakr

Aisha bint Abu Bakr was the daughter of the Prophet's clos-
est Companion, Abu Bakr. She was born in 614 C.E. and
betrothed to Muhammad when she was six, before the hijra,
the Flight to Medina. They were married when she was
nine, and the marriage was consummated when she
reached puberty. Of Muhammad's wives following the
death of Khadija, Aisha was his favorite, his Best Beloved.
She died in 56 A.H./678 C.E. at the age of sixty-four.

Aisha's beloved is buried beneath her floor. Beneath her feet.
  "Muhammad, what is your love for me like?"
  He was mending his sandal and Aisha was spinning.
  "Like a tight knot in a rope."
  "And what is that like?"
  "Always the same."
Hafsa bint Umar slips into the apartment and shuts the door
that leads into the mosque. It is late at night, when the believers
who crowd into the room to pray at the grave have at last gone
home to bed or collapsed outside the apartment to await the morn-
ing prayer. "A Prophet," Muhammad said, "must be buried where
he expires."

The night air is cool, the heat in the apartment is subsiding.
Aisha hardly slept while the Prophet was ill. She never left his side.
He lay with his head in her lap and she sat as still as she could to give
him comfort. The tiredness rests inside her shoulders, but her mind
will not be tranquil.

Hafsa, severe Umar ibn al-Khattab's daughter, sits beside Aisha, takes her hand, and gazes with her at the grave. Tears fall from Hafsa's large eyes into her skirt. Hafsa weeps less for her husband's death than for her sister wife, whose grief has left a gray pallor on her pert young face.

A tear lands on Hafsa's bracelet. She chuckles. She is as quick to laugh as she is to lash out. Aisha looks up, still ready for a joke. They have shared jokes from the beginning.

"I was just remembering the day we told Sawdah that the false prophet had arrived and was wandering through Medina."

"The *dajjal!* You were such a devil. It's you who taught me to be naughty. You who encouraged me to be outspoken. You sower of mischief!"

"No one had to teach you, Aisha, to be disobedient and unruly. Always spoiled, you! Always impudent and quick-witted. More than willing to test the Messenger's patience, though it only got you indulgence from him."

Aisha was to watch a captive. She was fourteen and suddenly distracted by some ruffle among the women. She turned her back. The prisoner sneaked out the door.

When Muhammad returned, he cursed her. "May God cut off your hand!" He rushed away to order a search.

Aisha sank to the floor, staring at her palms. First the left. Then the right. Back and forth, turning them over and over. He found her this way when he returned.

"What's the matter with you? Are you djinn-possessed?"

"I am waiting to see which of my hands will be cut off."

He lowered himself to the floor beside her. "O my Aisha, forgive my outburst. O God, All-merciful, All-compassionate, blessings on any man or woman I may have cursed."

"And from what I hear," Hafsa continues, "you were irrepressible as a child.

"You *knew* me as a child!"

"I wasn't much more when we met, when I became the third wife."

"You were twenty and widowed. A woman of experience. I was just eleven, a virgin, though I'd been married two years. I was," Aisha adds, raising her chin with pride, "the *only* virgin among the wives."

Her red-striped dress marked a ceremonial time. She was hard at play. Swinging with her playmates in the yard. Covered in dust, panting with the exertion of flying, pumping legs, flying higher than all her friends.

Her mother and Asmaa came. They took her to a little apartment in the new mosque. Muhammad waited. They washed her face and dressed her. He clapped his hands, delighted to see her decked out in wedding jewelry and her long hair brushed and brushed. Her mother placed her on his lap. "These are your family," she said. "May Allah bless you in them and bless them in you."

Her husband drank from a cup of milk, then handed it Aisha to drink, but child that she was, she did not want milk to drink at that moment and passed it on to her sister Asmaa.

"You and all the other wives had celebrations, but mine was hasty."

"Never mind, Aisha. You were the only one with whom he washed from the same bowl and drank from the same cup. You were his favorite. Your day was always the day the believers brought gifts to the Messenger of God."

The rival sister wives appealed to him to stop this practice, to tell the community to bring their gifts to other apartments, too. He received their plea in silence, though they asked again and again.

At last he reproached them. "Trouble me not about Aisha. She is the only woman in whose company I receive Revelations."

"Remind me again about Sawdah. I was not listening. I'm sorry, Hafsa."

Hafsa pats Aisha's hand. "I think we were jealous of her, for she has her own money, earned from that fine leatherwork."

"Yes, yes. What else?" Aisha does not want to remember her jealousies, how much she hated her sister wives, how she sometimes followed Muhammad to spy on him, how she and Hafsa taught new women to say, when the Messenger came to their rooms, "I take refuge with God from you."

None but his concubine, Maryam the Copt, had children by Muhammad. He was passionate for Maryam and visited her so often the sister wives banded together to complain. Hafsa caught them making love on her bed! He begged her not to tell Aisha, but Hafsa broke her promise. Aisha reprimanded him. Such indiscretions offended the harem and humiliated them all.

Then Ibrahim was born, with Maryam's fair skin and Muhammad's curls. He was happier than Aisha had ever seen him. When the baby boy died, he was more downcast than she had ever seen him.

She does not like to be reminded of how envious she was, especially of Umm Salamah and Zaynab, who boasted that Allah Himself had arranged her marriage to the Prophet.

She, so beautiful, and Aisha only nine and with nothing but the magnetism of a fun-loving child. Zaynab's adult allure enchanted her guests. They would not leave the wedding feast. God's Messenger was frustrated, anxious to be alone with his new bride. And Aisha, in whose presence he had received the Revelation to marry Zaynab, was carried to her bed by Asmaa and tucked in with a lullaby. Over Asmaa's song, Aisha could hear the gaiety, the dancing and musicians and Zaynab's laughter like rare, refreshing rain.

"You're still not listening."

"Tell me."

"Sawdah was so frightened of the *dajjal*, she hid in the kitchen tent—it was hilarious! Behind the pots and pans, she trembled and shivered and prayed against the false prophet. She would not come out."

Aisha giggles. "We ran to Muhammad, falling over each other with laughter…"

"…and he shook his head and rushed to the kitchen to rescue her! She was covered with dust and cobwebs, shaking like a frightened sheep!"

The two embrace, snorting and breathless, so used to laughing together they have only to glance sideways at one another to begin hooting and chortling until they are doubled up, holding their sides.

As more wives came into the family, old Sawdah feared divorce, for she had become fat and unattractive. If Muhammad divorced her,

THE SCIMITAR AND THE VEIL

she was afraid she would lose her place in Paradise. She gave Aisha her visitation days. But Muhammad would never have divorced her. He was too kind and grateful that she had cared for his household and his little Fatima, before the Flight, before Fatima's marriage.

"Listen to you two!" Safiyyah bint Huayy stands over the two young women, her face carefully arranged in amused reproof, fists on her hips. "You are irreverent sinners, you two, howling like monkeys at the Messenger's grave."

Safiyyah sits next to Aisha and the three wrap their arms around one another.

The Jewess arrived with Muhammad after a ghazu. *She was reputed to be exquisite and Aisha went with Hafsa, Zaynab, and Juwairiyah to inspect her.*

"I'm afraid," Zaynab sniffed, "that this woman will get ahead of us with Muhammad." The very beautiful are always troubled by the very beautiful.

"No," Juwairiyah replied. "She's not the kind who finds much favor with husbands."

"Aisha, what do you think of her?" Muhammad asked later.

"She is merely a Jewess," Aisha sneered.

"Be gentle, Aisha. Besides, she has become a good Muslim."

"Forgive me for taunting you when you first arrived." Aisha kisses Safiyyah's cheek.

"Forgive me, too," Hafsa says. "I was perhaps more jealous of you."

Safiyyah shrugs and smiles. It has been years since the awful teasing, when the Prophet taught her to put her sister wives in their places by replying, "How can any of you be above me, when Haroun is my father, Musa is my uncle, and Muhammad is my husband!"

It was as Juwairiyah predicted. He soon lost interest in Safiyyah. But he lost fascination for them all, including Juwairiyah. All but Umm Salamah—so clever—Zaynab—so pretty and bountiful—and Aisha.

He lost interest in Safiyyah, but she and Hafsa and Aisha became the best of friends. Any slight against one was a slight against them all.

110

Death is a time for reminiscences. Memories come thick and fast. Safiyyah and Hafsa look at one another over Aisha's head and nod. They kiss her and rise to leave. She smiles wanly at them as they depart. Her heart is so heavy, she's not sure she will be able to stand.

She came to this apartment when she was nine, small and skinny. During the day there were Barakah and her mother and Asmaa, when she could get away from her household duties. There was Sawdah.

There were playmates. Once when they were visiting, Muhammad came in and they ran away. He chased them and brought them back. "Have no fear, little ones. Amuse yourselves and my Aisha to your heart's content."

And when they were not there, he sat with her and played Solomon's horses with her and helped her dress her dolls.

Night was harder. A little girl, alone in this apartment. Fatima and Ali lived next door, but they cared not at all for Aisha. No doubt Fatima recalled when it was she with whom Muhammad played at Solomon's horses and dressing dolls.

At last Aisha became a woman. The nights were lovely with Muhammad. The nights that were hers. Her turn.

He was at Maimunah's apartment when he fell ill. He knew it was more than passing sickness. The other wives came visiting as he lay sliding in and out of fever.

"Where am I?" he asked. "Where will I be tomorrow?"

Umm Salamah called the wives to her.

"He is trying to determine which day is Aisha's," she said.

"Would it be a great offense if I retired to Aisha's apartment, though it is not her turn?"

They helped him up. They cooed at him and petted him as they laid him on Aisha's bed.

Now Muhammad and Aisha will share this room forever.

She fingers her wedding dress. The striped cloth is tattered, hem raised and lowered, sleeves frayed. So many in the *umma* borrowed this dress to bring luck to their own marriages.

"I know when you are pleased with me and when you are annoyed or angered."

"How do you know that?"

"When you are pleased, you say, 'O Muhammad' or 'by the Lord of Muhammad.' But when you're angry with me, you say, 'O Messenger of God!' or 'by the Lord of Ibrahim!'"

She drops to her knees on the floor over her beloved. She pounds the loose dirt. "O Messenger of God, by the Lord of Ibrahim, I am angered that you have left me."

She is eighteen years old.

She calls it her lucky day when her sister wives gave up their turns and sent the Messenger in his last illness to her. She had always fussed over him and pampered him. She took him to task when he pampered himself too much. She reminded him not to stay long in the hot sun, prompting him to hold court in the shade of his red leather tent. She loved to wait on him. To anoint his hair with perfume. She has no children. She will have no children.

*It is not fitting that you give any uneasiness
to the Messenger of Allah
or that you marry his wives after him ever.
This would be a grievous thing before Allah.*[36]

For Aisha and her sister wives to remarry would surely create factions and worse, dynasties. Hourly, someone comes to her to ask:

"Whom did he name as a successor?"

"None."

"Who?"

"No one."

"Whom did he name?"

"You visited him each day during his illness. You were here at night to help. You would know as well as I if anyone were named."

"Who?" they persist.

"None," Aisha again insists. "But he surely would have named Abu Bakr or Umar, for they were his staunchest supporters, his faithful counselors."

When she hears this, Fatima bint Muhammad winces.

112

Indeed, Aisha's father and Umar are bent on maintaining their advantages. Ali ibn Abu Talib, the Messenger's own son-in-law, holds back his resentment. Timid as she is, Fatima explodes and denounces Abu Bakr in public. Ali reminds Fatima that he is still young and there is still time for him to receive the caliphate. Yet Ali and all the others strive now to climb the ladder, to use any political advantage to achieve the position of Successor.

Abu Bakr is elected, the oldest and first Companion of the Prophet. Ali does not take the oath of allegiance for half a year, until Fatima is dead.

Abu Bakr is dead. Aisha honors his request to be buried next to the Prophet in her apartment. He has entrusted her to dispose of his properties and help rear his youngest children. She is twenty.

Now it is Umar ibn al-Khattab's turn as Successor. Ali ibn Abu Talib still waits. Umar expands the territories of Islam, and Ali, so skilled with his double-edged sword, leads the warriors.

Umm Habiba, the daughter of Abu Sufyan and Hind bint Utba, enters Aisha's apartment in a panic. "Umar has declared that women may not attend the mosque!" she cries. She is followed by a bevy of her sister wives, Zaynab, Umm Salamah, Maimunah, Safiyyah, Hafsa....

"He tries to prevent us from public worship!"

"He has forbidden his wife, Atikah, to attend public prayers and now he wants to stop us."

But Atikah, alone of all Umar's wives, disobeys him. She goes to the mosque, welts and all. She will not be dissuaded, even by beatings.

"The people come even to me now to protest my father's actions," Hafsa tells Aisha. "Men have visited me to ask that I intercede. I cannot. He will not listen to me. I have tried."

The Mothers of the Believers take their evening meal together. "Many are asking you to exert your influence," they tell Aisha. "You are Best Beloved. You can protest and Umar might hear you."

"We will be cordial to Umar and support him as much as possible," Aisha says.

Atikah is in the mosque when the assassin leaps upon Umar and stabs him.

Umar calls from his deathbed for Aisha. When she arrives, he dismisses his wives and children, even Hafsa, from the room. He chokes and sputters. He opens his mouth and blood trickles along his chin. Aisha reaches to clean him with a cloth. He waves her away.

"Will you, O Best Beloved, Mother of the Believers, allow me to be buried beside the Messenger of God and your father, the first caliph?"

Aisha does not hesitate. She does not refuse. Umar dies smiling.

She speaks these words of Umar: "He was harsh, but he was energetic. He managed the affairs of the community with fairness. He was equal to every occasion. He was a Qur'an reader. When he read or spoke, he made one hear. When he walked, he was brisk and quick of step, and when he struck, he hurt. He was not hesitant or ever wavering."

Aisha's head throbbed. She lay with a wet cloth on her head. She waited for Muhammad to return from a funeral. He walked in her door, preceded by sorrow.

"Are you ill?" he asked.

"My head hurts."

"It would not be to your disadvantage," he said, "if you were to die before me so that I myself could wash and shroud you and pray over you and bury you."

She sat up, ears ringing with the effort. His passion for Maryam the Copt still angered her.

"May that happen to another!" she said. "But I see that is what you wish for. You would then surely return to my apartment and there amuse yourself with some of your women!"

She looks from Muhammad's grave to Abu Bakr's and to Umar's. "It seems my apartment is now filled with men!"

She calls for a mason. "I could live with my husband and my father, but Umar is like living with a stranger. Build me a wall." *Hijab*, a curtain, between her and Umar.

There were so many visitors to whichever wife's apartment Muhammad was in, day or night, a constant stream, unremitting interruptions. At last, a Revelation:

Believers, do not enter the houses of the Prophet for a meal
without waiting for the proper time, unless you are given leave.
But if you are invited, enter; and when you have eaten, disperse.
Do not engage in familiar talk, for this would annoy the Prophet
and he would be ashamed to bid you to go;
but of the truth God is not ashamed.[37]

*The Messenger's wives were badgered for favors, harassed on the
streets of Medina, even at night when discretely leaving their apartments to urinate.*

If you ask his wives for anything,
speak to them from behind a curtain.
This is more chaste for your hearts and for theirs.[38]

*Now, the wives wore mantles when walking abroad. Aisha missed
her hair free. She who was ever forthright found speaking through a
curtain crippling. Only their male relatives were exempt, only their
sons, cousins, brothers, foster relations, fathers, uncles, and in-laws
could approach them face to face. Umar ibn al-Khattab applauded the
Revelation, and wanted even more austerity. He prodded Muhammad
for more rigorous restraints of the women. Muhammad left* hijab *as it
was—a curtain against strangers, a mantle covering the head. The
heavenly word indisputable.*

When the widows take their evening meals together, they play
a game. "Which of us will die first?"

The Prophet had said that it would be she of the longest hand.
She with the highest reach would be the first to follow him into the
next world.

Each time they meet, the nine line up against the wall to test
how far their arms will go. They stretch their middle fingers taut and
try not to stand on their toes.

Juwairiyah bangs hard on Aisha's door. It is morning, but Aisha
has been up all night long watching the stars, counting them, trac-
ing their patterns. She stumbles from sleep and lets her sister wife in.

"Zaynab has died. In the night! Zaynab! In her sleep."

They dress Zaynab's body. She is so small. The shortest of them all. She never won the hand-stretching game. What could the Prophet have meant?

They pray over her and praying they remember that although Zaynab had the flaw of boasting—God forgive her—she was charitable.

"Hers was the longest hand," Umm Salamah says aloud. "For she was openhanded. She had nothing she would not give away. She was the most generous of us, the kindliest and most industrious."

Aisha and Umm Salamah had accompanied Muhammad on an expedition. In the early hours of the morning, orders were given to break camp for the return journey. Aisha hurried to a hillock and squatted to empty herself of the night's urine. She was on her way back, when she felt the necklace of Yemeni agate missing from her throat. She turned again, retracing her steps and walking slowly, eyes to the ground, she found it.

But when she returned, the camp was deserted. She cried for help, but there was no answer. The others, assuming Aisha to be in her litter, had placed it on her camel and led it away. They thought nothing of the lightness of the load, for Aisha was a weightless and slender girl and none had noticed she was not in her hawdaj *when they lifted it back on her camel.*

She waited. Hoping someone would come back for her. The dawn was rising and Aisha fell back to sleep. She felt a movement. Her eyes fluttered open. A young man, Safwan ibn al-Muattal, stood in front her. He mounted her on his camel and without a word led her to Medina. They arrived just as Aisha's absence had been discovered, just as Muhammad was about to send a search party. He thanked Safwan. Aisha returned to her apartment.

By morning, Zaynab's sister Hamnah bint Jahsh—thinking to help Zaynab by ruining Muhammad's favorite—was whispering that Aisha and Safwan had met often, in secret. The gossip spread, until even Hassan ibn Thabit, Muhammad's court poet, was inspired to compose devious verses about a love affair between a handsome youth and the young wife of an old man.

Days passed into weeks. Outside her house, the rumors raged like wildfire, though none dared to tell Aisha. Yet she perceived Muhammad's growing coolness. At last, Hafsa warned her of the scandal.

"I am ill," Aisha told Muhammad. "Give me permission to go to my mother." She did not say that the pain in her heart was making her sick to her stomach.

"Take comfort, my child," her mother said. "Few are the young and beautiful women, more beloved than their rivals, who are not the victims of some scandal."

Aisha wept uncontrollably. Abu Bakr sent her home, where Muhammad sat helpless against the magnitude of the gossip, and afraid of his own doubts. No Revelations came, no word from God to guide him past the malice or reassure him of Aisha's love, though he loved her. He could not turn to Aisha's father. He would not turn to Umar, so severe and punitive to women.

He turned to Usamah, his grandson, son of his adopted son Zayd. Usamah ibn Zayd spoke only good of Aisha.

He turned to his son-in-law Ali ibn Abu Talib.

"O Messenger of God, Allah has placed no narrow limits on you. Many are the women like her," Ali said. "Examine her maid for the truth of the matter."

"She is full of childish pranks," the maid reminded Muhammad. "But there is no evil or infidelity in her."

While Aisha cried and could not stop crying, sleepless and hopeless, Muhammad took the matter up in the mosque. One accuses the other of spreading lies, until accusations turn to fighting. Muhammad at the pulpit, cool as a cloud, pacified the crowd.

Her parents were there, her mother daubing wet cloths on Aisha's tear-stained face, when Muhammad entered the apartment. He had not visited Aisha for a month. She could see he missed her.

"O Aisha," he pleaded. "If you are innocent, God will absolve you. But if you are guilty, ask forgiveness, for Allah pardons those of his servants who confess and repent."

She looked to her mother. Silence. She looked to Abu Bakr. Silence. She swallowed her tears and asked them each to answer Muhammad, to rise to her defense. "We know not what answer to make to the Messenger of Allah," they said. Aisha glared at them. Did they have so little faith in her? Did they know nothing of her? She turned to her husband:

"I see that you have listened to this talk about me until it has taken hold of you and you now believe in it. If I say I am innocent—and Allah most high knows that I am—you will not believe me. But if I confess to anything—and Allah most high knows that I am innocent—you will surely believe me. There remains nothing for me but to say, like the prophet Yusuf's father, 'Patience is becoming, and God's help is to be implored.'"

Then Aisha retired to her bed.

Her husband sat quietly, the symptoms of Revelation enveloping him. The others waited. At last his eyes opened and he called to his wife.

"Good tidings, my Aisha. Allah most high has exonerated you."

"Rise and go to Muhammad," her parents urged.

"I shall neither go to him nor thank him. Nor will I thank the two of you who listened to the slander and did not deny it. I shall rise," she said, "to give thanks to Allah alone."

The Messenger returned to the mosque and related God's words to the people:

But for God's bounty and His mercy in the present world
and the world to come
there would have been visited upon you for your mutterings
a painful chastisement.
When you received the scandal on your tongues
and were speaking with your mouths
that whereof you had no knowledge, and reckoned it a light thing,
but with God it was a mighty thing.
And why, when you heard it, did you not say,
"It is not for us to speak about this: glory be to Thee!
This is a mighty calumny"?
God admonishes you, that you will never repeat the like
of it again, if you are believers.[39]

The men who spread the scandal were flogged in public. Safwan struck the poet Hassan with the flat of his sword. Muhammad reprimanded Safwan and Hassan and gave them generous gifts.

Aisha called for the mason. "Build a wall where there is a door between my apartment and that of Ali ibn Abu Talib and Fatima bint Muhammad."

None would ever come between Muhammad and Aisha again, for God had affirmed her innocence and the Messenger's affections for his Best Beloved.

The men bear Zaynab's body to the cemetery. Her sister wives weep as Zaynab departs forever.

"In the Time of Scandal," Aisha says, surprised at herself for speaking of it aloud, "the Messenger of God asked Zaynab what she knew, what she had heard, or seen. Zaynab, my rival, swore by Allah that she knew nothing but good of me.

"May God grant Zaynab a high place in Paradise."

Uthman ibn Affan, Umar's successor, advances none but his own family. The Umayyads now hold all the positions of power within the *umma*. The governorships of newly conquered lands, the treasuries. Even the pensions of Muhammad's widows have been reduced and the money pocketed by Uthman's clan. The people appeal to the Mother of the Believers:

"The caliph is corrupt."

"Uthman's family misuses our resources."

"How can it be that one so loyal to the Messenger, his son-in-law, Ruqqayah's beloved husband, can be evil?"

"O Aisha, you must speak out against him." But Aisha bides her time. The Prophet would not approve of this dissension among the Muslims. It would break his heart. She wishes she might have a word from God to help her know what to do.

Ali ibn Abu Talib had at last stood for the caliphate and been rejected. Umm Salamah supports him. Aisha's youngest brother Muhammad ibn Abu Bakr supports him. Ali lurks now in shadow, silent, while, group by group, the people rise up against Uthman, some say with Ali's blessing. Some say Ali plans the rebellions.

Uthman has Umm Salamah's brother flogged in public. Aisha joins her sister wife on the front lines against the third Rightly Guided caliph. She visits him to demand his resignation.

"Allah himself has clothed me in the robes of caliph," Uthman tells Aisha.

There are threats of murder.

Aisha protests. There must be no bloodshed, no bearing of arms by believers against believers.

Uthman is trapped in his own house, besieged and surrounded. Humbled, he begs forgiveness. He promises everything the *umma* wants—except his abdication.

The siege continues. Weeks go by. Uthman's water and food supplies are cut off.

"This is cruel," Safiyyah tells Aisha. "Something must be done."

"Leave it alone," Aisha insists to her friend. But Safiyyah throws a plank from her window to Uthman's and walks across it with food for the hungry family of Uthman.

Now Umm Habiba stands amid the crowd, crying out against the treatment of her Umayyad cousin. The crowd throws stones at her and pulls at her mantle. Her sister wives comfort her, rub her with salve, and clean the cuts and bruises.

Aisha is outraged. "May God save a place in hell for those who threaten the Mothers of the Believers!"

A delegation again comes to her. It is time for Uthman's death, they say.

"Allah forbid that I should command the shedding of the blood of the Muslims and the killing of their imam!"

And Aisha packs her bags for pilgrimage.

A messenger arrives from Uthman. He pleads with Aisha not to leave Medina, but to help the caliph. Aisha forces calm into her voice.

"Do you desire that I should be subjected to the same treatment as Umm Habiba and then find no one to protect me?" she tells the messenger. "No, I will not be so dishonored! I have closed my bags and packed my camels, and I cannot stay."

The messenger mocks her in verse. In rhyme, he accuses her of cowardice.

"How dare you quote poetry to me!" she screams. "Would to Allah that you and Uthman each had a millstone round his foot and you were both at the bottom of the sea."

She is on the Pilgrim's Road with her sister wives when her youngest brother, Muhammad ibn Abu Bakr, stepson of Ali, breaks into Uthman's house with a gang of friends. Uthman knows what is coming and opens his Qur'an to die reading. His wife dives between the knives and Uthman and the fingers are cut off her hand.

"My own brother," Aisha laments to Hafsa when word arrives, "is an assassin! A murderer of imams!"

They make the *tawwaf* around the Ka'aba. They pray at the grave of Hagar and drink from the spring of Zamzam. They visit Mount Arafat, where their husband gave his final sermon.

In Medina, Ali calls a conference to elect the new caliph. The votes are cast in his favor, with swords at the throats of his rivals, Asmaa's husband, Zubayr ibn al-Awwam, and Aisha's friend Talha ibn Ubaid.

Twelve miles out of Mecca, on her way home, Aisha hears of Ali's election.

"Take me back! I did not think matters would take this course. This affair is not ended!"

Umm Salamah signals her drivers. Without a word to Aisha or her sister wives, she continues on to Medina, to ally herself openly with Ali and the People of the House.

Hafsa and Safiyyah beg Aisha to be cautious, but in Mecca she goes directly to the governor.

"I have come back because Uthman has been killed unjustly. Order will not be reestablished so long as this rabble has command. I demand revenge for the blood of Uthman and so restore and strengthen Islam!"

Before the governor can open his mouth, Aisha storms into the mosque. She takes her place at the sacred spot of Hijr, the foundation laid by Ibrahim.

The mosque fills with people, who gather close around her. Aisha, the Best Beloved, Mother of the Believers, slowly pulls her mantle across her face and thus ceremonially veiled, she calls out:

"O you people! Know that the rabble of the provinces, the men who wait at watering places to serve or rob and the slaves of the people of Medina, got together and killed Uthman. The mob reproached him for his cunning, for appointing young men to office while older ones had been appointed before him and for protecting for his party's use some of the districts prohibited to the people. In these matters he was rebuked and he desisted from those deeds, so as to conciliate. Then the rabble could find neither pretext nor excuse, so they agitated and began to show hostility. Their deeds were at variance with their words. They shed sacred blood, desecrated the sacred city, seized sacred funds, and profaned the sacred month.

"By God, Uthman's fingers are far better than a whole world full of the likes of them. Keep yourselves safe by not associating with them so that that others can inflict an exemplary punishment on them and scatter in fright those who are behind them.

"By God, even if that which they imputed to Uthman were indeed a fault, he has been purged of it as gold is purged of its dross or a garment of its dirt, for they rinsed him in his own blood, as a garment is rinsed in water."

The governor of Mecca raises his fist. "Here I am!" he cries. "The first to demand revenge."

Ali, the fourth Rightly Guided caliph, will not seek or punish Uthman's killers. He deposes all of Uthman's officials, gives those choice places to his relatives and those of his own party. But Mu'awiya ibn Abu Sufyan, son of Hind bint Utba, Umayyad governor of Syria, is left in his place. He is a man to fear.

"Ali is his own worst enemy," Hafsa says to Aisha. They are still in Mecca. Aisha will not return home. The Blessed City has become her headquarters, and many have left Medina to join her.

"He is losing his popularity," Safiyyah says. "There are those who believe he was behind the murder of Uthman."

"He is a dangerous fool," Aisha says. "A scandalmonger."

"O Messenger of God, Allah has placed no narrow limits on you. Many are the women like Aisha."

All the Mothers of the Believers, all but Hafsa, refuse to go to Basra with Aisha. From Syria she will launch her quest for justice for Uthman. A thousand strong join her caravan, but the Mothers accompany her only as far as Dhat Irq. They bid Aisha goodbye. It is the Day of Weeping, for such tears of farewell and lamentations have never been heard before or since.

Hafsa prepares to mount her *hawdaj* for the rest of the journey to Basra. There is shouting and commotion. Then standing before her, like a mountain, is her brother. She has no choice but to go with him back to Medina. She smiles wanly at Aisha, her best friend, a tiny, imperious figure mounting her camel, nose pointed toward Syria. Hafsa prays for Aisha. For her safety and her victory.

Ali is also marching north to Syria. To confront the armies of rebellious Mu'awiya ibn Abu Sufyan. Word comes to him of Aisha's travels. Ali halts and waits to intercept the Mother of the Believers. Umm Salamah offers the services of her son. "I would go with you, O Commander of the Faithful, but instead I offer my son. He is more precious to me than my soul."

She then writes to Aisha: "Desist from this unrighteous, unwomanly course, O sister. The Messenger would not approve. A woman's place is in the home, not on the battlefield."

"What an honor indeed to receive your sermon," Aisha retorts. "How well I know your right to advise me!"

She rides Askar, the best of Arabia's camels. She rides at the head of 3000 strong.

They pass the Spring of Hau'ab. Dogs howl like demons.

Once, as they traveled to a ghazu, they passed Hau'ab. The Messenger of God turned to Aisha. "Let it not be you at whom the dogs bark."

She will not go on. It is an ill omen, she tells her nephew Abdallah. He cannot pacify her.

"O Mother of the Believers," Zubayr lies. "The guides are wrong. We are not at Hau'ab."

"Aisha!" Talha lies. "We must not linger. Ali and his troops are close upon us."

She quiets her doubts and marches on.

In Basra, she states her intentions. She will avenge the blood of Uthman. She will set things right between Muslims. For it is written in Holy Qur'an that

> There is no good in their conspiring…
> O Believers, be securers of justice, witnesses for God
> Even against yourselves or your parents and kin,
> Whether rich or poor, for God stands closest to either.
> Do not follow caprice, so as to swerve.
> Though you twist and turn, God is aware of the things you do.[40]

Mu'awiya will not ally himself with her, though Uthman was his cousin. Mu'awiya ibn Abu Sufyan has his own plans.

She is seated alone in her red, mail-covered *hawdaj* on Askar. The battle is joined. Ali's forces are winning.

She shouts at K'ab, her driver, and he whips Askar into the fray.

"Leave me," she orders K'ab. "Go forward to the front ranks with cries of peace. Here is my own Qur'an. Carry the sacred book high. Secure the warriors' attention for the judgment of the Book."

K'ab is shot down.

"O my sons!" Aisha shouts. "Endurance! Remember God most high and the Reckoning."

Yet her warriors are beaten back and back.

"Curses upon you!" she howls at the warriors of Ali. "You murderers of Uthman! Assassins! God will find you on the Day of Doom!"

With these words, her army rallies. Now at last they return to the attack. They fight most heatedly around Aisha and Askar. She is fearless. Is she not Mother of the Believers? She pulls the curtains back from her *hawdaj* and, fully visible, she denounces strife and cries out against cowardice, she inflames her warriors with songs of heroes and victory. They defend her with more courage than they knew they had. Seventy win a hero's death protecting the Mother of the Believers.

Ali rides fast through the fray. He gallops past Askar and slashes the camel's sinews. Hamstrung, the creature falls. Her mail-covered *hawdaj* is pierced so thickly with feathered arrows, it might be a scarlet bird cut down from its high flight, and as it plunges, Aisha knows that her victory, her cause, goes with it.

Her brother, Muhammad bint Abu Bakr, rushes to her rescue. He who may have dealt the killing blow to Uthman, he who is loyal at all costs to Ali, cuts the pavilion from Askar and carries his sister away.

Ali approaches. He reprimands her. She glowers at him.

"You have conquered," she rejoins. "Now show forbearance."

"My day of defiance and opposition is over," Aisha tells Hafsa.

"It is right to make peace with Ali," Hafsa answers, a little unsure. Her friend and sister has returned to Medina. That is what counts.

Ali sent her back, handsomely equipped with generous funds for the journey and a large escort. Then he went himself to say farewell.

"My children," Aisha addressed the group that encircled her. "Do not harbor ill feelings. Do not hurt one another. I give testimony before all of Ali ibn Abu Talib's goodness."

"This," Ali said, "might have happened between any woman and her in-laws. Remember to uphold her, for Aisha bint Abu Bakr is the Best Beloved of the Prophet, in this world and the next."

"Many still wish I had died," Aisha says.

"And some that you had died so that Ali might live in infamy," Hafsa replies.

It comes to pass that Aisha's brother Muhammad is among those who go to war against Mu'awiya, who would take the caliphate from Ali. Word is brought to Aisha that Muhammad has been captured. She sends their older brother Abd al-Rahman to plead for his life. It is no use. Mu'awiya's henchmen kill young Muhammad. Then they wrap his body in the skin of an ass and roast it.

Aisha calls down curses. She weeps as she has not since the Time of the Scandal. She cannot stop. She closes her door against visitors. Only Hafsa and Safiyyah are allowed entry. So it is they she thinks are knocking at her door. She opens it. There is a man holding a roast ram, a gift from Umm Habiba, Mu'awiya's sister—Aisha's sister wife—and Na'ilah, the widow of Uthman. On it, there is a note: "So was your brother roasted."

Aisha never touches meat again.

She is forty-seven when Ali ibn Abu Talib is murdered. She mourns him publicly. She stands at the tomb of her husband, Muhammad the Prophet, and praises Ali, remembering the love between him and the Messenger.

She keeps the family finances and buys, sells, trades, invests. She arranges the marriages of her nieces and nephews. She cares for her sister Umm Kulthum, widow of Talha, and their children. She rears the orphans of her brother Muhammad. She writes poetry. She reads tearfully from the Qur'an. She fasts for long days and nights. She has accumulated great wealth through her dealings, but she lives modestly. She wears old clothes, she cannot bear luxury, remembering her husband's poverty and hardship and his advice that she content herself in this life with only a traveler's provisions, for we are only passing through.

She relates the Traditions, the sayings and deeds of the Messenger to the *umma,* and counsels them with words of her own wisdom.

Her life long, Aisha felt shame. Guilt for shedding blood, for causing the deaths of those near and dear. Sorrow for the loss of her prestige. "I wish I had died twenty years before the Battle of the Camel," she said. "It would have been more to my liking that I had not gone on expedition to Basra than to have born ten noble and heroic sons to Muhammad."

Again and again, she murmured to herself.

The Prophet is nearer to the believers than their selves;
his wives are their mothers....
Wives of the Prophet, you are not as other women.
If you are God fearing, be not abject in your speech...

but speak honorable words.
Remain in your houses.
Display not your finery, as did the pagans of old.
Perform the prayer, and pay the alms, and obey
God and His Messenger.[41]

11

Scholars of the *Hadith*

"*That does not
come from you,
but from her
behind the
curtain.*"

*A*isha's importance in the shaping of Islam cannot be underestimated. In addition to her—relatively brief—political activities, which had permanent impact, she counseled the *umma* in the teachings, acts, and behavior of the Prophet. These "customs" are called *Sunna*. Aisha originally related 2210 *Sunna*, for as Muhammad's favorite wife, and a keen observer, she was an essential authority on his life and religious practice. She is considered the first link among numberless women in the chains of transmitters, those with direct original experience of the Prophet's *Sunna* who passed it on to others.

Thousands of *Sunna* comprise the literary form called *Hadith*, or Traditions. While the *Sunna* is the saying or action itself, a *Hadith* is the report of the Prophet's saying or action by one of his Companions—male or female—who related it to someone in the next generation. There are many volumes of *Hadith*, and each *Sunna* became for the community a commanding guide for faith and order second only to the Qur'an.

In the eighth Islamic century alone, 170 prominent women Traditionists—those who collected the knowledge of the transmitters—are listed in one biographical dictionary, while a ninth-century A.H. "Who's Who" includes more than 130 women scholars. As the centuries move on, fewer and fewer are cited for their scholarship, a consequence of increasing misogyny, not for a lack of women's interest or education. In Egypt, female *Hadith* scholars lectured right up to the Ottoman conquest in 895 A.H./1517 C.E., when restrictions on women's movements tightened.

As well as saints and mystics, some of these women were also jurists, such as Fatima bint Abd al-Rahman (d. 312 A.H./924 C.E.), who was given the honorific *al-Sufiyya* for her great piety. Many were *hafzia*, meaning "one who knows the Qur'an by heart."

Women like Khadija bint Musa in Baghdad (d. 437 A.H./1056 C.E.) were considered persons of special wisdom, *wa'izah*, who in addition to their courses of studies, gave advice on ordinary matters to ordinary men and women. To Khadija bint Musa is attributed the Tradition: *He who provides in this world, God will reward him in the second world.*

Other scholars were additionally renowned for their poetry or, like Fatima al-Fudayliya in the twelfth Islamic century, as founders of colleges and libraries. Their knowledge of *Hadith* and the Qur'an created the basis for their other achievements. They were teachers, frequently in co-ed classes. Their concerns were not insular or limited to their personal edification or isolated within women's private space. Rather they worked and studied side by side with men.

Fatima bint Ahmed ibn Yahya in Baghdad in the ninth century of the Common Era was prominent in religious law, but apparently stuck close to home, where her husband, an imam, consulted with her whenever he was baffled by legal problems. She supplied her husband with the information, which he passed on to his pupils. They were not fooled, but occasionally confronted Fatima's husband with, "That does not come from you, but from her behind the curtain."

The Qur'an is the supreme authority and it confirms Muhammad's authoritative role:

You have indeed in the Messenger of Allah a beautiful pattern of conduct for anyone whose hope is in Allah.[1]

Naturally, while the Prophet was alive, and the *umma* still small and in close proximity to Medina, he could be consulted on any matter at any time and the community could observe and emulate his habits. But after his death, sources were needed to preserve his maxims and movements, his "beautiful pattern of conduct," and to be the ground for legal decisions. The *Hadith* complements the Qur'an, in a sense filling in the gaps.

"Without *Hadith*," Nasr writes in *Ideals and Realities of Islam*, "much of the Qur'an would be a closed book. We are told in the

Qur'an to pray, but were it not for prophetic *Sunna*, we would not know how to pray."

Hadith literature expounds on every domain from politics to metaphysics. A *Hadith* can treat a ritual problem—*prayer is not accepted without purification, nor charity out of what is acquired by unlawful means*—or it can discuss details of doctrine and faith—*religion is faithfulness to Allah and his Messenger and to the leaders of Muslims*—or it can describe the Prophet's behavior while eating—*say Bismillah (in the name of Allah) and eat with your right hand and eat from the side nearest to you*—or it can capture his countenance after receiving a Revelation—*when the Revelation was sent down on him, the Prophet felt like one in grief and a change came over his face.*

When Muhammad's daughter Fatima claimed she was entitled to an inheritance, the first Rightly Guided caliph Abu Bakr cited her father as having said that prophets "do not inherit nor leave an estate for inheritance. Whatever we leave is for charity." No one argued with this *Sunna*, coming as it did straight from the mouth of Muhammad's closest male Companion, and Fatima's claim was rejected. Daily problems like this demanded forms from which to draw resolutions.

The evolution of *Sunna* into the science of *Hadith* was a long process. Over time they unified into a well-defined standard of rules for living and of law, or *Shari'a*. The *Shari'a* provide knowledge of right and wrong and leave open the choice of which path to follow according to one's free will. They indicate what is obligatory, meritorious or recommended, forbidden, reprehensible, or merely indifferent. Muslims turn to both the Qur'an and *Hadith* for answers to all problems, legal or religious. *Shari'a* are considered an expression of God's will, although application depends on interpretation by jurists. Four legal indicators provide the basis for the *Shari'a*: the Qur'an; the *Sunna*; consensus of schools of law and the Muslim community across the centuries; and reasoning by analogy through which jurists formulate new laws based on the Qur'an or *Sunna*.

In the post-Enlightenment traditions of the West, religion and politics are separate. Religion is personal. But for Muslims, religion and politics belong together. Muhammad was political, his new

133

religion required social change and social justice. Islam knows no contradiction between the spiritual and material worlds. They were both created by God.

Sunni Islam has four schools of law, which differ on minor points, although each recognizes the jurisdiction of the other. The earliest, predominant in Upper Egypt and North and West Africa, is the Maliki School, which produced the first manual still in use as a text and emphasizes Tradition. Meanwhile, in Iraq in the seventh century of the Common Era, the Hanafi School was developing and presently concentrates less on Tradition than on juridical opinion. It is found today chiefly in Turkey, western Asia, India, and Lower Egypt. The Shafi'i School, founded nearly a century later, treats theology as a branch of jurisprudence and regulates human relations not only with ourselves and others but also with God. It is represented in Syria, Lower Egypt, India, and Indonesia. Finally, there is the Hanbali School, followed by today's Wahhabi sect of Saudi Arabia. It is the smallest and most orthodox, holding fast to the Qur'an and *Hadith* and rejecting *ijma'*, or consensus by those who are learned in religion and the law.

Shi'a Islam also rejects *ijma'* and has its own schools, laws, jurists, and theologians.

Outstanding female jurists include the notable *musnidas*—transmitters (an Arabic word related to *muezzin*, crier, the one who calls the faithful to prayer)—Umm 'Isa of Baghdad (d. 328 A.H./947 C.E.) took advantage of her father's enormous library to study Traditions, so that she eventually gave decisions of jurisprudence. Asma bint Kamal al-Din (d. 904 A.H./1498 C.E.) was consulted by sultans, viziers, and other government officials and her recommendations, it is said, were always accepted.

(The *fatwa*—a word made famous to Westerners by Iran's Ayatollah Ruhollah Khomeini when he placed a bounty on the head of Salman Rushdie for his 1988 novel *The Satanic Verses*—is nothing more sinister than a legal opinion issued by a *mufti*, a Muslim scholar. The *mufti's* opinion must be validated by a *mujtahid*, a qualified jurist or by a set of jurists who reach a consensus. A *fatwa* is not necessarily binding; it is an opinion, not a written law. In Islam things are always open for debate.)

Today, modern Muslims deliberate whether the *Shari'a* should be applied in all aspects of life and whether—and how—to refurbish it to address modern Islam's most pressing problems.

"The movement for reform throughout Islamic history has been to recreate and reshape human attitudes and social institutions so as to make them harmonious with the *Shari'a*....Such movements are brought about to a great extent not only through the weakening of religious faith...but also because the modern mentality, which originated in the West with its Christian background, cannot conceive of an immutable Law which is the guide of human society and upon which man should seek to model his individual and social life."[2]

Like some Christian and Jewish politicians and clerics who exploit the Bible to justify any number of agendas, explaining the same passage with opposite meanings, various Muslim politicians and clerics have used the Qur'an and *Hadith* to strengthen their arguments and propagandize. The "sledgehammer *Hadith*" used to exclude women from politics—as Mernissi puts it in *The Veil and the Male Elite*—is one which reads: "Those who entrust their affairs to women will never know prosperity." Reform, as it were—or re-formation—requires reinterpretation and delicate juggling of factionalism. Differences of opinion can flare quickly—among other reasons because the *Hadith* are many-sided and often contradictory.

And every party, every movement, every group of Muslims has supplied itself with a selection of Traditions, which would give prophetic authority to its particular point of view. Shi'ite Muslims have separate *Hadith* collections, wherein Muhammad's son-in-law, the fourth Rightly Guided caliph Ali ibn Abu Talib, and his followers are the major transmitters. Among Shi'ites, Ali's authority is recognized alongside Muhammad's and his sayings are assembled in *Nahj al-balagha*, "The Way of Eloquence."

In addition to Aisha, Muhammad's other wives and female Companions contributed their experiences and memories, though far fewer than Aisha's and perhaps not always as intimate. A good

135

many of these sayings are prosaic, but an equal number concern lofty religious issues. Considering that the caliphs Abu Bakr, Umar, and Ali did not share Muhammad's respect and affection—or admiration—for women, it's surprising that they gave much credence, let alone deference, to the women's transmissions and the counseling they, as Mothers of the Believers, provided to the community based on their recollections of Muhammad's behavior and statements. But the women's authority could not be denied. None were closer to the Prophet, especially in his day-to-day life and activities, which Muslims are not only expected to imitate, but which illustrate how to live within Islamic ideals. The *Sunna* and *Hadith* constitute the strongest force unifying Muslim peoples from Detroit to China.

Muhammad held multiple jobs as a spiritual guide, leader of a community, and organizer of a new social order. He was therefore concerned with the here-and-now, as well as the hereafter. How to rest the heart in contentment with the Divine while living in the world. How to live fully from a spiritual center, with harmony and human equilibrium.

Sunna were preserved and handed down from generation to generation, frequently within families. At first, ordinary Muslims were reluctant to reject any purported Traditions, however obviously false, for fear of showing disrespect to the Prophet. By the third century A.H., or ninth century C.E., action had to be taken lest Muhammad's message be completely garbled or perverted. Specialists in the emergent fields of law and theology began collecting *Hadith* far and wide, and critical schools of thought surfaced within both Sunni and Shi'ite factions.

Pious scholars set out to seek new and reliable *Hadith* or to hear masters speak about the Traditions. To travel in search of knowledge was crucial for scholarship in early times. People were largely nonliterate, so memories were sharper. Oral tradition was vital to the transmission of any history, whether political, religious, genealogical, or literary.

Those who spent their lives in the study of the Qur'an and its interpretation were highly revered, but even greater veneration was accorded scholars who enhanced their study of written texts, knowledge, and information by traveling to distant and frequently unique, oral sources. The journeys scholars took to find *Hadith* were arduous, and women undertook them with full determination and courage.

Early on, small collections of Traditions were written, but it was best to gather *Hadith* from the mouth of a teacher, who in turn had acquired her or his knowledge from another authority, thus maintaining a living lineage back to the Prophet. Each generation added new members until long lines of Traditionists arose. It was always necessary to sit at the feet of a master, and women such as Juma bint Ahmad in the fourth century A.H. became high masters of *Hadith* to whom students flocked.

A typical *Hadith* might go like this: "A said: I heard B say that he heard C telling that D said to him that E stated…" and so on. The "science of *Hadith*" culminated in the second and third centuries of the Islamic era in at least six respected collections. Although four of these canonical collections are held in high esteem and used for legal and doctrinal purposes, as well as for personal guidance, two of which contained Traditions that had survived the most rigorous tests were held above the rest: the *Sahih* (sound, immaculate) of Muhammad Ismai'l al-Bukhari (188 A.H./810 C.E. to 248 A.H./870 C.E.) and the *Sahih* of the theologian Muslim ibn al-Hajjaj (d. 253 A.H./875 C.E.). Al-Bukhari, an Arab scholar born in what is now Uzbekistan, traveled throughout the Muslim world gathering oral traditions of the Prophet. He collected more than 600,000 *Hadith* and reduced them to 7275 "genuine" traditions.

Al-Bukhari's *Sahih* is usually regarded as second only in importance to the Qur'an. In later centuries, notably in Mamluk Egypt, the whole *Sahih* of al-Bukhari was sometimes read aloud during the fasting month of Ramadan. Its completion—the *khatam al-Bukhari*—was then solemnly celebrated. An individual scholar who had completed the study of al-Bukhari invited friends to mark the auspicious event.

Using biographies that set forth facts about early Muslims, al-Bukhari could investigate whether A was even born when B was alive or C lived at one end of the Muslim Empire while D resided at another. Some reports were eliminated because they cut into a common and agreed-upon practice of the *umma* or did not correspond to the dominant school of thought. Traditions were divided into "genuine," "good," or "weak," but as the science of *Hadith* developed, at least fifty more categories of classification were employed.

Even where the sequence breaks in the line of transmitters, a report can be considered valuable for an oral society, which accepts that bits and pieces can be lost while the whole remains credible. *Hadith* of lower value—"weak"—can also have authority, in spirit if not in letter.

Conscious frauds may nonetheless have sneaked through the examinations (and it must be recalled that no historian can be sure of the authors of most sacred texts worldwide). Two *Sunna* take care of this: *Whatever good saying has been said, I myself have said it* and *You must compare the sayings attributed to the Qur'an; what agrees therewith is from me, whether I actually said it or no.*

Muhammad's prescience, his irony and awareness of how talk turns to hearsay, gossip, and exploitation, is evident.

Of the 2210 Traditions related by Aisha, Mother of the Believers, al-Bukhari preserved only 174. Scores of Aisha's Traditions were gathered by her nephew Urwah, whose daughter-in-law, Fatima bint al-Mundhir (d. 145 A.H./763 C.E.), became a renowned scholar in her own right.

Countless women seem to have specialized in the *Sahih* of al-Bukhari,[3] but others centered their expertise on other texts. Umm al-Khayr Fatima bint Ali (d. 532 A.H./1137 C.E.) and Fatima al-Shahrazuriyya (d. 524 A.H./1129 C.E.) lectured on the *Sahih* of Muslim ibn al-Hajjaj.

Muhammad Siddiqi notes in his *Hadith Literature* that few women scholars are recorded in any other culture or religion before modern times.

The science of *Hadith* forms an outstanding example in this respect. Islam, as a religion which (unlike Christianity) refused to attribute gender to the Godhead and never appointed a male priestly elite to serve as an intermediary between creature and Creator, started life with the assurance that while men and women are equipped by nature for complementary rather than identical roles, no spiritual superiority inheres in the masculine principle. As a result, the Muslim community was happy to entrust matters of equal worth in God's sight. Only this can explain why, uniquely among the classical Western religions, Islam produced a large number of outstanding female scholars, on whose testimony and sound judgment much of the edifice of Islam depends.

Since Islam's earliest days women had been taking a prominent part in the preservation and cultivation of *Hadith*, and this function continued down the centuries. At every period in Muslim history, there lived numerous eminent women-Traditionists, treated by their brethren with reverence and respect.

The names of these women, in the centuries following the prophetate, are recorded but life stories are not available. Rather, they are identified anecdotally, by their accomplishments. The lives of the first female Transmitters—Aisha, her sister wives, and the Prophet's female friends—however, have been written about extensively with devotion and pious adoration. Indeed, the *Sunna* they related were scrupulously recorded, for they were the stewards of knowledge and the future and were relied upon to give instruction to the other Companions and the *umma*.

Throughout Islamic history, scholars of the *Hadith* are considered the most devout of the religious scholars, trusted by their communities for authority.

The teacher regarded as the last truly distinguished *Hadith* scholar, female or male, of the Hijaz was Umm al-Khayr Amat al-Khaliq, a woman who lived for nearly a century, from 811 A.H./1409 C.E. to 911 A.H./1505 C.E.

Written collections of *Hadith* are indispensable for Islamic law, theology, and rules for living, as Frederick Denny writes in *Jews, Christians, and Muslims*. But, he cautions, "It should not be thought that the Prophet's *Sunna* is known only through a literary record. The way of Muhammad is known definitely through the behavior of Muslims and transmitted by example in many matters, as from mother to child in managing the humble personal tasks of the toilet and in simple courtesies; in the social relations of schoolmates who are taught to share and look out for one another's welfare; in conjugal relations wherein spouses are admonished to respect each other's rights to pleasure and dignity; in the rights of guests (who are entitled to three days' hospitality, no questions asked); in the behavior of fathers, who are encouraged to kiss their children" (in direct rebuke of some Bedouins who thought such behavior was soft: "I have ten boys but have never kissed any of them," a disdainful man said to the Prophet, after he'd seen him kiss his grandson Hassan. "He who does not show mercy will not receive mercy," Muhammad replied).

"The imitation of Muhammad," Denny writes, "is as fully developed in Islam as is the imitation of Christ in Christianity, if not more so. Muslims are utterly respectful of Jesus as one of God's greatest prophets. But Muslims are also aware that Muhammad lived a more complete human life—being businessman, husband, father, spiritual guide, military commander, judge, arbitrator, ruler—and thus can serve as a universal paradigm of the fulfilled human life."

From the very start, a strong feminine sensibility illuminated the spirit of Islam. The transmission, and hence, shaping, of many of its tenets—more than is the case with most other major religions— was in the hands of women.

Transmitters

Aisha bint Abu Bakr
Wife of the Prophet

Among the Traditions she related:

❖ God's Messenger never hit anyone with his hand—neither a woman nor a servant, but only when fighting in God's cause. He never took revenge for anything unless the things made inviolable by God were violated. He then took revenge for God, the Exalted and Glorious.

❖ When newborn infants were brought to God's Messenger, he blessed them and rubbed their palates with dates.

❖ The tooth stick is a means of purifying the mouth and is pleasing to the Lord.

❖ God's Messenger kissed some of his wives. He then went to perform the prescribed prayer without performing ablution. [It was said to her that it must have been her whom he kissed. Hearing this, she smiled.]

❖ God's Messenger hesitated to give such instructions to the men, so he directed the women to tell their husbands to use water for the purpose of cleaning their private parts and to tell them that the Messenger of God used to clean his private parts with water.

❖ She would drink when she was menstruating and would hand the vessel to the Messenger. He would put his mouth where hers had been and drink. She would eat meat from a bone when she was menstruating and then hand it to the Messenger of God, and he would put his mouth where hers had been.

141

❖ The Prophet used to recite the Qur'an with his head in her lap while she was menstruating.

❖ The Prophet said, "The sun and the moon are not eclipsed on account of anyone's death or on account of anyone's birth. When you see an eclipse, supplicate God. Declare His greatness. Give alms.

❖ Whenever God's Messenger saw the rain, he used to [raise both hands and] say, "O God! Let it be a strong, fruitful rain."

❖ The Prophet said, "If dinner is served and the declaration to perform the prescribed prayer is called, one should start with dinner."

❖ The Prophet said, "Disputants should refrain from taking retaliation. The one who is nearer should forgive first, and then the one who is next to him, even if [the one who forgives] is a woman."

❖ God's Messenger said, "There are three persons whose actions are exempt: a sleeper until he awakens, an idiot until he is restored to reason, and a boy until he reaches puberty."

❖ God's Messenger said, "The best of condiments is vinegar."

❖ The Messenger said, "Exchange presents with one another. Presents remove ill-will from hearts."

Umm Salamah
Wife of the Prophet

Among the Traditions she related:

❖ The Messenger said, "When you are afflicted with a calamity, you should say, 'O God, reward me for my affliction and give me something better than it in return.'"

❖ The Prophet used to say after the dawn prescribed prayer, "O God, I ask you for beneficial knowledge, acceptable action, and good provision."

❖ God's Messenger said, "When you drink milk, rinse out your mouth for it contains greasiness."

*The Messenger of God would be overtaken by the dawn when he was in a state of sexual impurity but would [still] perform the prescribed fast. (Aisha also reports this Tradition.)

142

❖ The Messenger of God taught her to say when the call to sunset prayer was made, "O God, this is the time when Your night comes, Your day retires, and the voices of Your summoners are heard, so forgive me."

❖ God's Messenger said, "He who drinks with silver utensils is only filling his abdomen with hell fire."

❖ The Messenger said, "One whose husband has died must not wear garments dyed with saffron or red clay or bejeweled garments. She must not apply henna or collyrium."

Hafsa bint Umar
Wife of the Prophet

Among the Traditions she related:

❖ The Messenger of God kissed his wives while fasting.

❖ The Messenger said to perform the bath lustration for the dead by washing the body an odd number of times. Three, five, or seven were mentioned, starting with the right side.

Umm Habiba (Ramlah)
Wife of the Prophet

Among the Traditions she related:

❖ God's Messenger said, "Perform ablution to purify yourself after [eating] what fire has touched [i.e., cooked food]."

❖ The Messenger of God would offer the prescribed prayer in clothes in which he had had intercourse if he did not see any impurity on them.

Zaynab bint Jahsh
Wife of the Prophet

Among the Traditions she related:

❖ The Prophet once came to her in a state of fear and said, "None has the right to be worshiped but God. Woe upon the Arabs from a danger that has come near. An opening has been made in the wall of Gog and Magog like this," making a circle with his thumb and index finger.

She asked if even believers and pious people would be destroyed. He said, "Yes, when evil persons will increase."

Asmaa bint Abu Bakr
Companion of the Prophet

Among the Traditions she related:

⊕ The Messenger said, "God's greatest name is in these two verses, 'And Your God is One God; there is no God but He, the Compassionate, the Merciful,' and 'There is no God but He, the living and eternal.'"

⊕ The Prophet said, "Do not shut your money bag, otherwise God too will withhold His blessings from you. Spend in God's cause as much as you can afford."

⊕ The Messenger said, "Give in charity and do not give reluctantly, otherwise God will give you in a limited amount. Do not withhold your money lest God should withhold it from you."

⊕ The Prophet commanded them to free slaves on the occasion of an eclipse.

Traditionists

Umm al-Darda the Younger
Medina (?)
Died 81 A.H./700 C.E.

A judge whose authority and ability are undisputed calls Umm al-Darda superior to all Traditionists of her time, better, he says, than the celebrated masters of *Hadith*, al-Basri and Ibn Sirin, whose daughter Hafsa is also a key Traditionist.

Zaynab bint Sulayman
Baghdad
Died 142 A.H./759 C.E.

She is the senior princess in Caliph Mahdi's court and the one to whom his favorite concubine, Khayzuran, turns for instruction in the behavior of royalty.

Zaynab's father is cousin to al-Saffah, founder of the Abbasid Dynasty, and she is reared in Basra, Oman, and Bahrayn, where he is al-Mansur's governor. Hers is the finest education and through it she acquires such a mastery of *Hadith*, she is reputed to be one of the most distinguished women Traditionists of her time. Many men are her students.

Amat al-Wahid
Baghdad
Died 377 A.H./987 C.E.

She is the daughter of al-Muhamili, a prominent jurist. He has given her an extensive education, teaching her himself and bringing her tutors. She's hardly grown before she's memorized the Qur'an and can command Arabic literature and grammar. She is known by the name Sutayah. Historians record her presence in the decisions of sacred law she makes with Abu Ali Abu Hurayah, and scholars copy her Traditions and transmit them on her authority alone.

She is known, too, for her generosity and the alms she gives liberally to the poor. Her son Abu al-Husayn ibn Muhammad ibn Ahmad becomes a judge, armed with the lessons she has taught him.

Abida al-Madaniyya
Medina/al-Andalus, ca. eighth or ninth century C.E.
Her dates are unknown.

She is a slave and learns many *Hadith* from teachers in Medina. At last her master gives her to Habib Dahhun, a Traditionist of Andalusia, when he visits the holy city on his pilgrimage to Mecca. He is so impressed by Abida, he frees her, marries her, and takes her to Andalusia, where it is said she relates 10,000 Traditions on the authority of her Medinan teachers. She is among those scholars who dislike and discourage the writing down of *Hadith*, preferring memorization. There are Traditions conveyed even by the Prophet's own scribe that forbid writing anything in book form but the Holy Qur'an. Abida's granddaughter, Abda bint Baishr, follows in her footsteps.

Karima bint Ahmad al-Marwaziyya
Mecca
Died 463 A.H./1069 C.E.

She is considered the best authority in her day of the *Sahih* of al-Bukhari, which she is able to teach in less than a week. Her name

146

occurs frequently as a narrator. The teaching of *Hadith* bears with it great responsibility and teachers must take care never to be misleading. "Keep exclusively to Karima," the illustrious Abu Dharr of Herat advises his students. "Study the *Sahih* under no one else."

Shuhda bint al-Ibari
al-Andalus
Died 574 A.H./1178 C.E.

She is called Fakhr an-Nisa, "the pride of womanhood." She is known both as a great authority on *Hadith*, and as a magnificent calligrapher. For that reason, she is also called Shuhda the Writer. Her father is passionate about *Hadith*. He obeys the *Sunna* that instructs men to give their daughters sound academic educations. She marries Ali ibn Muhammad, boon Companion of Caliph al-Muqtadi, who founds a college and a Sufi lodge. Yet she is better known than her husband because of the immaculate quality of her transmissions and her meticulous scholarship. Her lectures on *Sahih* al-Bukhari and other collections are attended by masses of students. It is an important credential to have studied with Shuhda and thus many people claim falsely to have done so.

She is more than 90 years old when she dies, a woman whose life has been devout and learned.

Zaynab bint Ahmad
Jerusalem
Died 740 A.H./1339 C.E.

She has acquired a "camel-load of diplomas," and is therefore called "bint al-Kamal." She delivers lectures and reads with another woman Traditionist, Ajiba bint Abu Bakr. Her travels have brought her to the Saxon Gotha Codex no. 59017—one of Europe's oldest and most sumptuous illuminated world histories, recalling events from the Old and New Testaments. Its authenticity is based on al-Kamal's authority. Many learned women work under her on the

codex, including the scholar Daqiqa bint Murshid. The traveler ibn
Battuta studies Traditions with bint al-Kamal.

Fatima al-Nishapur
Mecca
Died 227 A.H./849 C.E.

She guides her husband in matters of religion. She discusses
the most important questions of Traditions and law with illustrious
mystics and of them, Bayazid Bestami is her special friend, the one
with whom she most enjoys long discussions. She relaxes with
Bestami and raises her veil. Her husband is jealous.

One day, Bestami notices that Fatima has dyed the tips of her
fingers with henna. "Why did you do so?" he asks.

"If you have discovered that I have dyed my fingers," she says,
"then you have looked at me with eyes other than those of intellectual friendship. Thus, the familiarity between us must come to an
end."

III

Ascetics, Saints, and Mystics

*"Be like wax
and illumine
the world.
Be like a needle
and work naked."*

*W*omen were among the very first in Islam to emerge as ascetics, saints, and mystics, and it is here, more than in any other context, that they have participated and received acknowledgment on an equal basis with men.

Like Christian women, who were also excluded from the clerical state, individual women in Islam nonetheless wielded huge spiritual authority.

In every religion, there is a mystical element. In Islam, this was formalized in Sufism. Certainly there were Muslim mystics before the appearance of the Sufis. And there have been later ascetics and mystics who were not Sufis. To engage in a quest for immediate knowledge of and unity with God does not require participation in a proscribed order. But Sufism has drawn into its folds countless Muslims disinclined toward the external concerns of Sunni and Shi'a Islam, Muslims who prefer to devote themselves to repentance, abstinence, renunciation, poverty, patience, trust in God, and acquiescence to the will of God, toward a higher consciousness where knowledge, the knower, and the known are realized as one.

The concept of an afterlife is as strong in Islam as in Christianity. As in Jewish and Christian belief, no one knows the hour of death but God. Judgment is postponed until the Last Day. Meanwhile, the soul remains in the grave, until a trumpet sounds and the graves give up their dead. Then all will be judged. In Islam, all will be given an account book. If the accounting is put into the right hand, Heaven will be the soul's portion. If it is put into the left hand, the soul will be doomed to Hell.

There are two versions of Paradise described in the Qur'an, not necessarily contradictory. One is a garden fecund with fruit and shade trees and flowing with rivers of sweet water, milk, wine, and honey. The second, which appears in later verses, is more austere,

151

recalling the ziggurat of antiquity, wherein Paradise is a pyramid or cone of eight levels, its walls guarded by angels, the top shaded by a lotus tree. This version inspired Dante's *The Divine Comedy*. Heaven is located above the visible sky and rests on a number of seas. Above it all is the throne of God. The greatest reward of the elect, according to the Persian philosopher and theologian al-Ghazali (436 A.H./1058 C.E. to 489 A.H./1111 C.E.), was to be in the presence of God.

Hell is called *jahannam* (related to the Hebrew *gehenna*) and is the reverse image of Paradise, a crater of seven concentric rings or terraces, one fewer than in Paradise, as fewer souls will be there. Each ring is gated and punishments graded downward according to the severity of the sins. A bridge as narrow as a sword's edge spans Hell's mouth. This bridge, al-Ghazali says, is nothing more than the life of humans on Earth. The righteous cross it with ease; the wicked fall into the crater.

The terror of Hell naturally inspired the pursuit of perfect piety. Within a century after the Prophet's death—and to some extent in reaction to the excesses of the caliphs—Sufism took root as a way of life renouncing materialism in favor of quietism and spiritual poverty, *faqr*. In the early years, Sufis were primarily ascetics, attempting to abandon the world through practices of silence, seclusion, fasting, and *dhikr*, continual invocation and repetition of the various names of God.

Rabi'a al-Adawiyya, also known as Rabi'a of Basra, in what is now Iraq, was central to the beginnings of the mystical movement in the third Islamic century. She is universally revered as the first to transform solemn, gray asceticism into a bright poetic mysticism shaped by an all-consuming relationship of friendship and intimacy with God, the adoring embrace of the lover and the Beloved. Soon more such people emerged throughout the Muslim world advocating a loving bond with God. The nature of these relationships with the Divine depended on personalities, just as in human liaisons. Some are ferocious, the couple engaged in passionate combat, while others are gentle and affectionate.

A patched coat is bestowed upon initiates into the Sufi orders. The word *Sufi* derives from the Arabic *suf*, meaning "wool," referring to the coarse garments worn by the early mendicants—bringing to mind, for anyone who has experienced the high temperatures of the Middle East, the kind of hair-shirt self-mortification not uncommon to Christian ascetics. In all religions, there are those who encounter a god of wrath, who demands constant punishment, and there are those to whom the god is love. Certainly Islam, like Christianity, Hinduism, and others, has had its share of self-flagellators.

"To the Sufi, as to the Christian saint, the life of Purgation was the first stage toward the attainment of the mystic's goal, and asceticism was enjoined on all who entered the novitiate," Margaret Smith writes in *Rabi'a the Mystic and her Fellow Saints in Islam.* "Only when the novice had purged himself of the carnal Self and its desires, could he hope to enter on the way which would lead to Union with the Divine. Ascetic *(zahid)* was the most common appellation of the Sufi, and even those who had attained to sainthood, with few exceptions, practiced asceticism to the end of their lives. As a Sufi writer expresses it: 'If you ask, Who is the traveler on the road? It is one who is aware of his own origin. He is the traveler who passes on speedily; he has become pure from Self as flame from smoke.'"

Bayazid Bestami (d. 252 A.H./874 C.E.), a leader of the early period and the *Hadith* scholar Fatima al-Nishapur's friend, said, "Asceticism is no great thing. I was an ascetic for three days: on the first day, I abstained from the world; on the second from the hereafter; and on the third from all else besides God."

Ramadan is fourth of the Five Pillars of Islam, a period of daylight fasting that commemorates the month when the Qur'an was first revealed. It is a rigorous period for all practicing Muslims, physically and spiritually, an annual discipline enabling even ordinary believers to enter into a separate state of mind. Fasting is a familiar aspect of asceticism in any spiritual practice. Sufi manuals contain long lists of early ascetics whose fasting far and away exceeded the requirements of Ramadan. Hayyuna, a friend and contemporary of Raiy'a bint Ismai'li in the third century A.H., is said to have fasted "until she turned black."

Poverty and hunger were not the only means of abandoning the world on the path to the Divine. The annals of Sufism list hundreds of women who spent their days in copious crying. (The Prophet's mother Amina is said to have sobbed almost constantly—a sign, in the lore, perhaps of her devotion.) According to Javad Nurbakhsh's *Sufi Women*, a gnostic of Basra, Bardah-ye Sarimiyah (dates unrecorded), wept so profusely, she nearly lost her sight. "Let me be," she said to those who expressed concern. "If I am supposed to reside in Hell, let God estrange me from Himself and seize my eyesight. But if I belong among the denizens of Heaven, God will restore to me a vision superior to this eyesight."

In his hagiography, *Nafahat al-uns min hadarat al-quds*, the Persian poet and mystic Nur al-Din Abdur Rahman Jami (792 A.H./1414 C.E. to 870 A.H./1492 C.E.) tells of Sha'wana, who said, "It is better for me to go blind in this world because of tears, than in *that* world because of fire." She wept at any mention of the name of God.

Jami reports that incessant weeping rendered Ofayra Abeda of Basra completely blind. When asked whether blindness was difficult to endure, she replied, "More troublesome still is to be veiled from God, the Almighty."

Weeping oneself blind was not unusual among Sufis, "for it was felt that physical blindness enables a person to see the Divine Beloved all the better," Schimmel explains in *My Soul Is a Woman*. "The eye is no longer a veil between the person looking and the one being looked at."

The physical veil, *hijab*, also becomes a symbol of the barrier between the seeker and God. Jami tells of coming across a girl being stoned by children, who taunted her as "the infidel who claims to see God."

I followed her as she moved away...

"What are those children saying to you?" I asked. "They say that you claimed to behold God."

"True," she answered. "For ever since I knew Him, I have not been veiled."

154

Another Sufi woman, "lovely in appearance," entered Baghdad with one half of her face veiled.

"Why don't you veil your entire face?" a man asked her.

"First show me a man so that I might veil my entire face. There is only half a man in all Baghdad, and that's my brother. If it weren't for his sake, I wouldn't even cover this half."

The *salat*, required worship five times a day, is the second of the Five Pillars. Private supplications, free prayer, or *du'a*, are recommended as well. The best prayer is any that Muhammad first pronounced, such as this unadorned and beautiful devotional:

O God, create light in my heart, and light in my eye,
and light in my hearing,
And light on my right and light on my left,
light above me, light below me, light in front of me, light behind me.
Create light for me:
On my tongue, light; in my muscles, light; in my flesh,
light; in my hair, light; in my soul, light.
Make light grow for me.
O God, grant me light!

The call for radiance in Muhammad's prayer recalls nineteenth-century Celtic entreaties collected in the Scottish Highlands.

Du'a is a hallmark of mysticism, prayers created from the sincere depths of the soul, in close conversation with God. Of the hundreds of women saints and mystics, numerous seem to be famous for only a single prayer.

Bardah-ye Sarimiya of Basra prayed:

All eyes shut, the stars are setting, sweethearts have secluded themselves with each other—but Beloved, now we are alone together, just You and I. When Your love fills my heart, will You chastise me by hell-fire? O Love, never, never do this.

Nurbakhsh tells us of the Persian Sufi Habiba 'Adawiyyah (no dates recorded), who habitually ascended to her roof dressed in a

155

woolen frock and *chaddur* (in Persian, a veil, or Arabic, *burqa*) to pray:

Night is behind us, day again has arrived. O, how I long to know whether this night has been worthy in Your eyes.... I beg You inform me, as long as I live, of my worthiness or Your disapprobation. If You cast me out, I swear I shall not leave Your doorstep, as nothing but Your grace and bounty can be contained in my heart.

Rabi'a of Basra's younger contemporary Zahra, "The God-intoxicated," prayed:

You whose powers are without limit, You the munificent and eternal, make the eyes of my heart rejoice in the gardens of Your power. Join my anxious care to Your tender largesse, O Gracious One. In Your majesty and splendor take me away from the paths of those who only make a show of power, O Compassionate One. Make me a servant and a seeker, and be, O light of my heart and ultimate desire, my Friend.

Muhammad's Night Journey and Ascension informs the Sufi practice of wakefulness and keeping night vigil.

At nightfall, Hayyuna of Syria (third century C.E.) habitually prayed:

O my Beloved, One and Unique! You hinder me at night from the recitation of the Qur'an, then in the daylight hours estrange Yourself from me. My God, if only my days could be night so that I might benefit from nearness to You.

Once when Raiy'a bint Ismai'li was visiting Hayyuna and fell asleep in the night, Hayyuna nudged her awake. "Rise up, it is the hour of the banquet of those who are rightly guided," she scolded. "It is by the efforts of your prayers that the brides of night are beautified."

The struggle to stay awake through the long, drowsy night inspired Rabi'a al-Adawiyya to pray:

Eyes are heavy with sleep, unaware of their forgetfulness. And still Rabi'a the sinner abides in Your presence in the hope that You might look on her with a gaze that will keep sleep from diminishing her service of You. By Your power and majesty, may I not slacken in serving You either night or day until I meet You.

156

Sufi dancing is another form of prayer and exultation. It was introduced by the poet and Sufi master Jala al-Din Muhammad Rumi (585 A.H./1207 C.E. to 651 A.H./1273 C.E.), founder of the Mevlevi Order. Unlike those attempts toward unity with God that scourge the body, dancing brings body, mind, heart, and soul together. The dancer, the seeker, does not merely experience ecstasy but becomes ecstasy.

It is said that Roqiya (dates unrecorded)—a gnostic from Mosul in northern Iraq—used sheer concentration to suspend in midair a carpet on which her father and his disciples twirled, while the floor beneath them collapsed.

Culturally, as well as spiritually, Sufism has been a strong force in Islam. Along with dance, music provokes mystical love, and many women musicians are cited for their talent at arousing the spirit. Sufism gave rise to some of Islam's most striking and uplifting Arabic, Persian, Turkish, Urdu, and Malay poetry. It is in part this aspect of Sufism, the arts as sacred ritual—poetry, music, dance—as much as the doctrines of supreme experience of union and identity with God, which Westerners find so attractive. In *Responses to 101 Questions on Islam*, John Renard notes that a small number of Westerners "consider themselves at least incidentally Muslim by virtue of their belonging to 'Sufi' groups that trace their spiritual lineages to mystical organizations...I use the term *incidentally* because such groups often place greater emphasis on human unity than on membership in an Islamic faith community."

Dreams play a large role in guiding the mystic. They can be prophetic, as with Amina's dream of her unborn son, Muhammad. Khadija's dream of a full moon falling in her lap and shining across the world foretold her future husband who would become the Prophet of Islam.

"From earliest times Muslims have been recording their dreams and visions though they themselves are not always certain to which categories the experiences belong," Renard writes in *Windows on the House of Islam*. "Islamic tradition considers the prophet Joseph the foremost interpreter of dreams."

157

In subtle ways, whether or not we put stock in them, dreams help direct us through the tangles of our emotional and spiritual lives. Throughout history and even today, dreams are thought to be oracular and spiritual in origin, contacts with the divinity or a divine messenger, special revelations experienced in sleep while the turmoil of daily life is safely shut out.

For the Sufi, to dream of the Prophet might be an initiation. As Renard tells us in *Responses to 101 Questions on Islam*, some Sufis "have considered Muhammad as the ultimate *Shaykh*, the celestial spiritual guide who appears in dreams to initiate individuals into the Sufi Order by conferring upon them the symbolic patched frock. The more speculative mystics have even pictured Muhammad as a cosmic being, the Perfect Person whose spiritual presence suffuses all of creation. At this end of the theological spectrum, which majority theological opinion generally regards as at least innovation if not outright heresy, Muhammad bears some similarity to the cosmic Christ of the New Testament Letter to the Ephesians."

An early mystic tells of falling asleep one night.

And, lo, the Prophet came through the door and the whole room was lit up by him. He moved toward me and said: "Give me the mouth that has blessed me so often that I may kiss it." And my modesty would not let him kiss my mouth; so I turned away my face, and he kissed my cheek. I woke trembling. The house was odorous of musk from the scent of him, and the scent of musk from his kiss remained on my cheek about eight days. My wife noticed the scent every day.

A Jami poem with the rhyme-word *Muhammad* was sometimes used as a special prayer to induce a vision of the Prophet.

Dreams can help solve theological problems or open spiritual blockages. During a period of desolation, Sha'wana had a dream in which someone recited verses to her:

Spill sighs and tears of grief
to provide relief.
Strive to be straight
Try to be upright upon the Path

for the way of those acquiescent to God
is to live with sighs and burning grief.

Upon awakening Sha'wana resumed her devotion, weeping and
humming these lines to herself. After her death, she in turn made
dream visitations, appearing to a friend and offering the following
advice: "Let your heart be very sad and let the love of God override
your desires. Then nothing will harm you to your dying day."

While hundreds of Sufi women are documented, many have
drifted so deep into legend they are themselves dreamlike, nameless,
identified only by their dwelling places or as "daughter of...," "wife
of...," "disciple of..." or "master of...." Anecdotes about them resemble teaching tales, like this one told by the Sufi master of Herat,
Abdullah Ansari (384 A.H./1006 C.E. to 467 A.H./1089 C.E.):

*A devout lady was separated from her caravan and stranded in
the desert. She wandered here and there and finally paused to take her
bearings under a thorn-bush, where she laid her weary head upon her
knees and prayed, "O God! I am a stranger, sick and sorrowing, a
heart-burnt mendicant!"*

*At once from the Invisible World, she heard a voice reply,
"Though I accompany you, still you are afraid? Why should you pine
or feel alone? I am here, present in your heart, your soul's confidant."*

The wild, jolly poetry of the Sufi seems not to have appeared
until later and it would seem from much of the literature of the very
early period that women were chiefly relegated to symbolic roles, in
which women continually appear to seekers, then quickly disappear.
They are not identified as angels or djinn, but they are nevertheless
spiritual apparitions: disembodied voices, wraiths circling the Ka'aba,
like mirages, materializing alone in the desert or hovering like foxfire
on the banks of waterways. The Persian poet Farid al-Din Attar (ca.
523 A.H./1145 C.E. to 599 A.H./1221 C.E.), relates that

*One day I was walking by the bank of a river beside which stood
a pavilion. I went to the water and performed my ablutions. When I
finished my eye suddenly fell on the roof of the pavilion. There on the*

159

balcony, I saw a very beautiful girl. "Maiden," I said, "to whom do you belong?"

She answered, "When I saw you from afar, I imagined you were a madman. As you came closer, I supposed you to be a scholar. When you came still nearer, I thought you were a gnostic. Then I looked and saw you to be none of these."

"What do you mean?" I demanded.

"If you had been a madman, you would not have made ablutions. If you had been a scholar, you would not have gazed on what is forbidden. And if you had been a gnostic, your eye would not have gazed on that which is less than Reality."

So saying, she vanished.

Perhaps these specters, who come and go leaving traces of wisdom or tidbits for thought, are manifestations of the "woman-soul" venerated by Sufis. Women appear in Islamic mysticism as models of the longing soul that expresses loving devotion. Islam is very clear that life cannot exist without male and female polarity. Men and women are alter egos of one another, as is stated plainly in the Qur'an.

Women are raiment for you and you are raiment for them.[1]

Schimmel describes the *nafs*, "soul" or "self," as a "feminine noun appearing three times in the Qur'an in three specific senses, once as the 'soul inciting to evil'…once as the 'accusing soul'…and once as the 'soul at peace'….the feminine *nafs* in this role can be seen as a mirror image of the secular 'world' (*dunya*, likewise a feminine noun), and Muslim writers have made remarks and observations about 'Mistress World,' who seduces and swallows up men and children, in terms almost as uncomplimentary as those of the Christian theologians in the Middle Ages. With them, too, 'Mistress World' seeks to divert the man from his intellectual religious striving."[2]

The soul can also be represented as a maternal element. "It is only when the masculine and the feminine elements collaborate…that life can ascend to a higher stage."[3] In the tradition of the Indo-Pakistani region, Muslim mystics speak of the "bridal soul."

For Rumi, women are symbols of the loving soul. The twelfth-century C.E. Spanish theosophist ibn al-Arabi wrote that women could attain the highest mystical rank, for although the *nafs*, the "soul inciting to evil," is of the feminine gender, so also is the word *dhat*, "essence, nature." Thus, he concluded, the masculine and feminine—yang and yin, as Schimmel and other Islamic scholars put it, that is, creativity and receptivity—are contained in God. "Without the feminine mirror, God would not be able to contemplate his own beauty."[4]

In literature and poetry, the soul is personified as a woman. Male poets sometimes even assumed female identities, while dervishes occasionally dressed as women, so as to project themselves physically as God's handmaidens. As female dervishes twirled the courtyard, their male counterparts shouted to them, cheering them as if the women were their sweethearts.

Sufi masters practice meditation and retreat in their pursuit of union with God; some live in close observance of the *Shari'a*—Islamic law—while others are openly defiant of accepted forms of behavior, seeking only Allah's pleasure and approval. Some, probably the majority, are ecstatics, "drunk" on the love of God. Love, not justice, is the axis of devotion.

"Such a conception…left no room for the distinction of sex," Smith writes. "In the spiritual life, there could be neither male nor female."[5]

Attar, who also authored *Tadhkirat al-Awliya*, a twelfth-century prose work about the early Sufis, noted that the "Holy Prophets have laid it down that 'God does not look upon your outward forms.' It is not the outward form that matters, but the inner purpose of the heart, as the Prophet said, 'The people are assembled [on the Day of Judgment], according to the purposes of their hearts….'

"If it is allowable to accept two thirds of our faith from Aisha the Trustworthy," Attar continued, "it is also allowable to accept religious benefit from one of their handmaids. When a woman walks in the way of God like man, she cannot be called a woman."

The word *man* designates anyone who strives intently toward God. To embrace Sufism is to "profess manhood upon the Sufi way," and women have equal rank. There are periodic rumblings about the use of *man* as lopsided and unjust toward women, but this can seem like mere argument over semantics,[6] for as Smith points out, "in Unity there is no distinction. The Quest and the Way and the Seeker become one. All whom God had called to be saints could attain, by following the Path, to union with Himself and all who attained would have their royal rank, sainthood, as spiritual beings in the world to come."[7]

Some theologians name Fatima, the Prophet's daughter, as the first *quth* or spiritual head of the Sufi fellowship. As a kind of "mater dolorosa," her spiritual relationship to the Virgin Mary has been illustrated in numerous ways, most recently in Portugal in 1917, near the village of Fatima, founded by the Moors. "Our Lady of Fatima" first appeared to three children and afterward was beheld by thousands of people. Devotion to her has spread worldwide.

Nothing prevents women from reaching the highest rank in the hierarchy of Muslim saints. Indeed, one of the earliest recorded Muslim saints is Umm Haram, maternal aunt of the Prophet.

Martyrs, *shahid*, including women, are as abundant in Islam as in Christianity. And martyrdom naturally leads to sainthood. The first person said to have "suffered for the faith" was Summaya bint Khubbat, who accepted Islam while the Prophet was still in Mecca. Taunted and persecuted, she held fast, until one day, Abu Jahl— Father of Ignorance and dedicated enemy of Islam—passed by her on the street and stabbed her to death in the forehead.

Umm Waraqa bint Abdallah was the imam of a mixed community, personally instructed by the Prophet in leading prayers. She handed down the Qur'an before it was put in final written form, and had a great desire to be known as a martyr. She begged Muhammad to let her take part with his forces in the Battle of Badr. Muhammad acquiesced and allowed Umm Waraqa to tend the wounded. From then on he called her "the Martyress," perhaps somewhat teasingly, but with earnest affection and respect. That he bestowed on her the honor of martyrdom, although she was not killed, ensured her a place in Paradise.

Although the Prophet did not approve of the "idolatry" of saints or saint worship, Tradition recognizes Friends of Allah, who resemble Christian saints. Although they are distinct from prophets, Friends of Allah are also capable of manifesting God's power through miracles. Evidentiary miracles, which substantiate a prophet's claim, are called *mu'jzat*, whereas saintly miracles are called "wonders," *karamat*.

During a year-long drought, Jami tells us, prayers were offered up daily for rain, yet no rain fell. At last the people visited Umm Muhammad, imploring her to intercede. She stood before her house and prayed, "O Lord, I swept my doorstep, now You sprinkle the water" (a custom for settling the dust after sweeping).

It was not long before rain poured from the sky.[8]

"The influence which women saints exercised both during their lives and after their deaths," Smith writes, "is perhaps best proved by the fact that Muslim theologians, opposed to the Sufi movement, denounce also these women saints and the worship known to be given to them."[9]

Among saints, Zaynab bint Ali ranks lofty in Shi'a worship. The daughter of Fatima and Ali, granddaughter of the Prophet and sister to Hassan and Husayn, martyred during the wars for succession, she was tortured and imprisoned, but stood for "victorious truth." Poems, plays, and prose pieces—particularly in Iran—dramatize her suffering and that of her family. In various of these tales, as we've seen, Zaynab's persecution is forecast by Fatima, who while washing her daughter's hair a final time before dying, predicts that "one sad day, stones will be thrown at this precious head." Zaynab is the guardian of relics, such as the Prophet's teeth, knocked out in the Battle of Uhud.

Friends of Allah are eminent in public piety. There are shrines throughout the Muslim world, often elaborate architectural structures with staffs, endowments, and mosques. Many, we'll see, were founded by women, who then bequeathed their money to maintain them. As among Roman Catholics or Hindus, there are ritual practices for visiting saints' shrines and asking for spiritual blessings and

THE SCIMITAR AND THE VEIL

favors. There are processions and celebrations to commemorate them at particular times of the year.

Some places accommodate relics, such as various noble cloaks of the Prophet, the *khirqa-i-sharif* or *burda*, which are found in several mosques from Decca, India, to the treasury of the fabulous palace of Topkapi Serai in Istanbul. Another, also called the *khirqa mubarak*, is preserved at a mosque in Kandahar, Afghanistan, where millions of pilgrims visit annually.[10]

In *And Muhammad Was His Messenger*, Schimmel describes the Prophet's sandals, with two strings drawn between the toes, as an "amulet full of *baraqa*, particularly strong against the evil eye." These had touched the throne of God during Muhammad's heavenly journey. Pictures of the sandals became quite common in the Middle Ages and this inspired a poetical genre, especially in North Africa and Spain. The Andalusian female poet, Sa'duna Umm Sa'd bint 'Isam al-Himyariyya (d. 620 A.H./1242 C.E.) wrote:

> If I do not find a way to kiss the Prophet's sandal,
> I'll kiss the image.
> And perhaps the good fortune of kissing it
> will give me a radiant place in Paradise.
> By rubbing my raging heart on the picture,
> its burning thirst will be quenched.

Sufis first sought shelter and solidarity in small, informal circles in the homes of *shaykhas* and *shaykhs*, female and male spiritual guides. Formally constituted religious orders began appearing in the twelfth century C.E. The orders grew and spread rapidly, as in the Christian monastic tradition, splitting into suborders and variants identified with their founders. These monastic communities were frowned upon by more orthodox authorities, for, as we've seen, Muhammad spoke of marriage as his custom and that monks had no place in Islam. However, other *Hadiths* and biographies report that the Prophet—who before the *hijra* to Medina frequented the caves of Mount Hira to fast and pray (and often took his family with him)—spoke well of certain forms of asceticism.

In the beginning, Sufi women were admitted to the communal *dhikr* to invoke the name of God alongside men and that practice has continued in many regions. Women's sections were specially constructed. In some places, women watched the ceremonies from a nearby room or from the roof or balcony. Wealthy women who wished to enter upon or join the Sufi path often functioned as benefactors of a convent, providing shelter and food for a master and his disciples.

In the Middle Ages, women's convents, *ribats*, were started in Medina, Syria, and Cairo. Mecca had three, while Baghdad, then the center of the Islamic world, was renowned for its Dar al-falak, a convent founded by a woman on the west bank of the Tigris. In the seventh Islamic century, the last Abbasid caliph endowed a women's convent in Baghdad. His daughter was named its first director. The leadership of a convent was often handed down through families.

The director preached, led the women in prayer, and instructed them in mystical wisdom. The convents also served as safe havens for widows and divorced women, where they could spend the three months and ten days of the *idda*, the obligatory waiting period, before they were allowed to enter a new marriage. This is reminiscent of Christian convents during the Middle Ages, where women often retreated, not necessarily to take vows, but to relieve themselves of domestic burdens and social pressures and find some autonomy not otherwise permitted them.

Because celibacy in Islam is seen as against God's natural laws, most Sufi women were married and mothers. But some, Rabi'a al-Adawiyya among them, were faithful to a heavenly bridegroom, as are Christian nuns. Devotion to the Beloved requires a fidelity that cannot compete in the "normal" world of marriages and children.

The history of Sufism is peppered with bitter conflicts vis-à-vis conservative Muslim authorities, who accused Sufis of practicing pantheism, because of the belief that all creation is ultimately identified with God. Primal cultures were far more likely to accept and even venerate eccentric behavior, but so-called civilized societies everywhere have tended to look at exhibitions of ecstasy or pain, especially in public, not as signs of connectedness with the Divine, but as insanity.

Sufi men and women were sometimes confined to madhouses for their unconventional conduct. There are many paintings illustrating the "crazy" dervish acting out wildly or dancing under a young woman's window, "mad for love."

In *Sufi Women*, Nurbakhsh tells of an unnamed Meccan woman who was in "such a spiritual state" she wailed and shrieked *...at least once an hour. People pointed out to her that she was possessed by a state unlike that of anyone else and asked her if she wished to be cured of her pain.*

"Cure this pain?" the woman cried. *"Alas my heart is pierced with pondering about how to remedy it! Do you not marvel that I am still alive, sitting here right before you, yet my heart is a blazing fire of love and yearning for God? And these flames won't subside until I return to my Physician who knows my cure and possesses the proper salve for my heart. Yet it seems that my long-suffering in this house, in which even weeping provides no relief, serves to satisfy his goodwill."*

In Persian, the form for "sigh" is "heart smoke." Rumi noted that where there is no sighing, there is no ecstasy.

Jami wrote of a certain Sufi named Fedha, who encouraged her disciples to rejoice within until their happiness radiated outward to envelop others. "If hearts are joyous," Fedha instructed, "milk is likewise sweet, but if hearts are offended, milk is likewise sour. So endeavor to delight their hearts."

Ibn Arabi remembered a woman ascetic of Seville, Fatima bint al-Muthanna, whom he knew as a youth and who lived in extreme poverty. Yet "she was a consolation for the inhabitants of the Earth," possessed of irrepressible merriment, playing her tambourine while praising the glory of God.

Raiy'a bint Ismai'li (Rabi'a of Syria)

Her name was actually Rabi'a but in tales and anecdotes, she is often confused with her more famous namesake, Rabi'a al-Adawiyya of Basra. However, Raiy'a, as she was also called, was from Syria and a married woman. She died in 135 A.H./757 C.E.

Raiy'a is widowed when she proposes to the ascetic Ahmad ibn Abu al-Hawwari. He tells her he is preoccupied with his soul and does not trouble himself with women. His teacher, Abu Sulayman, warns him against marriage: "Not one of our friends has married without changing for the worse."

Raiy'a tells Ahmad that she has equally little inclination toward men, but her late husband has left her 300,000 dinars, lawfully earned, and she wishes to bestow her inheritance on Ahmad and his brothers, for they are pious men and this money might forge another road to God.

Ahmad again consults Abu Sulayman. The teacher puts his head under his garment and there is a long silence. When at last he lifts his head he says, "O Ahmad, marry her, for this woman is one of the saints of God, and this is the speech of those who are sincere in their faith."

The wedding is modest and afterward Raiy'a tells Ahmad, "I do not love you with the love of a wife. I love you with the love of a sister. My desire toward you is only to serve you."

Raiy'a attains high states of mysticism, sometimes Love, sometimes intense affection, sometimes terrible fear.

When overcome with Love, she exclaims:

O my Love—there is no one like You.
None but You may share my heart.
O my Friend—invisible
yet never absent from my heart.

When intimacy and affection possess her, she recites:

You are the Friend of my heart with whom I can converse.
You alone guard my heart; You alone are my heart's love.

When fear consumes her, she moans:

Should I weep for lack of provision
Or for the duration of this sojourn?
How shall I ever attain the real aim?
I fall short. Will You punish me by fire?
You are the ultimate aim of all desire.
In this desire lie all my fear and all my hope.

With each meal she serves Ahmad she says, "Eat from this food,
for I praised God all the while I cooked it."

And though she cooks, she eats nearly nothing. Ahmad over-
hears complaining: "I begrudge my *nafs* any good-tasting food and I
am grieved when I notice that my arms have grown plump."

Each night she purifies herself and comes before her husband,
saying, "Do you have any needs?" If he does, she performs them,
then leaves him to make her ablutions and remain in worship until
morning.

In time, she comes to him and gives him the sum of five
dirhams. "Take this money," she urges Ahmad. "Acquire for yourself a new wife or buy a slave girl, for I must excuse myself from
you."

Ahmad is stunned and perceiving his shocked look, she says, "I do not hold it to be lawful to deny you myself or any other woman. So go and choose another woman for yourself."

The man who was too engrossed in the state of his spirit to be inclined to marry accumulates four wives. To marry is God's will. With each marriage, Raiy'a prepares a meal for Ahmad. "You are a newly married man," she says as she serves him. "Eat this meat. You need it."

She serves household meals, saying, "Take this with your good and cheerful company to your wives."

"When I try to get close to her during the day, Raiy'a begs me, for God's sake, not to break her fast," Ahmad tells his companions. "At night whenever I try to approach her, she entreats me to allow her to be exclusively devoted to God for the night."

Once, when he is performing the prayers of the night vigil, he tells Raiy'a that he has never seen anyone remain so concentratedly awake the whole night long as she.

"God be glorified!" she cries, "Don't speak like this, Ahmad. When I am called, I arise."

Ahmad is filled with awe and reverence whenever he gazes on Raiy'a's face. His heart palpitates with dread when he sees her. Yet, when he is occupied with her, discussing the effects of devotion in their circles of remembrance, this awe eludes him.

Sometimes when he summons her, it is an hour before she responds. And when she does, her eyes are glazed with ecstasy. "My heart was so filled with the joy of God," she tells him, "I could not answer you."

A basin is set before her. Raiy'a gasps and orders it to be removed. "I see written on it that the Commander of the Faithful is dead." That day, indeed, the Abbasid caliph Harun al-Rashid—second son of al-Madhi and Khayzuran, husband of Zubaydah, the light of art and music and poetry—dies.

The hour of Raiy'a's death comes near. "I never hear the call to prayer, without remembering the trumpet call of the Day of

Resurrection," she tells Ahmad. "I never see the snow without remembering the fluttering of the pages of the Book of Deeds. I never see a swarm of locusts without remembering the Assembly for the Last Judgment."

Rabi'a al-Adawiyya

Rabi'a of Basra, Iraq, was probably born in 95 A.H./717 C.E. and is the most famous of Islamic women saints, called "The Crown of Humankind" for her enlightenment, piety, and asceticism and "a second, spotless Mary." A Sufi, she was on equal terms with the leaders of her day and was among the first to advocate the Way of Love, worshiping God in friendship rather than fear. Rabi'a died in 179 A.H./801 C.E.

On the edge of the desert near the town of Basra, the Sufi Ismai'l takes his wife to live in poverty. They have first one daughter and then a second and then a third. Ismai'l names the last girl Rabi'a, "the fourth."

There is no oil for the lamp and none with which to anoint the newborn's navel. There's no cloth to swaddle her. The tired mother begs her husband to borrow oil from a neighbor. Ismai'l goes, but he stands in front of the neighbor's door without knocking. He has made the vow of true Sufis never to ask another human being for anything, but to depend only upon God to supply his needs. He returns home empty-handed to a wife who weeps bitterly. Ismai'l buries his head in his knees and falls asleep.

He dreams that the Prophet Muhammad speaks to him: "Don't be sad. This infant will be a queen among women. She will mediate for 70,000 of my community."

The Prophet instructs Ismai'l to write a note to the governor of Basra: "Every night you send upon me 100 blessings and on Friday night 400. Last night was Friday and you forgot me. To set right your forgetfulness, give this man 400 dinars, lawfully acquired." Lawfully acquired, for the money used by a Sufi must only be earned according to the sacred laws of Islam.

When Ismai'l wakes, he writes the letter as the Prophet directed and sends it to the amir. The amir is astonished and ashamed. "Give 2000 dinars to the poor as a thank-offering, because the Prophet had me in mind," he tells his vizier. "Give 400 dinar to Ismai'l and inform him that I desire to see him, but that it is not fitting for such a blessed soul as he to come to me. Rather, I will go and rub my beard on his threshold."

Thus it comes to pass that the family prospers a while, until Ismai'l dies. The desert life is too harsh for a widow and her four daughters. She sets out for Basra with the children and they are set upon by bandits. Their mother is killed. The girls are sold into slavery.

Rabi'a is eleven years old and pretty. She is worth six dirhams on the slave market and there is a man who pays it gladly. He takes her home and teaches her to sing and play the oud and the flute. He leases her to sing and play at weddings and parties. Rabi'a is much in demand, for there is something in her songs that lifts hearts. She is singing to her Beloved.

And as she sings nightly to her True Love, her own heart is awakened. Soon she is fasting in the day and at night she prays until the sunrise. Now she refuses to perform in public, so her master beats her bloody. No bruises can persuade Rabi'a to sing for any but God. Then one night, the master is awakened by a strange light. He looks out the window and sees Rabi'a, whose head is bowed in prayer.

"O my Lord. You know the desire of my heart is to obey and that the light of my eye is to serve You. I would not cease, even for an hour from that service, but You have made me the subject of another human being."

Above her head is a lamp, suspended without a chain. The whole house is illuminated and Rabi'a is engulfed in a golden halo.

The master is frightened. He returns to his bed, cowering. He ponders until the day breaks. At dawn he calls Rabi'a to him and sets her free. She departs from that place and walks into the desert toward Mecca.

She plays a merry tune on her flute. Her feet dance. It is spring and she feels God's beauty within. She comes upon a holy man, who feeds her and asks for her hand in marriage. She thanks him and goes on. She visits Hayyuna in a cave. The hermit is famous for her great austerity. Rabi'a hears Hayyuna's prayer: "O God, I wish that the day were night that I might enjoy Your proximity."

After a time, Rabi'a is called to pilgrimage. She acquires a donkey to carry her baggage to Mecca. She joins a caravan and in the heat of the desert, the donkey drops dead. The kindly caravan folk offer to carry her baggage, but Rabi'a tells them she cannot depend on any but God for help. The caravan continues, leaving Rabi'a with bowed head.

"O my God, do kings deal this way with a woman, a weak stranger? You are calling me to Mecca, to Your own house, but You have caused my donkey to die and left me alone in the desert."

Hardly have these words been spoken than the donkey stirs and comes alive again. Rabi'a replaces her baggage on its back and continues her journey.

When she has fulfilled her pilgrimage, Rabi'a returns to Basra to occupy herself with works of devotion. She is always busy with God. She will be celibate so that she can pursue her Beloved without hindrance.

All the same, there are men who want her. Ascetics and amirs. To one suitor's request she replies scornfully, "Sensual one, seek another sensual like yourself! Have you seen any desire in me?" To another, who offers Rabi'a a generous bride-price, she answers, "It does not please me that you should be my slave and that what you possess should be mine. God can give me all you offer and even double it. It does not please me that you should distract me from God for a single moment."

She scolds yet another: "Renunciation of this world means peace, while desire for it brings sorrow. Curb your desires. Control yourself. And don't let others control you, but let them share your inheritance and the anxiety of the age. Give your mind to the day of death."

"The contract of marriage," Rabi'a tells still another, "is for those who are concerned with the affairs of this material world. For me, existence has ceased, since I have ceased to exist and have passed out of Self. My existence is in Him and I am altogether His. I am in the shadow of His command. Peace is in solitude, yet my Beloved is always with me."

To her Beloved she whispers: "I have made You the Companion of my heart. O my Joy. You are the source of my life and from You comes my ecstasy. My hope is for union with You."

For union with the Beloved Who is Allah, she must learn patience in the lover's bond. She fasts for seven days and nights. She sleeps not at all, but prays continually. A friend brings a cup of food, for Rabi'a is in extremity. She takes the food and goes to fetch a lamp. A cat leaps onto her table and upsets the cup. Food spills onto the clay floor. Rabi'a fetches a jug to break her fast with water. When she returns, the lamp has gone out. She sits down to drink the water, but the jug falls from her hands and smashes to bits. The water runs into the food on the floor.

Rabi'a weeps. Her fierce lamentations and howling anguish could catch the house on fire.

"O God," she sobs, "What is this that You do to wretched me?"

"Have a care, Rabi'a," a voice answers. "If you desire it, I will endow you with all the pleasures of this world. But I shall take concern for Me out of your heart, for such concern and the pleasures of this world cannot dwell together in one heart."

Love does not come with moaning and complaining at the Beloved. Love does not thrive in the foul air of fault-finding. She does not accept Him as a wrathful God and yet she herself has been wrathful with God. She cannot have it both ways. And with His warning that she cannot enjoy both material ease and divine friendship, Rabi'a separates her heart forever from earthly bounties.

"O God, whatsoever You have apportioned to me of worldly goods, give that to Your enemies. And what You have apportioned to me in the Hereafter, give that to Your friends. For You alone suffice me."

She performs each prayer as if it were her last.

"Everyone prays to You from fear of the Fire. Or they pray to You for the Garden, full of fruits and flowers. But I am not afraid of the Fire. I don't ask you for the Garden. All I want is the Essence of Your Love and to return to be one with You."

There are many days when she does not eat. When she denies herself even the most basic of comforts. Her friends offer food and gifts. She will have none of it. She looks only to God to provide her needs. When she has meat, she tears it with her teeth. A friend asks if she does not have a knife.

"I have never had a knife in my house for fear of cutting myself off, separating myself from God."

Rabi'a says prayers of praise and dozes off. She sees a green tree of immeasurable height and beauty. Upon it are three kinds of fruit, shining, otherworldly fruits, one white, one red, one yellow.

"Whose tree is this?" she asks.

"It grows from your prayers of praise," a voice replies.

She walks around the tree. Some of the golden fruit has fallen to the ground. "It would be much better if this fruit were on the tree with the others," Rabi'a says.

"This fruit was on the tree," the voice responds, "but during your prayer of praise, you thought about whether the dough was rising, and at that moment it fell."

She has no doubts about His Presence. She lives for Love that does not seek an answer. Love that does not ask rewards. Love that wants no reciprocity.

Her house is full day and night with those who seek her counsel, who long to hear her prayers or learn from her teachings, the first they have ever received about the Way of Love.

But when they ask her to pray for them, she shakes her head. "Who am I? Obey your Lord and pray to Him yourself, for He will answer the suppliant."

Sufyan al-Thawri is a constant visitor and a great authority on the *Hadith*. Rabi'a says he would be a good man if not for his attachment to the Traditions. "If only Sufyan did not love the gathering of people around him for discourse. They distract from the life with God."

Sufyan prays: "O God, be satisfied with us."

"Are you not ashamed to ask God to be satisfied when you are not satisfied with Him?" Rabi'a asks. Sufyan begs God's forgiveness.

He finds ways to provoke Rabi'a. He enjoys her retaliations. One day he says, "Alas for my sorrow and my sins!" He waits with a gleam in his eye for Rabi'a's retort.

"Don't lie, Sufyan!" she snaps. "Say rather, 'Alas for my lack of sorrow and sin!' If you were truly sorry, life would have no delight for you."

She is gentler with her friend the Sufi Hassan al-Basri. She gives him a piece of wax, a needle, and a hair. "Be like wax," she advises him, "and illumine the world and burn yourself. Be like a needle and work naked. When you have done these two things, a thousand years will be for you like a hair."

Rabi'a and Hassan are walking near a lake. Hassan throws his prayer rug on top of the water. "Rabi'a, come," he calls. "Let us pray here."

"Hassan, when you are showing off your spiritual goods in the worldly market, it should be things which your fellow men cannot display." She tosses her prayer rug into the air and leaps onto it.

"Come here, Hassan," she teases. He looks up at her sadly. She floats back to the ground to console him.

"Hassan, what you did, fishes can do. What I did, flies can do. The real business is not with tricks. One must apply oneself to the real business."

With increasing age comes illness. She accepts her suffering as God's will and endures her pains with fortitude. Once when she is afflicted with sickness, a merchant arrives at her door. He does not knock or enter, but stands there weeping helplessly. Hassan al-Basri appears and asks the merchant what is wrong.

"If the blessings of this ascetic upon us were to cease, we would perish," the merchant cries. He shows Hassan a purse of gold. "I brought this for her. It is lawfully acquired. But I fear she may refuse it." He begs Hassan to intercede that she may accept the gift and buy food and medicines, warm blankets.

Hassan takes the gold to Rabi'a. She peers at Hassan from the corner of her eye. "If He provides for those who revile Him, won't

He provide for those who love Him? He does not refuse sustenance to those who speak unworthily of Him. How then should He refuse sustenance to one whose soul overflows with love for Him? Make my excuses to the merchant, Hassan, that my heart may not be in bondage."

Seven years before her death, Rabi'a travels to the holy city of Jerusalem. She lives in a house on the Mount of Olives. She walks daily down the hill to the al-Aqsa Mosque, where she prays and gives teachings to men and women who flock around her. They come, as well, to hear her poetry, which are as prayers.

> I have loved You with two loves,
> a selfish love and love that rises to You.
> The selfish love occupies me with souvenirs of You
> to the exclusion of all others.
> The love that rises to You
> asks You to raise the veil that I may see You.
> Yet there is no praise for me in this or that.

She seems to her friends like an empty skin bag, withered and barely upright. In her house there is only a reed mat, a clothes stand where her shrouds hang, an earthen jug, and a bed of felt on the floor, which is also her prayer carpet.

She walks up the hill from the mosque to her house. She parts the palm-leaf curtain and enters. She lies down upon the felt bed. She closes her eyes. Her mouth moves in silence. She dies while she prays, smiling like a new bride at her Beloved.

They build her a tomb near the Christian Church of the Ascension. No day passes without a visitor. They say that Rabi'a was veiled with the veil of sincerity, inflamed by love and yearning, lost in union with God.

Nafisa

Nafisa was born ca. 140 A.H./762 C.E. in Mecca and grew up in Medina, the great-great-granddaughter of the Prophet through his grandson Hassan. She married Isaq ibn Ja'far, went to Egypt with him, and bore two children, al-Qasim and Umm Kulthum. She is still revered as a saint in Egypt, where she died ca. 201 A.H./823 C.E.

In Medina, her exalted family is renowned for its good works and Nafisa carries on the tradition of charity and almsgiving. She is well-educated and knows the Qur'an by heart. Jurists come to hear her relate *Hadith*. Imam Shafe'i transmits on her word alone.

She moves from Medina to Egypt with her husband Isaq ibn Ja'far, and there she fasts all day and prays all night. She makes the pilgrimage thirty times.

In Egypt, there is a prince who takes pleasure in torturing those who disagree with him. One such victim, Walid, takes refuge with Nafisa. She prays for him, and when she is finished, she tells him he can safely leave her house, for "God Almighty will veil the eyes of the unjust from perceiving who you are."

Walid is frightened, but he has faith in Nafisa, for she has already proven in many small ways that God is with her. There seems to be no end to those who come asking for her intercession.

He goes among the prince's companions and stands before his tormentor. The prince looks straight at him and asks his companions, "Where is Walid?"

"He is standing right in front of you," the companions answer.

"But, by God, I cannot see him," the prince insists, rubbing his eyes.

"He has been to Nafisa and requested that she pray for him. After praying, she informed him that God has concealed him from the sight of the unjust."

The prince blushes with shame. "If my actions have reached such extremes that merely through people's prayers God veils my eyes from beholding the oppressed, then, O Lord, forgive me! I repent! To You I return."

At that, the prince raises his head and sees Walid standing before him. He prays for Walid. He kisses Walid's head. He gives him a rich set of new clothes and sends him away in gratitude.

No sooner has Walid departed than the prince gathers all his wealth and gives it to the poor, sending 100,000 dirhams to Lady Nafisa as an offer of thanksgiving, for God has returned to him. Nafisa distributes the money among the poor.

"O mistress," says one of her women, "if you were to give me a small portion of this money, I would buy something with which to break our fast."

Nafisa refuses, handing the woman instead a small skein of thread. "Take this and sell it. With that money we'll break our fast, for the prince has no claim on it."

One Friday, an old woman, extremely poor with four growing girls, goes to the bazaar to trade as she does every week, to sell her home-spun woolen thread for bread and this time a little extra to buy a book for her daughters. En route, a bird swoops down and seizes her package. Now there is not only no money for food, but her daughters will go without the book as well. The people gather around the wailing woman and tell her to hurry to Nafisa.

At Nafisa's house, the old woman relates her story and asks Nafisa to assist with her supplications.

"O God!" Nafisa prays. "Your power over all is preeminent. Your reign prevails over all. Restore to these people what You have seized, for they are Your creatures, Your family, and You are omnipotent."

When she has finished praying, Nafisa says to her guest, "Sit down. God is powerful over all things."

Worried about her children at home, the woman nonetheless sits and waits. She has waited an hour, when a group of travelers appears at Nafisa's house.

"A strange thing has happened to us," they tell Nafisa. "A party of us were voyaging on the ocean in the utmost peace and safety, but as we approached your harbor, our sailing ship developed a hole in the hull. Water gushed into the ship and we almost drowned. We tried to stop the leak, but were powerless. Suddenly, a bird carrying a red bundle miraculously flew overhead and dropped it into our vessel. By God's will we used that bundle of thread to stop the leak. We have brought 500 dinars with us to express our gratitude for having survived."

Nafisa shouts with joy. "O my Lord, my God! How kind and generous You are to Your servants." She summons the old woman and asks, "What would you have sold your thread for?"

"Twenty dirhams," the woman tells her.

Nafisa gives her the 500 dinars, which the woman in turn gives to her daughters. They put aside their thread-spinning business and come to wait on Nafisa forever.

One year the Nile fails to flood. The farmers fear drought; the people fear famine. They crowd along the narrow alleys of Cairo, marching to Nafisa's house. She gives them her veil and bids them cast it into the river. When they have done so, the river rises higher than any flood anyone can remember.

Her miracles are myriad. She cares for a small, crippled Jewish girl and prays beside her and the girl regains the use of her limbs.

Nafisa digs her own grave with her own hands in her own house. She descends into it and prays there and there repeats the Qur'an 6000 times.

As her death approaches, Nafisa fasts, though her friends encourage her to eat for she is coming upon the end.

"What an odd request," Nafisa marvels. "All my life, I have aspired to meet God while fasting. Is it now time to break it? Impossible!"

And as she recites from the holy book—*They have an abode of peace with their Lord*[11]—she passes on.

The people assemble from throughout the nearby villages and towns and light candles and pray over her body.

Her husband, Isaq ibn Ja'far, wishes to convey Nafisa's body back to Medina, but the people of Cairo beg to let her be buried among them in the grave she has dug with her own fingers. At first he refuses, but the Prophet comes to him in a dream and tells him, "Do not debate with the Egyptians concerning Nafisa, O Isaq, for through her grave, Divine Mercy will favor them."

Jahanara

*Jahanara's original name was Fatima. She was born in 992
A.H./1614 C.E., the eldest and favorite daughter of the fifth
Mughal emperor Shah Jahan and his beloved wife
Mumtaz Mahal (whose tomb is the Taj Mahal). Jahanara
wrote* Risala-i Sahibiyya, *an extraordinary exposition of her
initiation into Sufism. In addition to her mystic calling, she
was a patron of the arts and a builder of great monuments
(many of which are no longer standing). (In 1857, the
British destroyed the imperial Mughal gardens built by
Jahanara, as well as fifty-eight acres of palaces and gardens
in Delhi's Red Fort.) She also acted as an administrator of
Shah Jahan's household after her mother's death, and to
some extent, his government. Jahanara died in 1059
A.H./1681 C.E.*

After Fatima, Mumtaz Mahal gives birth to thirteen more children,
four of them sons. That the brothers Dara Shokoh, Shah Shuja,
Aurangzeb, and Murad Bakhsh have the same mother does not
soften their rivalries. The first bitterness is toward Dara Shokoh, their
father's favorite and heir to the throne. Dara Shokoh is a year
younger than Fatima, whom they call Jahanara. Sister and brother
are especially beloved of their father Shah Jahan.

Jahanara is sixteen when Mumtaz Mahal dies giving birth to
her fourteenth child. Jahanara's mourning is cut short by her father's
despair. Within a week of Mumtaz Mahal's death, his beard and hair
turn white. He abjures perfume and loses interest even in listening

to *dhrupad*, his favorite music. Jahanara understands she must care for her younger siblings, as well as bring Shah Jahan out of his grief or the realm will be lost. Her brother Aurangzeb is already distinguished for his shrewdness in military matters and matters of state—and for his deceptions.

Dara Shokoh and Jahanara are bound by strong affection, by their search for God and desire for union with Him. Dara Shokoh is scholarly and gentle. He becomes a Sufi novice, following the teachings of the celebrated saint Mullah Shah. Dara Shokoh tells Jahanara of each step along the mystic Way, and listening to his accounts the princess wants nothing more than to also be admitted as Mullah Shah's student.

She writes him letter after letter. Each letter expresses her aspiration to renounce the world and each letter is stronger than the one before.

Mullah Shah leaves them unanswered.

Meanwhile, Jahanara tends her father and little by little she manages to return normalcy to the court. At eighteen, Dara Shokoh is betrothed to his cousin, Princess Nadira. Jahanara, taking her mother's role, arranges the wedding. Shah Jahan comes out of mourning to attend, for this marriage had the blessing of his adored Mumtaz Mahal.

The letters to Mullah Shah keep coming. Years of letters, posted daily, until the Sufi master is at last convinced that Jahanara, despite her many duties, is sincere and determined. They have never laid eyes on one another, but he consents to her initiation.

She recalls how, in Kashmir, she finally saw the blessed form of Mullah Shah from her hiding place behind the curtain and that he seemed to be filled with light and Love. She writes that now, watching Mullah Shah and her father Shah Jahan, her faith becomes a thousand times more fervent and ecstasy saturates her soul.

The next day, Dara Shokoh initiates Jahanara into the Sufi way. Dara Shokoh acts for the saint and leads his sister in a recitation of the formula of the Qadir dervishes and the order of Mullah Shah. When it is finished, Jahanara repairs to the chapel in her palace and prays until midnight. When she returns to her apartments, she becomes absorbed in contemplation. She has a vision of the Prophet and the saints. She is overwhelmed with gratitude. Her heart can barely contain this sign of Divine favor. When her breath returns and she is calmed, she prostrates herself before the throne of the Absolute Being. She pours out her soul in thankfulness to God for the immeasurable happiness He has conferred upon a weak and unworthy woman to attain the knowledge that raises human beings out of brutishness.

In the daily life of the court and the administration of her father's household, his health, and even his government, she is hardly weak or unworthy. Her father has built a monument to her mother, a tomb called Taj Mahal, and there he spends many sad hours. As the years pass, Jahanara causes the monuments of Jama Masjid in Agra and the Chandni Chowk in Delhi to be built. In Delhi she builds gardens and inns. Her work earns her the title of Baadshah Begam, First Lady of the Realm.

She strives to attain knowledge of God. Her asceticism is moderated by her position; her service is not only to the Divine but to her people, to represent the perfection of created things. She strives to become Love, to be absorbed into absolute existence, to become as a drop in the ocean, a mote in the sunbeams, a part swallowed up in the whole.

She is thirty years old. She wears modest clothing of fine muslin, perfumed with amber and musk. She passes by the open torches in the Red Fort and catches fire. She is enveloped in flames. Her maids-in-waiting throw themselves on her to put out the blaze. They, too, burst like candles into hot flame and two of the sweet friends of Jahanara crumble into embers. Jahanara hangs between life and death.

Again, Shah Jahan falls into despair. He is sick with anxiety for his daughter. He calls for all the physicians to create a salve that will heal Jahanara's burns. A purse is kept under her bed with 1001 rupees of silver to be distributed among the mendicants each morning, in hopes that this will bring God's blessing upon the charred princess.

Shah Jahan prays constantly by his daughter's bedside. His prayers are answered when a slave named Arif prepares a salve that helps mend her damaged skin.

She gives thanks for her survival. She studies assiduously with Mullah Shah to reach exultation. Mullah Shah has great affection for all his students, but he is especially attached to Jahanara. Her mystic knowledge is so vast, he says, she would be worthy to act on his behalf as his deputy.

This, too, is the feeling of Shah Jahan, for as he grows older he relies more and more on her. She is forty-three when he becomes ill and the rivalries between her brothers erupt with cruel intensity.

Expecting their father's death, his four sons begin desperate bids for the throne. Dara Shokoh is his father's choice, but the younger Aurangzeb's appetite for power is insatiable. While Dara Shokoh spends his days translating Upanishads into Persian, Aurangzeb spends his in military maneuvers and scheming. Jahanara spends her days giving voice to moderation and family love. Her brothers respect her authority, but ambition corrupts even the best intentions.

Shah Jahan is old and helpless. He can do nothing but watch as hostilities between his sons break into war. The contest is savage, but Aurangzeb is easily the winner. He imprisons his father in the Agra fort and crowns himself Emperor, World Conqueror, *Alamgir*.

Shah Jahan is imprisoned for eight years before he succumbs. Jahanara tends him throughout. He lies on his deathbed and never takes his eyes from the Taj Mahal, the tomb of his dearest wife. He dies and is buried beside her.

Jahanara steps fully onto the path of ecstasy and Love. It is said she reaches such perfection that she attains pure union with God and the gnosis which comes from the Vision of God.

IV

Warriors and Amazons

"If you do not fall in battle, someone is saving you as a token of shame."

The Prophet Muhammad taught that there are two *jihads*, a greater and a lesser. The greater *jihad* is each Muslim's struggle with her or his own behavior and relationship with God. To speak the truth, to act justly and demand justice, to sacrifice material and physical well-being for the benefit of individuals or the community, these are the greater *jihad*. "The best *jihad*," the Prophet said, "is a just word before a tyrannical authority." Tyranny can be external or internal.

Non-Muslims usually translate the word *jihad* as "holy war," but it means "exertion," "constant striving in the way of God."

The Prophet defined the greater *jihad* as that which is "against the *nafs*," the base instincts (in the Qur'an: the "soul inciting to evil" and the "accusing soul"). As all spiritual practitioners understand, the most difficult exertion is to subdue these instincts and transform them into positive thought and action. This labor becomes all the more complicated when one believes, as Muhammad did, that "God is gentle and loves gentleness."

There is a lovely *Hadith* about a young man who told Muhammad he desperately wanted to join his fellow Muslims in defense of the faith. The Prophet told the boy that his *jihad* was to care for his aging parents. "All God's creatures are His family; and he or she is the most beloved of God who tries to do most good to God's creatures."

The pilgrimage, the *hajj*, with its hardships, is also a *jihad*.

The lesser *jihad* is armed conflict against the enemies of Islam and Muslims. However, only religious authorities, the *'ulama*, may legally declare whether an armed response will be a genuine *jihad*. If Muhammad's model is analyzed honestly, fostering peaceful relations between conflicting groups will take priority. The Qur'an, *Hadith*, and biographies of the Prophet illustrate that his overwhelming preference was for reconciliation. Because he was who he was—known even to enemy Meccans as al-Amin, the Trustworthy, the Reliable—the people of Yathrib (Medina) invited him to negotiate between disputing tribes. And in the bargain, Muslims would escape persecution in Mecca. When Mecca was at last regained, after a bloody journey along the road to peace, Muhammad insisted that no vengeance be taken on the people of that city and named only a handful to be punished for special crimes. For most, punishment could be avoided by surrendering to Islam. Thus they were integrated into the *umma* and unity was established among the Arabs, no longer as separate, sometimes warring tribes, but now as Muslims.

In war, women fought, women commanded, and like Hind bint Utba and her bevy of cheerleaders, women supported the troops with song and verse. Throughout the world, women of all cultures have participated fully on the battlefield, as combatants, nurses, and encouragers, sometimes concurrently.

In the first centuries of Muslim expansion, lesser *jihads* were undertaken for conquest and subduing others in the name of Islam (and, as Christians have fought Christians, so have there been sad times when Muslims launched *jihads* against other Muslims). The lesser *jihad* has taken forms of resistance to aggression, including colonialism. But the Prophet denied Paradise to the "violent speaker" and said, "Faith is a restraint against violence, let no Muslim commit violence." The calls for peace and charity by prophets of every Abrahamic religion are invariably among the first things forgotten or interpreted to suit the politics of the moment.

Yet the majority of Muslims—like the majority of Jews and Christians—deplore extremism. In Islam, individual moral responsibility is stressed. The innocent may not be blamed or punished for the sins of others. Islam, like all other world religions, forbids suicide and those who commit it cannot be buried in consecrated ground or given a Muslim funeral prayer. There is no room for martyrdom in Islam by means of homicide, suicide, or the harming of innocent people.

"People who have been brought up on the Sermon on the Mount may find it rather disedifying that Muhammad did not turn

190

the other cheek," Armstrong writes in *Muhammad: A Biography of the Prophet.* "But in the Gospels, Jesus himself often cursed his enemies in good round terms. He prophesied a terrible fate for the towns of Bethsaid and Korozaim, which had not listened to his words, and in the Gospel of St. Matthew, he's said to have abused the Pharisees and Sadducees in a diatribe which was positively libelous....

"Instead of a pacifist religion that turns the other cheek, Islam fights tyranny and injustice."

The lesser *jihad* does not make Islam a violent religion. It is akin to the Christian and Zionist ideal of a "just war," that is, a religiously justifiable war. The lesser *jihad* is interpreted as war for the sake of establishing a Pax Islamica, an all-embracing peace.

"The Prophet embodies to an eminent degree this perfection of combative virtue," Nasr writes. "If one thinks of the Buddha as sitting in a state of contemplation under the Bo-tree, the Prophet can be imagined as a rider sitting on a steed with the sword of justice and discrimination in his hand and galloping at full speed, yet ready to come to an immediate halt before the mountain of Truth....His rest and repose was in the heart of the holy war itself and he represents this aspect of spirituality in which peace comes not in passivity but in true activity. Peace belongs to one who is inwardly at peace with the Will of Heaven and outwardly at war with the forces of disruption and disequilibrium."[1]

The so-called Sword of Islam is much-maligned, although the words "Forgive him who wrongs you; join him who cuts you off; do good to him who does evil to you and speak the truth although it be against yourself" were inscribed on the hilt of the Messenger's blade.

Echoing political leaders everywhere and always, Muhammad declared that all means should be undertaken to ensure his people were not subjugated by outsiders. "Islam," he said, "is the dominant force and not to be dominated." It must be recalled that Muhammad was both prophet and politician. His mission was about political and social as well as spiritual reform, for, it cannot be emphasized

191

enough, this world *and* the next were created by God. The Prophet's "constitution" for Medina is still praised as a model of modern democratic institutions.[2]

Islam respects the other Peoples of the Book, and wherever they conquered, Christians and Jews were *dhimma*, "the protected minority." The Qur'an reminds Muslims that

> *You will surely find that the nearest in affection to believers*
> *are those who say, "We are Christians."*[3]

The Muslim Empire expanded quickly, and—as usual with conquerors—Muslims were the privileged class wherever they landed. Others were nonetheless free to practice their own faiths, though in reality, this too often applied only to Christians and Jews. But the Qur'an clearly eschews forced conversions and although Muhammad's tolerance far exceeded many of those who followed him, the few forced conversions that took place were generally aberrations.

> *No compulsion is there in religion.*
> *Rectitude has become clear from error.*[4]

Indeed, as the empire grew, Jews and Christians became advisers to caliphs and generals. It was not unusual for Muslims and Christians to share places of worship, such as at St. John's Cathedral in Damascus: the Muslims on Friday, the Christians on Sunday. Islamic Spain enjoyed a hefty period of *convivencia*, the living together in near harmony of Jews, Christians, and Muslims. Jews held top positions in government as grand viziers to the sultan.

> *Surely they that believe,*
> *and those of Jewry, and the Christians, and those Sabaeans,*
> *whoso believes in God and the Last Day, and works*
> *righteousness—their wage awaits them with their Lord,*
> *and no fear shall be on them, neither shall they sorrow.*[5]

192

In Muhammad's view uncorrupted Judaism and Christianity were early manifestations of Islam. The first real wedge between Christianity and Islam came with the Crusades, when Western European Christians sought to capture the Holy Land from the Muslims beginning in 473 A.H./1095 C.E. In fact, it was, by and large, as Alfred Guillaume notes in *Islam*, a shameless, land-grabbing venture that lasted into the thirteenth century C.E. and was labeled a "just war" by its zealous advocates.

The word *crusade* was originally applied to European efforts to "free" the city of Jerusalem—holy to Jews, Christians, and Muslims—from the Seljuk Turks then in power. Pope Urban II, in a speech at Clermont in France, called for a great Christian expedition, whose ulterior motive was to unite Europe behind a single, centralized papacy. But *crusade* soon came to designate any military effort by Europeans against non-Christians, as well as dissident Christians. The First Crusade, marching east from France, became also an excuse to attack, in the name of Christianity, the Jewish communities of the Rhine.

Muslims in the Near and Middle East, in al-Andalus and along the Mediterranean were in the midst of one of many golden ages in arts and sciences. In Europe, meanwhile, savage, illiterate petty lords were preoccupied warring constantly with one another, while the peasantry starved and kept its head down. Europe's population was exploding and in need of space. Merchants were looking elsewhere to satisfy a greater demand for goods and to control trade routes and profits. What better way to accomplish this and to distract a despairing populace than to mobilize a righteous enterprise?[6]

Emperors and kings became enthused later on. Urban II's appeal at first drew mostly minor European nobility from French lands. Thus Westerners were all generally referred to by Muslims as Franks, galumphing toward Jerusalem, gathering thousands of men and women. The insignificant knights and their families, and the even less significant peasants and theirs, had no idea what to expect and no concept about Islam or Muslim life. Pilgrims to Jerusalem were not uncommon, but this was a "pilgrimage" of astounding proportions! Nonetheless, the Muslims ignored the hungry, ragtag

Christian masses, unable or unwilling to anticipate their effectiveness. The ruthless and destructive siege of Jerusalem ended in 477 A.H./1099 C.E. with a Christian victory, after many massacres of its Muslim and Jewish inhabitants. The crusaders eventually overcame the Muslim states and principalities of what are now Syria, Lebanon, and Israel, and thus Islam was disunited.

Meanwhile, throughout the crusading centuries, women on both sides fought or directed military campaigns. Armida of Damascus triumphantly defended her city against the First Crusade. Shajarat al-Durr of Egypt routed the army of Louis IX in the Seventh Crusade. And on the Christian side, Queen Melisande of Jerusalem in the twelfth century C.E. successfully attacked the Muslims controlling the expanses beyond the Jordan River.[7]

There is a third "exertion" in Islam, that of *ijtihad*, independent legal decision-making; the word is based on the same Arabic root as *jihad*. This is serious application, or striving, toward responsible understanding and administration of God's law, and among many Muslims today is sincerely undertaken to adapt, renew, revise, assimilate, and reform. As Denny writes, "the legal and theological discourses of Muslims, although they often have an enduring quality, are nonetheless open discourses in certain respects. That is, Muslims do not imagine that they have exhausted the possible meanings and applications of God's revelations and the Prophet's *Sunna*."[8]

Women throughout history have been fighters. And they have tended the wounded, and brought water and provisions amid the fiercest battles. Worldwide, they also went among the enemy, killing off the wounded. In his poem, *The Young British Soldier*, Rudyard Kipling, a spokesman for imperialism and the Raj, presented this as an act of barbarous cruelty:

> When you're wounded and left on Afghanistan's plains,
> And the women come out to cut up what remains,
> Jest roll to your rifle and blow out your brains
> An' go to your Gawd like a soldier.

All things considered in premodern warfare—no hospitals, no way to transport the wounded enemy, and not enough to feed him or nurses to spare—killing the severely wounded on the battlefield was often an act of mercy. Hind's bloodthirsty disemboweling of dead and wounded Muslims after the Battle of Uhud was repellent even to Meccans and their allies. When prisoners were taken, it was the Arab women who took charge of them. Aisha failed at this when she inadvertently allowed a prisoner to escape and in a temper, Muhammad cursed her hand.

The Turkish women of Scutari on the eastern shore of the Bosphorous Strait (where Florence Nightingale tended British troops during the Crimean War) are said to have carried the mutilated bodies of their loved ones through the battlefield to excite the combatants to vengeance.

Why women's voices are thought to invoke whatever magic is required to win battles is an archetypal mystery. Like the Greek Furies—Tisiphone, Megaera, and Alecto, the daughters of the Night—or the Irish Morrigna, the triple goddess of war and peace, women led the troops crying out for vengeance and fanning the flames of rage. As the Furies are merciless pursuers of justice, each army convinces itself that it, too, is engaged in a virtuous cause. Otherwise, it could not be easy to kill or to die. The penetrating cries of women have been ever emboldening, enjoining fighters to clash to the bitter end.

Pre-Christian Celtic women went to war and frequently trained young warriors. In battle, they charged first onto the field, screaming, howling, banging war clappers, and chanting verses. There have been women battle criers among Native Americans, north and south, and among Africans and Asians. Battlefield chants by women to spur the forces have survived as poems and songs, like these lyrics from a Central Asian melody:

> Better that a bullet find your heart
> than I hear news of your cowardice.
> My love is so brave,
> the other girls envy me.

It was customary for young women, *amriya*, to accompany the Murra Bedouin to war seated in camel litters above the fray. Women marched before the army singing to the accompaniment of tambourines. During battle, they sang and recited poetry and stopped those who were fleeing, urging them to return to the fray. This is the tradition that puts Hind and the other Meccan women at the Battle of Uhud, dancing, beating drums and tambourines, and chanting verses of encouragement:

> With horses hard by
> every long-bodied charger,
> let us attack Yathrib.

Like the Furies, Hind and her women exhorted death and punishment.

> We are the daughters of the Morning Star,
> our necks adorned with pearls,
> our hair perfumed with musk.
> Fight fiercely and we will crush you in our arms...

Such vocal appeals to men's pride, promises of favors for victory or threats to withhold them for cowardice or defeat, are perpetually successful.[9]

That women fought side by side with their men is further evidenced in an anonymous poem by an Afghan warrior:

> Give me two things,
> then let the British come.
> Give me a gun that won't jam
> and a girl to fight next to
> who will love.

One of the most revered persons in the history of Afghanistan is Malalai, about whom little else is known except that she carried the Afghans to victory over the British at the Battle of Maiwand in

1880. As the warriors retreated, Malalai leaped into action, shouting a *landey*, or couplet:

> Young love, if you do not fall in the battle of Maiwand,
> by God, someone is saving you as a token of shame.

The Afghans wheeled around and returned to the field behind the maiden, who used her veil as a standard. The most famous girls' school in Afghanistan was named for the legendary and eternal Malalai.[10]

The tradition of Arab Bedouin and North African Berber women warriors goes back millennia. They are familiar in the histories of the Assyrian king Sargon II, who ruled from 722 to 705 B.C.E., consolidating and expanding his empire from Mesopotamia to present-day eastern Turkey. Sargon II described the Bedouin as folk who "know not governors or overseers and have never brought tribute to a king." To prove him and his son Sennacherib right, Bedouin queens led troops against Assyria, battled for their tribes' autonomy and negotiated as tribal representatives.

The Greek geographer and historian Strabo (ca. 63 B.C.E. to 24 C.E.) encountered the "belligerent women of Libya (now including Morocco, Algeria and Tunis)...Amazons against whom Perseus waged war." They were, he said, "people of great courage," horsewomen 30,000 strong.

Helen Diner, drawing on the writers of antiquity in *Mothers and Amazons*, tells of women herders and warriors flourishing at the foot of the Atlas Mountains "clad in red leather armor, snakeskin shoes and with python-leather shields." They led camel raids on other tribes, chose their own husbands, spoke in council, and served as heads of encampments.

These are likely the Amazigh women, today called Berbers (probably from the Greek *barbaroi*, barbarians, a word used to describe almost any non-Greek). Around 60 A.H./682 C.E., the Amazigh Dhabba, queen of Carthage, drove Islamic Arabs from her city and, in order to leave nothing to successive Arab invaders, laid waste to her own country. Even after Islam established itself, these women were still notably liberated. In 1854, an Amazigh warrior, Lalla Fatima, led North Africans against the French invaders in the Berber Kabylia region of Algeria.

As late as the nineteenth century, armed, unveiled Muslim Albanian women were entrusted with truce and peace negotiations. The terms of peace treaties were often discussed between the women of hostile parties in the privacy of the women's quarters.[11]

In *The Underside of History*, Elise Boulding suggests that "all-women armies [may have] first organized in nomadic societies." She is rightly emphatic that nomadic life anywhere allows women far greater breadth of freedom than an agricultural or urban existence. "Everything she owns is piled on a couple of camels and she is the one who decides where the tents shall be erected when the camp is moved. She is interested in a politics which will preserve her freedom of movement and that of her children."

Hind bint Utba, though she was an urban woman, had no interest in sitting at home. No less militant after her conversion to Islam and the peace she made with Muhammad, after his death she joined the Muslims in their march to conquer Syria. It was from Damascus that her son Mu'awiya (called, not surprisingly, "the son of the liver eater") eventually ruled as caliph, though Hind did not live to see him reach those heights. Her daughter-in-law, the poet Maisuna, wrote with profound, poignant yearning for the old nomadic life.

The Umayyad Age—when Mu'awiya took the caliphate from Ali and his descendants in 39 A.H./661 C.E. and founded the first Arab Muslim dynasty—was one of military conquest, which completed Muslim control of the Mediterranean region. They penetrated India, crossed North Africa, eventually conquered Spain, and effectively met no opposition until they confronted the Franks under Charles Martel.

The Abbasid Dynasty—which defeated the Umayyads and ruled Islam from 128 A.H./750 C.E. to 636 A.H./1258 C.E., expanding the empire farther than ever—was an era of wealth and culture. With the development of the Muslim Empire came the standardization of behavior and the establishment of institutions—the organization of a military class, sedentary agricultural practices, schools and universities, and the seclusion of women. Women's open participation and influence in war, tribal headship, and political negotiations dwindled. Femininity and woman's "place" were redefined. Pre-Islamic Persian cultural influences are responsible for the introduction of harems and the suppression of women's leadership in Arabic society, but settlement and wealth also had a jeweled hand in quashing women's sovereignty. This did not mean, however, that women lost political clout. No society can survive, let alone flourish, without cooperation between men and women. But how women's influence and authority were manifested necessarily changed, for women were progressively suppressed, and restrictions on their movements grew tighter and tighter after Muhammad's death.

Muhammad had improved the lot of Arab women and for a brief time after he died, they enjoyed most of the privileges and some of the honor bestowed on them by the Qur'an and the Prophet's own example. The *umma* diversified as soon as outsiders arrived to embrace Islam. The changes in cultural outlook, however subtle, could only continue with time and the proliferation of the religion, even as Arabs considered themselves the elite among the believers. Under the Umayyad Dynasty, political and social ascendancy remained in the hands of a few Arab families from Mecca and Medina and discontent was therefore sure to follow. In shaping the Muslim community, Muhammad was creating a new, universal "tribe," whose values were based not on lineage or clan ethics, but on the principles of Islam. Islam also meant that accountability rested on individuals and *not* the tribe.

In the formative years, we hear of women combatants like Umm Omara, Umm Salim, and Nisiba bint Ka'ab. Muhammad's paternal aunt, Safiyya (sister of Hamza), is noted for killing a spy with a tent peg while her terrified male guard cringed nearby. His sister-in-law Asmaa bint Abu Bakr always fought side by side with her husband on horseback. After the Prophet's death, historians document Umm Hakim, who disposed of seven Byzantine soldiers single-handedly at the Battle of Marj al-Saffar. Entire battalions of women are also recorded as having participated in the fighting.

At the battles of Qadisiya, Maisan, Damascus, and Yarmuk, as the Muslim Empire drove on, the women of Quraysh are said to have flung forward with swords flashing in the battle until they were ahead of their men. Umm Aban avenged her husband's death with his own bow and arrow. She dispatched many a non-Muslim, including her husband's killer, the governor of Damascus. Following Fatima's death, the fourth Rightly Guided caliph Ali was married several more times, and among his wives was the renowned woman warrior Khawlah bint al-Kindiyya.

Aisha was, as we've seen, politically active and led a resistance against Ali. She visited mosques to rally thousands to her cause. In a counterspeech, Ali's son Hassan said, "She is the wife of the Prophet in this life and the hereafter. But it is a test from God to know whether you will obey Him or her."

It is said she was the only woman at the Battle of the Camel, where her troops were defeated by Ali, but this seems doubtful. Although the wheels of repression had already begun turning, especially with the second Rightly Guided caliph Umar, women may well have still been on the battlefield. Aisha as the only female presence makes a more powerful telling, and speaks of how biographers were beginning to draw the curtain around women's less "modest" activities.

In the mid-seventh century C.E., a dissident Arab political movement among the Kharawrij had women in its ranks, who according to the histories of the time, "won renown for their prowess in battle, among them Ghazala, who defeated [the Iraqi tyrant] al-Hajjaj in a duel." Orthodox leaders later objected to Kharawrij women's participation in battle—"naked and exposed"—and thus they were forced to withdraw from the field.

The Kharijites—Kharawrij, or "the leavers"—are the earliest Muslim sect, who originally believed that God decreed Ali's caliphate. It seems plausible that their women warriors were on the field battling Aisha's anti-Ali contingent.[12] The Kharawrij later turned against the party of Ali, and indeed one of their members was his assassin.

In *The Forgotten Queens of Islam*, Mernissi reports on Ghaliyya al-Wahhabiyya, "a Hanbali from Tarba near Ta'if, who led a military resistance movement in Saudi Arabia to defend Mecca against foreign takeover at the beginning of the eighteenth century. She was given the title of *amira, amir* being the title of the leader of armies....Her boldness and strategic ability led her enemies on the battlefield to credit her with the magic gift of making the Wahhabi forces invisible. Historians noted her appearance at the head of the Bedouin army as a memorable event."

It was primarily through the stories in *The Thousand and One Nights*, or *Arabian Nights*, that Westerners became acquainted with the women of Islam—sadly, as we'll see, through highly warped translations. The tales often present women as coquettish, sensuous, wily, amoral simperers and schemers or as nasty old hags. Only a few female protagonists, such as the Princess Arbiza (whose origins are probably Persian) and the Princess ad-Datma, qualify as warriors. Male and female caricatures in the *Arabian Nights* are simultaneously appalling, loveable, entertaining, delightful, and stereotypically offensive, like formulaic characters in any fiction or folklore. Unfortunately, Westerners have not been offered other sorts of widespread literature, properly credited, from Islamic cultures beyond *The Thousand and One Nights*.

These include ubiquitous tales featuring warrior women trained in the chivalrous art of combat. The popular literature still enjoyed today in Muslim countries is full of clever, armored, sword-slashing, arrow-shooting, acrobatic women who more often than not best their men (and if it comes to it, there's nothing like baring a breast to toss a fellow completely off his guard). Hundreds of warrior women appear in *sira* literature—Arabic popular romance—and in folk epics throughout the Islamic world. Tales of ancient Turks positively abound with high-spirited young women, as well as older women who broach no guff.

These and other magnificent stories feature battling maidens who will not marry any man unable to defeat them, or young brides who, having hidden their talents for the sake of their husbands' egos, must unmask in order to save the day (and the hero). John Renard, in *Islam and the Heroic Image*, notes that in Bedouin narratives "the

heroines usually exhibit courage in battle equal to their male counterparts....they possess in addition a measure of wisdom that bal-
ances the male tendency to swift and sometimes precipitous action."

In Persian poetic romances there is the frequent motif of a local
hero being challenged to battle by a foreign princess, whom he marries. Some scholars believe that these tales may have symbolized the
formation of new political and cultural alliances as the Muslim
Empire grew.

Little more than a hundred years after ferocious female combatants such as Umm Omara and Khawlah bint al-Kindiyya fought
for the faith, it was suggested to Zubaydah, favorite wife of the
Abbasid caliph Harun al-Rashid, that she should avenge her son
Amin's death as Aisha had avenged the murder of Uthman.
Zubaydah demurred: "What have women to do with avenging blood
and taking the field against warriors?" she asked.

Yet just two generations before, in 145 A.H./762 C.E., Zubaydah's
great aunt, Princess Asma, sister of the Abbasid caliph al-Mansur,
helped defeat a rebellion at Medina by unfurling the Abbasid standard
from the tall minaret, where the enemy awaited Mansur's forces. They
therefore concluded that the Abbasids had made an effective entry
into the city and were further demoralized by the princess's well-
placed "criers of flight." They deserted in droves. Princess Asma was
apparently not an armed woman, but she led the victory.

During the Persian Safavid Dynasty (879 A.H./1501 C.E. to 1100
A.H./1722 C.E.), Khayr al-Nisa Begam, the Iranian spouse of Shah
Muhammad Khudabanda, ruled the state for about seventeen
months when the shah, disabled by an eye illness, withdrew to his
religious preoccupations. Despite the deep repression of women by
the Safavids, Khayr al-Nisa Begam actually commanded its royal
army in war. During the campaign against the Ottomans in the winter of 956–57 A.H./1578–79 C.E., she was present at the war council
of the Qizilbash amirs. There are, throughout Islamic history, a
goodly number of such women, who carried on for their kingly husbands, even making military decisions.

The Egyptian sultana Shajarat al-Durr and Radiyya, an Indo-
Muslim queen of the thirteenth century C.E., named by her father as

his successor, were members of the Mamluks, slaves trained as an elite military class, who gradually supplanted their masters. The Mamluks fought on land and sea, repelled the Mongols, and defended Islam head-on for generations against the crusaders. They were the mainstay of Islam's military might. Without them, the expansion of the Muslim Empire would have been much restricted. The Mamluk institution lasted a thousand years, from the first half of the ninth century C.E. to the first half of the nineteenth.

The Mamluks were purchased as infidel children precisely to be trained for military service. Perhaps because they originated on rough steppes and wild lands, where to be tough was to survive, where boldness and bravery were not restricted to gender, the Mamluks seemed to be somewhat more amenable to female power than were the caliphs, imams, and sultans to whom they were bound.

A kind of female Mamluk watched over the Indo-Muslim *zenana*, the women's quarters of rulers and other members of the ruling elite. These women, frequently recruited from Ethiopia and Central Asia, were called *urdubegi* and served as personal attendants and bodyguards to ensure the safety of the *zenana* and as enforcers. For centuries in India, they were used to escort *zenana* women when they left their quarters, whether to accompany their menfolk on military campaigns or go on pilgrimage, or take pleasure jaunts or to hunt, play polo, and visit gardens.

The historian Khwaja Nizam al-Din Ahmad recorded Indo-Muslim Sultan Ghiyath Shah (873 A.H./1469 C.E. to 906 A.H./1500 C.E.) as having 500 Abyssinian slave women and another 500 Turki women all highly trained, uniformed, carrying swords, shields, bows and arrows, mounted on horses, and watching over the *zenana*, which included not just the shah's wives and concubines, but a giant retinue of extended family, aunts, sisters, cousins, in-laws, and all their children. The *urdubegis* are also documented as having accompanied the women of the courts of the Mughal emperors Babur (861 A.H./1483 C.E. to 908 A.H./1530 C.E.) and Humayun (886 A.H./1508 C.E. to 934 A.H./1556 C.E.).

The *urdubegis* divided into battalions, each with its own name and commissioned and noncommissioned officers. There are hundreds of Indian drawings and paintings dating before the nineteenth century illustrating these women. Some went unveiled or partially veiled and some wore modified women's dress, perhaps to avoid the kind of criticism leveled against the sultana Radiyya who wore men's clothing as a strategy to hold authority over her disdainful male courtiers, advisers, and generals. Indeed, Radiyya's staunchest supporters were the Turkish Mamluks, who were not only loyal to her Mamluk father, but who evidently saw nothing wrong with a woman as head of state, since she was the best choice.

Neither were the *urdubegis* necessarily confined to guarding the *zenana*. Some were palanquin bearers, a job requiring immense physical strength. They also protected the person of the ruler. According to William Knighton, an English traveler writing about Lucknow in the early nineteenth century, "The head [of the *urdubegis*], a great masculine woman, of pleasing countenance, was a special favorite of the king. The *badinage* which was exchanged between them was of the freest character—not fit for polite ears, of course; but the extraordinary point of it was, that no one hearing it, or witnessing such a scene, could have supposed it possible that a king and a slave stood before him as the two tongue-combatants."[13]

In nineteenth-century England, where women were bustled, buckled, trussed, laced, and crinolined, the very concept of armed women was anathema. In India, Knighton was further astonished to see

> men, like women, pacing up and down before the various entrances to the female apartments for many days before I was informed of their real character. I regarded them simply as a diminutive race of soldiers, with well-wadded coats....These women retained their long hair, which they tied up in a knot upon the top of the head and there it was concealed by the usual shako. They bore the ordinary accoutrements of sepoys (soldiers) in India—a musket and bayonet, cross-belts and cartridge-boxes, jackets

and white duck continuations, which might be seen anywhere in Bengal....They were drilled by one of the native
officers of the king's army, and appeared quite familiar
with marching and wheeling, with presenting, loading
and firing muskets, with the fixing and unfixing of bayo-
nets—in fact with all the ordinary detail of the barrack-
yard. Whether they could have gone through the same
maneouvres in the field with thousands of moustachioed
sepoys around them, I cannot tell—probably not.[14]

Knighton's speculation that the *urdubegis* he saw could not
compete on the battlefield is contradicted by an 1815 English
account which relates that the reigning Nizam Ali of Hyderabad had

two battalions of female Sepoys of one thousand each,
which mounted guard in the interior of the palace and
accompanied the ladies of his family whenever they
moved. They were with the Nizam during the war with
the Mahrattas in 1795, and were present at the Battle of
Kurdlah, where, at least, they did not behave worse than
the rest of the army. One of these battalions was commanded by Mama Burrun and the other by Mama
Chumbebee....They carry musquets....They are called
Zuffer Putuns, the victorious battalions, and the women
composing them *Gardunees*....Their pay is five rupees a
month.[15]

Many *urdubegis* were married and apparently took several
months off a year to attend to domestic duties, but returned to their
ranks and stayed as long as age and circumstances allowed.

In December 1600, Queen Elizabeth I signed a charter titled
"The Governor and Company of Merchants of London Trading into
the East Indies." The East India Company was granted a monopoly
of trade in the East Indies, with the formal restriction that it might
not contest the prior trading rights of "any Christian prince." Soon
after, the first trading posts were established in what would become

Madras and Bombay. In 1689, with the establishment of administrative districts called presidencies in Bengal, Madras, and Bombay, the company began what was to be more than 200 years of British domination of India.

More than one woman—Muslim and Hindu—resisted the foreign rule. In the late eighteenth and early nineteenth centuries, Begam Somru commanded a mercenary army of Indians and Europeans, who first fought the British, then joined them. In the late nineteenth century, the British, attempting to take Lucknow, faced another woman, Hazrat Mahal, Muslim queen regent of Oudh, who commanded an army of women. The East India Company's John Low called her "one of those tigress women, more virile than their husbands, who when finding themselves in a position to gratify their lust for power, have played a considerable part in Oriental history."[16]

Women have been spies, scouts, and couriers. They have been bandits and pirates such as al-Sayyida al-Hurra, an honorific meaning "the free lady." Her name was actually Aisha bint Ali ibn Rashid and in the sixteenth century, she was governor of the city of Tetouán, an agricultural center in northern Morocco, near Tangier. Of Andalusian origin, al-Sayyida al-Hurra's noble family had returned to North Africa fleeing the Inquisition after the fall of Granada.

"She found no better way to ease the humiliation of defeat than to launch into piracy," Mernissi writes. "Conducting expeditions against the Spaniards became the obsession of the bravest among [the Muslim refugees] and piracy was the ideal solution. It allowed the expelled to obtain quick revenues (booty and ransom for captives) and at the same time to continue to fight the Christian enemy."[17]

Under the leadership of al-Sayyida al-Hurra's husband, the Andalusians rebuilt the ramparts of Tetouán, constructed their dwellings, and erected the Great Mosque, then launched a holy war against the Portuguese.

Al-Sayyida al-Hurra received the title "al-Hurra, that is, a woman exercising sovereign power...upon the death of her husband....She then made contact with the Ottoman pirate Barbarossa, assembled a fleet and launched into privateering in the Mediterranean."[18]

206

Liat Kozma, in a working paper titled "Writing Women into Moroccan National History: The Case of al-Sayyida al-Hurra," speaks to al-Sayyida al-Hurra's role as a "feminist model in the re-writing of history, first by feminist political activists, later by academic writers and then, as incorporated into an official narrative of history."

Kozma notes that the story of al-Sayyida al-Hurra was and is cut at various angles to justify political and social orders: before the advent of feminism in Morocco—when she has mostly reemerged as a heroine—historians ignored her or "talked about her…in terms of asceticism, as a noble saint and sometimes she was intermingled in popular memory with a violent and frightening evil spirit Aisha Kandisha."[19] The ferocious life of piracy, particularly for a woman, has always inspired fearsome and wondrous tales.

Wild legends follow all warriors, perhaps especially women. In 1854, according to Lucy M. Garnett, "there passed through Constantinople on their way to the seat of war a band of Kurdish cavalry led by a woman named Kara ('Black') Fatmé Hanum." She was renowned for her formidable and heroic deeds. But, "save for the dauntless fire which blazed in her eyes there was, however, nothing Amazonian in the aspect of this female warrior, who is described as having been a little shriveled up old woman."[20]

Kurdish women, Garnett reported, were "treated as equals by the men, who are most affectionate in their relations with their parents, sisters, and children, and in the character of husbands most considerate, kind, and forbearing…. a girl of the Bulbassi tribe had killed with a spear a Turk who insulted her. This young Amazon was dressed like a man, and served the chief…as his faithful henchman, accompanying him on all his expeditions. The women of this tribe are particularly hardy and intrepid. They sometimes take to the road as brigands, and unlucky is the trader or traveler who falls into their hands."[21]

There are scanty records of sportswomen (or female adventurers) in any era or culture before the twentieth century. In the Muslim and Hindu paintings of India, we find scenes of women riding horseback and elephantback. Indian paintings show women straddling their mounts. In the West, "lady-like" women rode sidesaddle—a terrific accomplishment, much more dangerous and imprudent than riding astride. Journeying on horseback, the Indian women are illustrated as veiled, but in miniatures where women are shown hunting tigers and lions or playing polo or going to war, they are sensibly free of headgear. To restrict her vision would be foolhardy for a sporting or fighting woman.

Gul-Badan Begam was a sixteenth-century Mughal princess, whose memoir, *The History of Humayun*, bears witness to the reigns of her father the emperor Babur, her brother Humayun, and her nephew Akbar. In her book, she mentions two remarkable athletes, Mihr-Angiz Begam and Shad Begam. They were fast friends who wore men's clothes and were "adorned by varied accomplishments, such as the making of thumb-rings and arrows, playing polo and shooting with the bow and arrow." A thumb-ring was worn on the right hand to protect against the fret of the bowstring in drawing and release. Some of these were magnificent, made of gold or carved from whole gemstones. Creating them was a gentle art of the day. The inseparable princesses also played a variety of musical instruments together.

Here and there, we find daughters reared as their doting fathers might have wished to rear sons. Aside from the lovely natural closeness that fathers and daughters often enjoy, paternal intimacy was "safe," for girls were not going to compete for succession, and therefore favoritism carried no political weight.

The Abbasid caliph al-Mahdi, as we'll see, loved his daughter, Banuqah, above all his children. He took her on hunting expeditions, military excursions, and jaunts throughout the empire, and had her disguised as a page to avoid scandal. She was dressed in turban and trousers, carried a sword, which she presumably knew how to use, and learned to shoot a bow.

When Banuqah died, al-Mahdi sank into inconsolable grief, and in an unheard of gesture by bereaved fathers for their daughters, appeared in public to receive condolences from his people.

Umm Omara

Nusayba bint Ka'b, or Umm Omara, was one of numerous early Muslim women who fought with the Prophet Muhammad against the Meccans, as well as in subsequent conflicts. She is said to have been married three times and had children from each marriage. Little is known about her and her dates are unknown, but the stories of her contributions in battle are oft-repeated and she is held in the highest regard for the active part she played.

The defeat at Badr is a disgrace the Quraysh cannot bear. "Revenge" is cried day and night in the streets and marketplace of Mecca, and in every home vengeance is plotted. The loudest voice is Hind bint Utba's, for she has lost her father, her brother, and her sons.

Her husband Abu Sufyan forbids lamenting. Lamentation exorcises anger and replaces it with quiet grief. Anger fuels aggression.

Abu Safyan sends poets into the tribes to foment their fighting spirits for the battle against the Believers. Abu Azza goes into the low country and calls on the Banu Kinana:

Listen, sons of Abu Manat, the steadfast.
You are stout warriors like your father.
Do not promise me your help a year from now.
Do not betray me.

Musafi goes to the sons of Malik and stirs them against the Messenger:

O Malik, foremost in honor,
I ask in the name of kindred and confederate,
those who are next-of-kin and those who are not,
in the name of the alliance in the midst of the holy city,
at the wall of the venerable Ka'aba.

By the turn of the year, the Meccan army swells to 3000 men and women, ready to march on Medina.

A scouting party rides to the top of a hillock below Mount Uhud. Quickly, before they're spotted, the Muslims scurry down again. They dismount and climb stealthily back up the hill to peer below. Thousands of Meccans are encamped in the gully. Lying on their bellies, looking around rocks and dry shrubs, the scouts follow the enemy army's every move, sending reports back to the Prophet, step by step.

"I have had a dream," Muhammad tells the men and women assembled to plan their defensive. "I implore Allah that this is a dream of bounty, for I dreamed that cows were slaughtered and that there was a groove in the point of my sword and that I had inserted my hand into an immune armor."

Umm Omara is known for her skill in interpreting dreams. She is a healer and dreams inspire cure. The assembly turns to her. She nods and looks to the Prophet for assurance. His eyes give it.

"The slaughter of the cows," she says, "surely means that some of us will be killed.

"That there is a groove in the point of the Messenger's sword means that a member of his own household will be hurt.

"The armor," Umm Omara concludes, "is Medina. Unharmed."

There is a collective sigh and the assembly turns back to debate the merits of staying within Medina's walls or emerging to meet the enemy face to face.

"It is time to fight," they tell the reluctant Prophet. "Our 300 defeated their 3000 at Badr. Now we must go out and fight them lest they think we've lost heart and don't dare encounter them, lest they think God has deserted us."

Hamza ibn Abd al-Muttalib is at the forefront of the argument. "By Allah," he tells his nephew, "I will not taste food until I fight them with my sword outside Medina."

And so it's agreed.

And so the battle is joined.

Umm Omara comes to the field with a skin of water and a bag of herbs and salves. There is a sword at her waist, which is thick with many girdles she wears to tear for bandages.

Hind bint Utba leads the other wives of Quraysh chieftains. Umm Omara recognizes Umm Hakim and Fatima bint al-Walid, Bazra bint Mas'ud, Rayta bint Munabbih, and the freedwoman Umm Anmar, the female circumcisor of Mecca. There are more, all trilling and cheering, some brandishing swords, others aiming arrows, still others beating tambourines.

Hind rides ahead screaming:

On, sons of Abdul-Dar.
On, protectors of Mecca!
On, sentries of the sanctity of al-Lat, Uzzat, al-Manat
Smite with every sharpened spear!
Brandish every sword across a Muslim throat!

The battle begins slowly enough, but it is soon so hot the dust storms made by warriors' feet and horses' hooves nearly blind the Believers as well as their enemy. Salaym bint Malhaud fights with swords and daggers around her pregnant belly. Asmaa bint Abu Bakr rides her husband Zuabyr's one mare, straight into the hoards, lopping heads.

Umm Omara rushes to each wounded Believer she sees and drags him as far off the field as she can over bodies and around the clashing weapons. Her own son, Omara, staggers toward her, a gash in his left hand spitting blood everywhere. He has tried to fight on, but the Prophet has sent him to his mother and looks on while Umm Omara rips at her waist wrapper and swaddles the hand.

"Now get up, my son," she tells him, tying off the cloth. "Go back and fight."

Her son obeys and bounds away.

"Who could bear your burdens, Umm Omara?" the Prophet says and moves back into the fray.

The battle seems to be going in favor of the Muslims, but Umm Omara is too busy to assess anything except the wounds she is washing and binding or the eyes she is closing. Now a man, tall as a palm tree, rushes by. Umm Omara pulls the sword from her girdle and cuts him on the thigh. The man who struck her son falls hard and heavy on the ground. The Prophet is watching from a few feet away. He smiles so broadly the back of his teeth gleam.

"You have taken your revenge, Umm Omara!" he shouts and laughs.

Someone yells that the fight is over, that Muhammad has won, and now there is a swarm for plunder and the Muslim archers have charged up the hill to high ground. The Prophet calls them back, but they will not hear or obey.

Meccans charge toward Muhammad. Umm Omara leaves her tasks and leaps to his side, thrusting this way, parrying that way into this chest, across that neck. She takes her first wound and then her second. She takes another and another and another until she is nearly swooning, fighting on though there are fourteen cuts upon her body and some so deep the bone shows.

"Your mother! Your mother!" the Prophet calls to Omara. "See to her wounds! She has fought better than any man today!"

A rock smacks the Prophet's mouth and two teeth are dislodged; the blood runs down his chin.

Omara backs toward the Prophet and his mother holding a gash in her shoulder. He moves cautiously, clashing swords with one Meccan after another as he makes his way. Umm Omara is nearly blinded by her own blood, though she, too, tries to fight on. She is nearly blinded, but looks up in time to see a Quraysh attack Omara from behind. She swoons and someone catches her and takes her into a grove, where she is laid out and where she bites her tongue so as not to scream in grief.

Sitting next to her is Sulafa. Her two sons wounded by Asim have laid their heads in her lap to die.

"Who has hurt you, my son?" Sulafa sighs to each and swears an oath that if God ever lets her have the head of Asim, she will drink wine from it.

Mus'ab bint Umayr remains to defend the Prophet. Ibn Qami'a takes all his courage in hand and charges full into Mus'ab. Mus'ab falls and ibn Qami'a runs to the Quraysh, breathless, excited, saying, "I have killed Muhammad! I have killed Muhammad ibn Abdallah!"

The Prophet gives the standard Mus'ab has dropped to Ali ibn Abu Talib and is carried from the field, dizzy and covering his mouth to stop the flow.

In the grove, he is seated beside Umm Omara, who lies bleeding. Fatima has stuffed Umm Omara's own bandages into the wound in her shoulder. Ali has given the standard to another and comes with water in his shield. Someone arrives bearing Omara, but his mother is drifting into the shades of pain and does not see him.

"Bring him here," the Prophet says softly, and stretches his feet as a pillow for Omara's head. And Omara dies with his head on Muhammad's thronged sandals, the shoes that have touched the throne of Heaven.

The Quraysh are victorious. Hind and the Meccan women dance off the field mutilating corpses. Hind chews Hamza's liver, then spits it out. She mounts a high rock, her ankles and wrists and waist and throat dangling with entrails. She screams into the air and her taunts weave with the calls of scavenging birds:

> We have paid you back for Badr,
> and a war that follows a war is always violent.
> I could not bear the loss of Utba,
> nor my brother nor my sons.
> I have slaked my vengeance and fulfilled my vow.

A woman's voice calls back across the quiet, gory fields:

> You were disgraced at Badr and after Badr,
> O daughter of a despicable man.

God brought on you in the early dawn,
tall and white-skinned men from Hashim,
everyone slashing with his sharp sword:
Hamza my lion and Ali my falcon.
Your evil vow was the worst of vows.

And Hind replies across the fetid air:

I have devoured my enemy's liver.
I have devoured his strength!

The Muslims carry their dead and wounded back to Medina.
They bury the dead and care for the wounded. The Messenger of
God hears that Umm Omara is mended again, though her heart will
always be scarred. But hers was not the only calamity at Uhud, and
her son, like so many others, was honored with martyrdom.

The Messenger smiles upon Umm Omara. Whenever he sees
her, he tells all nearby: "At the Battle of Uhud, wherever I turned to
the left or the right, I saw her fighting for me."

In Abu Bakr's time, when the First Caliph must fight Musaylima
the False Prophet in Yamamah—he who claimed the archangel
Jibril had come to call him to be a prophet to all the countries on the
Earth—Umm Omara takes up arms again. She receives eleven
wounds and loses her hand. The days of sword and bow are over for
Umm Omara, but she heals the wounded, midwives the babies,
cures the sick until she meets again the Messenger of God—this
time in Paradise.

Khawlah bint al-Azwar al-Kindiyyah

Although the biography of the Prophet signals the earliest historical writing produced in Arabia, not much is known about its heroes on the battlefield. Like many women, Khawlah bint al-Azwar al-Kindiyyah is found in the lists of fighters on the side of Islam, but with few details of her life. She married Ali ibn Abu Talib, shortly after he became the fourth Rightly Guided caliph in 34 A.H./656 C.E. She was a Bedouin and probably trained as a warrior from a very early age. Khawlah's dates are unknown.

Heraclius the Byzantine has gathered a huge army. The emperor's troops are Greek and Syrian, Mesopotamian and Armenian. There are 200,000 amassed against the Muslims led by Khalid ibn al-Walid at the river al-Yarmuk on the Syrian front.

The fighting is terrible. The Greeks have chained themselves together so that none can flee.

From the rear, Hind bint Utba waves a sword and shouts, "Cut off the arms of these uncircumcised!" But the battle seems nearly lost.

The Muslims drop back. Panic quivers through their ranks. More and more withdraw. Out of nowhere a tall, imposing knight, enveloped all in black, with gleaming gray eyes, gallops into the fray, sword flying. Heads roll. The Muslims stop their retreat in awe at the

215

reckless courage of this Arab warrior, penetrating the lines of the Byzantines, rushing right into their center.

Three horsemen charge in behind the knight. One of them has slashed the head of a Greek and holds it high. Inspired, the Muslims turn to fight again. As one body, they raise their swords and follow the black knight into the smoky battle and soon the Byzantines have fallen or run away.

Khalid cocks his head in wonder. Who is this wild and mysterious warrior who's won the day? When the battle ends, he canters up to the black knight. The knight's captains close in like a shield.

"We are grateful to you," Khalid says. "But who are you?"

The black knight's gray eyes meet Khalid's, then drop. A thin hand rises and unwraps the cloak that encircles the face.

"I am Khawlah bint al-Azwar al-Kindiyya, sister of Dirar ibn al-Azwar and descendant of Arab kings. I only avoided you out of modesty, for I am a woman of rank and honor. I came to you with the Arab women to strengthen you in your fight."

One by one, the captains reveal their faces: Alfra, Oserrah, and Wafeira, whose fingers are stained with the blood of the headless Greek.

Ali ibn Abu Talib has moved his headquarters from Medina to Kufa. The skilled and fearless fighter 's hair and beard are white. The Commander of the Believers is stocky and, though Kufa's wealth is plentiful, he wears the simple clothing of a warrior. He marries the Bedouin battle-queen, Khawlah. It is said she is more ferocious than the rain cloud over the Yemen. She will not live in Ali's household, but resides with Oserrah, her boon companion. Ali watches, absorbed by admiration, as daily his wife and her captains practice at swords and spears and riding. At every battle, Khawlah, Oserrah, Alfra, and Wafeira storm into the enemy's ranks at the head of the Muslim troops.

Khawlah and her captains ride to Subhara near Damascus and there engage in battle. This time, it does not go well. They are captured, taken by surprise, like sheep. Their weapons are confiscated. They are confined to their tents, while the Byzantine troops taunt them with abuse and insulting language, with threats to their honor, for the Greek women are restricted from birth to death within their homes and only allowed to go out covered from head to toe as if they wore tents instead of only living in them as Bedouins do.

"Do you accept the Byzantines as your masters?" Khawlah whispers to her captains. "Are you willing for your children to be the slaves of the Byzantines?"

The women shudder and move in closer to hear Khawlah.

"There's nothing we can do," they hiss. "We have no swords or spears, we have no mounts."

Khawlah clicks her tongue. "Where is the famed courage which has become the talk of the Arab tribes? Where have you left the skill that is renowned in the cities?"

Afra nods. "You speak the truth, Khawlah. We are as courageous and as skilled as they say. But in these cases, a sword is useful…"

"Women!" Khawlah growls. "How did we train when we were girls, and what did we use?"

"The pegs," Oserrah gasps, and the women one by one move cautiously to the tent walls.

Slowly, they back into one another, forming a circle, and slowly they emerge.

Wafeira ululates the attack.

They kill their captors, one and all.

They leap to horses and ride to join the *umma*.

Shajarat al-Durr

Shajarat al-Durr's name means "Pearl Tree" or "Spray of Pearls." A Mamluk of Armenian descent, she married the last Egyptian Ayyubid ruler, al-Malik al-Salih Ayub, who died in 627 A.H./1249 C.E., shortly after the Seventh Crusade. A Syrian historian observed that she was "the most cunning woman of her age, unmatched in beauty among women and in determination among men." Shajarat al-Durr died in 635 A.H./1257 C.E. Her brief reign signaled the beginning of the Mamluk Dynasty in Egypt.

The woman is like a tree of pearls. She is a slave of Abbasid caliph Mustasim, who sends her as a gift to Sultan al-Salih Ayub of Egypt. The moment Ayub lays his rheumy old eyes on her he falls in love and never falters. He is aged and ill, she is young and the energy sparks through her bones right to the very ends of her mahogany curls. He coughs and chokes, and sometimes blood runs from his nostrils and mouth. There are days he cannot visit her, but lies in his bed longing for her, while the physicians mutter over him, days when the tuberculosis is upon him, scurrying through his chest like rats.

Shajarat al-Durr defies all convention and moves into his chambers to nurse him. A sultan need not be ashamed—of his age, of his illness—for he is sultan. She nurses him with a devotion that surprises the courtiers. Does she truly love this ancient, ailing man?

She gives birth to a son. The baby dies.

They are in Syria. How they got there is a tale of logistical complexities, but here they are and word has come that Louis IX, king of France—someday to be called a saint—is leading his crusaders to invade Egypt. The sultan collects his army and again they travel. It is April when they reach Mansura in the Nile Delta. In June Louis lands in Damietta and takes the northern town in a day.

Sultan Ayub's lungs are rotting. What is left of them rise from his chest into his throat. He coughs up tissue and blood. Shajarat al-Durr holds him as he dies in their tent at Mansura. Louis advances from Damietta.

The woman who is like a tree of pearls assumes command. She tells no one her beloved sultan lies dead in his bed. She sends for Turanshah, Ayub's son, forging the sultan's signature. Messengers are dispatched, but it will be months before Turanshah can reach Mansura. The sultan's officers come, one by one, in a constant stream to report on Louis's approach and each is met with orders in writing, signed by the sultan.

Shajarat al-Durr, alone in the tent with her dead husband, listens from behind a curtain to each officer's report. She shapes a strategy from each account of Louis's progress and the sultan's armies.

Does she have the sultan's decomposing body wrapped daily in perfumed cloths by slaves sworn to secrecy? Does she have a grave dug in the ground under the tent, covered with plush carpets? Certainly this is the case, for she must conceal her husband's death, and the stench would surely unveil her secret.

Louis's Franks are camped opposite the Muslim army, with only the channel of the Bahr al-Saghir separating them. Shajarat al-Durr knows the enemy will not be able to cross here. But within a month, Louis's scouts find a ford at Salamun. It is night when his army begins to cross. But the ford is deep and the banks are slippery. Only Louis's advance guard can make it to the other side and they charge the Muslim camp, taking them by surprise.

Shajarat al-Durr calls on her own guard, the Bahri Mamluks, those she knows to be fearless, for they are her own people. They exterminate the crusaders' advance guard; they meet the Franks full-on. In the weeks that follow, Louis's troops are confronted with hunger and dysentery. Shajarat al-Durr signs the order in the sultan's name: the Muslims pursue the Franks as they withdraw, bellies aching, guts liquid. The Franks surrender. King Louis IX of France is captured. Perhaps it is Shajarat al-Durr who suggests a ransom of a million gold dinars. Until it arrives, the Muslims care for the sick and wounded crusaders.

At last Turanshah appears at the camp in Mansura. At last Shajarat al-Durr admits that Sultan Ayub has been dead for months. There is no successor but Turanshah, yet Ayub had refused to name him, and now his reluctance is proved justified. Turanshah has no more sense than a bag of offal. He has brought his profligate play-mates from Syria and now he gives them military ranks senior to the veteran commanders of the army. Each night he and his companions indulge in drunken revels. Shajarat al-Durr has kept the throne for him, despite his father's unwillingness. Yet Turanshah quarrels with her. She warns him that his behavior will be his undoing. He reminds her she is merely a woman, a former slave, what would she know?

Turanshah rests in his tent when the Mamluk Baybars enters and runs the young sultan through with his sword. Turanshah screams for help, crying out that a Bahri Mamluk has tried to kill him. Before anyone can rescue the young sultan, the Mamluk troops advance on his tent. Turanshah, wounded, runs to the river and wades into the water. The Mamluks follow, surround him, and skewer him like a goat.

Shajarat al-Durr takes her seat again, the shadow sultana. Resources are too low to continue supporting the crusader prisoners and the Mamluks demand their death. In Damietta, Louis's wife Margaret and the Knights Templar struggle to gather the ransom money. When at last it is paid, Louis IX and the remnants of his army set sail from Damietta to Acre. The Seventh Crusade has been a dis-aster. Louis returns home to a life of penance. Never again will he wear fine clothes or indulge in wines and fancy foods. The failure of his crusade was God's way of teaching him humility, he says, but someday he will lead an army east again, for God wants him to fight the devil's Saracens. But God moves in mysterious ways. Louis is fifty-six years old when he embarks on another crusade and dies in Tunis.

The Mamluks proclaim Shajarat al-Durr queen of Egypt. Her courage has shown her worthy of rule. The people swear the oath of allegiance to her and she carries on the business of government. Her name is spoken in the Friday prayers like that of any sultan. Coins are minted bearing her title.

Caliph Mustasim remembers the slave girl, exquisite as pearls, whom he gave as a present to Ayub. He is outraged that she has become ruler. He writes to Cairo: "The Prophet said, 'Unhappy is the nation governed by a woman'—if you have no men, I will send you one."

The caliph's disposition must be taken seriously, for though he has little military power, he is esteemed, God's anointed. Shajarat al-Durr and the Mamluks confer. She will marry Mamluk Amir Aybak. But Shajarat al-Durr insists he must divorce his first wife with whom he has a son, Ali. He may then be declared sultan. He, and not Shajarat al-Durr, queen of Egypt, will now be supreme commander of the armed forces. In his name, not hers, orders will be issued and power will be maintained. Once again she signs declarations in the name of a husband and rules the realm. And she is still called sultana.

Aybak is impressed with his new position as sultan of Egypt. He takes on airs and demands the power the sultana will not relinquish. He wants the treasure of Sultan Ayub, but Shajarat al-Durr has hidden it. She will not reveal where the vast delicious sum lies. Aybak dispenses harsh treatment to the River Mamluks for their devotion to Shajarat al-Durr. He takes another woman as his co-wife. The sultana writes to Al-Nasir Yusuf, ruler of Syria and offers to murder Aybak, then marry him and reunite Eygpt and Syria.

Aybak returns hot and tired to the citadel after a hard game of polo. He goes straight to his bath, where he is strangled by Shajarat al-Durr's servants.

The amirs and other nobles fly into panic. Who will succeed Aybak? It cannot be a woman. It cannot be Shajarat al-Durr. The caliph forbids it; none but her Mamluks approve. Aybak's supporters triumph and proclaim his son Ali to be sultan.

In her chambers, wind billowing the red and green and blue and gold silk curtains, Shajarat al-Durr grinds her jewels and pearls to powder. Ali's soldiers kick the door and burst into the room. The sultana is waiting. A pearl rests on her tongue. The soldiers seize her by the arms and march her to the quarters of Aybak's divorced wife, the mother of Ali. She is mad for vengeance. She and her servants beat Shajarat al-Durr to death with their clogs.

Days later, the woman who was like a tree of pearls is found floating half-naked in the citadel moat.

V

Rebels and Concubines

*"Drink from this cup,
then be gracious
to her who sent it
by paying a visit
after sunset."*

he period of the four Rightly Guided caliphs ended in 39 A.H./661 C.E. with the death of Ali and the defeat of his descendants, the People of the House, by Mu'awiya I, the "son of the liver eater," who established the Umayyad Dynasty. The Umayyads hung on only a century, before the Abbasids—descendants of Abbas, an uncle of Muhammad—seized the caliphate, led by Abu al-Abbas al-Saffah, "The Shedder of Blood." They ruled for nearly five centuries, until the Mongols sacked Baghdad in 636 A.H./1258 C.E. The grandeur of the Abbasids depended on slavery.

Along with women, the majority of Islam's earliest converts were slaves. The Qur'an discourages slavery, but does not outlaw it, for doing so would have created considerable social upheaval and in the beginning, compromises had to be made. The *umma* at Medina was strained, and the pagan Meccans laughed off the very idea of eliminating the practice, let alone treating slaves with justice and kindness as the holy book dictates. The Qur'an plainly states that to release slaves is a good deed to be done whenever possible to compensate for moral shortcomings.

> *God will not take you to task for a slip*
> *in your oaths; but He will take you to task for such bonds*
> *as you have made by oaths,*
> *whereof the expiation is to feed ten poor persons*
> *with the average of the food*
> *you serve your families, or to clothe them,*
> *or to set free a slave.*[1]

We read of numerous folk giving thanks through manumission. And owners are enjoined to allow slaves to enter into contracts by which they could earn their freedom.

Those your right hands own
who seek emancipation, contract with them accordingly,
if you know some good in them; and give them of the wealth of God
that He has given you.[2]

Slaves were captured from caravans or rival tribes. The ransoms paid for captives and wealth that slaves brought by their labor were a vital part of the economy, not unlike that of the southern United States before the 1863 Emancipation Proclamation. However, the idea of slavery in North and South America after the European invasions of the fifteenth and sixteenth centuries did not have the same associations as within Muslim societies. Slavery was recognized by Islamic law, which stated that no freeborn Muslim could be enslaved. Only *kafir*, non-Muslims, the Prophet said, could be slaves, as long as they were captured in war or purchased outside the boundaries of Islam, or they were born into slavery. Often reared in the homes of their masters, slaves were, to a large extent, considered part of the family and that relationship could continue after the slave was freed. Freedmen might wander the world their whole lives long, but return "home" to die. Unlike other slave-holding societies, Muslims recognized the validity of slave marriages. The master might marry a slave and even marry his daughter to a freed slave. Male slaves were often his most trusted associates, conducting his business and financial affairs or inheriting the crucial custodial task of raising his sons.

There were agricultural slaves, brought from East Africa, who cultivated the land in the upper valley of the Nile and the oases of the Sahara. Most female slaves were domestic servants, but in a wealthy household, favorites could be consigned to be concubines, *jawari*, sometimes with slaves of their own. The master had unrestricted sexual access to his slave-concubine, *jarya*, and absolute rights over his children by her. They were free, but belonged to their father and his kin, that is, their care devolved upon his female relatives, not their slave mother. The mother, however, earned the status of *umm walad*, "mother of a child" (regardless of the child's gender), a step below the standing of a legitimate wife, *umm al-babin*, "mother of sons." As a mother of his children, the *jarya* could not be sold during the master's lifetime and had to be manumitted after his death. He could marry the *jarya*, but not until he had freed her. Men could not make money on their female slaves by pandering; if the master did not want her himself, he was to arrange for her marriage.

> *And constrain not
> your slave girls to prostitution, if they
> desire to live in chastity.*[3]

Although the Qur'an specifies no more than four wives, there is no limit on concubines. The Prophet had, depending on the source, at least one, a gift from a Christian ruler of Egypt, the Coptic Maryam, who presented him with a son in his old age. (A very few sources claim Maryam was married to the Prophet, but this is generally dismissed as prudishness or an attempt at whitewash, partly in reaction to Western labeling of Muhammad as a "seducer.")

> *If you fear that you will not be equitable,
> then [take] only one [wife] or what your right hands own.*[4]

Quite simply and obviously, concubines—what your right hands own—provide an opportunity for men to use slaves as sexual objects without interference or accusations of adultery, and this, too, has a long, ghastly global history. Sally Hemings, politely called the "mistress" or "lover" of Thomas Jefferson, was in fact, his slave concubine and as such, had no choice regardless of her feelings. In tale after tale of the Old Testament, concubines appear, usually as mistreated, blamed victims. (Concubines were not forbidden to Jews until the Middle Ages.) While adultery is frowned upon in most world religions, the rule applies primarily to women, who are restricted to a single male.

In her 1924 *Woman in World History: Her Place in the Great Religions*, E. M. White sniffs: "No modern thinker with high standards wishes to uphold polygamy among Mohammedans or any other peoples, but the practice can be explained, and in some respects it compares favorably with the more hypocritical customs of

Western Europe and America. At least polygamy is open; there is no lip-service to monogamy, and the secret use of prostitution, and early marriage prevents much prostitution. Polygamy does not imply sexual immorality in its worst forms."

(Prostitution did and does exist in Islamic countries. In various eras and empires, sex workers were accepted like any tradespeople, could be highly talented in music, dance, or poetry, and were even taxed. These women often accumulated great wealth and had freedoms not available to their more "respectable" sisters. Some were concubines who had lost favor and were turned out to prostitution, if they were not married off to minor officials.)

Muhammad's intention was to shape a cohesive, comprehensive, and principled society, with carefully articulated conventions for marriage, child rearing, divorce, and so on, regulating the social and familial conduct of pre-Islamic Arabs. He also had to compromise with customs his people were hard-put to give up. And he was, after all, himself a product of his era, even as he attempted reform. A pagan practice, banned by the second Rightly Guided caliph Umar, and unique today to a small segment of Shi'a Muslims (but illegal among Sunnis) is *mut'a*, a contractual temporary marriage in which women receive remuneration for a fixed period. These "marriages of pleasure" are referred to in the Qur'an:

> *You may seek,*
> *using your wealth, in wedlock and not*
> *in license. Such wives as you enjoy thereby,*
> *give them their wages apportionate; it is no*
> *fault in you in your agreeing together,*
> *after the due apportionate.*[5]

The verse has been read as an endorsement of sanctioned prostitution, but perhaps this "law of desire" also addresses a love match, a marriage that was not arranged by families for their advancement.

Rape earned the death penalty. Adulterers could be stoned to death. Sex between unmarried men and women became punishable by a hundred lashes and a year's banishment. Illicit sexual acts must have been almost impossible to prove since the Qur'an requires four witnesses. Such a number of observers would put a crimp in any assignation. The Qur'an's Verses of the Slander, revealed after Aisha's ordeal, call for severe punishment for false accusers.

These laws prescribing death and flogging are not written in the Qur'an, but come from *Hadith*, which are of varying authenticity, recorded at varying times. Habitually forgotten by despots is the *Hadith* that calls for punishment to be tempered with mercy: "Avert the infliction of penalties on Muslims as much as you can. And if there is a way out then let a man go, for it is better for a leader to make a mistake in forgiving than to make a mistake in punishing."

(*Hadith* are often recorded without context. Who knows, for instance, whether, when Muhammad purportedly said that more women would be found in Hell than in Heaven, he might not simply have had a tiff that day with Aisha? That he is the most accessibly and vulnerably "human" of spiritual leaders cuts in a lot of different directions.)

Multiple wives and concubines did not go down easily with second-generation Muslim women such as Aisha bint Talha and Sukayna bint Husayn during the Umayyad Dynasty. Their commotions over shared or straying husbands were epic.

Sukayna's divorce was the stuff of marital infamy. In Islam, as in other religions, divorce is discouraged and there must be an interval of three months before the dissolution can be complete. The waiting period, *idda*, would ensure that there was no pregnancy, and allow breathing space for the possibility of resumption of conjugal relations.

> *In such time their mates*
> *have a better right to restore them, if they*
> *desire to set things right.*[6]

Should a couple regret the divorce after the fact, an interlude is required before they can remarry. Once the divorce is concluded, women keep their dowries and are to be sent away "honorably," "kindly," and not against their wills. They are never to be abused.

> *If he divorces her finally, she shall not*
> *be lawful to him after that, until she*
> *marries another husband. If he divorces her,*
> *then it is no fault in them to return*
> *to each other, if they suppose that they will*
> *maintain God's bonds.*

> *When you divorce women, and they have reached*
> *their term, then retain them honorably*
> *or set them free honorably; do not retain them*
> *by force to transgress; whoever does that*
> *has wronged himself....*

> *Do not debar them from marrying*
> *new husbands.*[7]

Umm Salamah, wife of al-Saffah, "The Shedder of Blood," and her sister-in-law Umm Musa, wife of the second Abbasid caliph al-Mansur, also insisted on fidelity in monogamous marriage and got their way. These rebels are legendary for thumbing their noses at convention, which indulged men's whims by treating, as patriarchies do, women as mere property.

Umm Musa, a royal woman of the ancient tribe of Himyar, married Mansur before the Abbasids took power and he rose to the caliphate. She would not marry him unless he signed a written agreement to take no other wife or concubine as long as she lived. He signed and later, as caliph, regretted it. But each time he tried to have the contract legally voided, Umm Musa got to the judge first, and her case, not to speak of her bribes, proved effective. When at last she died, al-Mansur was presented with a hundred virgins by his sympathetic friends.

Umm Musa was alert not only to her own situation, but was also mindful of other women's welfare. Among her charitable deeds, she established an endowment for those unfortunate concubines whose children were girls.

These uppity women were all of the elite, with high pedigrees, from powerful families, and with assertive personalities. They signify the rebelliousness of women throughout Islamic history. For all that we may envision Muslim women to be violets shrinking beneath their veils, the truth is much more complex and the women far more influential and insistently spirited than many Westerners imagine.

Aisha bint Talha and Sukayna bint Husayn had their heydays within the century of the Prophet's death when the memory of women's contribution to the establishment of Islam was fresh in people's minds. As the Umayyad Dynasty progressed, so did the oppression of women. Yet even the Prophet's wife, Aisha—who treasured her freedom and against whom the Verses of the Curtain were used repeatedly—eventually spoke (although "muttered" may be more accurate) in favor of *hijab*, of veiling, a reaction it is thought to the excesses of the Umayyad Dynasty, during which slave women began to make their appearances as entertainers and courtesans at the mercy of men's desires.

Rebellion hardly ended with the eighth-century ruling elite. Among other feisty women throughout Islam, in the nineteenth century the Persian poet Bibi Khanum Astarabadi foreshadowed the Muslim feminist movement by writing a famous treaty, *Ma'ayib al-rijal*, "The Faults of Men," in response to a tome by one Khwansari entitled *Ta'ib al-nisvan*, "The Punishment of Women." By the early twentieth century, Turkish women were in full swing, demanding their rights. Indeed, the suffragists of England and the United States were not too far ahead of Muslim women in beginning to demand their rights and freedoms. And the refusal of Muslim women, like that of Western feminists, to accept subjugation and injustice, continues to this day.

For all that Muhammad disliked slavery, for all the ethical encouragement in the Qur'an and *Hadith* to free slaves—which makes it apparent that the Prophet expected Muslims to move away from the practice (as they have, of course)—nevertheless, as the

Muslim Empire grew, so did slavery. By the Abbasid period, it had developed into a thriving industry.

Ibn Batalan, an eleventh-century Christian doctor, was renowned in Baghdad for his data on the qualities of women from various regions: "He who wants a *jarya* for pleasure should choose a Berber; he who wants a reliable woman to look after his possessions should take a Roman. For the man who wants a *jarya* to bear him children, the best choice is a Persian. If he wants a *jarya* to suckle a child, he should choose a Frankish woman. And for singing, a woman of Mecca cannot be equaled."

In *Risala fi shari al-raqiq*, Ibn Batalan's meticulous instructions for the purchase of slaves, he lays out telltale signs for determining character. Wide eyes mean languor; blue eyes are stupidity; those with fine hair are thoughtless, while those with wiry hair are brave; large noses illustrate idiocy; low foreheads describe ignorance, and so on. Ibn Batalan's classifications recall the Spanish *conquistadores'* lengthy *casta* lists, detailing the unalterable traits inherent in every conceivable combination of ethnicities as intermarriages between Spaniards, Native Americans, and African slaves took place in the "new" world. Across the centuries, such labels have wormed into all our minds and stuck there as stereotypes.

Al-Mansur (r. 132 A.H./754 C.E. to 153 A.H./775 C.E.), who succeeded his younger brother al-Saffah to the Abbasid throne, was born of a Berber slave woman. He reminded those who taunted him for being the son of a concubine that Ismai'l was the son of Ibrahim's slave woman Hagar. Al-Mansur's success and power put to rest any stigma against the sons of *jawari*, and enhanced the prestige of concubines, though it also affirmed that no woman, slave or free, had much more than nominal rank. Marriage alliances still had political significance, but they did not guarantee succession.

In 500 years, only three Abbasid caliphs were sons of free women. Al-Mansur, who defended his slave-lineage so bitingly, nevertheless named as his heirs his two sons by his freeborn wife Umm Musa. To produce sons who might inherit the throne stirred deep ambitions among concubines. The *jarya* Khayzuran, as we'll see, produced two caliphs, Musa al-Hadi and Harun al-Rashid.

That Muslims were not permitted to take other Muslims as slaves did not apparently apply to women. When al-Mansur asked Khayzuran about her family, she replied, "I have none but Allah," perhaps intending to inform the caliph that she was a Muslim and therefore entitled to her freedom. It had no effect.

In the centuries to come, favored concubines in the Persian Safavid and Turkish Ottoman empires would be Georgian and Circassian women. The Turkish term for a young slave woman was *odalisk*, which comes from *oda*, "room," and means "woman of the room." The most beautiful and talented of the *odalisk* became concubines and the best of these were selected as *gedikli*, maids-in-waiting, who were responsible for dressing, bathing, and serving food to the sultan and even doing his laundry. The *odalisque* was a favorite fantasy for European painters and photographers.[8]

Khayzuran's lover, al-Mahdi, was the bane of his frugal father's existence. Al-Mansur tried and failed to keep Mahdi out of the harem, even advising him in his will not to let women interfere in affairs of state. (As spartan as al-Mansur was, his attitudes were libertine compared to those of tenth-century C.E. Shi'a sovereign Adud al-Dawla, who had his favorite *jarya* drowned because, as he complained to the executioner, "He who gives way to pleasure will become a bad politician and inevitably lose earthly power.")

When politics were not involved, Mansur allowed Abbasid women some freedom. Yet observing the effect of women on Mahdi, and the frequency with which he enjoyed the women's quarters, Mansur was alarmed.

"On one occasion, as [al-Mansur] approached the palace," Nabia Abbott relates, "he heard the sound of singing and the beat of a tambourine. When he entered, he found a group of servants seated on the floor singing, while one of them beat upon the tambourine.... slave girls were dancing and singing. Enraged, al-Mansur rushed in and scattered them all in flight with the exception of the luckless tambourine player, upon whose head al-Mansur proceeded to beat the instrument until it broke."[9]

No one paid any attention to the grumpy old ruler. Mahdi spent fortunes on slaves and each successive caliph outdid him. "The slaves gained great power at the court, for they became the wives of the caliph or the mothers of his children. The caliphs, who spent most of the time in the harem, were always under the subtle influence of the slaves who could raise or lower the fortunes of any individual they wished."[10] Westerners often imagine that harems were promiscuous places full of endless earthly delights. In fact, for busy sultans and caliphs, the harem was mostly merely home.

Slaves may have been legally powerless, but they did not lack initiative when it came to protecting themselves. It's thought that, like other aristocratic Arab women of her era who carried on businesses of their own, Aisha bint Abu Bakr probably traded slaves. She promised her personal slaves their freedom when she died. To hurry that day along, one of her slave women cast a death spell over her. Indeed, Aisha became ill, but a wise doctor pronounced that she was not really sick, she was bewitched. The slave confessed and Aisha sold her, delaying her freedom indefinitely.

And the histories tell of an abusive fifteenth-century sultan who was poisoned by his female slaves for his cruelty toward them.

The great conquests of the fourth Abbasid caliph Harun al-Rashid—the son of Mahdi and his concubine Khayzuran—resulted in Harun's acquisition of a thousand *jawari*: Persians, Kurds, Romans, Armenians, Ethiopians, Sudanese, Hindus, Berbers, and more. Subsequent caliphs boasted upwards of 4000 concubines.

Competition was stiff and produced an atmosphere of rivalry and intrigue. Slaves were sent to be educated, according to the talents they exhibited—to become poets or musicians or dancers—and the more erudite, the more possibility a *jarya* had for advancement into the caliph's good graces and his bed, the axis of power. A surprising number of *jawari*, like Khayzuran, came to wield incredible authority behind and on the scene as rulers, regents, and queen mothers. Among other things, Khayzuran carried on correspondences discussing the state of the empire with provincial governors, who considered her the caliph's equal.

The Abbasids loved and nurtured knowledge and arts. Thanks largely to the Abbasid harems' cultural diversity and the meticulous education of its members, a Golden Age of Islam burst forth with a vigor that continues to capture our imaginations, and which is responsible for scientific and artistic discoveries and inventions that are still unsurpassed. Poets, scholars, architects, musicians, scientists, and artisans produced the great Muslim civilization which began in Baghdad and was carried on elsewhere, notably in Iberia, where the last Umayyad prince, Abd Al-Rahman, escaped the massacre of his family by al-Saffah, "The Shedder of Blood," in the mid-eighth century C.E. and established the magnificent kingdom of al-Anadalus. New blood, new ideas, and new cultures acted as powerful stimuli toward the creation of a new society that linked into one state the many diverse racial and cultural elements in the Arab kingdom. The period may have been the pinnacle, but Muslim invention and creativity blazed for centuries beyond the Abbasids, in Arabia, Persia, Spain, India, Asia, and into Eastern Europe with the Ottomans.

And much of it spun straight out of the harem, the women's sanctuary, where arts and scholarship flourished. No wonder Mahdi found the harems irresistible. They were marvelous places, the centers of culture, filled with some of the most enchanting, beautifully educated women in the world, each skilled in fields that ranged from dancing to astronomy and astrology, from music to mathematics and history. They were poets and calligraphers. The *jawari* were versed in the Qur'an and Islamic law. A caliph might disappear happily into this realm of cultured women, into entertainment, ideas, and sharp conversation.

Wives or favored concubines commonly gave the gift of finely educated and artistically talented slave women to their royal men, thus increasing their own honor by demonstrating their unselfishness. Indeed, it was her duty to present the sultan with a girl from her own bevy if he desired her. Naturally, jealousies abounded: jealousy of the heart or covetousness of one's position and the succession of sons. While such an atmosphere would encourage powerful

235

intrigues and there were scheming, vicious rumors spread to undermine a rival's reputation and even murder, harem women, like the wives of the Prophet, were also united into communities, extended families and political "parties."[11]

During the Abbasid period, the caliphs began recruiting peoples of Central Asia (and eventually the Caucasus, the Maghrib, and al-Andalus) into their armies. They formed, as we've seen, a distinct category of slaves called Mamluks. The word *mamluk* in Arabic means "owned," and has the same root as *malik*, meaning "owner" or "king." In the case of the Mamluks, infidel children were sought, again because Muslims may take only *kafir* for slaves (and perhaps also for strategic purposes having to do with nurturing loyalties early), but the Mamluk institution was so renowned and respected that many Muslim parents are said to have sold off their sons, pretending to be pagans. Little girls were captured for the harems or quite commonly sold by their impoverished parents, both to gain profit (a girl might sell for a little less than a horse) and to provide for their daughters, who could, if they were pretty and clever enough, look forward to a life of luxury.

The boys were trained as soldiers, converted to Islam, then freed to serve in the armies. The Mamluks were first supporters of dynasties, then founded dynasties of their own. They, too, used marriage and concubinage to strengthen their power and wealth. It was not unusual for a Mamluk to marry the daughter, sister, or widow of his master.

Beginning with the brief reign of Shajarat al-Durr, the Mamluks ruled Egypt and Syria from 628 A.H./1250 C.E. to 895 A.H./1517 C.E., when they were defeated by the Ottomans, who continued the practice of taking non-Muslim children to be prepared for the harem and the ranks of Janissaries, the sultan's special troops.

Centered in what is now Turkey, the Ottoman Empire was established in the late thirteenth century C.E. Its original founders, beginning with a tribal chief named Osman, formed political, and multiple marriages, but within a few generations, marriage became anathema for the Ottoman sultans.

Acquiring a wife for any ruler is serious business. And, as al-Mansur learned with his marriage to Umm Musa, not so easy as taking and discarding concubines. There were property rights and family connections to consider, and if he should divorce her, a proud ruler might have to see his ex-wife remarried to a lesser man, as it was her right. Since the children of slave/master unions were freeborn and perfectly legitimate and could inherit, why bother with marriage?

The Ottomans, "more than any other Muslim dynasty," Leslie Peirce writes in *The Imperial Harem*, "raised the practice of slave concubinage to a reproductive principle: after the generations of Osman and [his successor] Orhan, virtually all offspring of the sultans appear to have been born of concubine mothers."

The Ottomans outdid the Abbasids and, Peirce writes, "by the end of the fourteenth century, if not earlier, the dynasty had come to practice reproduction through concubinage to the exclusion of reproduction through legal marriage." It was a matter of state policy, for marriage, aside from its other drawbacks, introduced complications about succession, and since "from the point of view of dynastic succession, the son of a Muslim ruler by a concubine was in theory no less eligible for the throne than his son born of a free Muslim woman," there was no reason to muddy the waters with convoluted alliances. "The manner in which [the Ottoman Dynasty] produced and raised its princes and princesses…had two goals: the preservation of the House of Osman and the minimization of political challenge to the individual sultan."

This is not to say that others of the royal Ottoman lineage did not marry. They did. Polygamy was in fact rare among the middle and upper classes of the sixteenth century. But the sultans themselves eschewed marriage, preferring what Peirce calls a "one-mother/one-son" policy, whereby a concubine who gave birth to a son could no longer be sexually available. Her childbearing days were over. Her title became Mother of a Prince. When her princeling was old enough to strike out on his own, he was given a province and his mother was sent with him to govern it. No longer did she live in the harem palace. Mothers seemed to have had profound effect on their lone sons, seeing to their educations, advising them, boosting their popularity and political credibility, as the princes vied for the throne. When the goal had been accomplished or the mark missed—and the prince killed off by his brothers or his father to end challenges—their grieving mothers withdrew to the city of Bursa, a kind of retirement community for concubines, where they lived out their lives in style, doing good works until they were reunited with their sons, buried next to them. This surely created a kind of "mama's boy" culture among the Ottoman sultan class, for good and ill.

The winning mother took the title *valide sultan* and, as First Lady, held tremendous power and influence. A few weeks after her son's accession, she was honored with a ceremonial procession that carried her to the palace, where she continued to reside in close proximity to her child as supervisor of the harem. All sorts of protocol had to be observed around her. Audiences were especially difficult to get with the *valide sultan*, for she had unfettered access to the sultan—and powers of persuasion—as no other did.

Suleyman I (r. 872 A.H./1494 C.E. to 944 A.H./1566 C.E.)—called The Magnificent by Europeans and The Lawgiver *(kanuni)* by his own people—was acutely devoted to his mother, Hafsa Sultan, a Serb concubine. A man might have thousands of concubines, but he has only one mother. Who knows but that Suleyman, so very doting on his mother, craved a kind of familial intimacy that carried on the closeness he had to Hafsa Sultan. Perhaps this is why he broke the mold by actually marrying his favorite concubine, Khurrem, and establishing a nuclear family. Khurrem held Suleyman's heart—by feeding him love potions, according to those who were appalled and outraged by the union—and worked with him to bring the Ottoman Empire to its zenith of might and splendor. Yet Khurrem was never acknowledged by Suleyman's court or his people as anything more than a *haseki*, the favorite.

Their unprecedented relationship did not change Ottoman reproductive politics. When Suleyman died, his unmarried successors picked up the old one-mother/one-son policy where it had left off, though the notion of *hasekis*, who may have functioned in some measure like wives, took hold.

Ottoman sultan Mahmud II (r. 1186 A.H./1808 C.E. to 1217 A.H./1839 C.E.) was the son of a Frenchwoman, Aimée de Rivery from Martinique, a cousin of Josephine Bonaparte. Kidnapped by Levantine pirates on her way to French convent school, she was sold into the harem of Sultan Abdul Hamid I, became Nakshedil Sultana, and promptly introduced French culture, building pavilions and gardens and throwing dance parties by the Bosphorus. She converted to Islam, but on her deathbed called for a priest to give her last rites. Mahmud, allowing a Roman Catholic priest into the harem for the first time, honored the *valide sultan*'s dying wish, then mourned his mother deeply.

The one-mother/one-son custom may have accounted for the longevity of the Ottoman Empire, which lasted until Mustafa Kemal Ataturk abolished it in 1922 and proclaimed the Republic of Turkey the following year.

From this distance, we can only imagine the daily life, the emotions, the private thoughts of these women, most taken from their native lands and installed in harems for the pleasure of a caliph, sultan, or man of wealth. What we can know is that it must have been complex, a mélange of homesickness, loneliness, danger, and oppression jumbled with liberation from poverty, fulfilled ambitions, the satisfaction of an otherwise elusive education, even contentment.

Aisha bint Talha

Aisha bint Talha was the niece of the Prophet's wife Aisha, daughter of the elder Aisha's sister Umm Kulthum. Her dates are apparently unrecorded. She and Sukayna bint Husayn were rivals in beauty and elegance among the Meccan aristocracy during the Umayyad Dynasty. The two women were called "two pearls of Quraysh."

Aisha the Younger is a replica of her aunt. The younger Aisha loves and admires Aisha bint Abu Bakr, but disdains her modesty. Aisha bint Talha sees no reason to behave. She is, after all, the granddaughter of the first Rightly Guided caliph, and will do precisely as she likes.

The same beauty. The same wide hips. The same intelligence. The same defiance, though in Aisha the Elder it is subdued now under the weight of experiences, responsibility, and the honor the *umma* offers her.

They say the younger is named for the elder, because her father Talha had desired Aisha bint Abu Bakr and Aisha supported him against Ali for the succession. Had she been permitted to remarry, Talha would have asked for Aisha. Instead, he took Umm Kulthum, Abu Bakr's youngest child.

Abu Bakr died when Umm Kulthum was only four and left Aisha, Mother of Believers, in charge of family interests. The second Rightly Guided caliph Umar demanded Umm Kulthum in marriage and such a union, when the child came of age, seemed advantageous.

"Aisha, he beats his women," her co-wife Hafsa bint Umar reminded her. "Atika—your brother Abdallah's widow—still walks about with a welt on her head where my father hit her with a carpet from Persia simply because it was a gift to her.

"Remember, Aisha, how Umar constantly took you to task. How he ran to Muhammad whenever he saw what he imagined to be a woman's show of independence."

"I will insist he cannot abuse my Umm Kulthum," Aisha replied.

"Insist away. Once she is out of your hands and into his, you will have no control," Hafsa said.

Umm Kulthum played on the floor with toy horses and camels, not three feet from the Prophet's grave.

"Look at her. Would you not prefer she have a handsome youth?" Hafsa asked. "One who will shower her with attention and gifts?"

"Fetch me Amr ibn al-As. He will be able to negotiate with Umar and break this arrangement."

Amr visited Umar. "We fear you and know you will not change your character," Amr said. "Would you assault the child should she disagree with you? Let me lead you to a better match, Umar. Someone who will bring you even closer to the Prophet's household."

"Yes, but who?"

"The other Umm Kulthum—the daughter of Fatima bint Muhammad and Ali ibn Abu Talib."

The suggestion appealed to Umar. "But what of Aisha? If I call off the marriage, will she not be angered?"

"Leave her to me."

Thus Aisha the Elder began her career of protecting the women in her family, and when Umm Kulthum came of age, she was married to Talha. When Talha died in the Battle of the Camel, Aisha once more took Umm Kulthum, now with her children, under her wing. Aunt Aisha watched over the proper conduct and training of Talha's son Zakariya. She taught her namesake poetry and ancient Arabic history and astronomy. The girl is a star-gazer and brilliant.

The graybeards are startled at the resemblances between the younger and elder Aishas. They remember Aisha bint Abu Bakr when she was a girl, before the Verses of the Curtain. They can see the resemblance between the younger and elder, because Aisha bint Talha refuses to wear the veil, when even the Umayyad princes are hiding behind screens to avoid the people's gaze.

"God Almighty has honored me with beauty," Aisha says. "I want the people to see this and understand what rank I enjoy before them. I will not veil myself. Nobody can reproach me with a fault."

Was it not the Prophet himself who said, "God is beautiful and loves beauty"?

Her first marriage to her cousin Abdallah ibn Abd al-Rahman is arranged by her aunt. The fur flies, vessels crash against walls, the screaming deafens the neighbors. "Aisha will not obey me!" Abdallah complains. She abandons him and goes home to Aisha the Elder.

The Mother of the Believers does not approve of such impatience between couples or such separations. The two are spoiled, brought up with far too much pampering, too many riches, too many advantages, too many sycophants breathless in the presence of these descendants of the first revered generation. The Prophet's widow lives simply, as he did. She has few luxuries and wants none.

Her niece adores luxury, loads herself with jewels and embroidered clothing, sits and sleeps upon the softest cushions, eats only the choicest meats. And at night, Aisha bint Talha perches on her balcony, watching the stars and scribbling notes she shares the next morning with her beloved aunt.

God removes all obstacles to happiness. Abdallah ibn Abd al-Rahman receives his reward in Paradise.

Aisha the Elder arranges Aisha the Younger's marriage to Mus'ab ibn al-Zubair, the most handsome man in Mecca. So desirable he wins both Aisha bint Talha and her rival in beauty and refinement, Sukayna bint Husayn. For a time, they are co-wives.

Mecca is festive. The life of wealth and radiant conversations, of poets and singers and scholars, agrees with Aisha bint Talha. She

242

puts all her cleverness to work and vies with the other women for attention and admiration and social position until finally only Sukayna stands in her way.

Mus'ab adores Aisha. When she is good, she is very, very good and her virtue is lauded by everyone. Nevertheless, she will not wear the veil. Her will could move mountains. When Mus'ab, who is as hard and unyielding as he is beautiful and generous, can bear Aisha's disobedience no longer, he beats her and calls her spoiled and indecent and threatens to lock her in her chambers. She nurses her bruises and still she does as she pleases.

He cannot be angry with her for long, though she continues to ignore his orders and desires. She has as usual spent a long night first with poets, then watching the stars until dawn and is sound asleep in the afternoon. Mus'ab enters her chamber and pours pearls on her lap. She opens her eyes to slits. "I would have preferred to sleep," she grumbles and closes her eyes again.

Mus'ab despairs that she will never give in to him.

"I can, I promise, force Aisha to give in to you," Mus'ab's secretary tells him.

Mus'ab is encouraged. "Do as you please, for she is the best of all earthly things I have."

That night, the secretary calls for two slaves to dig a grave in Aisha's house.

She is enraged. "What are you doing?" she shouts.

The secretary shrugs. "Mus'ab has ordered this grave to bury you alive."

Aisha gasps and backs away in horror. She is genuinely frightened. Beatings do not scare her and threats mean nothing. But this? And the grave is almost finished, a box perfectly cut in the earth, just her size.

Almost pleading, her proud bearing softened, she promises the secretary that she will be kinder to Mus'ab and much, much more obliging from now on.

God removes all obstacles to happiness. Mus'ab ibn al-Zubair receives his reward in Paradise.

Aisha bint Talha rejects all suitors. She will not marry again. Her beauty is praised in verse after verse. She will not wear the veil. She will not fight a man for her autonomy. She will do as she pleases and spend her nights and days and her money as she alone wishes. The governor of Mecca is dismissed for delaying the hour of prayer so that she can complete her *tawwaf* around the Ka'aba. The learned men of Mecca click their tongues and shake their heads at Aisha bint Talha and how she flaunts convention. But they cannot deny that she is their equal in knowledge of history and poetry and the stars, the gifts she received from her namesake, Aisha bint Abu Bakr, Mother of the Believers.

Sukayna bint Husayn

Sukayna bint Husayn was the daughter of Husayn ibn Ali, the son of the fourth Rightly Guided caliph, Ali ibn Abu Talib. Her dates are apparently unrecorded. She and Aisha bint Talha were rivals in beauty and elegance among the Meccan aristocracy during the Umayyad Dynasty. The two women were called "two pearls of Quraysh."

God removes all obstacles to happiness.

When Mus'ab ibn al-Zubair goes to receive his reward in Paradise, his widow Sukayna bint Husayn parts ways with her rival and co-wife Aisha bint Talha. The wags tell one another that poor Mus'ab could not survive two such spirited, rebellious women.

Sukayna swears she will only remarry the man who will never repudiate her, never refuse her what she wants, and never touch another woman.

She can have her way, after all. She is the granddaughter of the fourth Rightly Guided caliph Ali and the daughter of his martyred son Husayn. For all that her family is revered in piety and devotion, Sukayna relishes society, and like Aisha bint Talha, adores poets and musicians, revels in luxury and wealth. Her pranks are imitated around Mecca, her keen jokes repeated by everyone.

"My sister Fatima is always solemn," Sukayna says, "because she was named for our Islamic grandmother, Fatima bint Muhammad. But I am jovial because I am named for our pagan great-grandmother!"

Her home—husbanded or not, and there have been at least four—is a gathering place for poets. Annually Sukayna gathers them to judge and reward those who describe their beloveds in the most delicious verses.

When she piles her magnificent hair upon her head and elaborates on it with braids and curls and jewels, all the Meccan women rush to mimic the style they call "the Sukayna." Soon, even the men are demanding "the Sukayna" of their own hairdressers. Caliph Umar ibn Abd al-Aziz is appalled. He has the men whipped and their heads shorn. Sukayna laughs.

It is no laughing matter when the tumor below her eye grows to such proportions she can no longer see. The eye bulges like a toad's. Sukayna calls the best physician in Mecca, and demands it be removed then and there. The physician operates. Sukayna endures the unmitigated pain without flinching. She does not move. She does not cry out or moan or groan. Everyone at court agrees: the scar is exceptionally attractive.

No one can keep track of Sukayna's husbands, so no one is quite sure where Zayd ibn Amr, grandson of the third Rightly Guided caliph Uthman, who will himself become caliph, strides into her heart. As always she demands that he never repudiate her, never refuse her what she wants, and never touch another woman.

He swears, but can he know what he is really up against? They quarrel often and finally, enraged, Zayd leaves Sukayna and retreats to one of his estates. There he has *jawari* at his disposal and peace and quiet. He stays for seven months.

Every day of his absence is a nick in Sukayna's pride. At last she complains to the governor and petitions for divorce. The governor has Zayd brought from his estate to stand before a judge.

Nothing can stop Sukayna's rage. She turns it first to Zayd. He shrinks with every verbal blow. On and on she rants and when she has had enough of Zayd's timidity, she levels her wrath at the judge.

"If you were not a woman, I would have you whipped," the judge shouts, twitching and flicking his eyes toward the niche where his wife sits, hearing it all. Suppose his wife takes courage from Sukayna's audacity and becomes herself audacious?

246

Whipped? Sukayna turns crimson with wrath. She stomps her feet and bangs her fists and the judge, not to be outdone, responds in kind. Zayd keeps close to the judge's raised seat, wishing he could crawl into it, creep under it, and get away.

Sukayna twirls at him. "Coward! Cowering and cringing!" She shoves her face into Zayd's. He blushes and tries to back away, nearly toppling on the judge's lap.

"Have a good look at me, craven man! From now on you will no longer see my face!"

The governor, awaiting the meeting's end in an ante room, laughs until his sides split.

Umm Salama

Umm Salama was an aristocrat of the Makhzumite clan of the Quraysh. She was married to the first Abbasid caliph, Abu al-Abbas al-Saffah, who died of smallpox in 132 A.H./754 C.E., just four years after the founding of his dynasty and the fall of the Umayyads. They had two children: a boy who died young and a daughter Raita.

All the talk is about how Umm Salama has proposed to Abu al-Abbas. "Like the Prophet's radiant wife, Khadija!" She has even been married twice before, like Khadija. And handsome Abu al-Abbas is also younger than she. It is love and it is destiny.

Umm Salama sends her proposal through one of her freedwomen. He sends back a message that he cannot in honor accept, for he is poor and has nothing but his keen military wits to recommend him.

Umm Salama supposed it would be so. Her next messenger brings funds for the wedding. Now Abu al-Abbas accepts. When he arrives at Umm Salama's house, she is sitting on a bridal couch, covered head to toe with jewels. She is gracious and lovely and wins his favor. He promises her, on oath, that he will never marry another woman or take a concubine.

The years pass and the Abbasids plot for the caliphate. The future al-Saffah makes no decision without consulting his wife. Together, they succeed in bringing down the Umayyads. Al-Saffah is called "The Shedder of Blood."

There are those in the court who cannot understand al-Saffah's fidelity to Umm Salama. A man who is caliph, a man who is a *man,* surely owes no such devotion to only one woman. Khalid ibn Safwan speaks out.

"How, my master, can you be content with one woman when this vast empire of yours offers such beauteous bounty?" he asks. "Let me tell you of the charms and allures of the lovelies you are missing." And Saffah leans back to listen, his eyes dancing with delight.

Khalid leaves and Saffah is writhing with eagerness, when Umm Salama enters the room. She takes one look at her husband and demands to know what is wrong. He shakes his head. She asks again. He still refuses to answer. She demands a reply. And on and on until at last, as always, he gives in and tells her of Khalid's lyrical portrayals of all he, the Commander of the Faithful, could have, if only.

Khalid sees the messengers from the caliph's palace approaching his house. He smiles to himself, anticipating the large royal gift they must be bringing. Closer and closer they come until Khalid ibn Safwan begins to realize that they don't walk like gift givers, but like killers. They do not carry boxes of jewels or bolts of cloth, but rest their hands on knives at their belts. He is just about to run into the house, to bolt the door, when one of them grabs him and in the name of Umm Salama, turns him and kicks his rear end, while the others gather round him and pommel him with feet and fists. They pick Khalid ibn Safwan up and toss him, bloodied and breathless, through his gate, then march away again. His wives rush to him and carry him in to bed.

His cuts and bruises are barely visible when, in a few weeks' time, al-Saffah calls once again for Khalid ibn Safwan to visit him and tell him again of the assorted charms of the women of his empire.

"Oh my master, it is monogamy, fidelity to one woman that is the most satisfying," Khalid stutters, and loud laughter rings from behind the curtains. Khalid clears his throat and raises his voice. "And did I not say that the Makhzum are the flower of the Quraysh and that you, possessing the flower of flowers, need not covet any other woman, free or slave?"

"You speak truth, indeed," Umm Salama says from behind the curtain. When next Khalid sees men approaching his house, they are indeed bearing rewards of jewels and cloth, suitable, the messenger says, "for those who are truthful."

Umm Salama's laughter is driven from her heart and she will never overcome her sorrow when al-Saffah dies. She retreats and al-Saffah's brother, al-Mansur inherits the caliphate. Her daughter, Raita, marries al-Mansur's heir, al-Mahdi.

Khayzuran

Khayzuran was a slave in Yemen, sold to the Abbasid caliph al-Mansur around 140 A.H./758 C.E., to be a concubine for Mansur's son and heir, Muhammad al-Mahdi. She was Mahdi's favorite and bore him three sons and a daughter, Banuqah. Her eldest sons, Musa al-Hadi and Harun al-Rashid, were named heirs to the caliphate. Khayzuran's birth date is unknown. She may have been of Berber origin, for Berber slaves were thought to be among the most desirable concubines. However, the earliest records list her simply as "a woman of Jurash (Yemen)." She died in 167 A.H../789 C.E., probably in her early fifties.

Khayzuran dreams of greatness. She is barefoot and clothed in frayed cotton. Nightly, she has visions of damask and emeralds as big as her toes.

It is an art to decipher dreams. Her master prides himself on this skill. He listens daily, enrapt as Khayzuran presents her tangled fantasies. He unravels predictions of royalty.

She holds her head high, rehearsing her regal future. She is young and slender as the reed for which she's named: Khayzuran.

After a time, her master takes her to Mecca, to the grand slave market. She is dazzled by the journey, dazzled by the opulence of the bazaar, where those on display are strong and beautiful. A slave herself, yet Khayzuran covets these slaves like jewels.

She is bought by a trader who readies her for sale again. Her skin and hair are oiled and polished. Her eyes shine, illuminated with kohl. She admires herself in a copper disk.

She dreams of embroidered silk in colors of rainbows. In the morning, she stands among other young girls, when al-Mansur, the caliph himself, appears. He is called Father of Farthings, for he has amassed sums and sums of money and treasure. His frugality ensures a glorious future for his Abbasid Dynasty. And all are amazed as a new capital, Baghdad—the Round City of Mansur—blossoms from barren desert.

The caliph inspects Khayzuran and questions her. The girl is at once modest and bold. She lowers her eyes and kneels, but even in this humble gesture there is robust imperiousness betraying her dream that providence will bestow prominence.

Mansur lifts the girl's chin. He scrutinizes her face. "What are your origins, girl?"

"I was born at Mecca and brought up at Jurash," she says.

"Have you any relatives?"

"I have none but Allah; my mother bore none besides me."

Mansur calls an attendant. "Take this one to Mahdi and tell him she is good for childbearing!"

It is not merely filial obedience that makes Prince Mahdi willing to pay whatever is asked for Khayzuran. He takes to her immediately, as a fly to honey. They are charmed by the same music, the same poets, the same lyrical verse, the same satire, the same jokes. Mahdi showers Khayzuran with gifts. She is groomed daily, with lessons in poetry and *Hadith* and the Holy Qur'an and even music, though unlike Mahdi's other favorites, Khayzuran has no talent for melodies.

Mansur worries and fusses over his son's profligacy and pleasure seeking, over Mahdi's mild and easy-going ways. In his will, the caliph has outlined instructions for his son's reign: "take care not to spend money on music and dancing girls"; "keep the money that is stored in thus-and-such treasury always for safekeeping"; "attend in person to the affairs of state"; "do not put off the work of today until tomorrow"; "sleep not at your post, even as your fond father has not slept since he came to the caliphate." He ends each directive with the lament, "But I know that you will not."

Does Mansur, like Khayzuran's first master, have the dream-reading gift? Did he look inside Khayzuran's body and see that she is good for bearing the heirs of princes?

She suspects she's pregnant and in secret, sends her maid with specimens of her feces to the palace apothecary. Isa analyzes its color and texture and contents. She must have a boy. A male child will bring Khayzuran ever more favor with her beloved Mahdi and his Father of Farthings.

At last Isa sends back word: she is indeed with child and the child will be a boy. She sends the apothecary lavish gifts.

"Send, too, for a doctor," her old servant advises. "The princes will prefer it." And he recommends Abdallah al-Taifuri.

The physician confirms Khayzuran is with child. "But it is impossible to determine the sex of an unborn child," he scowls.

She, who comes from humble country folk, is taken aback but thanks him for his honesty and sends him away with gifts.

She thanks God for her good fortune by manumitting five slaves. She tells Mahdi the news and he is overjoyed. She is a *jarya*, a concubine and slave. She must keep her jubilance still. She must keep firm hold on her dignity. But Mahdi dances about like a madman, singing loud praise with his wonderful voice.

Pursuing dreams takes patient training, like falconry or weaving. The bird, the dream, learns who is master and returns from soaring with prey it drops at the master's feet. The weaver merges and unites mere red, yellow, blue, orange, gold, purple, and green to construct a pattern, a tactile image out of fragments.

"How," Khayzuran asks Mahdi, "can I improve myself?" She has ambitions.

"Fashion your deportment after Zaynab bint Sulayman," he says. The next day, she seeks out the famed Traditionist. A girl who would be queen can learn much from the most revered princess of the Abbasid.

Khayzuran is a willing pupil, a happy student, and the two form a bond like no others in the harem. When Khayzuran invites the princess to be entertained in her quarters, Lady Zaynab is seated always in the place of honor.

Khayzuran dreams of the child about to be born. And when it comes forth from between her legs, a boy, she is surprised at how closely he resembles the child of her visions. Yet Musa al-Hadi is not quite *that* perfect. Allah has given him a flaw, a mouth like a wine jug with a pinched lip that will not close. He wheezes at his nurse's breast, snorting and flailing for breath.

Still Khayzuran and Mahdi celebrate. Isa the Apothecary is rewarded beyond his wildest dreams, though his dreams are pale, modest compared to those of the prince's favorite concubine. Before he can count his new wealth, another child is on its way, the specimens are delivered, and the question is posed again. Again, Isa sends the maid back to Khayzuran with the word she wants to hear: boy.

Harun al-Rashid is flawless. Even Mahdi looks upon Isa the Apothecary with favor now and names him Abu Quraysh, Father of the Noble Quraysh, the lineage of caliphs back to the Prophet. It is an honor indeed. Khayzuran and Abu Quraysh form a powerful blockade, for Isa the Apothecary is now called upon by all the women of the harem who long for auspicious news. He delivers the gossip, reports all the details to Khayzuran, who discovers she has a talent for making good use of information.

With two sons, Khayzuran has an unyielding foothold in Mahdi's affections and loyalty. Now is the time to exhibit her realized dreams to those buried farthest back in her youth, those forgotten like flies shooed away.

"It is true, as I told Mansur, that Allah is my closest relative," she tells Mahdi, who nods absently. They are listening to a chorus of slave girls whom the prince has sent to the best schools for music. He does not like to be interrupted as he listens. But the Persian wine is smooth and rare. Khayzuran leans close to her lover. He smiles blearily and lies back on soft carpets.

"But He is also related to my two sisters and my brother."

"Who?" Mahdi's eyebrow rises ever so slightly. He cocks an ear toward her.

"Allah."

"Allahu Akbar." Mahdi's eyes have never strayed from the musicians.

"So you see, my mother did bear me alone," Khayzuran drawls. "I am *not* a twin."

Mahdi turns to Khayzuran. He stares at her in astonishment. "What?" Then he bursts out laughing.

She had wanted to make her way without encumbrance, she confesses. She had wanted to move into her dreams-come-true with no one hanging on her. Her family is poor as mud and mud will drag a swimmer down and drown her. Mahdi has turned away to admire a new singer.

Khayzuran is astonished then, when in a few weeks, Mahdi calls upon her with a woman, two girls, and a clumsy farm hand, so filthy he had to be stripped of his rags before entering Mahdi's presence.

Her mother beams at Khayzuran and runs her rough hands one after another on all the exquisite luxuries that fill her apartments. Khayzuran is at once ashamed of her mother's pride in her, embarrassed by a family of bumpkins, and overjoyed to have, at last, her own in whom she can confide and with whom to remember even underfed goats and fields of dust.

Her brother Ghitrif is given estates and the governorship of Yemen.

"You see how my prince loves me?" Khayzuran says to her mother. Her mother grins and bobs her head up and down, up and down.

Her sister Salsal catches the eye of Mahdi's half brother Ja'far and soon she is delivered of a son and daughter she calls Sukayna. The old caliph, al-Mansur, hard as rock, is charmed, his heart is caught in plump little Sukayna's hands. He calls her Zubaydah, Little Butter Ball, and bounces her on his lap, lets her sit on his shoulders and play at his feet even as he dictates state policies, confers with his viziers and generals and engineers.

Caliph Mansur's hard heart has been given to Zubaydah. His confidence has been given to Mahdi's stalwart wife, Raita, daughter of his half brother, al-Saffah, The Shedder of Blood. To her alone, al-

255

Mansur gives the keys to certain rooms and tells her to guard well the locks and not to open them until his death.

Yet he sees Mahdi's weakness for women and warns him: "Beware of taking women into your counsel and your affairs...But I think you will take them in."

Khayzuran is pregnant again, but Abu Quraysh the Apothecary refuses now to make predictions. In her fondness for him and their little intrigues together, Khayzuran forgives him, even giggles, when he admits that his prediction for Prince Hadi was a casual remark and his prediction for Harun was a lucky guess on which he was gambling his future. Khayzuran is familiar with gambles on the future.

She gives birth to a third son, Isa. Mahdi adores this boy, too. When Isa dies, Mahdi gives the lovely garden town east of Baghdad the name of Isabadh.

Khayzuran gives birth to a daughter, Banuqah. For all that she has prayed for boys, it is Banuqah her father loves most.

Poor Prince Hadi with his pinched lip. Neither Khayzuran nor Mahdi can look at him without comparing him to his brother Harun. It is not much of a defect, but it is a step away from perfection. Mahdi engages physicians to watch carefully over the health of the child who will be caliph, and a servant to follow the boy everywhere reminding him to close his mouth. In the harem, the child is known as "Musa-shut-your-mouth." Some say Musa al-Hadi is ill-tempered and quarrelsome, hard-hearted and suspicious, filled with cunning and jealousy. The honest doctor, Abdallah al-Taifuri, becomes like a father to Hadi, and sees the boy through a proud father's eyes: noble, gracious, equitable, just, generous, brave, energetic, and self-confident in spite of everything.

Prince Harun is showered with favors. His birth has brought ill-luck to Hadi, though other than the handicap of Hadi's pinched lip, they are alike in stature, tall and handsome and heavily built. Harun feels their father's bright lenience. Hadi senses his dark disapproval.

Banuqah is pretty as a field of cotton flowers, the light of Khayzuran's eye and the little queen of Mahdi's soul. He gives her a palace. He takes her with him on his travels, disguised as a page, with turban and trousers, a sword and a bow to avoid scandal. He is happiest when he is with his Banuqah.

With her three children, Khayzuran's position is assured. Even Mahdi's legal wife and friend, Raita, cannot—and does not care to—upset Khayzuran's standing. Her *jarya's* high, secure nest is slightly shaken, her confidence only slightly rattled, when Mahdi falls head over heels for first this singer, then that one. More children are born to him, chicks chirping from the nests of his favorite songbirds.

To Khayzuran's ears, their voices are not sweet or eloquent or angelic or compelling, but the sounds of fabric tearing her from Mahdi.

There is Sakhlah, who gives Mahdi a dark-skinned boy she calls Ibrahim. He will grow to be a poet, a musician, and a scholar. He will challenge the caliphate.

There is Makhnuna, with slender hips and high chest, for whom Mahdi pays 100,000 silver dirhams (he does not dare tell al-Mansur) and who in turn gives Mahdi his talented daughter Olayya. "No other of his women makes my position so difficult," Khayzuran tells Princess Zaynab.

Mahdi calls for his inkwell and book and writes notes from a lecture delivered by the historian Waqidi. Suddenly, he drops his pen and rises. "Stay here until I return," he tells Waqidi.

He ambles off toward the harem and is back shortly, infuriated, red in the face, his robes torn.

"What is the cause of this change from scholarly serenity to rage?" Waqidi backs toward the safety of the door.

"I went to Khayzuran. No sooner had I entered her apartments than she flew at me, shrieking, 'O you picker of leftovers! What good have I ever received at your hands?'"

Mahdi sputters and shakes. He is angry and he is afraid of Khayzuran.

"And it was I—I!" he shouts at Waqidi, "*I* who bought her from a slave trader and *I* who have lavished her with favor and riches. *I* who made her two sons heirs to my throne! Am I, then, a picker of leftovers?"

Waqidi tries to calm Mahdi and succeeds by quoting the Tradition, "Woman is like the rib from which she was created. If you

257

straighten her, you break her. If you enjoy her, you do so by accepting her crookedness."

Mahdi thanks the historian with a gift of 2000 dinars.

That night, Waqidi returns home to find Khayzuran's servant with a note: "I heard all that you said to the Commander of the Believers. May Allah reward you." The servant gives clothing and the sum of 1090 dinars to Waqidi. Khayzuran is wise not to match the king's gifts.

He always returns to her from his forays into the beds of siren slave girls. She, the victor, welcomes him happily. He writes long verses to her, even in the midst of straying. They long for one another when separated. From his retreat at Isabadh, he writes:

We are in great joy
but no joy is complete without you.
Hurry, if you are able.
Fly to us with the zephyr.

Her attachment to this man who purchased her but whom she has captured is strong and honest.

She sends him a crystal cup. On it are etched her plea, "drink from this cup, then be gracious to her who sent it, by paying a visit after sunset." The sunsets pass, one, two, and three, before he leaves.

They are suited, as if Allah made one the hand and one the glove.

So suited, in fact, the court jester Abu Dulamah exploits their harmony for practical jokes.

He comes weeping before Mahdi. His wife, Umm Dulamah, is dead and he has not the wherewithal to outfit and bury her.

Mahdi is touched and makes him a gift of clothes, ointments, and money.

Umm Dulamah comes weeping before Khayzuran, bewailing the death of her husband. She, too, is touched and gives Umm Dulamah clothing and ointments and money.

Mahdi and Khayzuran dine together.

258

"Did you know that my jester's wife, Umm Dulamah, has died?"

"No, no, you must be mistaken. It is Abu Dulamah who died."

"It was a trick," they say at the same moment and fall hilariously into each other's arms.

Al-Mansur is dead. Word comes in secret to Khayzuran. No one must know until the viziers have located al-Mahdi. The old caliph has met his end on the Pilgrim's Road to Mecca, on his way to the *hajj*. Mahdi sobs, for Mansur was a family man who loved his son openly and was his mentor, leaving his upbringing and education to none other. The Father of Farthings prepared the way for his son to rule in security and opulence, paved the path for the Abbasid Dynasty unto generations.

Mahdi as caliph takes his full quota of four legal wives. He liberates Khayzuran to make her his second wife. In this way, he can assure that her sons will succeed him. First Musa al-Hadi. Then Harun al-Rashid.

Khayzuran is manumitted and to celebrate she will go on pilgrimage. When she returns, Mahdi promises, they will marry. The caravan leaves the city carrying a joyful Khayzuran, her goods and servants.

Asma, the youngest of Khayzuran's siblings, has grown up. She is more fetching than Khayzuran. And younger. Mahdi is seized with passion for her. As Khayzuran's caravan trudges along the Pilgrim's Road, Mahdi marries Asma and settles her with one million dirhams.

Isa the Apothecary, Abu Quraysh, sends word to Khayzuran. She is furious. She orders the caravan back to Baghdad, competing with the wind for speed. It was she who was to be his legal wife, not her sister, and by the law a man may not have sisters as co-wives.

Mahdi hears of her return and rushes to meet Khayzuran outside the city.

"What is this affair of Asma? And how much did you settle on her?" she calls down from her *hawdaj*. She towers on her white she-camel over Mahdi on his black mare.

"Who is Asma?" Mahdi asks innocently.

"Your wife!" Khayzuran snaps.

"If Asma was my wife, she is now divorced."

"You divorced her when you heard of my return."

"Since you know it all, well, then, I gave her a marriage portion of one million and made her a gift of a second million."

And then Mahdi marries Khayzuran.

Raita is his senior wife and Khayzuran is his favorite. There are two other political alliances, but they are of no account.

Khayzuran's sleep is blank, without color, without voices, without pictures. She dreams no more for fear of seeing her beloved daughter. Banuqah is dead.

None have ever seen a man's grief for his daughter such as al-Mahdi's for Banuqah. There is no music but elegies in the court. Hilarity has been laid to rest with the little princess who was Mahdi's delight and in whom Khayzuran saw herself transformed—born not in poverty but as royalty, not scrambling and scheming to keep her place in the harem, but naturally and easily and unarguably at the top. It is a year before the music becomes lighter and the verses are no longer eulogies.

Hadi is kept close to home, first in line to the throne. Harun, second in line, is sent on an expedition against Byzantium's Empress Irene. Hadi's companions do not meet with Mahdi's approval. The caliph has them beaten. But not even flogging will keep Hadi from his closest friend Ibrahim al-Harrani. Hadi and Mahdi grow farther and farther apart. The young man's devotions and affections attach themselves firmly to Ibrahim and to his concubine Amat al-Aziz. His desire for her is fanatic. She is his closest confidante. He tells her of his agonies and joys. And Hadi's spiritual father remains his physician, Abdallah al-Taifuri. The young man is not outgoing, and lacking love, or so he believes, he has cultivated this small family of his own apart from his parents and siblings, who seem to despise him and disdain his each and every move.

Khayzuran is busy planning her sons' marriages and their harems. Harun has fallen in love with Zubaydah, Little Butter Ball.

Khayzuran finds two legal wives for Hadi. One is Khayzuran's niece, the daughter of her brother Ghitrif. The other is Mahdi's niece, daughter of his half brother.

Should not Hadi's line have the throne after him? Why should it be his brother, the one who is favored and loved, while Hadi—Musa-shut-your-mouth—has been rejected? Khayzuran is the first he informs that it must be his own son Ja'far who will inherit. Khayzuran chafes but says nothing until she speaks that night to Mahdi. The caliph sends Hadi to distant Jurjan east of the Caspian Sea. This time he allows Hadi to take his dearest friend Ibrahim.

"The reports from Jurjan are displeasing," Mahdi tells Khayzuran. "Hadi is devising his own state policies and Ibrahim is behind it. He puts ideas in the boy's head."

"Recall Ibrahim," Khayzuran advises, but Hadi will not let his companion go.

"Withdraw his heirship," Khayzuran advises. With that threat, Hadi reluctantly parts with his friend.

"Hadi is rebellious. Disobedient," Mahdi tells Khayzuran.

"Put Harun ahead of Hadi," Khayzuran advises and Mahdi sends members of the royal family to secure the elder son's acceptance. Hadi refuses.

Mahdi sends freedmen to bring Hadi back forcibly. He fights them and will not answer the summons.

Khayzuran seethes. Mahdi determines to go himself to subdue and fetch his son. Harun joins the cavalcade, an entourage that includes Mahdi's current pet *jawari*, especially Hasanah. It will be a long march to Jurjan. They may as well make it pleasurable. The hunting on that route is reputed to be excellent.

Khayzuran stays home. She reigns supreme in the harem and Mahdi gives her a free hand. She is one of the powers behind the throne and everyone knows it and fears it. She has lobbied for—and won—high positions for men she favors. She avenges herself on judges whose decisions she dislikes and turns Mahdi away from those with whom she disagrees. She cajoles, flatters, and truly loves Mahdi. She uses charm and tact with him, even though they are often of the same mind and he relies on her to look into corners where he cannot see.

261

She reminds her sons that it is thanks to her and the favor she found with their royal father that they were singled out for the caliphate. To be queen mother will be to reach the pinnacle of the dream.

The jovial party proceeds to Jurjan. Hunting, exploring, playing at games. Poets write verses to the fresh landscape. Hasanah, his new favorite, sings to Mahdi at nightfall.

Now it is Mahdi's turn to dream. He wakes early and calls for food and when he has eaten his fill, he resumes his sleep and gives orders not to be disturbed. His companions sleeping nearby are awakened by Mahdi's loud cries. They hurry to him.

"Did you not see what I saw?" He is panting with fright.

They admit they did not.

"A man stood at the gate," the caliph says. "I would not fail to recognize him if he were one among a thousand, no, a hundred thousand men. He was tall and encased in a red aura. He wore his shield on his back, a double shield that looked like folded wings. His eyes blazed black. His face betrayed no feeling…"

"You have seen Azrail, Angel of Death," the court astrologer pronounces.

Ten days later, word is sent to Khayzuran and the harem that Mahdi is dead. And although Khayzuran questions the messengers closely, none can say whether the accident of his death was on the hunt or from his traveling harem. Whether in chasing hounds chasing an antelope, the caliph's frightened horse dashed him against an ancient wall where the blows killed him cleanly, or whether Hasanah, envious of another *jarya* whose favor was rising, sent a poisoned pear to the rival concubine only to have it waylaid by Mahdi, who ate the fruit with relish and died in pain.

Hasanah screams and beats her face. "I desired you for myself alone and now I have killed you, my master!"

Mahdi is laid to rest far from Baghdad in the village of Radhdh, under the shade of a walnut tree. Raita's son Ali and Khayzuran's son Harun perform the last services for their dear father.

Khayzuran and Raita stand together on a balcony, holding hands, as the ill-fated caravan filled with al-Mahdi's concubines enters the city. They had departed in brocade and are returning in sackcloth.

Khayzuran, who had not dreamed since the death of her darling Banuqah, now reaches in her sleep for Mahdi. The vision of her caliph fades in and out of her mind's eye and floats away, a thread suddenly snarled into nightmares about Hadi. He leers over her, wheezing, lip pinched like a flute. Her mornings begin with trepidation. She goes from her bed to the mirror. Her youth is over. Her dreams have been realized. Her happiness with Mahdi is ended. She steadies herself for a new life of maturity. Nothing will change in the harem. She will still be the power behind the throne. Her son's throne. Why should it not be so?

Hadi rides posthaste to the capital, certain that his mother plots against him. Men riot in the streets against the caliphate, the army is restless in this vacuum of power. Khayzuran quiets and secures them with three years' pay. The streets are calm, the army is committed and loyal by the time Hadi enters Baghdad.

Nevertheless, he has convinced himself, as always, that Khayzuran has summoned his enemies to take control of his government. He is advised to declare a truce in his resentment of Khayzuran. For a time, he is obedient, a good son, trying hard to please. He allows her all the freedoms and privileges she enjoyed under his father. The men of whom she approves are solidly in office and Harun is heir to Hadi's throne, still second in line. She sighs in relief and busies herself erecting drinking fountains in the city and throughout the empire. She builds canals. She furthers the textile industry by ordering more and more gowns until it is said she has 18,000 of embroidered brocade.

Hadi appears to settle into the throne. He cultivates majesty and dignity. He hears petitions in person every day. He acts sensibly. He is, in spite of everything, a ruler more like his father and grandfather than anyone, especially Khayzuran, had expected.

Despite the veneer of peace, tranquillity, and cordiality, Hadi moves his residence to Isabadh, far enough from his mother to—as she well knows—avoid her, but close enough to permit frequent messages and occasional visits. She exercises her will upon him, she imposes decisions and makes excessive demands.

Sycophants crowd Khayzuran's apartments hoping to achieve their ambitions, begging for influence. It seems unlimited. Nobles, generals, retainers flock to her gates, until the truce finally cracks. The young caliph is calling upon his mother when she asks that he appoint her brother, Ghitrif, Hadi's own father-in-law, to a new and wealthier governorship.

"Remind me of it before my cups," he says and goes home. He dines with precious Amat al-Aziz and calls for bedtime wine. Just then Khayzuran's maid Khalisah appears to remind him of her request.

"Return," Hadi orders Khalisah, "and tell my mother to choose for Ghitrif either the governorship or divorce."

The befuddled maid returns quickly. "I have already chosen for him the governorship," comes Khayzuran's message.

Hadi divorces Ghitrif's daughter then and there.

"Do not," Hadi tells Khayzuran, "overstep the essential limits of womanly modesty and overdo in person the role of the generous donor. It is not dignified for women to enter upon affairs of state. Take to your prayer and worship and devote yourself to the service of Allah. Hereafter, submit to the womanly role which is required of your sex."

Khayzuran ignores his warning.

He becomes ever more jealous of the honor and reputation of the harem, watchful and prideful as neither his father nor grandfather was before him. He flogs a prince for marrying Ruqayyah, one of Mahdi's widows, though it is only the Prophet's wives who were forbidden to remarry.

He is with his friends one night when a servant enters and whispers in his ear. He is up and gone, shouting at his friends to wait for him. He returns breathing heavily and throws himself on his couch. A servant enters behind him bearing a tray covered with a towel. It is an hour before Hadi's countenance turns to normal. Finally, he sits up and orders the trembling servant to uncover the tray.

There, like gory jewels, the disembodied heads of two of the harem's most beautiful *jawari*. The scent of blood mixes with the perfume in their hair. The guests recoil.

"Do you know their offense?" Hadi asks. Silence.

"I was informed that they were in love, so I set my spies to watch them. I caught them in the immoral act and killed them myself."

The two heads, eyes surprised, sit placidly on the tray as Hadi resumes his conversation.

Hadi will not grant Khayzuran's requests for promotions of her favorites. She does not heed him. She persists. "You absolutely must," she insists.

"I will not," Hadi replies.

"I have already promised," she says. Has she lost her wisdom and wiles? Does she not see that her son is not her husband? That her son, like Khayzuran, is stubborn and cannot yield as al-Mahdi did so effortlessly, confident in himself and his authority?

"A plague upon these sons of strumpets!" Hadi rages. "I refuse you!"

"Then, by Allah, I shall never ask anything of you again!" Her skin aches with anger. She rises to depart.

"Stay where you are!" Hadi roars. "And heed my words. I swear by Allah and on the forfeiture of my descent from the Messenger of Allah, that if I hear that any one of my generals, retainers, or servants is at your door, I shall strike off his head and confiscate his property. Let him then, who will, take that course. What is the meaning of all these daily processions back and forth to your door? Have you no spindle to keep you busy or Qur'an to remind you of Allah, no house to shield you? Beware and again beware! Open not your doors hereafter to either Muslim, Christian, or Jew!"

Khayzuran reels out of the chamber, her mind clouded, her heart pummeled by this show of defiance from her own son. His nature is as hot as hers and she had never noticed. She reaches her chambers and holds her hands to her head. Her maids bring cloths to stop the throbbing. She stares at the ceiling. The astrologers, at least, have forecast a short reign for Hadi.

Hadi calls his generals.

"Who is better? You or me?" he demands.

"Most certainly you, O Commander of the Believers," they grovel.

"Then, what do you mean going to my mother and making requests of her, making me the object of your conversations with her?"

And the generals cease their visits to Khayzuran. She has never known such humiliation, even in the slave market, on display, for sale to the highest bidder. Thereafter, she speaks no word to Hadi, bitter or sweet, and never enters his presence.

Hadi summons his brother. Harun has had a dream and Hadi is much disturbed.

"O Harun, it seems that like our mother, you allow yourself to dwell too much on the fulfillment of a dream. You hope for that which is not now within your reach."

Harun knows what is coming and does not blink. He has seen their father, al-Mahdi, who has given them each a rod. Al-Hadi's rod put forth a few leaves and no more at the top; Harun's rod put forth leaves from top to bottom.

Harun falls to his knees. "O Musa, my brother, the haughty are humbled, the humble are raised to honor, and the unjust are deceived. I do certainly hope that the authority will in time be mine. I will then be equitable to those whom you have oppressed and generous to those whom you have cut off from your generosity. I will place your sons above my own and give them my daughters in marriage. I will bring to pass that which is worthy of the memory of our father."

Hadi's fears are for a moment allayed. Harun's dream seems undestined, and Hadi's dream that his own son will inherit the throne seems unthreatened. Assured, he dispatches to Harun a thousand thousand dinars and land and treasuries.

Hadi sends his mother a dish of rice. "I have enjoyed this and wish you to share it." Is it a gesture of peace? Khayzuran wants badly to share her son's victuals and find her way back to her place of action. She is bored and lonely.

Khalisah insists Khayzuran must test the food. She spoons some on the floor and whistles for the dog, who gobbles it with relish. Within an hour, the dog is dead.

Hadi sends a messenger to inquire how his mother likes the dish. She sends the messenger back with praise, she liked it very much.

He sends the messenger back to Khayzuran again. "You did not eat it, for if you had, I would certainly be well rid of you by now. When did a caliph ever prosper who had a living mother?"

She fears for herself. Equally, she fears for Harun.

Al-Hadi demands a precious ring that al-Mahdi gave Harun. Harun refuses. Death is threatened until Harun announces he will take the ring to Hadi himself. He gallops from Baghdad across the bridge to Isabadh and stops halfway across. He pulls the ring from his finger and throws it in the Tigris. "Let Hadi do whatever he wishes."

Hadi insists that his followers renounce any loyalty to Harun and give it instead to his son, Ja'far. Some are willing to make the pledge, others hang back. Hadi visits Amat al-Aziz. He craves her friendship, her sweet and quiet attention.

"This morning we were full of hopes for the child," she tells him. "This evening we are full of fears for him."

Hadi takes her hand to comfort her. "I have hopes that Allah will gladden you yet."

The next morning he orders the physician Abdallah al-Taifuri to devise a poison for Harun. The man who has been like a father to Hadi begins the work of grinding and mixing deadly powders, while Hadi rides to his gardens at Mausil. He has called forth all his governors to meet him and confirm that Ja'far will be heir to his throne.

He has hardly dismounted, when he is taken desperately ill. The pains in his gut wrench him double.

A messenger brings Khayzuran the news that her older son is dying.

"What am I supposed to do about it?" she snarls to her faithful maid, Khalisah.

"Arise and go to Musa, Noble Lady. For this is no time for resentment, reproach. or anger."

Only Khayzuran seems sure of Hadi's impending death. She calls for the viziers to prepare state papers to send to the provinces announcing Musa al-Hadi's death and Harun al-Rashid's accession.

Hadi grows worse. Abdallah al-Taifuri and Abu Quraysh the Apothecary sit helpless beside him. He chides them. They take his money and yet cannot help him in his hour of extreme need.

"We do our best," Abu Quraysh says, "but Allah alone is the bestower of health."

Weak as he is, Hadi rants at the Apothecary, rages at his fatherly companion Abdallah al-Taifuri. He threatens them with execution. Another physician is sent for.

"Have you seen the specimen?" Hadi asks.

"Yes, O Commander of the Believers," he answers. "I will now prepare you a medicine and in nine hours you will be free from your pain."

But outside the sick room, he tells the other doctors, "Do not trouble your hearts, for today you will depart to your homes." He sets them to pounding medicines within the caliph's hearing and Hadi is calmed. Each hour he asks after the medicine and is reassured by the sound.

As the hour approaches the ninth, Khayzuran enters and sits silently by his bedside.

"I will perish," he tells her. "And my brother Harun succeeds me this very night. I had forbidden you to do some things and commanded you to do certain others out of the demands of state policy and not for lack of filial devotion. I was not in opposition to you but sought only to shield you, filially and sincerely."

She makes no reply. He reaches for her hand. He places it on his breast. When he has breathed his last, Khayzuran removes the signet ring from Musa al-Hadi's hand.

Hadi's sleeping son is stormed at sword point and made to swear allegiance to Harun to whom a son, Ma'mun, is born to his favorite *jarya* that very night.

Khayzuran herself tells the leading princesses, Zaynab and Raita, that her older son is dead. Khalisah enters the room to announce that the Commander of the Believers has been buried. Khayzuran sighs and calls for refreshments. She orders Khalisah to give each princess a million dinars.

"And what is my son Harun doing?"

"He has sworn," Khalisah says, "to be in Baghdad for the midday prayer."

"Then saddle the horses!" Khayzuran cries. "What point is there in my staying here when he has departed?"

Harun al-Rashid lets her do as she wishes. These days, good works come more naturally than intrigue. Yet she is ever Khayzuran and, true to the dreams of her youth, she does not let her reins drop too loose.

She travels to Mecca and there rescues and sets apart as a shrine the birthplace of the Prophet, and then the house of Arqam where Muhammad and his earliest converts met in secret. Next door, she builds a house of her own.

When death claims her, not long after Raita's passing, it is autumn. A dreamy day of rain. Her son Harun al-Rashid dresses in the simple cloak of mourning and, barefoot, leads the procession to the cemetery, where Khayzuran is laid to rest beside her daughter Banuqah.

He offers the prayers for the dead. He washes the mud of the streets from his feet. He steps into the clean earth of the freshly dug grave. He emerges from the tomb expressing the sorrow of a loving son.

Leaving the cemetery, Harun al-Rashid, Commander of the Faithful, removes the royal signet ring from his vizier Ja'far al-Barmakid and transfers it to Fadl ibn al-Rabi. He explains that Ja'far was not his choice, but his mother's. She was not, the caliph reminds the assembled company, a woman to be loved and mourned, but a woman driven by her dreams to be feared and obeyed.

Amat al-Aziz

A slave and singer, Amat al-Aziz was the favorite of Abbasid caliph Musa al-Hadi, first son of al-Mahdi and Khayzuran. This story may be apocryphal, but it is irresistible. There are records of Harun al-Rashid's barefoot journey to Mecca and it is thought that his vow to Hadi was the reason he did so. Amat al-Aziz's dates are unknown.

Amat al-Aziz sings to Hadi. He lies with his head in her lap, content as he is nowhere else with no one else. A tear falls onto her skirt.

"What is it, my master?" she asks. Her voice is honey. She smooths his wet cheek with her long fingers.

"I have had a vision that I will die and Harun will marry you, my beloved." Hadi chokes on the words and stands suddenly. He claps for an attendant and sends for his brother, Harun al-Rashid.

When Harun arrives, Hadi insists that he and Amat swear an oath that they will never marry on pain of taking the pilgrimage by foot and shoeless.

Amat is amazed by this show of jealousy. Not that she hasn't heard and seen it between the brothers, especially Hadi, many times before. But never has she shown interest in Harun, nor he in her.

It is less than a month after Hadi's death and Harun visits Amat al-Aziz in her quarters. She gives in to him—what else to do with a caliph? But when he asks her to marry him, she balks.

"What of your oath and mine?" she asks.

"I will redeem them," Harun says.

And so they are married. Harun changes Amat's name to Ghadir and she finds even more favor with him than she found with Hadi. Harun will do anything for her. He showers her with attentions and gifts.

He sits motionless for hours, while she sleeps with her head in his lap. One night, while she is sleeping thus, she wakes with a scream. Her teeth chatter with terror.

"My Ghadir! What is wrong?" Harun embraces her trembling body, holding it still so that she can speak.

"I dreamed of Hadi," she weeps. "In my dream, he recited verses to me and reprimanded me for breaking our vow. 'You married my brother after all,' he shouted. 'In truth did he name you Ghadir! By morning, you will join me.'"

Harun grips her shoulders and holds her away from him to look firmly and with reassurance into her eyes. "These are but confused dreams, my beloved."

But she cannot contain the shuddering, the strangling in her throat, the heart that beats violently, as if trying to escape her body.

She whose name meant Handmaid of the Almighty and was changed to Deceiver is dead within an hour.

Harun al-Rashid mourns Amat-Ghadir for months, ignoring all his duties and even his dearest wife Zubaydah.

In the month of *hajj*, he sets forth along the Pilgrim's Road. He will redeem their vows to Hadi. He travels on foot and shoeless, on soft reed mats spread out before him every step of the way.

Roxolana/Khurrem

The favorite concubine and eventually wife of Ottoman Empire sultan Suleyman I, the Magnificent, Khurrem was born in 883 A.H./1505 C.E., the daughter of an Orthodox priest in the Ukraine, then part of Poland. Her original name was Aleksandra (sometimes Anatasiya or Nastia) Lisovski. Her wedding in about 912 A.H../1534 C.E. to Suleyman marked the first time an Ottoman sultan had married in generations. She died in 936 A.H./1558 C.E.

Ottoman forces drive deep into gore. Across the steppes and plains and rivers and into cities and villages, east, west, north, and south. Killing and looting. Slaves mount to the millions. They sing the Lament of Captives.

> Will they sell us beyond the Red Sea?
> Will our price be silver, gold or brocade?
> Iron shackles eat our flesh down to yellow bones…

In Manisa, near the Persian border, Suleyman governs, awaiting his ascent. He is twenty-five. It will be a year before his father, Selim the Grim, dies. Suleyman and his mother, Hafsa Sultan, bide their time. The prince writes poetry, studies military and naval strategy, mathematics, maps, and astronomy. Like all Ottoman princes, he must master a craft, for "sultan" is not a true profession. Suleyman fashions exquisite gold pieces, goblets and jewelry, boxes and crowns.

At night there are seventeen concubines. The Circassian, Madidevran, Moon of Fortune, has given birth to his first son, Mustafa.

In Poland, the Crimean hordes are constantly at the ready, like packs of hounds baying to be let loose for the hunt. When the gates open, they rush barking and snarling through the countryside and bring home to their Turkish masters the richest human booty of the Ukraine.

Blood runs in the streets of Rohatya. Gore dries between the cobblestones. The daughter of the priest Havrylo Lisovski is ripped from her father's house. Aleksandra is fourteen. No one would call her a beauty, but she is small and comely and graceful and lively. This has become her situation. She sizes it up and decides that nothing will interfere with her happiness, not even slavery. She is sold to Ibrahim Pasha, the Greek. He is fascinated by her relentless charm, her clever ways, and her good cheer, then all the more intrigued, for Aleksandra, the daughter of the priest, knows Greek and Latin. Ibrahim calls her Roxolana, Ruthenian maiden, and Aleksandra recedes into the past.

In Istanbul, Suleyman receives his throne. The gifts pour in. Among them is Roxolana, presented by Ibrahim Pasha, Suleyman's best friend, companion of his boyhood, brother-in-law. Roxolana is barely noticed on that festive day. She is sucked into the harem, into the crowds of concubines and eunuchs. She is named Khurrem, Joyful, and Roxolana recedes into the mouths of Europeans who will call her nothing else.

The foreign ambassadors report to their governments:

"The sultan is very lustful and visits the palace of women often."

As a courtesy, for she is after all a gift from Ibrahim Pasha, Suleyman sends for his newest concubine. She arrives at his bed chamber in a procession of musicians. From the start, as Ibrahim knew, Suleyman cannot get enough of Khurrem. He writes to her every day.

I am at your door to glorify you.
Singing your praises, I go on and on.
My plant, my candy, my treasure

Who gives no sorrow, but the world's purest pleasure.
Dearest, my turtledove, my all.
My revelry, my feast,
My torch, my sunshine, my sun in heaven.
My orange, my pomegranate,
The flaming candle that lights my pavilion.

The affection Suleyman lavishes on Khurrem begins to gain attention in the court. The *effendis* whisper angrily:
"She has the bridle of the sultan's will in her hands."
The foreign ambassadors report to their governments:
"The sultan has two highly cherished women: one a Circassian, the mother of Mustafa the firstborn, the other a Russian, loved as no woman in the Ottoman House ever has been. It is said she is agreeable and modest and that she knows the nature of the sultan very well. The Circassian, naturally proud and beautiful, and who already has a son, Mustafa, understands that Roxolana, the Russian, has pleased the sultan, wherefore she insulted her, and as she was doing so, she scratched Roxolana all over the face and mussed up her clothing saying, 'Traitor! Sold meat! You want to compete with me?'

"A few days later, the sultan had this Russian summoned for his pleasure. She did not let the opportunity pass, and angrily told the eunuch Agha, who had come to fetch her, that she was not worthy to come into the presence of the sultan, because, being sold meat, and with her face so spoiled and some of her hair pulled out, she recognized that she would offend the majesty of such a sultan by coming before him. These words were related to the sultan and induced in him an even greater desire to have her come to him. He wanted to understand why she would not come and why she had sent him such a message. The Russian woman related to him what had happened with Mustafa's mother, accompanying her words with tears and showing the sultan her face, which still bore the scratches, and how her hair had been pulled out. The angry sultan sent for the Circassian and asked her if what the other woman said was true. She responded that it was, and that she had done less to her than she deserved. She believed that all the women should yield to her and recognize her as

mistress, since she had been in the service of His Majesty first. These words inflamed the sultan even more, for the reason that he no longer wanted her and all his love was given to this other."

Khurrem receives a new name from Suleyman. He calls her *haseki*, favorite. Khurrem the Joyful is moving forward. The people are troubled by Suleyman's increasing attachment to one woman. It is, they say, unnatural and harmful.

The foreign ambassadors report to their governments:

"There is only one male heir, the six-year-old Mustafa. It is imperative that the sultan produce more sons quickly. The empire will be in great confusion should Suleyman die leaving only infant heirs."

Khurrem accommodates. She gives birth that year to Mehmed, her first child. She is sixteen.

Still Mustafa is dearly loved by Suleyman. A father's love that will bode ill.

The foreign ambassadors report to their governments:

"Mustafa has extraordinary talent. He will be a warrior, is much loved by the Janissaries and performs great feats."

A provincial governor presents Suleyman with two beautiful Russian captives, one for his mother and one for him. Khurrem flings herself to the ground, weeping. Hafsa Sultan gives her maiden to the sultan, but as soon as the tears start to flow, she takes the slave girl back and sends her off to marry. Suleyman follows suit, for Khurrem says she will perish of sorrow if these women remain in the palace.

Suleyman then defies custom and marries off as virgins nearly all the eligible concubines in his harem. It is his gesture of fidelity to Khurrem. He foreswears all other sexual partners.

My life, the gift I own, my be-all,
My elixir of Paradise, my Eden,
My spring, my joy, my glittering day,
My exquisite one who smiles on and on.

Mehmed's birth is followed in a year by the birth of Mihrimah, a daughter, then Abdullah, who dies when he is three, then Selim

275

and then Bayezid. At last there is Jihangir, a hunchback. Khurrem has accomplished what no other Ottoman concubine has before her: she has produced a family with a sultan.

Hafsa Sultan, Mother of a Prince, captured from Serbia to serve Selim the Grim, custodian of her son's behavior, keeps her own counsel about these breaches of custom. The foreign ambassadors report to their governments:

"Such love does Suleyman bear Roxolana that he has astonished all his subjects, who say she has bewitched him. Therefore they call her 'witch.' For this reason the entire court hates her and her children, but because the sultan loves her, no one dares to speak. Yet everyone speaks well of the firstborn, Mustafa, and of his mother, Madidevran the Circassian, who has been repudiated."

Mustafa is eighteen. He leaves the imperial household to take his place as governor in the same post his father held before he became sultan. Clearly Mustafa is to inherit the throne. Manissa is on the border of the resistant Safavid Empire, the Persian holdouts. Madidevran accompanies her son. Mustafa is her whole joy. She organizes his court so that it is almost as glorious as his father's. She approves or disapproves of his concubines. She instructs him as to how to make himself loved by the people, but it does not take much. Like his father, he has a natural ability to be admired.

Ibrahim Pasha's power is soaring. He receives honors and titles from Suleyman, and is closest to the sultan in authority and rank. They confide in one another, as they did when they were boys together, and once a week they dine together in private.

Hafsa Sultan dies. Suleyman's heart breaks. Only Khurrem can mend it.

> My darling with that lovely hair, brows curved like a bow,
> Eyes that ravish: I am ill.
> If I die, yours is the guilt.
> Help, I beg you,
> My love from a different religion.

He mourns his mother and then Suleyman departs on his campaign for Iraq.

Flames engulf Khurrem's chambers in the women's palace, in the harem. She escapes the mysterious fire with her children. She moves into the palace of the sultan, the Grand Turk. It is to be a temporary move—whoever heard of a concubine living with the sultan?— but Khurrem never leaves.

The foreign ambassadors report to their governments:

"The palace of the favorite, Roxolana, is in that of the Grand Turk, and one can go through secret rooms from the one to the other...Her chambers are very splendid, with chapels, baths, gardens, and other amenities, not only for herself but for her maids as well, of which she keeps as many as one hundred."

Suleyman returns from Iraq and there is a wedding. The priest's daughter, Aleksandra, Ibrahim Pasha's slave Roxolana, the sultan's concubine Khurrem, his *haseki*, is to become Islamic empress of the immeasurable Ottoman Empire.

My very own queen, my everything,
My beloved, my bright moon;
My intimate companion, my one and all,
Sovereign of all beauties, my sultana.

The foreign ambassadors report to their governments:

"This week there has occurred in this city a most extraordinary event, one absolutely unprecedented in the history of the sultans. The Grand Signior Suleyman has taken to himself as his wife a slave-woman from Russia, and there has been great feasting. The ceremony took place in the Seraglio, and the festivities have been splendid beyond all record. There was a public procession of the gifts. At night the principal streets were fairly illuminated and there is much music and feasting. The houses are festooned with garlands and there are everywhere swings in which people swing by the hour with great enjoyment. In the old Hippodrome a place is reserved for the empress and her ladies screened with a gilt lattice. Here Roxolana and the court attended a great tournament in which both Christian and Muslim

knights were engaged, and tumblers and jugglers and processions of wild beasts, and giraffes with necks so long they, as it were, touched the sky....There is great talk about the marriage and none can say what it means."

A few speculate that Khurrem has refused to have anything to do with Suleyman unless he makes her his lawful wife. Few can believe the sultan is motivated by love.

For the first time, a Mother of a Prince does not accompany her firstborn son to his provincial post when he comes of age. Mehmed goes alone to Manisa, and his half brother Mustafa is sent on to Amasya. Khurrem's sons are moving into the field to compete for the succession. Selim is sent to Konya. Bayezid goes to Kutahya.

Jihangir receives no provincial governorship; deformity disqualifies him for rulership. He is in constant need of medical attention.

Khurrem writes to Suleyman on campaign:

"The success of the operation on Jihangir makes me hopeful."

Suleyman takes the deformed boy with him everywhere. When Jihangir dies, the sultan's heart cracks.

So alien is Suleyman's marriage that none can comprehend Khurrem's devotion to her sultan, nor understand his to her.

The foreign ambassadors report to their governments:

"It is commonly reputed that Roxolana retains Suleyman's affection by love-charms and magic arts. She stays at the royal palace by Suleyman's side and runs his household affairs and acts in place of his late mother. She does not accompany any of her sons to his post as the Mother of a Prince has done before and as the Circassian has with the ever-popular Mustafa. Should Roxolana have chosen to accompany Mehmed, that son would have the advantage over the rest. Instead she visits one after another in the company of her daughter, the Princess Mihrimah, and her husband Rustem Pasha. They say Roxolana has fashioned a nest of potential successors out of her own offspring and she summons them often to family reunions, where they plot who knows what."

Khurrem writes to Suleyman on campaign:

"My Sultan, you wrote that if I were able to read myself what you write, you would write at greater length of your longing for me. I will learn.

"There is no limit to the burning anguish of separation. Now spare this miserable one and do not withhold your noble letters. Let my soul gain at least some comfort from a letter...When your noble letters are read, your servant and son Mir Mehmed and your slave and daughter Mihrimah weep and wail from missing you. Their weeping has driven me mad, it is as if we were in mourning. My Sultan, your son Mir Mehmed and your daughter Mihrimah and Selim Khan and Abdullah send you many greetings and run their faces in the dust at your feet.

> Go gentle breeze, tell my Sovereign:
> 'She weeps and pines away;
> Without your face, like a nightingale,
> She moans in dismay.'"

Is it any wonder Suleyman is seduced by this woman? By the intimacies of family, by hearth and home so unfamiliar to an Ottoman ruler? He wishes he could hurry to them. His letters to his wife fuss about her finances: Is she sufficiently comfortable? Has she been taking care?

Khurrem's sharp intelligence—Aleksandra's lessons in Greek and Latin—serves her well. She becomes the sultan's source of information, his political confidante, essential in every way. Only Ibrahim Pasha rivals her closeness to Suleyman.

The foreign ambassadors report to their governments:

"Whatever Ibrahim Pasha wants done is done and nothing is done without his advice. He was much hated at first, but now that they see the sultan likes him so well, all have been made friendly to him."

Khurrem's letters are filled with long and intricate details of events in Istanbul: an epidemic that has killed many; rumors of succession and the contenders; rumors, when there has been insufficient word from the front, that he has died. She tells him the news of naval campaigns and diplomatic endeavors. She praises his accomplishments.

Khurrem writes to Suleyman on campaign:

"The good news of the conquest in the east has arrived. My Emperor, my Sultan, God knows that I have died and been granted a new life. Thousands upon thousands of thanks to the Lord God the Almighty! My Shah, my Sultan, may you undertake many wars, give the enemy their due, take many lands and conquer the seven climes!

Don't think your power can heal her heartache.
In your absence no one has found
A cure for her woes."

The foreign ambassadors report to their governments:

"Competition is fierce between the four princes for the succession. Mahidevran Khatun tries to protect her son by exercising great diligence to guard him from poisoning and reminds him every day that he has nothing else but this to avoid, and it is said that he has boundless respect and reverence for her. She maintains a network of informants to protect him from his political rivals.

"It is impossible to describe how much he is loved and desired by all as successor to the throne."

The foreign ambassadors miss the mark: not everyone desires Mustafa's accession. Accusations circulate, growing stronger and stronger. Prince Mustafa is plotting with the Safavids to dethrone his father! Treason! No one knows where the accusations started, but many have their suspicions. Whispers about the *haseki* witch follow on the heels of these unproven charges of Mustafa's treachery.

Mahidevran sends messenger after messenger to warn her son of his father's growing suspicions, his increasing wrath. Generations of Ottoman rulers have eliminated their brothers and sons to shield their power. Yet which son wants to believe it? For the first and only time, Mustafa ignores his mother.

Suleyman the Lawgiver lays down the law. His son, his eldest, his firstborn, is executed for treason. The crack in the sultan's heart widens. Again he defies custom and will not let his eldest son, the boy most like himself, be buried for days. Instead, he sits by Mustafa's body weeping and staring into the space his dearest son once occupied.

Rustem Pasha, grand vizier and Mirimah's husband, is dismissed for two years to assuage those who are outraged at the loss of such a prince as Mustafa.

The foreign ambassadors report to their governments:

"Mustafa was the envy of all the princes in his gloriousness, lofty titles, comma and learning, and in his liberality, justice, and munificence. Nearly all the soldiers were of one heart and mind in their love of him and it is said that the Grand Turk himself claimed that Mustafa would become sultan and deprive all his brothers, even the cripple Jihangir, of their lives."

Mahidevran Khatun retires in sorrow to Bursa, where her son is buried. She is disgraced. She cannot pay her rent. Her servants are taunted. She is cheated wherever she turns.

Khurrem writes Suleyman on campaign against the Safavids:

"There is discontent everywhere over your recent decisions, my Sultan. I ask you, I beg you, to send news quickly, very quickly, because—and I swear I am not lying—no messenger has come for the last week or two. The whole world is clamoring. All kinds of rumors are circulating. Don't think it is only for myself that I am asking."

The letters fly thick and fast.

Khurrem writes Suleyman on campaign in Syria:

"There is great talk in the city that a messenger bearing good news is coming. Everyone is saying that he'll be here in two or three days and they are getting ready to decorate the city with lights. I don't know if it is rumor or if it is true. Now, my fortune-favored, my Sultan, it is very odd that a good-news messenger should come when you yourself are wintering in Aleppo. Furthermore, my Sultan, neither the son of the Safavid Shi'a heretic shah nor his wife has been captured. Nothing has been happening. Now if a messenger arrives saying 'No progress here, nothing there,' no one is going to be happy, my Sultan...I was going to visit Bayezid soon, but now I'm not going to go until news comes from you."

Khurrem courts the ambassadors. She treats them to pomp and gifts of her own embroidery, her own servants, her own enormous wealth. She is the sultan's voice in diplomatic correspondence.

The foreign ambassadors report to their governments:

"Suleyman speaks through Roxolana when peace is his aim. She has made frequent diplomatic contacts with her native Poland, which has sent eighteen embassies to the sultan, more than any other power. King Sigismund is able to maintain peace with the empire and Roxolana enjoys a private correspondence with his son."

Khurrem writes to Sigismund II:

"I have transmitted to the sultan assurances of your friendship. He has expressed pleasure and says, 'The old king and I were like two brothers, and if it please God the Merciful, this king and I will be like son and father.'

"I will be glad to petition the sultan on your behalf if you inform me of your wishes.

"I am sending a gift of two pairs of pajamas, six handkerchiefs, and a hand towel."

She corresponds with Sultanim, sister of the defeated Safavid Shah Tahmasp. Sultanim writes Khurrem:

"The carpets for your newly completed mosque have been sent. All the people of Iran pray for Suleyman and the continuation of his sultanate."

Khurrem writes Sultanim:

"We thank you for your donations to our mosque. I cannot express strongly enough the sultan's devotion to a peaceful alliance between him and Shah Tahmasp. Make no mistake, the Emperor Suleyman's campaigns into your territories were not for the purpose of destroying the lands of Muslims, but in order to repair the houses of religions and to adorn the lands of God's law. We pray for continued peace."

Suleyman yearns for home. He writes to Khurrem and dedicates his conquests to her:

My Istanbul, my Karaman, and all the
Anatolian lands that are mine;

My Bedakshan and my Kipchak territories,
My Baghdad and my Khorsan.

Suleyman returns. His boon companion, Ibrahim Pasha, too, has been away campaigning. His rank, Khurrem complains, is nearly that of sultan. Suleyman gives him anything. He is grand vizier, he has the post, too, of governor general in Rumelia. She is vexed by his ambition and his power, by Suleyman's insistence on seating Ibrahim Pasha beside him at ceremonial occasions. She sits uneasily in her seraglio and fretting to her daughter, Mihrimah, that Ibrahim Pasha could take the throne, if not from Suleyman—for surely he is loyal to his best boyhood friend and cannot harm the most powerful man on Earth. But, she complains, Ibrahim Pasha must be capable by now of destroying her own sons, chances for the throne when Suleyman dies.

Ibrahim Pasha comes to Suleyman's quarters, as always, for their weekly suppers when they are home. They laugh and talk, reminiscing about their teachers and their games, plotting the empire's expansion. They eat and drink late into the night and Ibrahim Pasha staggers back to his quarters.

In the morning, Ibrahim's body is found in his bed, throat twisted, face swollen from strangling.

And the crack in the sultan's heart widens.

There are those who whisper that the *haseki* witch has caused Ibrahim's murder. Yet there are others who say that Suleyman himself ordered the execution.

Khurrem writes Suleyman on campaign:
"My Sultan, my health is not good. I do not mean to be the object of distress, and yet I miss you and wish you were by my side. I spend many days and nights in the hospital in the Old Palace of Women.

The hand of grief pierces her heart with its painful arrow.
In your absence, she is sick
And wails like a flute."

The ambassadors report to their governments:

"The Empress Roxolana appears to be in ill health. Suleyman departs on fewer campaigns, for she is unwilling to let him part from her for fear of death."

He is by her side. He holds her hand. Aleksandra, Roxolana, Khurrem—the women she was across fifty-three years—merge into one as she departs this Earth.

The crack in the sultan's heart is like a gorge. He cannot bear the sorrow. He retreats into poetry and will be consoled only by Mihrimah.

> Even if your reign on the imperial throne
> seems everlasting,
> do not be taken in.
> One day, a hostile wind will blow
> and bring to your land of beauty
> Heaven's misfortune and suffering.

Khurrem has left mosques and hospitals, parks and fountains, endowments for poets and artists, especially goldsmiths. As lavish as her gifts are to the people of the Ottoman Empire, never will they admit she was their queen, rightful wife of the emperor. Each building's inscription bears only the title of a favorite concubine: *haseki*.

With Khurrem dead, Suleyman determines the succession in the true tradition of the Ottomans. He executes his son Bayezid to ensure that Mehmed receives the throne. Fate's twists and turns, destiny's ironies, cannot be managed by murder. Mehmed dies of smallpox. The sultan builds a mosque in Mehmed's memory and comes out of retreat to go on campaign. In the expansion of empire, he may be truly comforted; in the excitement of war, he might be consoled and forgetful.

The Grand Turk, the Magnificent, the Lawgiver, the Emperor Suleyman whose heart has at last cracked open and broken in two, dies in his imperial tent on the eve of battle.

His son Selim, known to all as the Drunkard, succeeds him. The least favored of all his sons takes the throne. Selim follows his father's precedent and marries his *haseki.*

Mahidevran's pleas are finally heard. Selim pays her debts and purchases a house for her. She receives an income and creates an endowment for the upkeep of the tomb Selim builds for her son. When Mahidevran Khatun dies, she is buried beside Mustafa.

VI

Musicians and Dancers

"*Listening stirs
the heart
to see God.*"

*I*n the Time of Ignorance, the *jahiliyah*, before the Revelations of the Prophet, music, poetry, and dance flourished in worship and for amusement. That kings and chiefs practiced the arts is testimony to their deep-seated significance. Under the pre-Islamic reign of the Quraysh in Mecca, poets and minstrels from throughout the Arabian peninsula gathered to contest for supremacy. Women ruled the musical world as singers and players. The lute, the psaltery (which was taken to Europe by the crusaders, where it became immensely popular during the Middle Ages), the flute, the reed-pipe, and the tambourine were a few of the instruments women used.

The Hijaz was a vital trade and cultural center. Long before Islam and the vast spread of the Muslim Empire, there were cultural exchanges. Musical and poetical styles from Greece, Persia, and Byzantium were being assimilated, but although their influence was considerable, Arabian music was predominant. Persian princes visited Arabia to study poetry, while Arab songstresses, in high demand, performed throughout the region.

The arts, which truly define cultures and societies, too often recede in the legions of proud, bombastic annals about kings, politicians, and generals. When it comes to music and musicians, and recognition of their magnitude, the history of Islam is exceptional. Song and music follow Muslims from crib to crypt. Before Islam and the coming of the Prophet Muhammad, women were at the musical center and they have continued to be.[1] Many a caliph's wife, favorite concubine, or mother was a musician. Princesses engaged in the arts of music and poetry, and countless were remarkably talented, often having inherited their abilities from their skilled mothers. The patronage of women such as Abbasid queen Khayzuran and her niece Zubaydah, to name only two out of hundreds across the centuries, helped music prosper.

Both Khayzuran and Zubaydah had musical rivals for their caliphs' affections. Khayzuran contended with the singer Makhunna, who gave birth to Mahdi's daughter Olayya, and Zubaydah vied with the singer Dananir, on whom her husband, Harun al-Rashid, showered fortunes. Harun and his half sister Olayya were the best of friends. He fell head over heels for Dananir, a member of the Barmakids, an influential clan that later fell out of favor with the caliph. The singer, who had charmed Harun and alarmed Zubaydah, met with a grim execution.

Slave women were the primary purveyors of the performing arts, meticulously trained for the pleasure of the ruling class. Through them, music, poetry, and dance were largely perfected. These women were not only entertainers, but the best of them became important composers, teachers, and innovators. So-called singing girls were essential to the development of music throughout the Muslim world. The history of music in Arabia, the womb of Islam, is profoundly dependent upon women.

The first sacred art is thought by some scholars to have been dancing. Music is doubtless a close second, when harmonies were made by pounding on rocks or hollow logs and songs imitated bird and animal calls and Nature's melodies in wind or water, long before spoken language. In all three Abrahamic religions, spoken language has overtaken the language of the body.

Among the Arabs, the first song, an elegy on the death of Abel, was said to have been composed by Jubal, the son of Cain, or in Arabic, Qain. The architects of musical instruments were Cain's daughters, hence *qainat*, or singing girls. In fact, the Persians invented the oud—which in Arabic means wood—and called it *barbat*, after the word *bar* or breast, the contour of the oud, and yet another reference to the women who played it. But in legend, Lamak—Lamech in Hebrew—is said to have conceived the oud, ancestor to the lute, while his son Tubal fashioned the tambourine and the drum called *tabla*. His daughter Dilal introduced open-stringed instruments. Some Arabic histories claim the *tanbur* (*tambura*, or Greek *pandoura*), a long-necked stringed instrument like a lute, came from the people of Sodom, the ancient biblical city near the Dead Sea. The Persians are credited for the flute, the double-reed pipe, and the harp.

Some Arab historians believe the first song was the *huda*, or caravan song, which they trace to the biblical Almodad, one of the sons of Joktan, progenitor in Genesis of the first tribes of central and southern Arabia. That Almodad's name means "measure of God," or "immeasurable," seems to speak to the heavenly qualities of melody.

Universally, however subtly, each art form relies upon the other. In ancient epochs they were tightly linked. The visual arts and calligraphy require rhythm and precision and are dances of color, texture, poetry, and narrative. Dancing takes place to music or the beating of time, and dancers often tell stories in their gestures and movements. Tales of princesses and princes, of ghouls and djinns and hidden treasure, might likely be punctuated by music. Marathon epics were recounted in hypnotic poetic cadences. Music and poetry were inextricably bound, frequently one and the same, and poems were set to music. The troubadours, who sang stories, poems, and later the poetry of courtly love, are thought to have originated in Arabia and to have perfected their art as the *trobars* of Islamic Spain. The Arabic *taraba*, "to sing," is the root of the European word *troubadour*.[2]

In the Near and Middle East and Central Asia, instruments include lutes and other stringed devices, reed-pipes, tambourines, bells, clappers, and the clapping of hands and feet. The most robust instrument is the human voice. Tribal matrons dance, play, and sing in family gatherings and festivities. The arts fulfill community: women singing and dancing at weddings, births, circumcisions, burials, and others of life's principal events.

In *Arab Folktales*, Inea Bushnaq observes that among rural women "from Morocco to Iraq" and obviously far beyond, the names given to the patterns in peasant embroidery—"eye of the camel," "tree of life," "tent of the pasha"—"could well be titles to fairy tales…like a commonly told tale, the decoration of a dress displays a number of well-known elements, unchanging and recognizable by name, but arranged and combined according to the taste of the stitcher." The same rings true with designs in weaving, patterns in ceramics, and more.

The tales are old as time. They are told in palaces or tents. The raconteurs might have been members of the harem or they might be nannies regaling children with wondrous adventures, or a skilled woman or man entertaining a nighttime gathering of ordinary folk. In Arabic, they are called *raweya*, and today are often grandmothers.[3] Women chant and recite tales while they work or sing verses of love as they walk, skirts swaying, jugs or bundles balanced on their heads.

Favorite at-home Ottoman diversions, along with music and dance, Fanny Davis wrote in *The Ottoman Lady*, were visits by a *masalci*, a female storyteller, as well as *karagöz*, shadow and puppetry theater, and numerous parlor games. Although she did not relate which tale was told, Julia Pardoe recalled the entertainment of the *masalci* in her 1836 *The City of the Sultans and Domestic Manners of the Turks*: "A very pretty old…tale-teller had been invited to relieve the tedium of the evening with some of her narrations. This custom is very general during the Ramadan, and is a great resource to the Turkish ladies, who can thus recline in luxurious inaction, and have their minds amused without any personal exertion."

In his novel *A Year in Istanbul* (translated into German in 1905), Turkish writer Mehmet Tevfik describes a winter evening in which the *masalci* entertains a cozy household. Tevfik makes clear that the storyteller is a very important personage. It's known that in the eighth century C.E. Abbasid court of Harun al-Rashid, the story-teller ranked high, along with musicians and poets.

Mernissi, in *Dreams of Trespass: Tales of a Harem Girlhood*, tells of magical nights when the children and women of the household congregated in the small quarters of a storytelling aunt, and of her grandmother, who spun fables of young girls growing up to realize their aspirations, and of her mother, who recounted the marvelous fictions of Scheherazade.[4]

"I was amazed to realize that for many Westerners," Mernissi writes, "Scheherazade was considered a lovely but simple-minded entertainer, someone who narrates innocuous tales and dresses fabulously. In our part of the world, Scheherazade is perceived as a courageous heroine and is one of our rare female mythical figures. Scheherazade is a strategist and a powerful thinker, who uses her psychological knowledge of human beings to get them to walk faster and leap higher....she makes us bolder and more sure of ourselves and of our capacity to transform the world and its people."[5]

And so it is with storytellers worldwide.

Travel along the Pilgrim's Road and the assembling of people from throughout the Muslim world in Mecca for the *hajj* closes the cultural distances between Muslims. Motifs are shared from country to country; legends, stories, and songs exchanged from North Africa to Southeast Asia, though the names of heroes and heroines and the landscapes in which they perform may transform to match their new environments. Vocalizations of epics—such as the long and vivid tales of Antar or Rustum, two of Arabia's greatest heroes—still thrill audiences from Fez to Jakarta.

The storyteller uplifts the community, teaches the children through allegory, describes the origins of a people, and celebrates their accomplishments. It is an art that encompasses physical gesture, poetry, music, and sometimes, dance. Although Middle Eastern dance is "pure," that is, its movements do not tell stories, dance in other Islamic cultures can be highly narrative.

In any place or era, the arts arouse magic and through them the mysteries are joined. Music played a large role in the rituals of pre-Islamic Arab soothsayers, in the ecstasies of *majnun*, the mad poets, and the "street prophets" called *kahin*, such as those Muhammad feared he had become when the first Revelation shook him to the bone.

As in the European folktale, *The Pied Piper of Hamlin*, music draws souls away from daily life. For the Arabs, djinn could be conjured by music, recalling the Irish who brought forth the fairies with tunes. One notion has it that the djinn inspired poetry and music, like the Greek Muses. The voice of the djinn is called *azf*, for which the

293

instrument *mi'azf*, a kind of lyre, is named. The *mi'azf* in Hebrew is called *kithara*, whose sound Jews equate with God's Holy Spirit.

The spiritual effects of music are well known to Sufis. Echoing a prayer of the Prophet, "O God, let us see things as they are," in the eleventh century C.E., the Sufi al-Hujwiri wrote that "Listening to sweet sounds produces an effervescence of the substance molded in humans. It is true if the substance is true and false if the substance is false."

For the Sufi, music and dance are sources of spiritual inspiration, revelation. It is said that "Listening *(sama)* is a divine influence which stirs the heart to see God"; and "The listener can find Truth behind the Veil." In Sufi practice, music provokes mystical love and, as we've seen, women musicians were cited for their talents at awakening the spirit.

No one really knows what part music and dance actually played in the pagan worship of Arabs. The songs of pre-Islamic pilgrims on the road to Mecca still exist in the *tahil* and *talbiyya*. Saint Nilus of Sinai (d. ca. 430 C.E.) reported that northern Arabs chanted while circling the sacrificial stone dedicated to the goddess al-Lat. Pre-Islamic poets sang of this as "maidens circling a pillar."

In *Mohammad: The Man and His Faith*, Andrea posits the theory that the *tawwaf*, the circumambulation of the Ka'aba, originally a pre-Islamic ritual, was a magico-religious dance, akin to European rites of circling sacred trees, fires, or Maypoles. Such dances bind the dancer to the divinity of the object, protect the object by enclosing it in a ring, and contain the Divine chaos within the circle.

One indication that the encirclement of the Ka'aba was a dance may be that today the *tawwaf* is not done at a slow walk, but at a trot or run as it was in antiquity.

Dancing worldwide was once part of religious ritual. Some historians propose that even dances for "entertainment" originate in fertility and other rites. Yet there is also pure enjoyment, pleasure for its own sake. And dancing, Jane Ellen Harrison suggests in her 1912 *Themis: A Study of the Social Origins of the Greek Religion*, could be the vehicle through which people taught their tribal lore. Writing of

294

the Cretans, though her theories most certainly apply more broadly, Harrison says that through dancing, leadership, order, and religious concepts were developed. Women everywhere, throughout time, have been principal innovators of dancing—spiritual, as well as physical, choreographers.

The elite of pre-Islamic Arabia kept *qainat*, singing women, as well as dancers, in their households to entertain or commemorate solemn and joyful events, to lead warriors into battle and make supplications, especially for rain. Song and dance went hand in hand, particularly in ritual. Arabs and Jews both had their "well songs," entreaties for water in a chronically thirsty land. Regrettably, dancing is rarely mentioned, though it's a fair guess that dances accompanied these appeals, with prayers made through the body. Throughout time, dancing has been indispensable in appeals to the divine.

Arab singing women were sometimes called *jaradatan*, grasshoppers, probably because "grasshoppers" are associated with rain. A common pet name for a *jaradatan* was Thumad, "preserver of water." Other Arabic words for singing women are *karina* and *darjinat*, from the root word *dajana*, "cloudy." Many a poet praised these women for the beauty and intricacies of their playing, the turns, trills, and timbres of their voices, their extraordinary vibratos and otherworldly antiphonal chanting. And many a versifier wrote adoringly of tavern singers and musicians: Arabs, Syrian Greeks, Persians.

Surprisingly, the names, if not the stories, of famous pre-Islamic female singers and musicians have survived: Sirin, Zirnab, Khaula, al-Rabab, Sallama, Ra'iqa. The redoubtable Hind bint Utba was renowned as a poet and musician, although, as we've seen, she is mostly remembered for demonstrating those talents on the battlefield.

Azza al-Maila of Mecca was one of the first important female professional musicians in Islam, famous for her rendering of old Arabian songs, singing Persian melodies, and carrying on the musical traditions of pagan singers such as Ra'iqa, who was Azza's teacher. Azza played the oud and the *mi'zaf*, and coined whole new rhythmic styles.

In *Jews, Christians and Muslims,* Denny notes that Muslim peoples have nurtured an immense musical oeuvre, from flamenco to Javanese gamelan to the marching band (the Turkish army was the first to march into battle with full-blown military brass, doubtless terrifying the enemy; Beethoven's "Ode to Joy," the closing movement of his *Ninth Symphony,* was inspired by the Turkish marching bands). Hymns are sung for the Prophet's and saints' birthdays and at other religious festivals.

For all its diverse array of music, its uses and significance to the history of Islam, it is nonetheless a source of controversy. Dancing as performance is less so, for like many of the Christian church fathers, Islamic lawmakers simply dismissed most dancing, including that of Sufis, as outright immoral, without debate.[6]

Music for entertainment is condemned today in the Islamic Republic of Iran. Gone are the public venues, from cafés to nightclubs, where music and dancing took place during the era of Shah Muhammad Reza Pahlavi. The Taliban of Afghanistan viciously persecuted musicians, even destroying their tombstones, and burned instruments in public pyres. Yet happily, neither contemporary leaders nor lawmakers of the past have ever managed to silence music or stamp out dance.

There is not a word against music or dance in the Qur'an. Rather, in *Surah* after *Surah,* there are reminders that what humans possess are gifts from God the Creator, which He increases and which must be applied and appreciated:

> *Surely God is powerful over everything.*
> *Whatsoever mercy God opens to men, none can withhold.*[7]

Neither may anyone prohibit the exercise of God's gifts:

> *Say: Who has forbidden the ornament of God*
> *which He brought forth for His servants, and*
> *the good things of His providing?*
> *Say: These, on the Day of Resurrection, shall be exclusively*
> *for those who believed in this present life.*[8]

Nonetheless, some protest that singing is "unlawful" because it uses poetry and they say the Prophet denounced poetry:

There is one who buys diverting talk
to lead astray from the way of God
without knowledge, and to take it in mockery;
those — there awaits them a humbling chastisement.[9]

This reference, however, is to a specific poet-minstrel, al-Nadr ibn Harith, who satirized the new religion. Although the Prophet employed his own poet, Hassan ibn Thabit, he had an ambivalent relationship to poets and poetry, for poetry could be used against an enemy as a deadly weapon. But Muhammad's aim seems never to have been to eliminate music, poetry, or any other art. Rather, he sought to denounce the practices of the old religion. He had his own favorite singer, a woman named al-Sayma.

Although music is fundamental in Arab life, for centuries lawmakers have squabbled about whether it is permitted under *Shari'a*, and which music and where and how much. All cultures have their puritans and killjoys, all religions have their fundamentalists and extremists, strident and intimidating. Wine, women, and song are forbidden by sophistic factions everywhere. Islamic lawgivers who condemn music find their most potent weapons in the *Hadith*. They quote Traditions that allege the Prophet cursed singing and singers and called singing women and stringed instruments signs of the end of the world. Aisha gave out a Tradition that Muhammad had once said, "Verily, Allah has made the singing girl unlawful, and the selling of her and her price and teaching her." Yet this is considered by some scholars to refer only to tavern singers (and would also indicate another of the Prophet's assertions against slavery and mistreatment of women, as well as decadent behavior).

On the other hand, *Hadith* being what they are — fortunately broad enough to embrace argument — it's not difficult to find numerous Traditions illustrating how Muhammad loved music and listened to it. Aisha also handed down three Traditions that uphold Muhammad's enjoyment of music. In one, she recalled that her father, Abu Bakr, visited her apartment while two women were play-ing tambourines. The Prophet was there, wrapped in a robe. When Abu Bakr, with his usual starchiness, rebuked the musicians, Muhammad chided his Companion to leave them alone, "for it is the time of the festivals."

Typically, Abu Bakr would not let up. On another occasion, Aisha reported, he entered his daughter's home to reprimand her for singing with two other women, but the Prophet again told him to stop.

Umar, too, was narrow-minded, indeed he could be downright mean-spirited, though his devotion to Islam and the Prophet was absolute. One day he visited Aisha's apartment and heard the singing of a slave woman. When he entered, Muhammad was smiling.

"O Prophet of God," Umar said. "What makes you smile?"

"A slave was singing here, but she ran away as soon as she heard your step."

"I won't depart," Umar gruffed, "until I hear what the Messenger heard."

Muhammad called the woman back to resume her singing, then listened to her intently.

Innumerable other testimonies show his support for music. It is reported that Muhammad and Khadija's wedding was celebrated with "mirth, music, and dancing," as were the nuptials of Fatima and Ali. The Prophet counted many musicians among his friends and associates, including a singer named Shirin, who may have been the sister of his Coptic concubine, Maryam, although she may in fact have been the famous pre-Islamic musician called Sirin.

The *taghbir*, the cantilation or recitation of the Qur'an, is truly music, not mere modulation of the voice as opposers to song would have it. So is the *adhan*, or call to prayer, inaugurated by the Prophet in the second year of the Hegira, when he made Bilal the first *muezzin*, caller to prayer. Bilal had been a slave of a certain Quraysh in Mecca, cruelly abused by his master for his conversion to Islam. Abu Bakr heard the slave's cries, his testimony to the One God, even as he was brutally beaten, and bought him and freed him. Bilal is the patron of *muezzins*. The Prophet called him "The First Fruit of

Abyssinia," and often asked him to "sing us a *ghazal* (love song)." Muhammad made frequent reference to the "Beautiful Voice," likening the chanting of singers reciting his Revelations to "the pipes of David."

The music of Muslim peoples is hugely diverse, but the *taghbir*, the recitation of the Qur'an, remains uniform, although there are several styles.

There is a belief that when Moses received the Ten Commandments, God ordered him to read them: *"Musa ki!"* "Moses, recite!" In Farsi, the Persian language, *Musa ki* became *musiki*, "music."[10] Qur'an derives from *iqra*, the word for recite or read and *ki* also comes from *iqra*.

Muhammad's tolerance was buried with him. His successors, Abu Bakr and Umar, the first two Rightly Guided caliphs, had more interest in the sword than in the arts and busied themselves securing Islam. During his two-year rule, Abu Bakr managed to ordain that music and dance were among the "forbidden pleasures," or *malahi*, although it's believed he did not interfere with the *qainat* of noble and wealthy households. But public musicians and tavern singers were restrained. In that period—so characteristic of the severity that follows the death of an enlightened spiritual leader—two singing women's teeth were pulled and their hands cut off. Chances are, however, that the punishment was not because they were musicians, but because they used their talents to ridicule Islam.

In Abu Bakr's time, the words for female musicians became synonyms for courtesan and adulteress. Bit by bit, lists grew of "dishonorable" people, who followed "infamous" professions. Christian Europe, too, saw the demonization of artists: as Karin van Nieuwkerk reminds us in *"A Trade Like Any Other,"* in fourteenth-century Germany, for instance, singers, musicians, and dancers were blacklisted and it was assumed that any woman practicing these arts was a prostitute. By the Middle Ages, Muslim singers and dancers were considered to be of questionable morality, even as they were members of elite households; even as they may have been slaves with no alternatives; even as caliphs acquired hundreds of them. Attitudes of disdain for artists continue to suffuse elements of many societies; performers were often looked upon as a class far below the rest of the respectable world, marginalized in part because of their itinerancy, which marked them as thieves, beggars, wantons, and panderers.

"In spite of the austere regime of Abu Bakr," Henry George Farmer writes in A History of Arabian Music to the XIIIth Century, "there appear to have been a goodly few who indulged in the malahi. Nature is not to be forever thus pent up. The rebound too often comes; and in casting off its shackles, humanity not seldom bursts likewise through the barriers of Faith."

Umar, the second Rightly Guided caliph, was something of a Muslim Calvin, tramping through the streets of Medina at night checking on its residents to see that there were no infractions of the law. But having heard the singing woman in the Prophet's own household, Umar favored them, or at least held his tongue, except for momentary outbursts, as when he referred to singing as "the braying of asses." He was, however, enthusiastic about the gloriously melodious recitation of the Qur'an and defended it when others questioned its appropriateness.

The third Rightly Guided caliph Uthman came from the upper classes of Mecca, was wealthy, and had financed Muhammad during the worst of times. He was exceptionally fond of diversion and display. By then, the Empire of Islam had grown and so had its riches, along with slaves, palaces, and sumptuous living. Music, musicians, dancers, and poets were part of these new treasures.

It was during Uthman's reign that the male professional musician first appeared. Women carried so much authority in music that these men affected feminine habits, right down to applying henna to their hands.

(In what must have been an astonishing piece of ritual theater in Lucknow, India, an eighteenth-century Indo-Muslim court expressed its devotion to the Twelve Imams of Shi'a tradition by dramatizing their births. The emperor himself played a pregnant woman, acting out the pangs of labor. He then produced an imaginary infant, who received the customary sixth-day ceremony after the birth. These dramas seem not unlike puberty rites in primal cultures, where men pretend to take on women's attributes and thereby their power.)

The fourth Rightly Guided caliph Ali was himself a poet, and not only authorized the study of arts and sciences, but protected them. His patronage, as well as that of Uthman, Aisha bint Abu Bakr (in spite of her father), her niece Aisha bint Talha, and Ali's grand-daughter Sukayna bint Husayn during the Umayyad Dynasty, put the stamp of respectability and allowableness on music, despite conservative opposition. When one of the Quraysh elite thrashed one of Aisha's favorite musicians, she refused to speak to the man until he'd begged the artist's pardon.

It is said that the four Rightly Guided caliphs made Islam a religion, while the Umayyads who followed upon the death of Ali made it into an empire. In the century of their reign, Islam reached the Atlantic and China. They shifted the capital from Arabia to Damascus, an auspicious move for the arts, which could more freely flourish in a cultural crossroads, and introduced the first of many golden ages of Islam.

The Umayyad Dynasty was launched with an artistic bang. The first caliph of the House of Umayya, Mu'awiya, surrounded himself with scientists and artists of all disciplines. His wife, Maisuna, was an accomplished and renowned poet. Her descendants, the subsequent Umayyad caliphs, were endowed with her talents, interests, and tastes. No house was without its singing woman. Throngs of musicians, poets, and dancers crowded the Umayyad court, a golden age, auguring the next, more extravagant golden age led by the Abbasids. During the Umayyad regime, the musician Yunus al-Katib began collecting biographical and historical materials about Arab music, introducing the first musical literature. In the Abbasid era, Ibn al-Kalbi (d. 197 A.H./819 C.E.) created the *Kitab al-nagham* (Book of Melodies) and *Kitab al-qiyan* (Book of Singing Girls). The lively *Kitab al-aghani* (Book of Songs), assembled in the fourth Islamic century, is a vibrant description of Baghdad court life and contains a wealth of anecdotal and biographical detail about musicians. Clear distinctions are made between popular and serious art and separate lists are given of each.

While it is thought that Antoine Galland introduced *The Thousand and One Nights* to the West in 1704—having constructed the tales into a cohesive, Europeanized text and expurgated the naughty bits—in fact, many had been floating around Europe for centuries, brought back by the Crusades. (Various beloved romances, such as *Tristan and Isolde*, are believed to originate from literary and folkloric traditions of the Near and Middle East and North Africa, although they are rarely acknowledged as such.) The "evening stories" told in the streets and markets of Baghdad and Cairo, some of which would be compiled into *The Thousand and One Nights*, were circulating by the fourth century A.H., indeed were being collected in Persia in a book called *Hazar Afsa*, "The Thousand Stories." Featured are the powerful and generous Harun al-Rashid and glamorous Zubaydah. It introduces the filibustering Scheherazade, whose victory is not thanks to her charms but to her good education, quick wits, and power of endurance. Sadly, as Naguib Mahfouz writes in his modern Egyptian novel, *Middaqq Alley*, today in much of Cairo as elsewhere, the bard has been discarded, replaced by radios and television.

The Abbasids boasted such women as Basbas, a slave imported from Medina, where she had been the idol of the Quraysh; Shariyya, a native of Basra, who married an Andalusian prince and taught another famous singer, Farida; Badhl, who is said to have had a repertory of 30,000 songs, composed her own book of songs, and taught Harun al-Rashid's ill-fated concubine Dananir.

Competition was great. In the ninth century of the Common Era, Shariyya and another singer, Arib, were deadly rivals and divided the entire city of Samarra, then the capital of the Abbasid caliphate, situated on the Tigris River, such that fans of one did not speak to aficionados of the other.

Arib, not only renowned for her singing, was also a marvelous cook. The caliph al-Mu'tamid would eat nothing that was not prepared by her. At her request for "a share of his table," the governor of Mosul sent Arib bread, meat, and confectionary.

"O you stupid barbarian!" she wrote him. "In the name of Allah, Merciful and Compassionate! Do you think I belong to the Turks or wild soldiers? May Allah protect me from you!" The note was accompanied by delicacies of her own kitchen: vegetables, palm blossoms, pockets of bread with partridge—all served on a plate covered with gold brocade.

There was an ulterior motive for rulers to support singers: as in many cultures, singers like poets, were the journalists of the day and if paid well enough could help consolidate the empire by praising its glories and the ruling elite and their genealogies, while they traversed the territories.

That clerics outlawed the performing arts did not matter a whit to the Commanders of the Faithful, the caliphs in their glorious palaces made content by musicians, dancers, poets, and tellers of tales. With the Abbasid Dynasty, the arts thrived in Arabia as they never had before. Music was the axis; the harem was the hub. The ruling elite of the Abbasid and other dynasties spent massive amounts of money on the professional music and dance education of slave women. These were the cream of the slave crop. Harun al-Rashid kept an orchestra of a hundred musicians in constant attendance. His wife, Zubaydah, was also fond of music, and had an "orchestra" of fifty slave women trained to recite the Qur'an from sunup to sundown, so that the Revelations echoed constantly throughout the palace.

Harun's father, al-Mahdi, while an enthusiastic patron, gifted with a fine singing voice, nonetheless frowned upon the practice of the art by noble Arabs and would not allow musicians to perform before his sons and heirs, Musa al-Hadi and Harun al-Rashid. He neither wanted them exposed to that which was deemed unlawful nor to invite "degeneracy" into their lives, when they had an empire to run. Shades of Mahdi's father, caliph al-Mansur, the "Father of Farthings."

Rulers endowed the best singers with fortunes, gave them high positions at court, and supported their families. Some, like the singer Abdah al-Tanbuirya who was married to the Abbasid caliph Mutawakkil, reached the highest positions in society.

In 128 A.H./750 C.E., Abd al-Rahman ibn Mu'awiya, a young man in his teens, the only surviving member of the Umayyads, who had all been slaughtered by the Abbasids led by al-Saffah, escaped Syria, traversed North Africa, and appeared in Iberia. There, in al-Andalus, Abd al-Rahman (r. 134 A.H./756 C.E. to 166 A.H./788 C.E.) reestablished the House of Umayya, a sovereignty of magnificent accomplishments that more or less lasted until the fifteenth century C.E. The center of Umayyad power dwindled across the centuries (splitting into city-states, or *taifa*); nonetheless, the artistic achievements continued, until the Christian rulers Ferdinand and Isabela succeeded in ridding Spain of all Muslims and most Jews, with the help of the Inquisition. The arts and sciences under the Muslim reign "flourished with such brilliance," Farmer notes, "that their light was reflected to all parts, not only the world of Islam, but of Western Europe."[11]

Abd al-Rahman, Menocal writes in *The Ornament of the World*, was bent on re-creating the culture from which he'd been forced to flee and to which he could never return (therefore nostalgically introducing, for example, palm trees to Spain). Thus for a long time, the music of the Muslims in al-Andalus was notable for preserving Arab forms, while in Baghdad, where the Abbasids ruled, it was experiencing all sorts of changes. For a while in al-Andalus, the purity of Arab music was cherished, even horded. The courts filled with musicians and singers, and prominent among these, as always, were women.

Across the centuries, al-Andalus boasted of—and honored—musical women such as Afza, who sang and played the oud and was the favorite of Abd al-Rahman. The lengthy lists of women musicians include Fadhl, originally in service to one of Harun al-Rashid's daughters; Musabih, who was said to have "reached the highest point of excellence and skill, together with sweetness of voice," and in whose honor poetry was written; Hamduna and Ulayya, granddaughters of the greatest Andalusian singing and music teacher, Ziryab; Qamar, a slave who belonged to the amir of Seville and was noted for her eloquence, elocution, and compositions; Tarab; Bazya; Uns al-Qulub, and many, many others.

North Africa, Farmer writes, was "deeply influenced in the arts by al-Andalus. The influence of the Andalusians in Africa was especially marked after the fall of Seville [to the Christians in 626 A.H./1248 C.E.], when 40,000 of its people went into exile."[12] Among them was the family of the pirate queen al-Sayyida al-Hurra.

As Islam broke into sects, many of their founders opposed music. As in religious institutions worldwide, control had to be exercised over the faithful. Dancing and music making are individually empowering. The worshiper alone can connect with the indwelling Divine spirit, completely apart from the dictates of the institution.

Nonetheless, the old pagan chantings of the pilgrimage, *tahil* and *talibiyya*, were allowed to stand and are legal, as are the musical instruments that accompany them. Like the Catholic Church, which absorbed local customs wherever it sought to conquer, despite the grinding machinations of the Muslim lawmakers, the customs of the people endured. The Islamic ethos is ever solid. Muslims are all part of one splendid *umma*, but all around, and in overlay and pentimento, the unique character of each original culture persists, along with its arts. Regardless of rules and laws and puritanical dictates, there could be no choice but to allow music, Farmer notes, "when joy was allowed, such as on days of private festivals like betrothals, weddings, births and circumcisions. Finally, the love-song was allowable."[13]

A compromise was struck at the Umayyad court in Damascus (though not necessarily outside it) that could satisfy the pious: *hijab*. When his wives and concubines were not with him, a thin curtain was drawn between the caliph and the female musicians. Azza al-Maila performed behind a curtain, as did the illustrious singer Jamila al-Medina and her troupe during their famous "musical pilgrimage." Jamila was noted, however, for dropping the drapery during special fêtes at her own house.

Judaism, Christianity, and Islam destroyed, while simultaneously assimilating, the ancient pagan rituals in order to establish themselves. Sexuality and fertility in female dance were vilified. In

305

the Bible, references are often made to men dancing, but there are few mentions of women's dances, which are frequently associated with polytheists, goddess worshipers, and slatterns.

The word *dance* is thought to come from the Sanskrit, *tanha,* "joy of life," which is apparently related to the Arabic *raks,* "to cele- brate." As music cultivates the spirit among Sufis, so is dancing the most acute meditation and profound exhilaration. The "Whirling Dervishes" were founded by Rumi in the thirteenth century C.E. The Mevlevi, and their style of dancing, are by no means the only Sufi form; there are differing modes worldwide, although the Mevlevi are best known to Westerners, occasionally performing on stages.[14] The elation produced by dancing is called *hadrah,* "the presence," and each step "[moves] us upward toward a new freedom of spirit, toward ecstasy," Iris Stewart writes in *Sacred Woman, Sacred Dance.*

"The word *darvish* translates as 'the sill of the door,' describing the dancer as standing at the door to enlightenment. Some Sufi orders, though not all, practice dance movements prescribed to achieve spiritual ecstasy."

The whirling dance may have come from a similar practice in ancient China, which was taken by the Mongols to Balkh (in what is now Afghanistan), where Rumi was born.

"In that [Mongol] dance," Stewart tells us, "the women acting as religious mediums, whirled with a flower in hand until they fell to the ground in a trance. Ketharas, shrill flutes and drums accompa- nied the rite."

The names of most dancers, in almost all cultures, are left out of historical records, and there are few if any acknowledgments of their artistic accomplishments. When dancers are spoken of in the Islamic biographies, it is not for and about their art, but usually an aside within an account of a romantic entanglement. Despite good intentions, therefore, modern scholars are adrift when it comes to discussions of dancing in the Islamic world.

In *Serpent of the Nile: Women and Dance in the Arab World,* Wendy Buonaventura[15] proposes that the European Orientalist painters, whose fantasies have so informed our skewed understand- ing of Muslim peoples, are, in fact, owed something of a debt "for the record they bequeathed us, for without them we would have no detailed knowledge of Arabic dance in former times." This is only true of a certain kind of publicly performed dance. Meanwhile, Persian, Turkish, and Indian miniatures also help us determine the motions of dancers.

Indeed, these paintings illustrate certain steps, gestures, poses, and movements, which might otherwise be lost to us. "Western expansion in the nineteenth century nourished the cult of otherness," van Nieuwkerk writes, "particularly of the exotic and bizarre other. Eroticism was one of the main aspects of the exotic 'Orient.' Travelers were fascinated by the licentious female dancers, who provided them with a means to express the differentness and sensuality of 'the East.'"[16]

The male European, American, and Russian painters and photographers who rushed to embrace the exotica of the Muslim world had no access to "respectable" women in the harems. So, they made it up. Yet they were free to watch dance in public—often in disreputable places or on the street and in the marketplace, where much entertainment took place. They were enthralled, smitten especially by the dancers, whose postures bore little resemblance to the stiff stances of European dancers at the time. As Kabbani notes in *Imperial Fictions,* "the Oriental woman was linked, like a primitive goddess, with cycles of the supernatural….Her beauty is linked to the darker elements…causes the unleashing of evil….Even the moon turned red as Salomé danced.

"The dance became…a metaphor for the whole East."

European women were invited to visit some harems and periodically recorded their experiences watching dance. Interpretations vary wildly and get snagged on the gentlewomen's cultural biases. They are habitually unspeakably "shocked" or "appalled" by what they regard as the sheer vulgarity of vigorous and sinuous hip movements, shaking, and torso undulations. In 1717, however, Lady Mary Montagu wrote of a native dance that "was very different from what I had seen before. Nothing could be more artfull or proper to raise certain Ideas, the Tunes so soft, the motions so Languishing, accompany'd with pauses and dying Eyes, halfe falling back and then recovering themselves in such artfull a Manner that I am very positive the coldest and most rigid Prude upon Earth could not have look'd upon them without thinking of something not to be spoken of."[17]

A century later, the unflappable Pardoe wrote of a dancer entertaining guests who gathered to pay their respects on the birth of a child: "she twisted the tambourine in the air with the playfulness of a child; and having denoted the measure, returned it to one of the women, who immediately commenced a wild chant, half song and half recitative, which was at times caught up in chorus by the others, and at times wailed out by the dancer only, as she regulated the movements of her willow-like figure to the modulations of the music. The Turkish women dance very little with their feet; it is the grace and art displayed in the carriage of the body and arms which form the perfection of their dancing; the rapid snapping of the fingers, meanwhile, producing the effect of castanets."[18]

Pardoe also attended an event in which some of the female dancers wore male dress.

Ancient miniatures from Muslim India show women performing what are traditionally thought of as Hindu dances, such as *khatak*.

The sixteenth-century Indo-Muslim Sultan Ghiyath Shah, whose retinue included a thousand warrior women, is said also to have owned 16,000 slave women trained in singing, dancing, and playing musical instruments, reading aloud, reciting the Qur'an, and even wrestling. The historian Shaykh Sikander ibn Muhammad Manjhu (961 A.H./1553 C.E. to 1020 A.H./1611 C.E.) wrote in his history of the Gujarat, *Mir'at-I Sikandari*: "It is said that the expenditure...on women's dresses and perfumes exceeded that in any king's palace. [The emperor] had four *akharas*, that is to say, 'bands' of dancing girls, who were each unrivalled in their special art. Forty women held the torches while dancing girls performed. Every dancing girl, moreover, had two attendants, one of whom held her *pan* box, and the other poured sweet-scented oil on the torches, for they never burnt any [except] oil scented with rose perfume. All the women's clothes were of gold brocade, or embroidered with gold."

It was not until the nineteenth century that Western historical documents describe dancers as individuals and give them credit for their attainments. Then, in a sudden shift of attitude in Europe at the turn of the twentieth century, dance actually took the forefront of the arts for a little while. The early-twentieth-century American choreographer Ruth St. Denis made dances with "Oriental" themes. Indeed, these were her most successful works, and while not necessarily authentic, ultimately influenced modern dance movements. Sadly, the so-called belly dance, a ritual thought to have originated long before recorded time as a way to teach maidens the facts of life and to invoke fertility and a happy married life, was largely transformed in the nineteenth century into "exotic" show dancing, largely for the Western trade. Nevertheless, folkloric dances whose beginnings are in ancient forms, remain.

Van Nieuwkerk notes, writing about contemporary Egypt in "A Trade Like Any Other," that professional dancing is not acceptable in Islam. In many regions, women and men are expected to dance separately in separate spaces, though there are vast differences from place to place and culture to culture. As Buonaventura wisely observes, however, there is something vital about this separation at certain momentous occasions, when dances become sacraments.

"Kurdish men and women, whether Muslim or Christian dance together at certain events," Garnett observed in the nineteenth century. "Kurdish warriors dance with their sweethearts customarily at small gatherings where no strangers are present. On other occasions the men and women dance separately, though the latter even then lay aside their veils, no matter how great the crowd of spectators."

The *tchopee* at weddings begins with the men dancing first, then the music struck up again and a string of about thirty ladies advanced, hand-in-hand, with slow and graceful steps, resplendent with gold spangles and parti-colored silks, and without even the pretext of a veil. This was a really beautiful sight and quite novel to me, who had never in the East seen women, especially ladies as all of these were, so freely mixing with the men without the slightest affectation of concealment....The line or string of ladies moved slowly and wavingly round the circle of men. Sometimes advancing a step toward the center, sometimes retiring, balancing their bodies and heads in a very graceful manner. The tune was soft and slow, and none of their movements were in the least abrupt or exaggerated....This exhibition lasted about half an hour. The music then ceased, and the ladies retired to their homes, first veiling themselves from head to foot, which seemed a rather superfluous precaution, as the crowd which was looking on at the dance far exceeded that which they were at any time likely to meet in the streets of Sulimania.[19]

Garnett's description seems to address those qualities in dancing that are personal, transporting, performed as if the exterior world does not exist no matter the numbers of observers, while the return to veiling "head to foot" signals reentry into everyday life.

Today, Kurdish women, usually matrons, perform with men to whom they are related in this one dance. It's thought that restrictions are more severe, because women no longer work side by side with the men.

That there are no personalities in religious dance is reasonable. In antiquity and even into modern times, movements were probably created collectively and handed down since prehistory. It may be that movements and gestures similar to those found in Arabia even today, distinguished by the action in the hips, were once found in dances throughout the world. Feet generally stay flat on the ground, and indeed, it was not until Westerners arrived that Turkish dancers were brought up onto their toes. The Ottoman sultan Selim III (r. 1167 A.H./1789 C.E. to 1185 A.H./1807 C.E.) imported French dancing masters to teach ballet, and perhaps social dancing, to his harem. In music, the West also made inroads into Ottoman traditions: Mahmut II (1163 A.H./1785 C.E. to 1217 A.H./1839 C.E.) abolished the Janissary marching band and brought Giuseppe Donizetti, brother of the opera composer Gaetano, to train an all-woman imperial band to play Western music. Selim's successor, Abdulmecit, was a great fan of the group, which consisted of forty slaves dressed in men's costumes.

Young women chosen for an Ottoman sultan's bed were brought to him in processions of singers and musicians—the marching band recycled for romance.

In his early-twentieth-century *Bihishti Zewar* (Perfecting Women), Maulana Ashraf Ali Thanawi, outlining rules for young women, deems certain customs including dancing and music at weddings as "sinful but inconsequential." There are two kinds of "forbidden and illegitimate" forms of dancing at weddings: the worst is performance in men's quarters by "dancers displaying and moving their hips and waist" for this is adultery and can also create disinterest of the bridegroom in his wife; but dancing arranged for the women is equally wrong, for, Thanawi writes, "the performances of monkeys are forbidden, isn't it much worse to have people dance?"

Perhaps reacting harshly to what he may have considered to be loose Western influences, Thanawi tars it all with one brush. But most religious opinion creates a hierarchy of the arts. Quranic recitation is the musical pinnacle, while dancing and singing are at the bottom of the heap—especially in contexts where other condemned activities, such as drinking, take place. The Qur'an expressly forbids intoxicating drinks. (The Prophet, however, was known to have enjoyed some grape and date juices. Thus, fermented wines passed frequently for juices.)

The Egyptian novelist and feminist Nawal al-Sadaw'i once remarked that Westerners see Muslim women in extremes: completely cowed behind the curtain of the harem or as bawdy belly dancers. Edward Said, in *Orientalism*, writes that, to the Orientalist, "an Oriental is that impossible creature whose libidinal energy drives him to paroxysms of overstimulation and yet he is a puppet in the eyes of the world, staring vacantly out at a modern landscape he can neither understand nor cope with."

The West, Said notes, "invented the East." Unfortunately, Said says little about the feminine. Yet Muslim women are precisely the seed of "Orientalism." The roots of Western perceptions are found in representations of the "Othered" female, the "East" sexualized and waiting to be penetrated. Nowhere is this more evident than in our perception of its dancers.[20]

Jamila al-Medina

The most famous singer of the early Umayyad period, Jamila was a freewoman of the Banu Sulaym, whose talents brought her wealth and fame. She was renowned as a singer and teacher. She died ca. 98 A.H./720 C.E.

Each day, Jamila sneaks away from her duties and goes to stand by the house of her mistress's neighbor, Sa'ib Khathir. She memorizes the notes of his songs and when she is ready, she sits her mistress down and sings the songs of Khathir and the songs she has composed while she washes clothes and sweeps floors and plumps pillows and chops mint and dates.

Soon, Jamila is the talk of Medina. The city of the Prophet rings with praise for the girl whose voice shatters hearts and sets minds to thinking of nothing but Paradise. Soon, the house of her mistress fills with men begging to be taught by Jamila, to learn the songs of Jamila. And Jamila gains her freedom.

She marries. She chooses well. A wealthy man, with a splendid house where she can hold concerts and teach the nobles and slaves who throng to her. The slave masters hire her to train their girls. They will bring high prices with the name of Jamila behind them. "In the art of music," her students say, "Jamila is the tree and we are the branches."

She collects fifty women of her own, and teaches them to play the lute and to sing. Jamila's orchestra of *qainat* becomes the center of attraction. Jamila is generous. She lends her orchestra to Sallama al-Zarqa, Azza al-Maila, Sallama al-Qass, Julaida, Rabiha, al-Fariha,

Bulbula, and Habbaba, who will win the deepest affection of Caliph Yazid and be his constant companion. When she dies, Yazid will cling to Habbaba's body until it is forceably taken from him. He will never lift his head again. He, too, will die within a week, the music in his heart silenced.

At Jamila's house, all is bright and happy. At Jamila's house the *qainat* perform in the open. She will not have curtains distorting the exquisite sounds that transport her guests.

And so it goes, delightful years, and to thank God for the blessings bestowed on her Jamila decides on a pilgrimage, a musical *hajj*. She invites all the musicians of Medina, men and women, and the poets, too. Her fifty *qainat* will go, as well. They pile into magnificent litters and sway along the Pilgrim's Road singing *tahil* and *talbiyya*. Do angels sing? The folk along the way stop whatever they are doing to listen to angels.

In Mecca, the greatest musicians and poets await Jamila's cortege and greet them with song and verse, with magnificent feasts, with the best of everything. They sing and pray, they circle the Ka'aba, and then they return to Medina to celebrate for three days. The fifty *qainat* sing and play on and on behind a curtain, and at the end, the grande finale, Jamila herself sings with her lute and her women.

Jamila's fame cannot be contained, it seems to wrap the land and stars. One night she dreams and wakes fearing for her soul. She calls together all her friends for a final party, a last concert before she will retire to spend her days in prayer.

She tells the men and women gathered at her home of her decision. She asks them to tell her what they think: Did her dream portend the condemnation of her soul? Opinions are divided. Some must surely be in fear themselves, for the lawmakers have opposed song and dance.

An old man full of wisdom, experience, and knowledge of the law raises his voice. Do not give up, he tells her. "Singing is one of the greatest pleasures and is more pleasant for the soul than any of the things which it desires. It stimulates the heart, strengthens understanding, brings joy to the soul, and provides wide scope of great opinion. Difficult tasks are made easier by it. Armies become victorious through it. Despots are so captivated by it they despise themselves when they hear it.

"Singing heals the sick," the old man tells Jamila. "and those whose heart, understanding, and perception have withered away. It makes the rich richer and the poor more contented and satisfied when they hear it so that they no longer demand possessions.

"He who retains singing is a man of learning, and he who renounces singing is ignorant. There is nothing more exalted and nothing more beautiful than song. Why is it considered right to abandon it, and why is use not made of it in Divine service?"

Jamila al-Medina sings on for the rest of her life.

Olayya bint al-Mahdi

Olayya bint al-Mahdi was the half sister of Abbasid caliph Harun al-Rashid. She is the only known freeborn singer of the period. Her mother was the singer Maknunna, a serious rival to Khayzuran, who said of her that "no other woman has made my position so difficult." Olayya was born in 160 A.H./776 C.E., and was Harun's favorite sibling. She died in 210 A.H./826 C.E., outliving him by seventeen years.

Harun al-Rashid is angered with Olayya. His sister has fallen in love with not one, but two slaves, and writes passionate lyrics about them. Harun sulks. He reprimands her. It is improper, inappropriate. He will send them away.

Olayya lowers her chin, smiling at him while he rants. She knows he cannot stay angry at her long. She is too beautiful, her voice too heavenly, and they have been the best of friends since they were children.

Nevertheless, he shakes off the temptation to relent. These love affairs enrage him. He is caliph and she is a princess and it is unseemly. He orders one of the boys to be sold and forbids Olayya from ever mentioning the other again. He storms out of her quarters and when she knows he has safely gone, she falls onto her bed laughing and sobbing at the same time.

It is not in Olayya's nature to wallow in misery or hide in disgrace for long. She is a woman of solutions, as decisive as any caliph or vizier.

316

She calls on Abu Hafs, a blind poet, and asks him to compose verses that will soften Harun's heart. When he delivers the flattering lyrics, she shuts herself in her chambers and sets them to music. When words and melody are perfectly matched, lovers nestled like spoons, she sends for a bevy of Harun's slave women and teaches them every word, every note, every nuance, then rehearses them to perfection.

Harun is staggered when he hears the song and its story, which glorifies him and reminds him how much his sister loves him. He sends for Olayya and when she arrives, carefully downcast, he greets her with the old affection. She mutters an apology and he grins.

"Now sing the song yourself," he tells her, for hers is the finest of all the voices in the court. As the song tumbles out of Olayya's mouth, the tears plummet from the caliph's eyes.

"I will never be angry with you again, my dearest," he says.

That night the slave boy, one of the two she had loved, appears at her door, a gift from Harun al-Rashid.

She is merry. Optimistic. Full of fun and quick with answers. Her clothing rivals even that of Harun's extravagant wife Zubaydah. When a blemish appears on Olayya's otherwise flawless brow, she designs a magnificent headdress that is the talk of the court. Soon everyone is wearing them.

Olayya and Harun, dearest brother and sister, ride together, dine together, play music together, write poems to one another. Zubaydah sometimes joins in their amusements, for she, too, admires her sister-in-law's beauty, talent, and courage. They are the weapons that bend Harun and his court to her pleasure.

One day, Zubaydah appears in Olayya's quarters.

"I have," she tells Olayya, "a problem that I believe you can help me solve."

"Do you mean the new slave woman? That paragon of beauty? Whatshername?"

"Yes, Whatshername!"

"Sister, you are jealous."

"Who would not be? You were there when Harun produced in her honor an entertainment where everyone, hundreds, were pres-

317

ent, all dressed in finery, all awed by this woman! I must do some-thing. I cannot sit back in silence while she distracts my husband!"

"Sister," Olayya assures Zubaydah, "don't let the incident alarm you. For by God, I will bring him back to you. I shall compose a new verse and set it to a new melody and teach it to all my maids. Your maids will learn it along with mine."

A few evenings later, Harun takes the fresh air in the palace courtyard. He is composing verses in his head to his new, exquisite *jarya*, thinking of words that rhyme with sunset, with twilight, with dusk—musk, husk, tusk, brusque, mollusk, and west, best, rest, lest, impressed, breast, digest...

Behind him he hears a faint tune, which is surely the sound of his smitten heart, but which grows louder and louder until suddenly he is surrounded by Olayya and Zubaydah, each at the head of a train of maidens, all splendidly attired, singing, as if with one voice, a song whose chorus begins, "Departed from me, though my heart will not part from him."

Harun claps his hands with delight. He had planned an evening of unparalleled enchantments with his new *jarya*, that paragon of beauty, but all thoughts of departing this marvelous com-pany disappear.

At dawn he declares to Olayya and Zubaydah that he has never before had such a happy day. He signals his eunuchs, who shower the party with thousands upon thousands of gold dirhams.

None mourn Harun al-Rashid more deeply than Olayya. In her great sorrow at his death, she forsakes wine and song, until the new caliph, Harun's son Amin, forces her to resume them for his own amusement. Yet never again does she laugh as heartily or sing as angelically as she had with and for her dear brother.

VII

Rulers, Regents, Queen Mothers, and Philanthropists

"We have left the account for the Day of Accountings."

*F*rom seventeenth-century traveler Raphael du Mans's *Estat de la Perse en 1660* to Lady Mary Worley Montagu's eighteenth-century *Letters from the East* to the nineteenth-century fable scenarios of pre-Raphaelite painters and printmaker Thomas Allom's fantasized engravings and missionary Henry Harris Jessup's railing on about lost souls in unnatural intercourse in his *The Women of the Arabs* to images by Henri Matisse and Pablo Picasso of languid, spread-leg courtesans, the harem has been an obsession to those who journeyed to North Africa and the Near East—and those who didn't. Among them was the French painter Jean-Auguste-Dominique Ingres, whose neoclassical 1814 *Grande Odalisque* virtually defined how for more than a century the West would view women of the Ottoman harems. Yet he never set foot outside Europe, and it's doubtful he ever laid eyes on a Turkish woman.

There's no question that the writings of some European visitors provided real and useful information. Yet while a few observers were truly perceptive and unprejudiced, most were apparently not. All were naturally hampered by cultural limitations in their understanding, and unless they were women, had little or no contact with female society.

The harem did not appear until the Abbasid period, when women came to be secluded behind walls, a practice said to have been introduced to Arab princes by the Persians. The Sassanid Dynasty, which ruled Persia from 224 C.E. until 29 A.H./651 C.E., fashioned a marvelous culture, with unparalleled architectural inventions and art that glorified the monarchy and its Zoroastrian religion. The splendor and pomp of the Sassanid courts and their large harems could not help but dazzle the conquering Arabs, sons of the desert.

Zoroastrianism had become an elitist religion. Downtrodden and thoroughly sick of the depraved aristocracy and the spiritual practice they'd made decadent, the people turned almost immediately to their Arab conquerors, who brought tribal democracy and a fresh faith that promised social justice and equality. But Arab liberalism was soon replaced by a feudal system patterned along grandiose Persian lines. Across time, with riches, conquests, and cross-cultural influences, the seclusion of women was institutionalized. Their isolation became Abbasid dynastic policy.

At the time of the Revelations, certain Arab tribes veiled and secluded their women for protection, but this bore no resemblance to Persian and later Arab segregation. Never mind that the Prophet spoke for the betterment of women's lots and therefore, it would follow, their increased visibility. Within two centuries of his death, the law books were providing for their seclusion.

Yet despite ancient Persian extremes that put them in positions of servility, women exerted effective social and political pressure. "At a period when the status of women in Iran had reached its lowest ebb," Minou Reeves writes in *Female Warriors of Allah*, "Parikhan-Khanum, the daughter of Shah Tahmasb [904 A.H./1526 C.E. to 954 A.H./1576 C.E.] played an active role in the Safavid state. Highly esteemed by her father, she had extensive influence. After her father's death she played a decisive role in the struggle for the throne; her support for one of her brothers, Ismai'l, was instrumental in his success. Yet it was also she who rid the country of him when her influence over him had waned. Finally, her efforts to maintain the same influence over the new ruler, Mohammed Khodabandeh, caused his wife to have Parikhan-Khanum assassinated." This wife then became regent and ruled in the name of her son for two years.

As noted earlier, the word *haram* simply means "sanctuary." It is rooted in pre-Islamic religion, when Mecca was a center of sacred sites called al-Haram. Mecca and Medina are the two most revered *harams* in Islam. The inner courtyard of a mosque is a *haram*. In Jerusalem, the Temple Mount, equally sacred to Jews, Christians, and Muslims, is called Haram esh-Sharif, the Venerable Sanctuary. In *Shari'a*, Islamic law, *haram* refers to behavior that is prohibited.

"Few aspects of Islamic civilization have been as misunderstood or as immersed in fantasy as the women's quarters in the households of Muslim rulers and other members of the ruling elite, quarters variously referred to as the harem, the seraglio or the zenana, words long assimilated into English from Arabic, Turkish or Persian," Gavin Hambly writes. "The original prototype of this institution was the simple division of a house into two parts: the private space occupied by women...and the public space occupied by men.... The latter, by extension, reached [into]...streets, bazaars, bathhouses, mosques, shrines...accessible to women in comparatively restricted circumstances."[1]

"The word *harem*," Peirce notes, "is a term of respect, redolent of religious purity and honor, and evocative of the requisite obeisance. It is gender-specific only in its reference to the women of a family."[2]

Mernissi, born and reared in a harem in twentieth-century Morocco, writes in *Scheherazade Goes West* that whatever the connotations of the harem are for Westerners, for her it is "a synonym for the family as an institution." In her enchanting memoir, *Dreams of Trespass*, she reminds us that there are two distinct kinds of harems, the imperial and the domestic. The first are those that so mesmerize the West. The second, she says, "are rather dull, for they have a strong bourgeois dimension....What defines it as a harem is not polygamy, but the men's desire to seclude their wives, and their wish to maintain an extended household rather than break into nuclear units."

Only men of means could maintain "imperial" harems, which demanded vast resources to feed and clothe the hundreds residing in these cities of women. The population included wives and concubines, in-laws, widowed mothers, their co-wives, unmarried aunts, sisters, and cousins, as well as young children of both sexes. Then there were the caliph's friends and retainers: tutors, musicians, poets, astrologers...

Such an environment was hardly erotic nor did the caliph necessarily choose the women who were to be his wives and concubines. That task was frequently performed by his mother.

To keep the infrastructure running smoothly, there had to be servants at all levels: hairdressers, midwives, concierges. Battalions of eunuchs squired the women from place to place on pilgrimages or to the bazaar, supervised their lessons and their dress, reported on them to officials and did the bookkeeping, acted as secretaries, performed myriad other duties, and, most important, held the keys to the locked doors. Most of the harem staff were slaves, a savings, at least, in salaries.[3]

What was a ruler to do? He had, like all monarchs, to keep up appearances. The Abbasids, Abbott reports, were determined "to make the caliph the symbol of the new age. His court was to be the center out of which radiated all the splendors of the Muslim world, and that world, in return, was to be a fitting setting for the magnificence of the court."[4]

When royal women emerged on rare occasions in public, they were swathed from head to toe. They rode in closed palanquins or veiled on horses or mules. Today, Saudi Arabia, more than any other country, practices the most rigid form of veiling, where the whole body and face are covered. But the facial veil, as we've seen, did not enter Islam until after the Prophet's time. In pre-Islam, a woman such as Khadija might have worn a headdress of some sort to distinguish her from slaves. Late in his life, his wives were only required to wear mantles to avoid unwanted and inappropriate attention. Ironically, other women of the *umma* adopted the fashion, for it symbolized high status. Even now, in some places, rural women — whose lives of cooking, cleaning, farming, herding, drawing and transporting water, and raising children are not conducive to heavy shrouds — yearn for this emblem of luxury and ease.

In *The Women of Turkey and their Folk-lore*, Garnett showed that in diverse Muslim societies — Kurds and Albanians, among others — ordinary women did not bother with *hijab*, illustrating the difference between social custom and religious precept.

"When the wives of the Crusaders saw the respect in which Muslim women were held," Armstrong writes, "they took to wearing the veil in the hope of teaching their own menfolk to treat them better."[5]

324

Zarrin-Taj, in the nineteenth century, was the first woman to unveil publicly in Iran. She was a preacher, a member of the Babi movement, today known as Bahai. Babism was developed in Shiraz, Persia, in 1852, out of the Shi'a branch of Islam by Mirza Ali Muhammad, who was called the Bab, "the Gate." He claimed that the prophets were divine manifestations of God and that he was equal to Muhammad in importance. He wrote a new holy book, *Bayan*, "The Explanation," to supplant the Qur'an and proclaimed the coming of an era when all religions would be united. Babism forbade polygamy and concubinage.

Zarrin-Taj is said to have torn off her veil before a group of men as she proclaimed herself the herald of a new day when women and men would be equal. One man was so shocked, legend has it, that he slit his throat in horror. In 1852, Zarrin-Taj was executed by strangulation, but not before she proclaimed, "You can kill me, but you cannot stop the emancipation of women."

Ibn Battuta (682 A.H./1304 C.E. to 747 A.H./1369 C.E.) journeyed for twenty-six years throughout the medieval Muslim world from his home in Tangiers to the Russian steppes. His book, *Rihlah*, "Travels," is a valuable source for history and geography. In it, he wrote with some astonishment of the freedom of Muslim Turkish women, observing that they did not wear the veil. Upon seeing a Turkish woman come into a bazaar with her husband, he remarked scornfully that "anyone seeing [the husband] would take him to be one of her servants."

> On the morrow of his arrival in the camp [Ibn Battuta] presented himself before the khan....He found Ozbeg seated upon a silver gilded throne in the midst of an enormous tent whose exterior was covered, after the fashion of all the Kipchak rulers, with a layer of bright golden tiles. The Khan's daughter, his two sons, other royal kinsmen, and the chief *amirs* and officers were assembled below the throne, but his four *khatuns*, or wives, sat on either side of him....If wives and mothers often influenced politics in the palaces of the Moroccan Marinids, as we may assume

they did, counsel was given in the confines of the *harim*. But in the Mongol states the women of the court shared openly and energetically in the governing of the realm. Princesses of the blood, like their brothers, were awarded...landed properties, which they ruled and taxed as private fiefs quite apart from the state domain. The *khatuns* sometimes signed decrees and made major administrative decisions independently of the khan.[6]

Ibn Battuta was shocked and amazed, especially when, at a ceremonial event, the sultan welcomed the senior *khatun* entering the golden tent by advancing toward her, greeting her, taking her by the hand, and seating himself only after she had mounted the couch. And all this without veils!

"There was a precedent for the important role of the royal [Ottoman] concubine as the elder in a household separate from that of the ruler," Peirce tells us. "It resembled in some ways the Mongol *ordu*, the separate camp or household maintained by each of the khan's wives, vividly described by Ibn Battuta in his visit to the Uzbek khan of the Crimea....However, the Ottomans quickly moved away from this Turco-Mongol pattern to limit the authority of wives and sons."[7]

In *The Ottoman Lady*, Davis notes that among some pre-Islamic Turkic peoples, the women were shamans, which may explain why they continued to enjoy positions of power and privilege after the advent of Islam. One could speculate, too, that this ancient female spiritual leadership among Turko-Mongol peoples leads with perhaps a somewhat tattered thread to the Ottoman rulers' regard for their mothers (notwithstanding, as we've seen, that a mother was a prince's only trustworthy friend against his father and brothers who might be out to kill him).

In the middle decades of the sixth century A.H., two Mongol princesses ruled over the Qara-Khitan Empire in Turkestan, founded by refugees of the Liao Dynasty of northern China. One of these was Sati-Bek (ca. 717 A.H./1339 C.E.), who conspired her way through three husbands and uncounted interfamilial assassinations.

Mernissi relates the tale of Padishah Khatun, a fifteenth-century "poet raised as a boy among boys...in order to deceive the Mongols, who would have married her off among them. Her mother was Kutlugh Khan, who upon being widowed took the reins of government. Eventually Padishah was married off to a Mongol...a Buddhist. After she was widowed, she was married to her stepson Gaykhatu and demanded...that he give her the throne as proof of his love. He did so."[8]

By all reports, harems were loud and lively places, fertile with ideas and inventions. Yet, as Mernissi emphasizes in *Dreams of Trespass*, privacy was at a premium—at least in domestic harems, and no doubt imperial ones, too.[9]

"The explanation of why some women were able to gain...distinction lies in the very fact of seclusion," Abbott writes, "for when the Abbasids established the custom of housing all the women of the court in special quarters...they introduced a completely new social order."[10]

Notwithstanding, *purdah*—the Hindi word for seclusion, which is still practiced by some Hindus—a number of women became rulers in their own rights and by the consent of the people.[11] Some, like Radiyya and Sitt al-Mulk, were beloved daughters, favored by their fathers over their incompetent sons, but who had to wait until their brothers' deaths to rule. In doing so, these women rescued their fathers' legacies. The fifteenth-century Sufi princess, Jahanara, ran the government for her ailing father, the Mughal emperor Shah Jahan, who, having lost his wife Mumtaz Mahal, entered a lifelong melancholy.

The formal succession belonged mostly to men. The infamous saying of the Prophet, "Those who entrust their affairs to women will never know prosperity," continues to be exploited on many levels to prevent women's rise to power—not only in government. No one is sure whether this *Hadith* was inspired when a woman ascended to the Persian throne years before the Arab conquest, or by a widow who led her tribe in battle against the Muslims. It seems to lack solid context and therefore, among feminist scholars, credibility. Regardless of what excuses may be used to bar women from equality, Islam has been no more opposed to female leaders than most other cultural traditions.

327

In every Islamic dynasty there have been women who exerted political authority. As in other societies, women's political clout emerged more often than not during periods of disunity or internecine strife. It had potential to stabilize, and often did for a time, until new turmoil arose among male factions, which resented female command.

Ultimate legitimacy meant having the name of the ruler spoken in the Friday prayers, the *khutba*, and was further enhanced with coins minted in the sovereign's name.

In the Indo-Muslim state of Bhopal, it was purportedly the eldest child, boy *or* girl, who inherited the throne with the weight of the *khutba* to authorize it. In the late nineteenth century, Bhopal's orthodox Nawab Sultan Begam wrote an autobiography titled plainly, *An Account of My Life*, describing her reign and focusing with special attention and affection on her mentor, her grandmother, Nawab Sikander Begam (d. 1247 A.H./1869 C.E.), who was apparently a great reformer. One of her earnest injunctions to the granddaughter who was to succeed her was: "The cultivators of the soil are our wealth; that we are able to rule and to live in state and luxury is owing to the labor and industry of these poor people. When you become ruler of the State, look upon the fostering of this humble but useful class as your first and highest duty."[12]

The eleventh-century C.E. Yemeni queens, Asma and her daughter-in-law Arwa, ruled side by side with their husbands, making policy decisions equally, until the men's deaths, when they ruled alone. Al-Sayyida al-Hurra, the pirate queen of Tetouán in Morocco, governed first with her husband, then carried on alone after his death with the endorsement of her people, and perhaps more significantly for her security, other male officials. Zaynab al-Nafzawiyya, a Berber queen of the eleventh century C.E., shared power with her husband, the Almoravid sovereign Yusuf ibn Tashfin. Their empire included North Africa and Spain and they founded Marrakech in Morocco. According to Mernissi, historians call Zaynab *al-qa'ima bi mulkihi*, "that is, the main actor running the show."[13]

Examples abound of women as "virtual rulers," regents for their sons, or counselors to their husbands, providing them with military, political, and financial advice, admonishing them against too narrow points of view, giving them the straight scoop on how to rule justly, or even nudging them into despotism. Turkan Khatun (d. 472 A.H./1094 C.E.) had 10,000 horsemen at her service during her two-year rulership of the Turkish Seljuk Empire. A Persian, she was called "Master of Isfahan," and had begun as the sultan's concubine, borne him a child, was subsequently married to him and later poisoned by those who were not impressed that Turkan Khatun's sultan sought her direction and yielded constantly to her intelligence.

Some queens sat in for an ailing or disinterested sovereign spouse. Al-Malika al-Hurra Alam began as a singer in the harem of the king of Zubayd (in Iraq).[14] He fell in love with her, handed the administration of his domain over to her, and she kept right on going after his death.

Shajarat al-Durr, as we've seen, started her career as a disembodied voice for her deceased husband. Mughal Empress Nur Jahan is depicted in history as a schemer or as a true heroine, depending on the historian's point of view.

Imperial marriages are not necessarily satisfying. The Abbasid caliphs could take it or leave it and Ottoman emperors we know very soon eschewed it altogether, siring their successors exclusively by concubines.

"Acquiring a wife was a much more serious undertaking than stocking up on concubines who could be discarded, given away or even killed without any questions raised," Abbott notes about the Abbasids, though her words ring true in almost any royal arrangement.[15] Wives, after all, had legal rights to property and political connections through their families. With the exception of the Ottoman rulers (though not their relatives or the nonruling elite), marriage was vital to satisfying ambition. It opened new lands and loyalties. The Mamluks, having started as a slave class, were especially keen on the institution, which strengthened their ranks and eventually helped shape their dynasty. The geo-political history of the world has

329

depended largely on women, daughters or sisters given away as prizes for the benefit of men's ambitions.

Despite her prestige, a legal wife could mean little or nothing to her husband, but might be only a symbol—albeit dynamic—of territorial possession. And her sons might have no chance at all of succeeding to the throne, whether she was a senior wife or the daughter of another powerful ruler.

Within the harem, a wife might have seniority, based on her family, or where she appeared in the line of wives—first, second, third, or fourth. But the highest-ranking harem member could very well be someone else, like the Traditionist princess-of-pedigree, Zaynab bint Sulayman in Khayzuran's time.

Every rule has its inevitable exceptions: we've seen that Umm Salama and Umm Musa asserted their wills over their husbands, the first and second Abbasid caliphs, by not allowing them to marry others and that Umm Musa's sons were named successors of her husband, al-Mansur. These women arrived with position at a vulnerable time in their husbands' careers and they were not about to lose it. In fact, it was their families' prominence or their own wealth that brought their caliphs to power.

Marriages were almost always arranged, as they were in Europe, until love matches were invented in relatively modern times. Marriages were arranged to create close unions between families and therefore closer economic and political ties. These unions are by no means all cold and heartless, as we saw with, for example, Aisha's relationship with Muhammad. Couples within arranged marriages frequently cultivate the truest love and friendship.

Yet Mumtaz Mahal and Mughal Emperor Shah Jahan, Jahanara's parents, fell in love at a spring festival, while she was married to another. Sisters and daughters of a sultan, like most wealthy women in the first centuries of Islam, had the principal say in who they would marry. Here again, women's fate is tied to that of nations: as empires expand, so women's choices diminish.

As few choices as women of the ruling elite may have had in their marriages, it is well to remember that neither girls nor boys had options.

In pre-Islamic Arabia, few women had choices about who to marry. Islam provided for women to choose their husbands. The Qur'an allows for women to reject or accept proposals as they wish. The holy book insists, as well, on mutual respect, kind treatment, and the equal give and take of sexual pleasure in marriage.

The established order on the Arabian peninsula at the time of the Revelations was patriarchal, a culture of domination and subordination. The social reforms of Islam were built on existing practices regarded as far from ideal in today's world. Nevertheless, the Qur'an responds directly to the pressing need for the improvement of women's lot. Thus, among other things, the Qur'an never orders women to obey their husbands and any belief that women must be obedient is a remnant of pre-Islamic cultures. The Qur'an demands reciprocal honor, not subservience.

Marriage ceremonies and wedding feasts are everywhere chances to display family riches. Among the merchant and ruling classes of the Islamic empire, they were opulent affairs, where guests might even receive estates, horses, and slaves as gifts.

During the Safavid Dynasty (789 A.H./1501 C.E. to 1100 A.H./1722 C.E.)—yet another golden age for Islamic art, especially in miniature painting and architecture—Persians arranged their marriages through a *vakil*, an attorney. The rite took place at the house of the bride's parents. When the contract was signed by the men, the bride—who had yet to be seen—retired with her female friends and relatives and waited while those acting for her and the bridegroom stated the terms of the marriage settlement. When bride and groom had agreed aloud, the marriage document was validated by a cleric.

"The amount of pomp and ceremony on these occasions depended on the social status of those involved, as did the length and splendor of the accompanying processions and celebrations," Ronald Ferrier writes. "Humbler folk might dispense with an attorney and the bride-to-be might appear veiled with her father, exchange vows with her husband-to-be in the presence of a cleric, and declare her acceptance of the marriage terms."[16] His gifts to her were money, a ring, clothes, and jewels. Hers to him were toiletries and items she had sewn. The celebrations could last for ten days.[17]

In his *Book on Etiquette of Marriage*, Abu Hamid al-Ghazali, a Persian jurist of the twelfth century C.E., recalled the Prophet's instructions that no man may "'come upon his wife like an animal, and let there be an emissary between them.' He was asked, 'What is this emissary, O Messenger of God?' He said, 'The kiss and [sweet] words.'" Al-Ghazali went on to describe precise instructions on every possible aspect of sex relations, with an attitude that Mernissi compares to Freud's.

As Muhammad had married Christians and Jews, mixed marriages were acceptable, but only a Muslim man could take a *kafir* wife. A Muslim woman was never permitted to marry a non-Muslim.

Divorce was rare, and is discouraged in the Qur'an. To cast off a royal wife could have ugly social and political repercussions (sixteenth-century court historians document a vizier who beat his royal wife, the daughter or sister of a sultan, and was immediately divorced and fired). And there was, as Abbott put it, "the question of royal dignity to consider. Since remarriage was never legally forbidden to the divorced wives of caliphs...[he] might be put to the personal humiliation of seeing them the wives of other men of high or low station."[18] No surprise that royal marriages became rare.

In Ottoman Syria and Palestine, the Hanafi School of law articulated meticulous rules for child custody and child support. Briefly put, in cases of divorce or death, the patrilineal family had no claim on the child until after the period of female nurturance, which could last until she or he was nine years old. There was no question of child support. It was paid. And if the father was dead, his family must make the payments. The mother was to be paid at a level commensurate with her standard of living, which would cover costs of clothing, food, shelter, even servants. Her testimony as to his means was enough to override any claim that he was too poor to provide that support. All this was founded on the Qur'an, which states that

There shall be for divorced women
honorable provision—an obligation on the godfearing.[19]

Muslim jurisprudence, like that of most of the rest of the world, was usually partial to men. But life has a way of providing balance, for as it happened, sons were reared in the harem. In their formative years, boys were profoundly influenced by their mothers and the other women who surrounded them day and night. Of course, with each culture and era, customs differed, but generally speaking, at nine or ten, boys were removed to begin their "manly" training in military, political, and business matters. As we've seen with the Abbasid prince al-Mahdi, many a young man preferred harem life and their fathers were hard put to drag them from the pleasures therein, which included maternal sympathy. That boys were reared in the harem did not motivate them to change the custom of seclusion, quite the opposite, for few would disrupt their own safe, comfortable havens. For most children, however grown, "home" must always remain the same. But being brought up in the *zenana* did mean that rulers were often devoted to their mothers and inspired by their opinions and desires and thus mothers were likely to attain a good deal of power when their sons took the throne. In the Ayyubid Dynasty—descendants of the Kurdish military adventurer Saladin, who routed the crusaders from Jerusalem in 565 A.H./1187 C.E.—Baraka Khatun (d. 750 A.H./1372 C.E.) acquired such immense authority when her son became sultan, she was honored by a magnificent pilgrimage procession in what was declared "The Year of the Sultan's Mother."

Motherhood is of principal significance in Islam. "Attention has been drawn to the fact that the word *rahma*, 'mercy,' stems from the same Arabic root as *rahim*, 'womb,'" Schimmel notes. "It would be completely acceptable therefore to speak of the Creator's 'maternal love' in its widest sense. 'Paradise lies at the feet of the mothers,' the Prophet said, and one's mother deserves the never-ending care and support of her offspring."[20]

The Mothers of the Faithful, Muhammad's widows, were not so called merely for the sake of empty honorifics. They were indeed "mothers" of the *umma*, bearing the burdens and duties of motherhood, as well as the joys: they had crucial Traditions and examples to impart, which were to guide the young community into well-rounded maturity; they acted as counselors and judges; they suffered the slings and arrows of ungrateful, rebellious, and divisive children (and were themselves sometimes insufferable); and simultaneously, they enjoyed adoration and respect.

Garnett wrote admiringly (with a few culturally biased caveats) about a celebrated nineteenth-century Albanian woman, Khamko, who "had not, until the death of her husband placed the responsibility for the well-being of the family in her hands, given any signs of extraordinary strength of character and readiness of resources which afterwards distinguished her, qualities which were, however, sullied by an implacability of soul which only too nearly resembled that displayed by Olympia, the mother of Alexander, herself a native of Epirus." Thanks to her energy and ruthless courage, Khamko "changed the distaff for the sword" and as a result, her son Ali Pasha rose to become the Lion of Ioannina.

> Ali, who had during his father's lifetime been a wild and intractable boy, appears at his death to have submitted with the utmost docility to the authority of his mother. "To my mother," [he said] on one occasion to the French Consul-General — "I owe everything, for my father left me but a mere hole and a few fields. My imagination, fired by the counsels of her who had twice given me birth — for she has made me both a man and vizier — revealed to me the secret of my destiny."
>
> Such being the character of the Albanian women, it is not surprising that they have played a considerable part in the history of their country.[21]

Ten months before Columbus "sailed the ocean blue," the Spanish Catholic monarchs Ferdinand and Isabela reached the gates of Granada, the last stronghold of the Muslims. Its downfall and the triumph of the Christian *reconquista*, reconquest, brought exile and misery to Muslims and Jews, and is still a shadow on the heart of Islam.

Muhammad XII Abu 'Abd Allah, known in the West as Boabdil, was the last Arab ruler of Granada and had been hoisted to the throne by his mother Aisha al-Hurra. Although the particulars of her life are little known, she is considered by some Muslim historians to have been heroic in her actions to save her city-state for Islam. She was unhappily married to the sultan Ali Abd al-Hassan. In his dotage, Ali foolishly fell in love with a Christian Spanish captive, married her, and had children. As the Catholic armies closed in, the Muslim aristocracy was none too pleased with their sultan's amorous preoccupations. Aisha al-Hurra played on nationalist fervor and fled her quarters in the splendid Palace of the Alhambra to organize attacks on her husband, who was quickly overthrown.

She immediately installed her son in Ali's place. Boabdil held the throne briefly until 870 A.H./1492 C.E., a year after the fall of Granada. Then secretly, he negotiated with the Catholics to hand over the city in exchange for his safe passage out of Spain. As he left, Boabdil paused to look back at the Alhambra, the Generalife gardens, and all that had been the brilliance of Granada. Stanley Lane-Poole related the tale in his 1887 work, *The Moors in Spain*: "'Allahu Akbar!' [Boabdil] said, 'God is most great,' as he burst into tears. His mother Ayesha stood beside him: 'You may well weep like a woman,' she said, 'for what you could not defend like a man.' The spot whence Boabdil took his sad farewell look at his city from which he was banished for ever, bears to this day the name of *el ultimo sospiro del Moro*, 'the last sigh of the Moor.'"

Sweet testaments of love between mother and son the world over can't hold a candle to the excitement of stories about mother/son hatred, like that of Khayzuran and her older son Musa al-Hadi, who made regular attempts on each other's lives. The nineteenth-century English traveler William Knighton had this recollection in India: "Once during my residence at Lucknow, the female sepoys (*urdubegis*) were employed by the king against his own mother. The king...sent [them] to turn her out; but her retainers fought with and routed them. The balls firing on either side were whistling over my house at the time. Fifteen or sixteen of the Begam's attendants were killed in this attack."[22]

Women could sometimes take power by acting as regents for their underage sons and were occasionally reluctant to give it back. Tandu bint Husayn (d. 797 A.H./1419 C.E.) became ruler of southern Iraq during the Mongol Jalairid Dynasty after having her husband killed. His son by another wife ascended the throne, so Tandu had him eliminated, too. Claiming to be reigning for her own minor son, she took over as legal sovereign. Even when the boy came of age, she held on until her death, but issued her dictums from behind a veil or curtain, thus turning *hijab* to her advantage. She is listed in the books of dynasties merely as a regent and queen mother, but in fact, coins were minted in her name and she was mentioned in the *khatub*.

Regency has a way of unbridling ambition, but not all queen-mother regents were ruthless. A niece of Shajarat al-Durr, Ghaziyya (d. 635 A.H./1257 C.E.) ruled in the name of her minor son and is described in the biographies as modest and pious. Safiyya Khatun of the Ayyubid Dynasty administered the state for six years in the name of her minor grandson. She is said to have restored justice and compassion and eliminated unfair taxes.

The concubine mothers of the Ottoman Empire were sent with their sons to their provincial posts, where as governors, they trained for their possible succession. The *valide sultan* was the lucky and highly honored woman whose son made it through the literal slings and arrows of competing siblings to become sultan. For a century after Khurrem—who did not live to be *valide sultan*, though her son Selim acceded to the throne—queen mothers became so commanding, governing de facto, that the era was labeled the "Rule of Women." It was the sultan's mother who represented the "human" side of the dynasty to the people by appearing in royal processions in the city and countryside as an icon of benevolence and community.

During the seventeenth century, an old *valide sultan*, Kosem, and a new *valide sultan*, Tarkhan, struggled for dominance, each campaigning for followers. The argument ended definitively when Kosem was strangled with a curtain cord by Tarkhan's eunuchs. The notorious, mythic harem brings forth Western visions of "intrigue." We've seen that harems were convivial, familial places, but schemes and conspiracies often also meant survival for a mother and her children.

Zubaydah seems an archetypal queen mother. As the Abbasid caliph Harun al-Rashid's favorite wife—and a passionate character—she supported her son's succession adamantly. But when he was assassinated, she refused to take revenge. Not to be deprived of her place of veneration and influence, she instead embraced the new sultan, reminding him and the rest of the world that she had, after all, reared him when his concubine mother died in childbirth.

Much more than her glamorous image, political maneuverings, and expedient queen motherhood, Zubaydah is best known and esteemed for her extravagant philanthropy. To say that one is "generous to a fault" is usually a mistake: most kinds of generosity cannot be faulted. And this is where Zubaydah, for all her vanity and self-indulgent antics, came close to flawlessness. Her charitable enterprises were massive. She was following in the footsteps—as others have followed in hers—of Islamic women throughout history.

Shaghab, mother of the eighteenth Abbasid caliph, al-Muqtadir (d. 321 A.H./933 C.E.)—a queen mother who put anyone to death who would not recognize her adolescent son's right to the throne—is described as the most generous woman since Zubaydah. She donated a million dinars each year from her private estates and made many endowments, waqf, to Mecca and Medina. When al-Muqtadir was killed and Shaghab's wealth seized, she refused to abolish her endowments, though witnesses were ordered to testify that they were illegal. They could take anything else they liked, she said, but "what was endowed cannot be returned by Allah." She was tortured and killed, but never reneged.

Khurrem gave Zubaydah and Shaghab a run for their money, centuries later. Meanwhile, dynasties between the Abbasid and Ottoman were hectic with public building projects and the establishment of endowments by women.

The queens Asma and Arwa built roads, mosques, monuments, and buildings in Yemen during the Fatimid Dynasty. Aside from the obligations rulers such as Asma and Arwa understood to be merely good governance, these projects were zakat—almsgiving, third of the Five Pillars of Islam—and thus acts of piety. Women were the greatest philanthropists in Islam, and their patronage is evidence of the great property and wealth owned by them. While living in boundless luxury, they spent unimaginable sums on public projects and charity.

Personal deeds of charity and the establishment of charitable foundations by women of dynastic families broadcast their own devoutness and bounteousness as well as that of the ruling families. Again, they compensated for the sultan's aloofness by providing him with an image of munificence. Nevertheless, the giving was sincere, grounded partly in a story about the Prophet's wife Aisha. The Prophet, after a raid where a fortune of pearls was taken, was distracted and forgot to dispense the wealth to the poor. When he realized what had happened, he rushed to amend the error, only to find that Aisha had already distributed all the pearls to the needy.

There were two kinds of *waqf*: public and family endowments. The latter was often set up to create matrilineal inheritance. In Syria, old records show that one female endower excluded all males from benefiting until the female line died out. After herself, the beneficiaries were her sister's daughter and her own three granddaughters.

Women created public projects and made endowments for other, less privileged women, including hospitals and schools.

In a parched land, fountains, pools, wells, canals, and aqueducts were constantly needed and demanded continual upkeep and repair. Public-spirited women turned their attention and their means to this essential service. In Islam, it is as commendable as it is in Christianity to give a cup of water to the thirsty.

Women paid for the construction of some of the most beautiful structures in Islam, where extraordinary architecture and engineering are the rule. Most of these were mosques, but there were also *khanqahs*, or Sufi convents (favored by Shajarat al-Durr), as well as royal colleges, *madrassas*, or theological schools, mausoleums, and public libraries. Women also funded the restoration of historic edifices, as Khayzuran did with the birthplace of Muhammad in Mecca, or they might renovate existing sites to house pet projects.

In the fifteenth century C.E., Timurid queen Gowhar Shad built mosques, schools, public baths, palaces, and libraries in what is

338

now the Afghan city of Herat. Gowhar Shad built a beautiful fifteen-acre "Women's Garden," which was destroyed during Afghanistan's recent twenty-three-year war. Efforts are being made to restore the garden or at least keep it more or less alive until such time as a new benefactor can revive it.

Once, Gowhar Shad was inspecting a mosque and *madrassa* she was building on the outskirts of Herat, when it was discovered that not all the students had vacated the premises for the queen's visit. One was sound asleep, and awakened to see a gorgeous lady-in-waiting. When the maiden returned to the queen, she was disheveled and breathless, but rather than punishing her and the young man for making love, Gowhar Shad ordered all her ladies-in-waiting to marry the students in a mass ceremony, so that they might avoid future temptation. She gave each student clothing and a salary and allowed the couples to meet once a week as long the students worked hard.

About one-fifth of all the Ayyubid's religious structures and one-fourth of their colleges in Damascus were built by women. The royal colleges endowed by the women of the Ottoman Suleyman's family were renowned for their high levels of education.

Shajarat al-Durr's patronage, like that of other women, not only favored ascetics, but scholars and jurists. The Damascus noblewoman Zumurrudh Khatun (d. 539 A.H./1161 C.E.) built and endowed a mosque-*madrassa* for the Hanafi School. Rabi'a Khatun of the Ayyubid ruling elite built a college for the Hanbali School at the suggestion of a learned lady whose family of scholars benefited.

Philanthropists were not only queens and princesses. The Traditionist Fatima al-Duayliya, who excelled in the sciences and the art of calligraphy during the twelfth Islamic century, settled in Mecca and founded a rich public library.

All this giving required management. Women often appointed themselves as *mutawali*, endowment administrators, and if not, their first choice was likely to be a sister. Mumtaz Mahal was the administrator of the *zenana*, but she appointed the Persian Sati al-Nisa Khanum to manage her endowments. When Mumtaz died, Sati took over such maternal duties as supervising weddings and nursing one of the princes back from a bout of smallpox.

Shaghab appointed a woman named Thumal not only as *mutawali*, but minister of justice for the land. Thumal was apparently so successful that although officials of the court resented her, the people "loved her and appreciated her way of acting, and with good cause...[she] put an end to corruption [in the judicial system] and lower[ed] court fees."[23]

The Indo-Muslim *urdubegis*—armed women retainers—also acted as administrators for the *zenana*, and were *sadr-i ana*s or superintendents of the women's quarters, juggling everything from emotional disturbances and arguments to marriage arrangements and *zenana* bookkeeping. These women, like Bibi Fatima, chief *urdubegi* in sixteenth-century Mughal emperor Humayun's *zenana*, did not necessarily carry weapons, but were armed with the executive skills required to run a massive population. Bibi Fatima was also a skilled political negotiator sent by Humayun to deal with problematic queens and to arrange marriages.

Zubaydah bint Ja'far

Zubaydah was born ca. 147 A.H./765 C.E. to the Abbasid Caliph Mansur's second son Ja'far and Salsal, sister of Khayzuran. Her actual name was Sukayna, but her grandfather Mansur, with whom she was a great favorite, gave her the pet name Zubaydah, "Little Butter Ball," by which she would be known throughout history. She married Harun al-Rashid, second son of Khayzuran and Caliph al-Mahdi. Their romance and adventures in Harun's opulent court are legendary, fictionalized in The Thousand and One Nights. *She was profligate, even in an era notable for its excesses, and profoundly generous at all levels, bestowing innumerable philanthropic works on her people. Zubaydah died in 216 A.H./831 C.E.*

Travelers to Baghdad are stunned breathless by the radiance of the court. The Father of Farthings, Caliph Mansur, indeed assured his dynasty would prosper and it has done so in ever-increasing splendor.

Zubaydah commands 400 slave girls. When she displays jealousy, she apologizes to her husband by presenting him with bevies of the most beautiful and talented. One of these, Marajil, gives birth to Abdallah al-Ma'mun and dies in childbirth on the very night Harun succeeds to the throne. Zubaydah takes the little boy into her care and six months later gives birth, at long last, to her own child, Muhammad al-Amin.

Another *jarya* whom Zubaydah has given Harun gives birth to no fewer than five of his many children.

But Amin is all that Zubaydah has.

It is the murky side of her generosity that Zubaydah indulges when she gives Amin everything he wants and then some, until the boy's soul begins to decompose and his heart turns hard as the gems with which he covers himself head to toe to flounce about the harem. She fights for him on every front, coming close to alienating even her beloved Harun. Harun sees his sons for who they are and knows Ma'mun to be unspoiled, a scholar in arts and matters of state, and quick, where Amin is distracted by any shiny thing. Amin is a vicious little boy. There are those who seek audience with Zubaydah to express their fears for Ma'mun at the hands of Amin. Zubaydah could see for herself how different these boys are, for she has taken the orphaned Ma'mun under her wing, but she is blinded by love for her own.

Nothing shakes Harun's love for Zubaydah, even as he is disgusted by their son. Despite the romances that distract him, it is Zubaydah's company Harun enjoys most and always returns to. To entertain each other or send messages in the codes they have devised since they were children—double cousins fascinated with one another and destined to be together from the beginning—they pay huge sums to poets and musicians.

A verse that delights is rewarded with liberal dispersments of dinars and dirhams. A poet with a special turn of phrase might have his mouth filled with pearls. Poets seek Zubaydah's favor in hopes of profiting. Rarely does she disappoint even the least gifted. A young poet flubs his lines and her attendants step toward him to punish his blunder.

"Stop!" Zubaydah orders. "See how he meant well but only stumbled. Compare his well-meaning to those who mean ill and use their verses to spread lies and satire. Give him what he had hoped for and explain kindly to him his error."

Harun and Zubaydah exchange gifts of jewels and clothing, property and cash. Harun gives Zubaydah all that she asks and much she does not. Her holdings are enormous. Through the secretaries at her command, she lavishes her treasure on a life of such luxury it must appear to the poor that she is not of this Earth, but heaven-sent, that Allah's less fortunate are ruled not by humans but by angels of Paradise.

Zubaydah's extravagances spread to every art and every craft. The finest brocades are made for her, costing 50,000 dinars apiece. The cloth merchants sing Zubaydah's praises.

She rides in palanquins of silver, ebony, and aromatic sandalwood ornamented with gold and silver hinges and covered with sable, brocade, and silks in red, yellow, green, and blue. The sedan-chair makers, the fine woodworkers, the silver and goldsmiths, the furriers include Zubaydah in their prayers.

Her suppers are sumptuous: she is the darling of cooks, butchers, bakers. And candlestick makers, for she is first to burn candles made with ambergris. Far away, whalers and fishermen extol the distant queen in Iraq who so adores the scent of cuttlefish and the glands of sperm whales.

She wears slippers studded with jewels. All the harem follows suit. Glory to Zubaydah! cry the shoemakers. But the foot is not fleet enough for Zubaydah. She is first to organize men and women on horseback with messages between her palaces and Harun's.

Zubaydah's imagination is boundless. None can match her originality. Nor her wit and humor. She enjoys jokes on herself and playing jokes on Harun.

Her pet monkey, Abu Khalaf, wears a little sword and bejeweled vest. He is waited upon by thirty men and all who come to court to pay homage to her must also kiss the furry hand of Abu Khalaf. General Yazid ibn Mazyad is outraged by the demand.

"Shall I serve apes after having served caliphs?" he growls, drawing his sword and cutting the monkey in two before turning his back on Zubaydah. Courtiers who send her letters of condolence are abundantly rewarded.

Her greatest accomplishment is to persuade Harun, by whatever means necessary, intrigue or pleading, to name her son Amin to the throne, though Ma'mun, the Trusted, is his favorite and his choice.

From Syria, word comes that the saint Raiy'a bint Ismai'li has seen Harun's death in a basin of water.

Zubaydah is forty-five years old when Harun al-Rashid dies. Like his father al-Mahdi and his grandfather al-Mansur, he dies away from home. When the news reaches her, she gathers the women for public mourning at her palace. She sends for the poet Ishaq al-Mausili to compose an elegy.

> Do not blame us if we grow silent, overcome with sorrowful
>   emotion;
> We have come to keep close company with a painful malady...

Only her son Amin holds a stronger place than Harun in Zubaydah's heart. She loved Harun from childhood. Harun's sister Olayya, too, adored him and in her sorrow forsakes wine and song, though she is a singer of marvelous voice.

Zubaydah now gathers the fortune she has accumulated for her son's future and secures Harun's treasures, too, which she delivers personally to Amin at Baghdad. He causes coins to be minted in her name. Briefly they work in cordial tandem to rule the Abbasid Empire.

It is not long before matters of state begin to bore Amin. Within months of his accession, he hands the burden of government onto the shoulders of his vizier and devotes himself to pleasure. A hundred singing slave girls amuse him on his five river barges, shaped like a lion, an elephant, an eagle, a snake, and a horse, which traverse the Tigris day and night. For a time, he is happiest cavorting on the wooden hobby horse of a merry-go-round with crowds of acrobats and entertainers. Each new game wears quickly off. Amin must up the ante to be satisfied. He dresses his prettiest eunuchs as girls and divides them into Ravens and Grasshoppers, black and white. He becomes infatuated with the boy eunuch Kauthar. The poets are divided—some revile Amin while others curry favor with love verses for Amin and Kauthar.

Zubaydah dresses maidens in the costumes of page boys. The fashion takes root among the nobility, but the mother's motive is to

344

wean her son from his young eunuchs, in the desperate hope of providing a fresh novelty. She chooses the most gifted and attractive maidens and displays them in large numbers before her son. He is amused and shares the girls with his castrated paramours.

The scandals rock the empire. Is Zubaydah's son yet another pet monkey? Denouncements and rumors of plots to depose Amin sift through the palace walls.

Zubaydah's pride in Amin erodes. If he has any state policy it is to antagonize his half brother Ma'mun, to disclaim Ma'mun's right to succession in favor of his own sons, and to send expeditions against him. Degeneracy and spite go hand in hand. Amin's general, Ali ibn Isa, comes to take his leave of the queen mother. She knows the general will kill Abdallah al-Ma'mun at Amin's whim. She cannot hold back.

"O Ali!" she sobs. "Though the Commander of the Believers is my own son, my pity for him has reached its limits and my cautiousness on his behalf is ended. Indeed, I am favorably inclined toward Abdallah al-Ma'mun, for it was I who brought him up. He has my sympathy for the disagreeable and injurious events that befall him. For my son is a monarch who has contested his brother's legitimate authority and envied him his possessions. The better sort among his followers devour his worldly substance and the rest will be the death of him.

"Render, therefore, to Abdallah the recognition due the dignity of his father and brothers," Zubaydah begs the general. "Do not speak haughtily to him, for you are not his equal. Compel him not as slaves are compelled, nor hamper him by fetter or handcuff. Withhold not from him either maidservant nor manservant. Do not subject him to harsh treatment on the journey and travel not on an equal footing with him. Do not ride ahead of him and take not your seat on your mount before you have seen to it that he is first mounted. Should he abuse you, bear with him, and should he revile you, do not retaliate."

"I hear your commands," Amin's general replies. "And I shall endeavor to obey them."

Fraternal civil war now rages. Zubaydah steps in again and again to plead with Amin for reason. Her anxiety is overwhelming.

She tears up fine old poems that speak of disasters of any sort in any era and throws them in the river to allay catastrophes to come. She goes weeping to Amin.

"Silence!" he screams. "Crowns are not to be firmly secured through women's frets and fears. The caliphate demands statesmanship beyond the ability of women, whose function is to nurse children. Away! Be gone!"

In this Zubaydah hears echoes of the angry words spoken by Harun's brother Hadi to their mother, her aunt, Khayzuran.

No sum, large or small, can now curtail the calamity that marches toward Amin's pleasure palaces. Zubaydah bribes this one, pleads with that one, rewards another for loyalty, though it be ambivalent. At last there is no choice. Amin sees that destiny has come to claim him in the form of his abused half brother Ma'mun. He takes refuge with his mother and though in terror he experiences moments of seriousness and hours of despair, in no time, he reverts to his debauchery. He has no friend except his mother and she, though she loves her only child, is repelled by him.

As Baghdad falls, Amin takes his beloved Kauthar on a fishing expedition. The boat capsizes, Amin swims to shore. An enemy warrior recognizes him. His head is soon displayed at the city's gate, then sent to Ma'mun, where it keeps company with the severed head of the general Ali ibn Isa.

Ma'mun accedes to the throne and all Zubaydah's extensive properties are confiscated.

Zubaydah bares her head in mourning. None may visit the unveiled queen. Still, there are those outraged that a caliph, even a popinjay, could be thus deposed and killed. They beseech Zubaydah to follow in the footsteps of Aisha, to avenge the blood of Amin as the Mother of Believers avenged the blood of the caliph Uthman.

Zubaydah refuses: "What have the women to do with avenging blood and taking the field against warriors?"

She dresses in black haircloth. She consoles herself with poetry and some she directs to Ma'mun, whose heart is touched by her conciliatory verses. He writes to her addressing her as "mother."

"Mother," he assures her. "I have not taken part in, nor given the order for, nor even approved the murder of Amin."

He reinstates her properties and sends her gifts. She gives a magnificently munificent wedding party and a gown sewn entirely of pearls to Ma'mun's bride Buran.

Her husband is gone, her only child is gone, she is safe under the protection and affection of her foster son. Zubaydah now gives her attention outside the palace, outside the harem, outside the insular and blinkered world of royalty. The generosity that comes so naturally to her radiates into the world.

She builds gardens and canals. She founds the city of Tabriz and the town of Kashan. She causes forts, mosques, wayfarers' inns, and bridges to be constructed. She repairs the Umayyad fortress of Warathan and sees to its upkeep. On pilgrimage in Mecca and Medina she makes enormous cash disbursements to the poor and establishes stations where those who must make the pilgimage on foot can rest and refresh themselves at cisterns. The poor are her concern, for her mother Salsal, when revealed at last by her aunt Khayzuran, had been hungry and wretched.

Zubaydah builds guest houses, where she herself and her retinue stay on the 900-mile Pilgrim's Road. She undertakes the repair of a mosque associated with the Prophet Muhammad in Taif, where once he had known despair and rejection.

She renovates the tomb of the celebrated Traditionist Abdallah ibn Abbas. She takes 20,000 dinars of gold bullion to Mecca, where it will be used for nails and gilding on the door of the Ka'aba. The depth of the sacred well of Zamzam is increased to relieve thirst.

Drought parches the already dessicated Hijaz. Zubaydah orders waterworks—springs and reservoirs and subterranean aqueducts—to be built throughout the empire. The Mushshasah Spring in Mecca, whereby water is transported to the sacred city across miles of mountains and through hard rock, is an engineering feat of unprecedented proportions and new techniques are invented in the process. The costs are unyielding, but Zubaydah, who has never wavered in her commitments, urges the engineers to greater effort. "I will go through with this even if every stroke of the pickaxe were to cost me a gold dinar."

On the arch above Mushshasah Spring, where the water finally flows, is written: *In the name of Allah, the Merciful, the Compassionate. There is no God but Allah alone without any partners. The blessings of Allah be on Muhammad his servant and messenger. The grace of Allah be with us all! Zubaydah, the daughter of Abu al-Fadl Ja'far, son of the Commander of the Believers Mansur—may Allah be pleased with the Commander of the Believers—ordered the construction of these springs in order to provide water for the pilgrims to the House of Allah and to the people of his Sanctuary, praying thereby for Allah's reward and seeking to draw nigh unto him.*

The long task is accomplished. The engineers appear before Zubaydah to render an account of expenditures. She receives their ledgers and casts them into the river.

"We have left the account to the Day of Accountings. Let him who has a cash balance keep it, and he who is our creditor, him we will repay." Then she bestows upon one and all, honor and rewards.

Before her death, at sixty-nine, she establishes endowments for the upkeep of each of her myriad establishments and public works. That Ma'mun has given permission to the governor of Mecca for supplementary cisterns and canals without calling upon her, hurts her deeply. On her last pilgrimage, she takes the governor to task.

"Why did you not write to me so that I could have asked the Commander of the Believers to assign me that project? I would have undertaken its costs as I undertook the expenses of this other cistern so as to accomplish in full my intentions toward the people of the Sanctuary of Allah."

Ma'mun is absent from the capital when his "mother" dies. The role of chief mourner goes to her grandson, Amin's son, Abdallah.

In Arabia and Persia there are many places of respite, places where thirst is slacked and Allah's beauty is nourished, which will be called Zubaydah for hundreds of years.

Sitt al-Mulk

Sitt al-Mulk was born in Egypt in 348 A.H./ 970 C.E., the beloved daughter of the second Fatimid caliph, al-Aziz, and his Christian wife. The Fatimids were Ismai'li, a branch of Shi'a Islam. They began as ascetics, but with power succumbed to the sumptuous life of the Abbasids before them. The Ismai'lis were devotees of astrology. Sitt al-Mulk died in 402 A.H./1024 C.E.

There are no dogs. The young caliph has had them all killed. He has taken to parading at night. He has ordered the citizens of Cairo to light and decorate the streets. To live upside down, under the stars rather than under the sun.

The princess Sitt al-Mulk watches the city from her balcony, illuminated and loud with voices and music and the sounds of hammers. She is sixteen years older than her brother. For sixteen years she had the undivided adoration of her father and she thinks now of his tolerance, his generosity, his courage. He loved pardon and used it often. Christians and Jews were given rights and privileges they had never had before in Egypt. They held high offices. Caliph Al-Aziz protected them and their God-given right as Allah promised to practice their religions as they pleased.

That has all changed with this fourteen-year-old, this child who mounted the throne three years ago. This little caliph who is guided by the court astrologers and hard-bitten imams. Christians and Jews retreat, as if into the cracks of walls. They are forbidden now from buying or consuming wine, even for religious ceremonies. Their churches and temples are destroyed. Their cemeteries are profaned. It is their fault, *their* fault, that the economy of Egypt is collapsing. The Christians must wear large wooden crosses. The Jews must wear bells around their necks. They may not ride horses, but only lowly donkeys.

He processes with his garish entourage through the brightly lit night city. The gleam and glitter of lanterns bounce and dance on the jewels of his turban, as if he himself were a constellation descended to Earth.

Day for night and night for day. His attendants wake the people just as they are falling asleep at dawn and order them to prepare for a new appearance. And here he comes again, Caliph al-Hakim, beard barely sprouted, now on horseback through the streets, while the people stifle their yawns. Then back to bed with prayers for sleep at last. Again a royal pageant is announced and at noon he comes through the streets himself on a lowly donkey.

By early afternoon he sways past in a litter hoisted on the heads of porters. By early evening the people must assemble on the riverbanks to cheer their caliph as he passes by on a boat. This time, they notice, he is not wearing a turban.

And thus it goes, day for night, night for day. The people of Cairo are exhausted. The caliph cannot sleep, so he will not let others sleep.

Sitt al-Mulk never knows when he will appear in her apartments to accuse her of fornication. To tell her that she is copulating with this general or that general in his armies. To threaten her with death. She listens to his accusations and retires to weep herself to sleep, for this cruel child is so unlike his father. This juvenile tyrant is mad.

Can his obsession with her, these jealousies, explain his abrupt decision to lock the women of Cairo away?

He visits Sitt al-Mulk and bawls at her for her sins. He blames her for the epidemics and inflation and drought plaguing the city.

She represents all women and they represent her. He forbids women to laugh. When the laughter they must hold back turns to tears, he forbids women from weeping. The next day, he forbids them from attending burials. The following day he forbids them from visiting the cemeteries. Within a week, he has forbidden them

350

to walk in the streets with their faces uncovered. The following week he forbids them from leaving their homes altogether.

Having won his war on dogs, he has declared war on women. He bans them from stepping out at night, although since he has turned the world upside down, daily life must take place under the moon. How are the women to visit the markets, to fetch water?

And to make sure they remain prisoners, he forbids the shoe-makers from making shoes for the women. He forbids their visiting bathhouses.

They are confined, barefoot, and unbathed, for seven years and seven months. Those who defy the bans are killed, relegated to the fate of the dogs. Old women are exterminated quickly.

The women with no men complain. They have no one to care for them. How will they feed themselves and their children?

Caliph al-Hakim the Pubescent devises a solution. All the merchants will bring everything sold in the *suq* to the women so they can make their purchases in the confines of their homes. The vendors will equip themselves with a long-handled soup ladle and push the merchandise in to the woman hiding behind the door.

The men of Cairo grumble and show signs of discontent. Al-Hakim ignores them.

The people look toward the palace, where the daughter of the good caliph al-Aziz resides. They know of her goodness, too. They have heard of her endeavors to reason with her brother.

All pleasures of all kinds are now forbidden. Caliph al-Hakim the Prowler takes to the streets at night dressed in a mendicant's wool cloak. His head is bare. No more jeweled royal turbans. No more gems to catch the light of the stars. He has let his hair grow long and scraggly. He wanders alone through the Cairo nights, paying his beads, heading for the outskirts of town to watch the sky, to listen to the voices of planets and stars.

He no longer bursts into Sitt al-Mulk's apartments. Now he inundates her with humiliating letters.

He rambles, a solitary figure, who speaks to no one. He glides along like a peaceful beggar, then without warning seizes a butcher's chopper or a soldier's spear or a cobbler's blade and kills any unfor-

tunate standing nearby. Crowds are paralyzed. Sometimes, as if to
repent, the caliph sends his victims shrouds for burial.

The people of Cairo hide in the shadows when al-Hakim the
Madman floats by, muttering and murmuring.

Sitt al-Mulk writes to General Ibn Daws, the greatest in her
brother's army. The latest one he imagines to be her lover.

Caliph al-Hakim the Lunatic declares himself Divine. The
announcement is made with pomp and ritual in all the mosques by
all the imams. From this day forth each time his name is pronounced, all those who hear it must prostrate themselves and kiss the
ground.

The outrage could fuel the sun and burn the moon to cinders.
The people of Cairo send letters, thousands of letters, to this caliph-
who-would-be-God. They cover the walls of the palace with messages of insult and anger and ridicule. As quickly as the walls are
washed, the ugly words and curses reappear, promising disobedience
and professing hatred for the Commander of the Faithful, who will
lead them straight to hell.

He is endeavoring to live forever. His people are his sacrifice.

Sitt al-Mulk is his scapegoat.

He is enraged at the persistent dispatches scrawled on the walls
of his palace. He orders the city of Cairo to be set on fire. He watches
the city go up in flames and smiles.

Sitt al-Mulk meets with General ibn Daws. They conclude a
bargain.

Caliph al-Hakim the Arsonist walks out in the night. He wanders as usual, bareheaded in his wool mendicant's cloak, oblivious to
the charred and burned out city. It is spring.

The nights are gentle. Caliph al-Hakim Glorious and Great
retires to the desert to meditate. He is not missed. The palace is
serene. After a few days, Sitt al-Mulk sends troops far and wide in
search of her brother. They find nothing but bloody clothing torn by
knives.

Sitt al-Mulk moves quickly to enthrone al-Hakim's tiny son. He
is crowned with a diminutive royal turban, so encrusted with jewels
it shoves his flabby baby neck flat onto his miniscule shoulders.

Sitt al-Mulk becomes the wee caliph's regent. It is she who will run the country. But it is she who could be blackmailed, and worse, exposed by General Ibn Daws.

Guards appear at a meeting of viziers and generals. They burst in the door. They accuse ibn Daws of regicide. They kill him then and there.

Baby Caliph toddles and plays and grows, while, for seven years, Sitt al-Mulk restores justice to the people and order to the land.

Asma bint Shihab al-Sulayhiyya & Arwa bint Ahmed al-Sulayhiyya

Two Ismai'li queens of Yemen: Asma (ca. 406 A.H./1028 C.E. to 462 A.H./1084 C.E.) was mother-in-law to Arwa (430 A.H./1052 C.E. to 515 A.H./1137 C.E.). They were fully recognized as equal ruling partners with their husbands, Ali ibn Muhammad al-Sulayhi and Ahmad ibn Ali al-Mukkaram. Asma brought the orphaned Arwa to the court to be reared alongside her son and educated together. Arwa was eighteen when she married al-Mukkaram, just two years before Ali al-Sulayhi's death. She ruled Yemen for forty years.

Asma sits in her prison cell, breathing Ethiopian dust. She cannot see through the only window. Her view is obstructed by the impaled head of her husband. If she could watch the stars, she might know what's in store for her. She might perceive, as she has been taught, the hidden meaning behind this obvious circumstance: she has been kidnapped, her husband murdered.

She will sit and wait. Secrets will remain hidden behind her enigmatic face, and behind those secrets are more veiled secrets. No

354

one wants her secrets. They want only to lure her son and the armies of Yemen. It has been two years.

The head rotting outside her window contained the brilliance of sunlight mirrored on water. She wishes she could turn to look at it—the peeling then yellowed then bleached skull that was once her beloved husband—but she fears the loss of her dignity. It is all she has left in this dungeon. Her queenliness. Her nobility. Her faith.

They established their reign together. It was ordained. From childhood Ali ibn Muhammd al-Sulayhi was initiated in the Shi'a belief...and beyond. He studied law. He inherited his teacher's library and memorized each book from front to back. He rose from one level of knowledge to the next, gently removing the veils that concealed each secret, and he was recognized by the caliph in Egypt himself as the one who would bring the Fatimid Dynasty, the Ismai'lis, to the Yemen.

Asma, his cousin, waited for him. He journeyed as a guide for poor pilgrims and like Muhammad spoke gently to them in close circles about the seven successors and the last, Ismai'l, who will return on the Day of Judgment.

She does not need to turn to the window to recall how he dazzled her. And she him. Together, they planned the future carefully. She lived as his wife in modest circumstances for fifteen years until the moment the imams in Egypt empowered Ali to begin the conquest. He did so with the dispatch of one who has prepared all his life. In only a few months he installed her and their son Ahmad in San'a, now their capital.

What are Ahmad and his wife Arwa doing there now? Do they know what has happened? She stops the thoughts, for they will lead to longing and that will lead to restlessness and that will lead to grief.

In San'a, she conducted affairs of state, unveiled, unlike the women of Egypt. She built a new government and rooted out the old corruption. And the imams spoke her name alongside Ali's in the Friday *khatub*.

Meanwhile, he conquered Mecca. And the world bowed down.

What glory and what joy when at last he could realize his dream of a pilgrimage made in state, no longer a lowly guide, no longer a soldier, but arriving at the holy city in grandeur, yet with the humility of the truly devout.

This was his happiness, his crowning achievement. They gathered their splendid retinue of princes and set forth, leaving Ahmad and Arwa in San'a. A thousand horsemen. Five thousand Ethiopian warriors. Hundreds of *jawari* dressed in silks and cloth-of-gold and cloth-of-Damascus. Horses and white camels and banners and bells and trumpeters. The poets and singers Asma so treasured came, too. The caravan shimmered along the Pilgrim's Road and stopped for the night at the oasis of Bir Umm Ma'bad.

In her solitude, the vague picture Asma had of all that happened—the thundering, the chaos, the screams and shouts and blood—has gradually taken shape and come clear. Sitting for nearly two years, waiting and watching the secrets behind the secrets, the tale has revealed itself, unveiled itself, not like the mystic levels of the Divine, but like an onion, each layer drawing forth tears.

The tents were pitched. Asma attended to her duties. Ali attended to his. He was in his own tent talking with his brother, when Sa'id ibn Najah burst in, flanked by seventy fighters. Pandemonium as ibn Najah put to the sword all the princes of the Sulayhi. Men ripped open her tent flap and ordered her out. Her women screamed and pleaded, but Asma raised her head and walked forth into the presence of the prince of Zubayd, blood-splattered and triumphant now that he had avenged himself on his father's killer.

Why did the warriors not protect the king and the princes? Precisely because they, too, were Ethiopians. Ibn Najah's army increased that day by 5000. They gave her women to their officers. They escorted her here, to this little cell. They set her husband's head on a pole outside her window.

She jumps as one who is falling asleep stumbles on the step between consciousness and dream. An armored shadow stands in her cell door. Asma scrambles to sit up, to regain her posture. She will not let ibn Najah nor his henchmen see her in any other posture than that of a throned queen.

The shadow sways and greets her in all politeness, with subservient blessings.

"Who are you?" Asma says coldly.

"I am Ahmad ibn Ali," the masked warrior replies.

"There are many Ahmads, sons of Ali among the Arabs," she says.

He raises his helmet. She suppresses her smile; she holds back her elation. She stands and greets him—"I bid welcome to our master, al-Mukkaram"—not as a son but as a king.

It is not she who falls to her knees before him, but he before her. His eyes roll back in his head, he grips his left side. She rushes out the prison door, still unsure whether he has come to liberate her or to be her companion in this place. She calls to warriors wearing the colors of the princes of the Sulayhi and they come running. Indeed, they have defeated ibn Najah. Now they place their young king on a litter. They bear their queen and her son home.

She did not see him enthroned. It took two years before he discovered she was alive and could defeat the enemy and release her. Now she returns with him to the cheers of their people. And Asma rules for her son with her daughter-in-law by her side.

And the Friday *khatub* is spoken in the name of al-Mukkaram, Asma, and Arwa.

Like her mother-in-law, Queen Arwa bows to no superior authority. Like Asma, her subjects call her *balqis al-sughra*, the queen of Sheba reborn, for Asma and Arwa remind the people of that splendid ancient time when a woman ruled, a time that is forever observed in God's words:

> But he tarried not long, and said,
> "I have comprehended that which you
> have not comprehended, and I have come
> from Sheba to you with a sure tiding.
> I found a woman ruling over them,
> And she has been given of everything,
> And she possesses a mighty throne."[24]

She is only twenty-six, but she, too, possesses a mighty throne. Asma is dead. Al-Mukkaram grows weaker every day. It seems with every day another stroke overtakes that once bold warrior, vivid thinker, fair ruler, vital young man. His mother held the ambitious cousins at bay. Asma governed with such skill that the Yemenis stand firm against any pretenders.

Arwa is frightened. From Asma she learned to love knowledge, she learned the principles of good governance. Her father-in-law had told Asma to treat her "with respect, for God has ordained that she will be guarantor of our decendants, preserving this regime for those of us who survive." It is a daunting responsibility. She watched as Asma, widowed, her son debilitated, brought the kingdom to further greatness and vaster territories. Now it is hers to preserve and al-Mukkaram cannot help.

Her first act is to tour the domain. When she returns to San'a, she has al-Mukkaram bundled into a palanquin. They look out from highest point of the city.

"What do you see?" she asks her husband.

He sits up with great effort, gritting his teeth. "I see our capital. The sun flashing off swords and spears..." He gasps and collapses onto his pillows.

The small royal caravan moves away from San'a into the countryside. Soon, they are in Jabala, nestled against a mountain and embraced by two rivers. A fortress looms above the town, a sentinel guarding the gentle shepherds, the children, the women carrying vessels of honey and oil and water on their heads.

"Now what do you see?" Arwa asks her husband.

"I see no weapons. I see peace."

"Life is better here," Arwa says. "Here is where we will move our capital."

From Jabala, Arwa rules with efficiency and renewed confidence. She administers projects for new roads, new fountains, increases agriculture, the raising of cattle and trade. She builds hospitals for women, where they are taught family planning and birth control.

She builds schools and the Big Mosque at San'a, the al-Gurba mosque in Yarim to the south and the al-Game mosque in Jabala.

She lowers prices and supervises tax collection, making it fair for all. She keeps meticulous records, as she was taught by her father-in-law, Ali al-Sulayhi, when he put her in charge at the age of sixteen of collecting the tax revenues of Aden, given to her as a dowry.

She conducts the government with her face veiled. She is young and beautiful; her husband, the sultan, lies paralyzed in his bed. The strategy will vouchsafe the dynasty; the officials will take her seriously. As she speaks from behind the veil, they will sense that she is merely a conduit, a medium, speaking for al-Mukkaram.

She loves peace. She strives for peace. She abstains from the use of force, preferring persuasion, conciliation, and bribery. Better to purchase a fort from the rebel who has taken it than to fight. She is a woman and law forbids her from riding at the head of the army. The clans compete to seize local power. Without this authority, though Arwa appeases and uses diplomacy where others would use the military, the Sulayhi clan is weakened.

But there is one violent goal that Arwa cleaves toward. She will find and kill Sa'id al-Najah. It will be a victory to exhibit the might of the Sulayhi despite its misfortunes. And the Yemeni Sunnis, afraid that the Sulayhis may be vassals of the Fatimids in Cairo, will be silenced.

Al-Mukkaram had taken Zubayd when he rescued his mother. Sa'id had fled by sea. From her new capital of Jabala, Arwa begins to constrict al-Najah's movements. She negotiates new alliances and thus gains new terrain to which Said is unwelcome, where it is dangerous for him to tread. Arwa cannot command Yemen's military, and does not want to ask for it unless and until it's crucial. She spreads false rumors that her allies are preparing to abandon her. She persuades them to visit Sa'id al-Najah and let him believe that should he attack Jabala, they will be behind him. He attacks. Arwa's army crushes him.

When he is dead, his wife Umm al-Mu'arik is brought to Arwa. An act of cruelty requires its exact proportion in return. A balance.

One for one. Umm al-Mu'arik is placed in a small prison cell with one window. Her view is her husband's impaled head on a pole.

The grief nearly paralyzes her when al-Mukarram dies. All those whom she had loved from childhood are gone. She is alone, carrying the burden of a dynasty. Her first son is eight years old and he must accede, while she is his regent. From Cairo, the caliph al-Mustansur agrees.

Once again love deserts her. Her older son dies and within a few months his younger brother is gone, too. She is sole ruler of Yemen. Alone.

Saba ibn Adman is al-Mukarram's cousin. He is one of those they had kept at arm's length so as to preserve the dynasty within Ali al-Sulayhi's own clan. He proposes marriage. She rejects him. He attacks her castle in Jabala. She repels the attack. He offers her a measureless bride-price. She shakes her head and refuses with the words, "I will never consent to marriage except by order of the caliph."

Saba takes his case to al-Mustansur. In Egypt, they veil their women. In Egypt they have no *balqis al-sughra*, no queens of Sheba reborn. The caliph cannot imagine that Arwa should rule alone with no husband, no sons. He sends messengers telling Arwa to marry and let her spouse rule before her. They may say *khatub* in the mosque for her on Friday, and she may hold temporal power, but she cannot hold religious authority.

She wrangles. She sends ministers and ambassadors. They plead for her. They know their queen. She has been a successful ruler. She will continue to be. And back and forth and forth and back they argue against the implacable caliph al-Mustansur. At last Arwa gives in and signs the marriage document.

Saba sets forth to claim his bride. At Arwa's castle, the gates are locked. He camps outside and waits. A day goes by and then a week and then two weeks, and then a month has passed. Arwa sends his troops food, paid for with the bride-price he has given for her. All around him the people pass, ignoring him, though the caliph allowed him to be ruler of Yemen. Yet they refer to Arwa as *sayyida, malika, al-hurra—our* lady.

How does Saba bear the humiliation? He writes a letter to Arwa and sends it in secret.

"Lady, let me spend just one night in the castle. Let me keep up appearances, at least."

Arwa orders the gates to be opened and Saba rides into the castle. Arwa is nowhere to be seen. He is placed in a bed chamber. The door creaks open. A serving girl enters. She stands before him at the foot of his bed all night. A serving girl! To be ignored, of course. He never looks at her.

At dawn, he says his prayers and leaves.

It is this tale Arwa tells to remind the caliph that she had presented herself to Saba as his wife, she had been by his bed the night long. But he had rejected her. He had never glanced at her!

Never again will Saba appear before Arwa. He is sultan of Yemen, but he serves his queen faithfully and well. She makes him the titular head of the army and thus the conduit through which she can command her military forces. He lives eleven more years.

She is old now. The girl who had power thrust upon her, frightened of her own abilities, terrified of responsibilities, but well-trained and determined. The Yemeni viziers—Sunni who see little good in the Fatamid caliph to whom the Sulhayis have given their allegiance—are less and less trustworthy. They see in her aging fissures in her power. They look toward exploiting her aloneness. The veil cannot disguise her age, it cannot make her seem immortal.

Arwa sends to Cairo, to the Fatimid court for a minister she can truly rely upon. And he is. She shuffles and he marches with energy and enthusiasm to assert her will. She trembles and he holds forth a strong, steady hand.

In Cairo, the dynasty feuds within itself. Her vizier is recalled and he is executed on false grounds.

Arwa is devastated. And suddenly confronted by the new caliph in Cairo, who sends his troops to seize her kingdom. She is old. She is fragile. This is the moment.

The people love their queen. The Yemenis rally against this interloper. The army mobilizes behind her. The Cairo caliph withdraws.

In eight years she is dead. She is eighty-five. They bury her in the mosque she built in San'a.

Radiyya

Sultana Radiyya took power in Delhi in 634 A.H./1236 C.E. She was a Turk, descended from the military slave class of Mamluks. She ruled for three years, six months, and six days. She was called the "spinster queen" and given the honorific "Pillar of Women," and was a legitimate sovereign, who ruled in her own name. She died in 638 A.H./ 1240 C.E.

It is said her beauty is "sufficient to ripen the corn on the blade." And like her father, Iltutmish, she is immensely talented, skilled at everything she attempts.

She holds in her hand the diploma he signed giving her the throne upon his death. Of all her siblings, she is most like him and was taught by him and trained by him in the ways of a sovereign and a general. She can—and she will—have the inheritance that is rightly hers. He has written: *My daughter Radiyya will rule all India after me.*

Had she not been his regent? Had she not administered the affairs of the central government when Iltutmish departed Delhi with his great army to bring all Hindustan to its knees before Muslim rule? "Know," the sultan said to his court officials, "that the burden of power, too heavy for my sons, though there are three of them, is not so for Radiyya. She is wiser, stronger, and more spirited than any of them."

She did not disappoint. When Iltutmish returned, triumphant, she once again sat, as she had from childhood, beside him, his

363

favorite, his friend. And so it was for four more years: father and daughter, warm and affectionate, proud of one another, and she, guided in his image.

Now Iltutmish is dead. A Turk who had come to India as a slave who fought so valiantly to bring Islam to power in Hindustan that Sultan Qutub al-Din Aybak married Iltutmish to his daughter. Aybak died, Iltutmish took power and declared himself independent of his Ghaznah overlords, manumitted, for without the charter declaring his liberty, he could not be a legitimate monarch. He reigned for twenty years.

Now Iltutmish is dead and snug in his place as one of the greatest slave kings in history.

The Turkish *ghulams* accepted the diploma Iltutmish signed to hand his power to Radiyya, his eldest child. The amirs did not. At last, before he died, Iltutmish relented. Firuz Shah, his eldest son, profligate, womanizing, weak, will succeed Iltutmish.

Radiyya bides her time. There is no choice. Firuz Shah ascends the throne, and that moment of coronation is the only moment he spends acting as monarch. It is his mother, Shah Terken, who rules India from the *zenana*. While Firuz lavishes the treasury on musicians, dancers, and wine, Shah Terken plots tyranny and assassinations. She causes her son's half brother to be blinded and put to death. There are small uprisings. She conspires to murder Radiyya. There are widespread revolts.

For once, the amirs and ghulams, Turks, Tajiks, Ghuris agree: Firuz and his mother must go. In the seventh month of her son's corrupt reign, Shah Terken is overthrown in Delhi. Firuz Shah is put to death by his half brother Rukn al-Din, supported by those same amirs who had insisted upon Firuz's enthronement.

Who now will grip the imperial reins? The Turks remember the diploma signed by Iltutmish. They are loyal to their late sultan, who brought them unprecedented influence. They persuade other eyes to turn to Radiyya. Yet the insurgents who have deposed Firuz Shah will not recognize her. She mounts the throne no longer her father's pampered princess, but sultana in her own right, supported by the powerful Turkish slave officers and the people. Always the people.

Her half brother Rukn al-Din does all he can to frighten Radiyya back into the *zenana* like a mouse back to its hole. She is fearless. She mounts the tower, Qutub Minar, said to have been built by the last Chauhan king of Delhi so that his daughter could behold the sacred river Yamuna in daily worship. But it was Iltutmish who completed this finest of structures.

Standing atop the red sandstone tower covered with carvings and verses from the Holy Qur'an, Radiyya looks down upon crowds of people, here to lavish praise upon Sultan Iltutmish:

The great king; the exalted emperor; master of the necks of the people; pride of the kings of Arabia and 'Ajni; God's shadow on Earth; son of the world and of faith; redresser of Islam and the Muslims; crown of kings and princes; spreader of justice among humankind...

It is his justice they remember. They cheer for Radiyya's words, invoking the name of her beloved father.

She brings back his laws. As he did, she orders the oppressed to wear dyed garments, though the other inhabitants of India wear white clothes. She marches as he did through the streets and when her eyes fall upon one wearing colored attire, she looks quickly into his case and obtains justice from the oppressor.

She reinstates the bell he had installed at the palace on an iron chain between two marble statues of lions on two towers at the gate. Those who are demoralized, those who are exploited, have only to shake the bell in the night and Sultana Radiyya, on hearing the sound, awakens, looks into his case, and administers justice.

Rukn al-Dinn continues his threats. She is a woman, his half sister, by rights, he claims, he can put her to death. He calls on the people to help him avenge the death of Firuz Shah, though he himself had murdered Firuz, despised him with the same jealous fury he has for Radiyya.

Not for nothing did Radiyya sit at her father's side. He taught her well. Again, she follows his customs. On a Friday, she dresses in the dyed garments of the oppressed. She goes to the mosque where the faithful are gathered. Rukn al-Din emerges from the palace to attend services. Radiyya mounts the balcony and calls to the people and to the army:

"My brother killed his brother and he now wants to kill me! Remember my father Iltutmish! Remember his goodness and his benevolence!"

And the army arrests Rukn al-Din. They take him to her. She orders his death in retaliation for his brother's death.

She rewards some for bringing her safely to the throne. She exalts others in rank. Yet it is ever true that some are never rewarded enough. Disappointed amirs find one another and congregate in opposition.

There are men who cannot stomach the notion of a woman reigning over them. Never mind her intelligence, her skill in warfare, her diplomacy and righteous administration. Never mind that she is her father's chosen. The great Iltutmish is dead. The Turks never mind a woman ruler it seems, but what are they but slaves, albeit authoritative and compelling. Yet, the amirs tell one another, it is not God's intention to let a woman rule, let alone over an empire as vast and rich as this one. They gather an army. At its head is Iltutmish's old vizier. The army of grumbling grandees marches on Delhi and defeats Raddiya's forces.

What she cannot do with her soldiers, she will accomplish by her wit. A word of praise here, a smile there among her enemies and soon they are confused and arguing, until their confederacy dissolves. Some she puts to death. Most she offers mercy, even generosity, until quiet is restored.

Never again will she be criticized merely for her gender. She discards her feminine apparel and her veil. She dons tunic, turban, and trousers when she sits on the throne and gives public audiences. She rides abroad on her elephant with no attempt at concealment.

She gives herself over to affairs of state. She is a reformer. The amirs recoil in anger. She cleans out the corruption left by Firuz Shah. More anger. She revises laws. She judges important lawsuits. She has coins minted in her own name. Her name is spoken in the Friday prayers. The people call her "just" and "able." She determines to build her own power. She advances the loyal Turkish slave elite inherited from her father, but tries as well to check their ascent. And she extends the empire, even as she loses ground to those who will not abide her.

Radiyya is alone, the spinster queen, married to her father's memory and his legacy. There are suitors, of course. There are men ambitious for power and men who are simply charmed. Old, young, rich and wanting to be richer.

A woman who would rule as her father expected cannot afford a husband's interference. She turns a cold shoulder to them all.

But one man captivates her in spite of herself. He is handsome, strong, witty. He makes Radiyya laugh and this is the first step to love.

Jamal al-Din Yaqut is her equerry, amir of horses. He has come to India from Abyssinia as a slave.

The secrets of Radiyya's bedchamber will be safe throughout history. But it is no secret in court that Sultana Radiyya showers this lowborn Ethiopian with favors. The grumbling grandees go at it with renewed veniality. They spy on Yaqut to learn why he is promoted so quickly. They note that their queen takes great pleasure in his company. And then one day he is seen sliding his arms around her to hoist her on her mount. A familiar gesture that violates ethical behavior. A queen touched by her slave!

The accusations begin. Passion unbecoming a royal woman for a servant! Her army elects to depose Sultana Radiyya and marry her off.

Whether the light grip of Yaqut as he places her on the saddle thrills her is of less consequence than how it thrills her enemies. It is not only he who uplifts her, the courtiers complain. She will raise him to a place on her throne.

Indeed, she has raised the object of her favor to the office of amir of amirs, commander of commanders. And with that, the religious leaders and princes call on Ikhtiyar al-Din Altuniyya to lead a revolt. Word reaches the sultana: Altuniyya has taken the field and is launching a siege.

She calls forth what's left of her loyal army. She prepares a counteroffensive. She rides at its head to Altuniyya's fort of Batinda with massive strength. The nickering of horses, the clip-clop of

367

hooves, the trumpets of elephants, the clatter of swords and armor and spears, the beat of war drums deafen Radiyya to the sounds of discontent within the force, resentment from the ranks to the generals that the man who rides beside her, her general-in-chief, is a mere black slave. Suddenly, as they proceed with slow resolve, the army stops behind the sultana and men gallop forward to surround her and the former slave they are sure must be her lover.

They seize the Abyssinian and before Radiyya's eyes cut him down, stab him, behead him. Then, afraid she will nonetheless rally rebellion among the people—for the people see Iltutmish in her and love her for her justice and generosity—they lead her fast to the fort at Batinda and deliver her into the hands of the rebel Altuniyya.

Then fast again, fast as their steeds can carry them, they dash back to Delhi and swear allegiance to Radiyya's brother Behram, another brother as base as the first and the second. A brother the nobles can control.

Who will have the last laugh? How could her mutinous generals guess that by delivering their queen into the hands of Altuniyya, they were delivering her yet again to love?

Altuniyya receives Radiyya sumptuously, as a sultana should be welcomed. He dines with her and talks with her and by the end of the evening, his eyes are clouded with romance. Before she has wiped her mouth clean of the last morsel, Altuniyya has freed Radiyya, and before the week has passed, he has proposed to her.

Does Altuniyya resemble her father? Is he brave and single-minded, shrewd and vigorous like Iltutmish? Wise when wisdom is called for? Brutal when the time is right? Does Radiyya return Altuniyya's affections? Is she as fascinated by him as he is with her? The secrets of her heart will be safe throughout history.

Or does she, brave and single-minded, shrewd and vigorous, recognize opportunity when it presents itself? Power about to be regained?

They marry and there is great celebrating in the fort of Batinda.

And there Radiyya and Altuniyya stay a while rejoicing. All that while they assemble warriors, fighters who will erect the sultana's imperial banner and carry it back to Delhi to dethrone the usurping prince.

Two pitched battles. Radiyya and Altuniyya's troops are routed. Altuniyya is taken prisoner. The sultana, dressed in men's clothes, flees and runs until she is overpowered by hunger and strained by fatigue. A peasant is tilling the soil when Radiyya collapses by his field. She begs for food. He brings her bread. She eats and falls asleep. While she sleeps, the peasant's eyes fall upon a gown studded with jewels revealed by her torn tunic. A woman!

He stabs Radiyya, plunders her, and buries her in his field. In the morning, he takes her bejeweled garment to the market to sell.

There are those in the market who become suspicious. They seize him and drag him to the magistrate, who beats the peasant until he confesses. He takes the authorities to the furrow where he has disposed of the woman.

Sultana Radiyya is disinterred. Her body is washed and shrouded and buried in Delhi. Hearts were hard toward a woman who would be queen. A woman who dares wear men's clothing. For politicians, a just, able, and peaceful reign means little. They are never content to be content when contentment is possible.

But for the people dressed in dyed garments, Radiyya's tomb becomes a place of pilgrimage, where she bestows blessings from Paradise. A dome is built over her grave on the bank of the great river Jumna.

Nur Jahan

Nur Jahan's given name was Mihrunnisa. She was born near Kandahar, in what is now Afghanistan. In 989 A.H./1611 C.E., when it's believed she was about thirty-five years old, she was married to the fourth Mughal emperor Jahangir (r. 983 A.H./1605 C.E. to 1005 A.H./1627 C.E.). She was a devoted patron of the arts, and among other projects, built a magnificent tomb—the It-ma-ud-Daula in Agra, India—for her beloved father, a generation before her step-son Shah Jahan built the Taj Mahal. Legends surround Nur Jahan. The tale of her birth may have been embellished to increase her popularity or acknowledge her greatness.

Mirza Ghias Beg belongs to an impoverished if noble family in the town of Teheran. When he hears of the magnificent fortunes to be made in India, he determines to take his wife across the plains and over the mountains to the glittering city of the Mughal emperors.

They have one old horse and a few coins. They pass through Herat and on to Kandahar, when Ghias Beg's wife gives birth to a girl in the desert. For a few hours they await relief, in the vain hope that a traveler might pass by and help with food or water. Darkness gathers and wild beasts roar in the distance. Ghias Beg is afraid. He places the new mother back on the old horse. He hands her the child, but she is so weak she cannot hold herself fast on the horse, least of all carry the infant. Ghias Beg is exhausted. He can scarcely stand. He decides to leave the child to God's mercy by the side of the road. He places her under a tree and covers her with leaves to keep her warm.

Ghias Beg and his wife advance a mile, but when the eyes of the mother can no longer distinguish the solitary tree, she gives way to wild weeping for her daughter. She throws herself from the horse and pounds the ground, sobbing. "My child! I want my child!" She tries to rise, but cannot. She tries to crawl on hands and knees toward the tree, but drops into a faint.

Ghias Beg hurries back to the place where he left the child. A black snake is coiled around the baby. Its jaws are wide open—or is it merely shading the pretty infant with its hood? Ghias Beg shrieks in horror and the snake slithers into the hollow of the tree. The baby sleeps peacefully on. Her father sweeps her up and rushes with her to his distraught wife.

And at the moment they retrieve their child, the fortunes of Ghias Beg and his wife improve.

Travelers appear on the scene and give sustenance and companionship the rest of the way to Lahore. In Lahore, Ghias Beg begins his career upward to become high treasurer of the empire. He names his daughter Mihrunnisa, the Sun of Women, for she is beautiful and well aware of it.

She is educated in music and dancing, poetry and painting. Courtiers and warriors ask for her hand and when she is fifteen, Ghias chooses the Persian, Shaer Afghan, the lord of Bengal, the most accomplished noble of the emperor Akbar's court.

But Mihrunnisa has set her sights on Selim, the emperor's son and heir. She is sure that he has only to see her once briefly and his heart will be hers. When he visits her father, she lets her veil fall and Prince Selim is smitten. Ghias Beg will hear nothing of such a union. He has made his promise to Shaer Afghan and the betrothal will stand. Selim pleads with his father, but Akbar refuses to interfere or force Shaer Afghan to give up his claim on the Sun of Women.

And that is that. Until Akbar dies and Selim inherits the throne and gains the name Jahangir, World Conqueror.

In Bengal, Shaer Afghan and Mihrunnisa live happily. She has lost her girlish passion for crown princes and looks to her handsome, affectionate husband with love. Later, her enemies will claim she

371

never stopped corresponding with Selim, and that she collaborated with his designs on Shaer Afghan's life. But Mihrunnisa's youthful infatuation has turned toward her own daughter, Ladli.

Jahangir is infatuated by the rights of emperors to have whatever they wish.

He sends for Shaer Afghan, commanding his presence in Delhi without delay and ordering him to bring his wife. Shaer Afghan is received with cordiality. New honors are conferred upon him.

Jahangir organizes a tiger hunt. Shaer Afghan is tricked into facing the beast alone and unarmed. Shaer Afghan defeats the fearsome creature, but the tiger clawing at Jahangir's heart will not be vanquished.

The largest imperial elephant is driven into a narrow street where it meets Shaer Afghan's palanquin. The elephant charges. Shaer Afghan is knocked to the ground. He draws his sword and kills the oncoming creature. The leviathan propelling through Jahangir's heart cannot die.

Shaer Afghan and Mihrunnisa return to Bengal with Ladli. On their journey forty ruffians attack. Shaer Afghan dispels them one by one like insects. The flies aggravating Jahangir's heart buzz and drone incessantly.

A pikeman rides fast at Shaer Afghan's horse and pierces it. The horse falls. Shaer Afghan is surrounded. Cornered. Sword drawn, he challenges the oncoming assassins to single combat. They ignore his honorable challenge, advancing closer and closer in tight formation. Arrows and musket balls whistle and men shout. Shaer Afghan drops and turns his face toward Mecca. He scoops a handful of dust and tosses it on his head as ablution. He mutters a prayer, *Allahu Akbar, Allahu Akbar*. Shaer Afghan struggles to his feet as six balls enter his body. His enemies praise his valor. There is not a murmur from Jahangir.

The widow and her daughter are conveyed to the palace at Delhi and for nearly six years Jahangir and Mihrunnisa do not see each other's faces.

Some say Jahangir is ashamed. Others that Mihrunnisa refuses all overtures from the man who has murdered her husband. She keeps strict mourning for Shaer Afghan.

In the *zenana*, Mihrunnisa's name is changed to Nur Mahal, Light of the Palace. She occupies herself with the needlework at which she excels. She winds raw silk from the pod. She divides each pod into twenty degrees of fineness. She runs the thread through her fingers so swiftly the eye cannot perceive it. Soon nothing is so fashionable in *zenana* than to possess an item of Nur Mahal's handiwork. The astonishing designs reflect her Persian origins, as well as the Hindu art all around: embroidered abstract patterns of nature, as well as trees of life and potted flowers, elephants, peacocks, and even human figures.

With the money she makes, she beautifies her mean apartments. She buys slaves and clothes them in rich tissues and brocades. But Nur Mahal in mourning wears simple white muslin.

Then one day Jahangir arrives unannounced and unexpected.

Nur Mahal reclines on a couch. Her maids sit in a circle around her. She in white muslin, they in rich brocades. The Light of the Palace rises, confused by this sudden visitor. For a moment she does not recognize Selim, the passion of her girlhood. Then she touches the ground and her forehead with her right hand. She says nothing, no word. Jahangir, overcome by her still marvelous beauty and the idyllic scene he has entered, is stunned silent.

When he sits and motions Nur Mahal to sit beside him, when he opens his mouth to speak, he asks, "Why this difference between your appearance and that of your slaves?"

"Those born to servitude must dress as it shall please those they serve. These are my servants, and I alleviate their burden of bondage by every indulgence in my power. But I who am your slave, Emperor of the World, must dress according to your pleasure and not my own."

Jahangir begs her forgiveness. He sends her forty pearls. He sends his vizier to ask for her hand. The marriage is celebrated with pomp. The Light of the Palace is renamed Nur Jahan, Light of the World. Coins are stamped in her name with the inscription, "Gold has acquired a hundred degrees of excellence in receiving the name of Nur Jahan."

Her father becomes grand vizier. With Ghias Beg, her brother Asaf Khan, and her stepson Khurram, Nur Jahan is not only the

Light of the World, but its commander. Day by day her influence grows. No land grants are conferred without her seal. She keeps strict *purdah* and sits in the balcony of her palace, while nobles present themselves and listen to her dictates from behind the curtain. Her model for rule is the mandala of her Hindu subjects, power moving out from the center in concentric circles from court to countryside.

How has she come by such authority?

Jahangir lurches from alcohol to opium and back again, pausing only to write a poem or listen to one, to slur and drum happily along with court musicians, to, in his almost-sober moments, dabble in architecture or painting.

"I require," he tells his nobles, "nothing beyond a sir of wine and half a sir of meat. I bestow sovereignty on my empress, Nur Jahan."

In his diaries, he confesses, "I think that no one is fonder of me than Nur Jahan. Her skill and experience are greater than those of the physicians. She by degrees lessens my wine and keeps me from things that do not suit me, and food that disagrees with me."

She is nurse, she is governess, she is tyrant. At bedtime her husband drools and nods while Nur Jahan and her slaves undress him, chafing and fondling him like a child. Whatever Nur Jahan desires, he gives her. Some say that she does with him as she likes, that daily she rewards him with false words of love.

Say what they will: gradually, by degrees, she is sobering him. When she denies him a glass of wine, he weeps. At last Nur Jahan succeeds in getting Jahangir to agree to only nine cupfuls of liquor a day, so long as they are offered by her own hand. When he wants more, he attacks her, lays hold of her, and scratches and hits her. She grapples with him, biting and kicking until he, weakened by the exertion, lets go, then collapses into tears.

The emperor sleeps it off, while Nur Jahan attends to court intrigues. She promotes and demotes. She arranges marriages. She makes decisions about trade and taxes and spending of the treasury. Her authority is absolute.

Jahangir's son Khusrau observes all this and makes his move for the throne. Nur Jahan determines that he will be imprisoned in the fortress at Decca and that his brother Shah Jahan will accompany him. It will mean a quick end for Khusrau. A quick end to the revolt. It is officially recorded that Khusrau dies "from a disease of colic pains." The way to the throne is cleared for whichever man is chosen by Nur Jahan to marry her daughter Ladli. That man is Shahryr, Jahangir's weakest offspring. Some among the elite favor Shahryr, but most put their hopes in Shah Jahan to succeed his father.

Impatient, Shah Jahan breaks out into open rebellion and is defeated in the ensuing struggle. His father forgives him.

For Jahangir has taken a vow of nonviolence. He retreats into a period of asceticism. He is traveling and the party is faced with an approaching tiger. Jahangir prays while Nur Jahan takes up a gun and kills the tiger with one shot.

He is who he is and he admires his empress for her courage and wisdom. He writes in his diaries that "In the whole empire there is scarcely a city in which the queen has not left some lofty structure, some spacious garden, as a splendid monument of her taste and magnificence."

He notes the splendor she has brought to the court, that she has beautified the ladies' dress and introduced new designs and new ideas from Europe and Persia and China. Jahangir reels through twenty years drinking, eating opium, consuming the arts with bottomless contentment, while his wife and her retinue manage the empire—well and prosperously.

No sooner has Shah Jahan given up his rebellion than the empire's most exalted general, Mahabat Khan—once Jahangir's friend, now his enemy—takes the emperor captive while he is encamped with courtiers, friends, and family on the bank of the Jumna River.

Word is brought to Nur Jahan in the women's tent. She disguises herself and rides in an ordinary palanquin to her brother. She reproaches the royal troops for allowing their sovereign to be made a prisoner before their eyes. She makes immediate preparations to rescue her husband by force.

First, she directs a captain to swim the river with a small body of horses and dash for the tent where Jahangir is confined. The captain is caught and killed.

The next morning, the royal army is commanded to advance, headed by Nur Jahan herself, riding on an elephant and holding on her lap her granddaughter and a bow and four quivers of arrows. The bridge is destroyed, so they cross a narrow shoal, full of holes. Many must swim. They land with their powder wet, clothes drenched, and slogging armor. They are met by Mahabat Khan's soldiers, and wet and sloshing, some still up to their chests in the river, they engage in watery hand-to-hand combat.

Nur Jahan and her brother are among the first to cross. They face a furious assault. The empress's driver is killed. Musket balls and arrows fall thick around her. She shouts encouragement to her sodden and panic-stricken troops. She pours the contents of her quivers of arrows upon her foes.

An arrow strikes her grandchild and lodges in the little girl's arm. Nur Jahan pulls it out so fast and straight the child barely feels it. Blood spurts across the queen's garments. Just then the elephant is pierced on its trunk, and in pain and fear it dashes back into the river and makes for the farther side. At that, the royal troops flee in terror and dismay, unable to fight without their queen's encouragement.

Nur Jahan escapes to Lahore. Letters come from Jahangir, letters he is compelled to write, saying matters are amicably arranged and begging her to join him. Suspecting nothing, she sets off. A short distance from Mahabat Khan's camp, she is taken prisoner.

Mahabat Khan blames Nur Jahan for all the troubles that have brought him to this impasse. He charges her before the inebriated emperor Jahangir with treason and of conspiring to put her stepson, Jahangir's son, her son-in-law Shahryr on the throne.

"You who are Emperor of the Mughals," he snarls at Jahangir, "whom we regard as something more than human, ought to follow the example of God, who is no respecter of persons."

Holding a cup of wine, pupils dilated, Jahangir sways as he signs a warrant for the instant execution of his wife.

Nur Jahan's courage does not fail her. From her place of seclusion, for even at this encampment she keeps the strictest *purdah*, she hears of her husband's treachery with bland emotion. She requests only that she may see him before she dies.

"Imprisoned sovereigns lose their right to life as well as their freedom," she tells Mahabat Khan through the curtain that separates them. "But permit me once more to see the emperor and to bathe with my tears the hand that has fixed the seal to the warrant of my death."

She knows her husband well.

Mahabat Khan does not. He acquiesces. Nur Jahan enters the tent of Jahangir and removes her veil. She speaks not a word, her face betrays nothing, but tears cascade from her eyes.

Jahangir, too, begins to weep. He turns to Mahabat Khan and in the most pathetic tones begs him: "Will you not spare this woman? Do you not see how she weeps?"

Mahabat Khan is struck dumb at the beauty, even in age, that he has never seen, that he has only heard praised. "The Emperor of the Mughals should never ask in vain," he says. And Nur Jahan's life is spared.

The imperial couple, though ostensibly at liberty, is not allowed to leave the camp of Mahabat Khan. The general is everywhere with his captive and no one can explain why, at length, Mahabat is humbled. Months pass until at last he releases the emperor, who returns to his palaces with his wife.

Nur Jahan will have none of this passivity! She entreats Jahangir to declare Mahabat a traitor and to set a price on his head. Her wrath seems boundless until her brother, knowing the value of Mahabat's military skills, persuades her to let the emperor pardon him and to entrust him again with an army.

Within the year, Jahangir pays the toll for dissipation. Shah Jahan sends his widowed stepmother to Lahore, to exile. Nur Jahan is paid a handsome sum that provides her with the means to execute public projects, buildings whose beauty is unrivaled until Shah Jahan builds a tomb for his beloved wife, Mumtaz/Mahal.

Nur Jahan lives on for eighteen years. She wears no color but white. She will not speak of public affairs and politics. She gives herself up to study. She strolls her gardens, the Light of the World, the Sun of Women.

VIII

Tradeswomen and Learned Ladies

"To educate a woman is to educate the whole world..."

*T*he Prophet's early experiences in trade with his uncle Abu Talib and his wife Khadija's profession as a tradeswoman have given trading an honored place in Islam. In the desert and in lands that cannot sustain farming and self-sufficiency, survival depends upon mobility and commerce. The *hajj* grew from the annual Arab observance in Mecca that focused on worship at the Ka'aba and around the great fair to which tribes came from long distances to trade. *Hayat al-Dunya,* "the life of this world," is not despised, as in some faiths, so long as it does not get the better of believers and prevent them from striving toward the afterlife, *al-Akhira,* which includes sharing the wealth through almsgiving and acts of charity.[1]

A modern Sindhi children's song, Schimmel tells us in *And Muhammad Was His Messenger,* chides boys to learn trade, "'for the Prophet himself was occupied with it and made it important with all his energy."

Khadija continued her career even after her marriage to Muhammad, who traveled for a time as her agent. She, as we've seen, supported his every endeavor, spiritually and with her wealth.

While women in pre-Islamic Arabia were recurrently mistreated and their rightful inheritances habitually withheld from them, there was nonetheless some accepted practice, especially among widows, of independent women in business—of whom Khadija was one—and this carried over into the Muslim era.

Shaffa bint Abdallah was so skilled in matters of money and trade, the Prophet, without a qualm, appointed her to the position of overseer of the market in Medina.

Aisha was no slouch, either, when it came to money matters. Her father, the first Rightly Guided caliph Abu Bakr, left her (not his sons) with the responsibility of caring for the family and she did so shrewdly, providing for them well, arranging profitable, often very loving, marriages, dealing in real estate, and, it's thought, trading slaves. Like the other Mothers of the Believers, she received a stipend from the community treasury. As the Prophet's "Best Beloved," in whose company he had experienced Revelations, Aisha's portion was more lavish than the others. That the third Rightly Guided caliph Uthman reduced her income contributed to her opposition to him.

Buying and selling real estate was a primary occupation among women throughout the Islamic empire. They were prominent in their patronage, as we've seen, and used their wealth for innumerable building projects. They also invested for profit. A study of the Anatolian city of Kayseri in the early seventeenth century shows that women sold property three times more frequently than they bought it.[2] A further study of eighteenth-century Aleppo, Syria, illustrates that men bought and sold houses less often than women.[3] In eighteenth-century Egypt, women invested heavily in long-distance trade of coffee and spices, in textile production and artisan's workshops, in storehouses, which included living quarters and shops, in apartment complexes for rental income, and in cafes.[4]

In Egypt's Mamluk system of the seventeenth and eighteenth centuries, Mary Ann Fay writes, "women served as the conduits of status and property. It was not enough for a manumitted Mamluk to acquire his dead master's rank and title; in many cases, he also had to marry his former master's widow to legitimize his position. Insofar as she controlled her dead husband's property as his heir or as the *nazira* (overseer) of his [endowments], she brought to her new household not only her high rank and status but considerable wealth as well. Thus, women provided an important element of stability and continuity in an inherently unstable system."[5] The *valide sultans* of the Ottoman Empire owned ships and possessed huge estates.

The Muslim Acheh Empire, on the northern tip of Sumatra — now an impoverished, beleaguered territory gasping for independence from Indonesia — was ruled during the seventeenth century by four women in succession. Islam arrived in the region as early as the ninth century C.E. with Muslim trading ships from India, the Persian

Gulf, and the coast of Arabia. Marketing in Sumatra, as in many places, was conducted openly by women, a fact that shocked the Spanish and Portuguese who appeared in the fifteenth century. They might have found that the harbor master of Gresik was a woman, Nyai Gede Pinatech (ca. 906 A.H./1500 C.E.), who sent ships to trade throughout Southeast Asia.

The mercantile women of the region did not simply trade in local markets, but engaged in long-distance import and export, as well as money changing and other lucrative activities. Girls were educated to understand the workings of family fortunes, to keep the books and drive the bargains.

The four queens of Acheh were no exceptions to the custom of educating daughters to business. They were especially influential in enriching their tiny empire's prosperity, keeping food prices low, respecting property rights, expanding international commerce, and avoiding war so as to succeed in building wealth.

The Indo-Muslim Sultan Ghiyath Shah—he of the 16,000 slave women trained in the arts—had an additional 500 who were educated in numerous formal studies. One was required to join him for conversation every day at each of his meals. "He selected a number of them and entrusted them with various affairs of state, such as the office of demands and the watching of receipts and expenditure of the country and supervision of various factories."[6]

The Persian ruler Fath Ali-Shah (r. 1175 A.H./1797 C.E. to 1212 A.H./1834 C.E.) brought his daughters into the administration of the court, appointing his youngest, Zia-o-Saltaneh, as his political adviser, his middle daughter, Anis-o-doleh, to run the court secretariat, while his eldest, Khazin-o-doleh, was treasurer in charge of the crown jewels.

The intrepid Garnett wrote that "the Kurds generally leave to the women the business of settling accounts with that regular, but unwelcome visitor, the tax-gatherer." She relates an incident that could excite envy in anyone at tax day:

> On the arrival on one occasion of this functionary at the
> camp of...a large and wealthy tribe established in the

plains to the north-west of Van [Turkey], he was politely
received and treated with black coffee and tobacco in the
tent of the chief…who courteously informed him that he
was at liberty to enter the different tents for the collection
of the sheep tax. Once in the tents, however, the tax-gatherer soon perceived that while he was striving to get hold
of everything he could detect, the object of the women
was to conceal from him all they could. Out of interests
so opposed, a collision naturally soon arose and a shower
of vituperation, followed by an attack with sticks and
stones, assailed the unlucky official, who was finally rescued from the hands of these fair furies by the men of the
tribe, and carried for safety to the tent of the chief…[who]
now gave him friendly advice to get from the women all
they were willing to give and return at once to Van, thank-
ing Allah that no worse had befallen him.[7]

Sitt Nasra bint Adlan, daughter of the last king of Sennaar in
the Sudan was, according to an 1852 account by American traveler
Bayard Taylor, "a woman of almost masculine talent and energy and
may be said to govern Sennaar at present." Although she was not a
queen, she called herself "sultana" and was a major economic
player, a powerful high roller, who turned her inheritance into a
mini-empire. She is still legendary among the Sudanese people.[8]

In studies of Islam and the Middle East, the seclusion of
women has been a defining factor, Ruth Roded writes. "A growing
body of evidence, however, challenges this axiom. The documented
scope of women's public and social economic activities has raised
the question of how the seclusion and modesty of Middle Eastern
women were maintained. Some measures taken to guard women's
privacy or modesty in public were wearing the hijab and a face-
veil, being accompanied by a male family member, and maintaining a formal or informal division of public space by gender. But,
to what extent was seclusion a function of gender rather than
social status? To what extent did upper middle class and upper class

men 'seclude' themselves from the general population as a perquisite of their status?"[9]

In *The Imperial Harem*, Peirce expands on the point:

> In many ways male society in the Ottoman world observed the same criteria of status and propriety as did female society. The degree of seclusion from the common faze served as an index of the status of the man as well as the woman of means. Poor women and poor men mingled in the city streets and bazaars, for their cramped households and lack of servants prevented them from emulating the deportment of the well-to-do. Just as a woman of standing who appeared in public in the sixteenth century could maintain her reputation for virtue only if she were surrounded by a cordon of attendants, so no Ottoman male of rank appeared on the streets or in the public arenas of a city without a retinue. The more powerful the individual, the greater the extent to which her or his accompanying retinue took on the aspect of a ceremonial procession.

Women acted as legal agents for other women, as well as for men, appearing in court or functioning as financial advisers, secretaries, and trustees and therefore were obliged to be seen—or at least heard—in one way or another. That Muslim women were and are frequently the power behind the wallet seems to have little to do with seclusion and again raises questions about whether their dismissal by many Westerners as utterly subjugated is overemphasized. That old "sledgehammer" *Hadith* which states that "Those who entrust their affairs to women will never know prosperity," seems not to have been heeded when a steady hand was needed. Throughout history's undulations, as any given society feels threatened and hunkers down, the repression of women's visibility and activities—indeed, the suppression of all civil liberties—can be the first line of defense against a hostile world, as evidenced today with the burgeoning of hawkishness and fundamentalism of all makes or models. Nevertheless, even as political Islamists—a minority in the Muslim world—seek to increase their influence, the numbers and strength of Muslim women in business today are increasing.

Afaf Lutfi Marsot notes that women of the middle and upper classes gained terrific organizational skills through domestic management of huge households, with constant parades of relatives, retainers, and guests requiring lodging and feeding.[10] To an extent, this would likely also be true of women from the lower classes, although poor women are additionally occupied helping to support the family with daily income-generating endeavors, enlisting daughters as co-workers and assistants to produce marketable goods, trade, and run the home. Women everywhere have contributed to family revenue through numerous kinds of activities centered in the home, such as baking bread or making needlework to be sold on the street by one of the children or in a family market kiosk or shop.

As urban areas expanded, and a given city's quarters became less self-reliant, central market areas also grew and women entered these public spaces to sell their goods. "As late as the seventeenth century," Dina Rizk Khoury writes of the Ottoman Empire, "women who made cotton and woolen thread or fabrics hawked their wares directly in the market…More visible than ever, these working women were marginal women…drawn from a variety of social groups such as prostitutes or rural migrant women, who were beyond the strictures of what was considered good behavior among the urban literati and middle classes."[11]

Public entertainers, as we've seen, were considered "infamous" in both the European and Muslim middle ages. In fourteenth-century Europe, despite the necessity for them, others occupied in disreputable livelihoods included executioners, gravediggers, guards, surgeons and shepherds, chimney sweeps, trash collectors, bath attendants, and any sort of itinerant laborers.

Meanwhile, in Muslim cities, usurers ranked first among the disgraceful, while moneylenders and slave dealers were iniquitous, too, loathed on religious grounds. Traders of silver, gold, and silk were considered a lower form, although there was a great desire for their merchandise, as indeed there were for slaves. Professional mourners, sellers of pork and wine, camel and donkey drivers, butchers, stablemen, veterinarians, hunters, and waste scavengers fell into the dishonorable category, despised along with prostitutes and entertainers. In Mamluk Egypt, women were employed as bath attendants, matchmakers, or hairdressers. They laid out dead females and were professional mourners, paid to attend funerals to wail and keen in loud expressions of grief otherwise not acceptable to the bereaved.

Among the Balouch women of Kalpourkan in southeastern Iran, the making of pottery was passed on from mother to daughter and created at home. "Until the end of 1960 [when Empress Farah Diba built a community arts and crafts center in the region], the pots were fired by the potters' husbands in a large joint fire pit in the center of the village. When word got around that there was a firing, customers would arrive from nearby villages to buy the still warm pots. Whatever was left over the husbands loaded on their donkeys and sold in the bazaars of other villages. The price of a pot was often the amount of grain it could contain."[12]

The Prophet's wife Sawdah bint Zamah supported herself and her children by making fine leather goods. That she had such a skill and therefore her own income made her the envy of her two, much younger, co-wives, Aisha and Hafsa. Like many women, Sawdah was an artisan. We know of her occupation because of her position, but worldwide, the arts and crafts have been anonymous activities, so that it seems nearly impossible to discover what the particular contribution of an individual woman (or man) might be. Some crafts are customarily family undertakings, such as rug weaving, which requires all hands for each stage in a long, complicated process. A common trade for women was spinning, as miniatures attest with their depictions of women carrying a spindle under the arm. In 1674, the Italian traveler Pietro della Valle wrote with gushing admiration about Turkish women's skills in working linen, cotton, and silk and that their embroidery was so delicate as to be almost transparent.

We've seen that before her marriage to the Mughal emperor Jahangir, Nur Jahan, then Nur Mahal, raised her fortunes with her exquisite designs and needlework, which became all the rage in the *zenana* and the court. Did ordinary women design clothing and make jewelry or fashion shoes or headgear? Were they tailors or makers of tapestries, as well as seamstresses, fine needle workers, and makers of textiles? There's no reason to assume that, in the confines of home, surrounded by the demands of the family, Muslim women, like those of the West, were not also finding time (and fulfilling an economic need) to exercise their artistic talents and dexterities as creators and innovators in these and other crafts often assumed to have been men's work.

Few women in any culture are credited as inventors. A rare exception is Nur Jahan, who is also recognized for the invention of cashmere shawls and distilling the perfume attar of roses.

> *Men and women who have surrendered,*
> *believing men and believing women,*
> *obedient men and obedient women,*
> *truthful men and truthful women,*
> *enduring men and enduring women,*
> *humble men and humble women,*
> *men and women who give alms,*
> *men who fast and women who fast,*
> *men and women who guard their private parts,*
> *men who much remember God and women*
> *who much remember God —*
> *For them God has prepared forgiveness and a mighty reward.*[13]

With these words, the Qur'an declares equality between men and women. Their deepest meaning has been contorted to refer only to parity in religious duties and equality before God. But as feminist scholars note, before a genderless (and nonhuman God) there can be no difference. If women are required to fulfill the same religious obligations, so they should be endowed with the same rights on Earth.[14] The Unity of Islam would demand it.

These rights include education, which Muhammad admired and encouraged in both sexes. Proof is given in various *Hadiths*, including an appreciative statement made by the Prophet about the excellence of the "women of the Ansar [supporters of Muhammad in Medina]. They do not feel shy when learning sound knowledge in religion." And:

"O Lord, increase my knowledge!"

"It is the duty of every Muslim man and woman to acquire knowledge."

"There is no priesthood, but science belongs to everyone."

"To educate a woman is to educate the whole world. To educate a man is to educate a single human being."[15]

We've seen that record numbers of women were scholars of *Hadith*, skilled in religion, Tradition, and law, who transmitted what they gathered, then wrote, analyzed, and taught what they knew. Devout fathers who took the Prophet's words seriously educated their daughters, some of whom are still renowned for their important contributions. As well as *Hadith* scholars and female legists, women were knowledgeable on virtually every other subject. Among the most prominent of learned ladies listed in biographies of the Umayyad period was Mayasa bint al-Din, a famed grammarian. She originated among the tribes and studied Arabic dialects. Understanding of classical Arabic is prized, for it is the language of the Qur'an. Another woman of the era wrote a book titled *Rare Forms and Sources of Verbal Nouns*.[16]

A biographical dictionary of the fifteenth century C.E., devoted to more than 11,000 individuals who died during the ninth century A.H., features a thousand women, a third of whom had received licenses to transmit their learning and to teach others. Century by century, the numbers of females dwindled from the biographies, until finally they virtually disappeared. In the mid-twentieth century, Arab women at last began to be included again in the Who's Whos.[17]

In the arts and sciences, masses of slave women were carefully educated, as we've seen, to entertain caliphs and sultans. Harems overflowed with highly educated wives, sisters, daughters, and *jawari*. Tutors and famous instructors were employed not only for music, dance, and poetry, but also history, astrology and astronomy (considered twin disciplines), natural philosophy, and other sciences. Aisha bint Abu Bakr and her niece Aisha bint Talha were both

astronomers, the elder having taught the younger. Who knows but
that they may have contributed new ideas to the study of stars and
planets. Hafsa bint Umar, Aisha's dear friend and co-wife, could read
and write, skills that do not necessarily go hand in hand. Others of
Muhammad's wives begrudged Hafsa's abilities. Her father, the second Rightly Guided caliph Umar, was learned in both reading and
writing, which put him in a special position among Muhammad's
early Companions.[18] Despite his prejudices against women's rights, it
was no doubt through him that Hafsa was educated.

From earliest times, women were scribes. Some, such as the
Indo-Muslim Sufi princess, Jahanara, were memoirists. Gulbadan
Begam, sister of the sixteenth-century Mughal emperor Humayun,
wrote the *Humayun-nama*, an absorbing history of her brother's
reign. The work provides insight into a vital period of history, from
the inside out, that is, from the women's quarters, unavailable to
male historians.[19]

In nineteenth-century Nigeria, Nana Asmau applied herself to
repair the devastation of war by writing histories and eyewitness
accounts of battles, training women as teachers and directing reedu-
cation projects for women refugees.

During the Abbasid Dynasty, Baghdad exploded into a dazzling center of learning, as well as the arts. The Abbasid caliphs
spent fortunes attracting the best scholars to the court and encour-
aging scholarship throughout the empire with contests and prizes as
inducements. Each year, scholars met at the palace every Friday during the month of Ramadan to share all the latest discoveries and
ideas. These annual conclaves were free from official interference.
Harun al-Rashid, a formal, autocratic caliph, was humbled by scholarship and modest in the presence of scholars. Once at dinner with
a blind scholar, Harun himself poured water on the venerated man's
hands after the meal.

He was happily seduced by a pretty face and artistic talent, but
a woman of learning and culture could also win his heart. At one
point, he acquired two highly educated slave women. Wishing to test
them, Harun sent for Asma'i, the ranking scholar of the day. "Asma'i

found himself facing an imposing pair of girls. Turning to the more impressive of the two he wished to know what branches of learning she had studied. 'First,' answered the girl, 'that which Allah has commanded in his Book. Then, that which engages the people's mind in poetry, language and literature and historical narration.' The scholar then put the girl to an exacting test...and found her to excel.... Asma'i's verdict was that he had never seen a woman take hold of learning like a man, as did this first girl, and that the second girl, though not yet equal to the first, with proper training would measure up to her. Harun then gave orders to have the 'perfect' one prepared immediately for his company and pleasure."[20]

Tawwaddud was an erudite slave, familiar with theology and religious law and the arts, as well as the known sciences of mathematics, astronomy, and philosophy. She, too, was put to the test in front of Harun by a group of scholars, whom she not only bested in their examinations, but trounced in a game of chess.

Caliph Ma'mun, Zubaydah's foster son, encouraged scholarship by instituting empire-wide cultural clubs—some convened in shops where paper and books were sold. Scholars came together in these clubs for discussion and debate. The first Greek geometrical treatise, the *Elements* of Euclid, and Aristotle's *Physics*, a study of the science of bodies, of motion and rest, were all translated during Ma'mun's reign. He sent envoys to the emperor of Byzantium to acquire and have rendered into Arabic all the Greek scientific works available. Women were participants in the development of scholarship, though much of their activity was restricted to the religious field. This, however, was hardly insignificant, for law and behavior in Islam depends upon and is interwoven with the words of the Qur'an and the sayings of the Prophet.

"The colophons of many manuscripts," Siddiqi writes in *Hadith Literature*, "show [women] both as students attending large general classes and also as teachers, delivering regular courses of lectures."

The mystic Bibi Munajjima, in the fifteenth century C.E., was better known as an expert in astrology and astronomy. She was a mathematical genius who applied her talent to the difficult task of calculating calendars. She was also a poet and bitter rival of Jami, the Sufi poet, who she determined was far inferior to her in literary creation and religious thought.

Women occasionally apprenticed with their fathers. 'Ijiliyah bint al-'ijli al-Asturlabi followed in her father's profession in Aleppo, Syria, as a maker of astrolabes, a respected branch of applied science. She was employed at the court of Saif al-Daulah (r. 333 A.H./944 C.E. to 357 A.H./967 C.E.), part of the powerful Hamdanid Dynasty of northern Syria.

In al-Andalus, scholarly activity for women in various fields of knowledge is thought to have been accepted more widely than anywhere else, in part, perhaps because Jews, Christians, and Muslims for a time lived and worked and studied and played side by side.

As among Europeans, a woman's education was up to her father. Some, of course, valued education for women, while others were suspicious of it. Generalizations are easy to come by and obscure the diversity of attitudes—across a great deal of time—about education for women, whether conducted in the home or outside of it.[21] At various periods in various places, girls attended school in mosques or in secular institutions of learning. These, and libraries as well, were founded and maintained by private individuals, mostly, as we've seen, by women, on whose patronage so much depended. Wherever Islam spread, primary schools, *kuttabs*—where the overwhelming majority of students were boys—were established to teach at least a minimal knowledge of religion. This meant learning the Qur'an, which, while it involves rote and recitation, also taught children to read and provided a knowledge of classical Arabic, a starting point to learning altogether.[22]

Girls were given edifying guides to deportment, called *adab* books, not unlike the fare that still circulates today for young women in the West. In the nineteenth century, a princess of Bhopal in India, Shajan Begam, produced one called *Tahzibu 'n-niswan wa tarbiyatu 'l-insan*, "The Polishing of Women and the Education of Humanity." In the twentieth century, Ashraf Ali Thawani—whose opinions on dancing we've seen—wrote *Bihishti Zewar*, "Heavenly Ornament," a book which for many years was an essential part of an

Indian girl's dowry. It offers guidelines on proper behavior in every possible situation.

In any era, in any place, women of the ruling elite are most likely to be educated, while the poor are left to their own devices. As elsewhere in the world, compulsory public education for women came late, in some places not until the early twentieth century, although in others it was introduced as early as the mid-nineteenth century. Today, more than 50 percent of students in universities in the Arab world are women.

There were—and still are—separate girls' schools, yet boys and girls also studied together. A lovely miniature from the Persian *Khamsa* (Romance) *of Nizami* of the sixteenth century C.E. illustrating the exquisite love story, *Layla and Majnun,* shows the two as children meeting for the first time in school, sitting side by side with their writing boards in front of the teacher, while nearby other boys and girls pore over their books.

From the beginning and into the modern era, girls everywhere, as among Europeans, were most commonly taught at home. Daughters of the wealthy might have tutors, but others were taught by grandmothers, grandfathers, and fathers. Sometimes girls attended classes at the home of a female teacher.

Revolutionaries, primarily army officers, grouped under the name Young Turks, deposed the repressive Ottoman sultan Abd al-Hamid through a bloodless revolt in 1909. For years, the Young Turks had been instrumental in opening schools for women and overseeing legislative progress in women's rights. They started the first state-run girls' school in Istanbul in the 1860s and moved from there into wider and wider reforms for women (and in 1923, under Kemal Ataturk, ousted the Ottomans altogether).

Ayse Sidika Hanim was the daughter of a palace teacher of the Topkapi Palace in Istanbul. Her father, Mustafa Hoca, believed in educating women and sent Sidika to the Zaption, a Greek School, and then to the Women's Teacher's Training School in 1872. Thereafter, until her death, she was a teacher of "the science of education" and "the principles of instruction." "Sidika was not only a pedagogue, but also a musician and a painter and she embroidered beautifully. She died when still fairly young, or more would undoubtedly been heard of her."[23]

Hafsa bint al-Hajj (ca. 513 A.H./1135 C.E. to 568 A.H./1190 C.E.), one of Islamic Spain's most illustrious poets, attempted to mend a broken heart by retreating to Marrakech, where she lived out her life teaching the Almohad princesses. She won such esteem that some biographies list her as the greatest woman educator of her time.

In addition to her other abilities, the Abbasid slave woman Tawwaddud claimed a knowledge of medicine. The Prophet's wife Aisha was said to have healing skills. The Prophet's personal physician was Umm Omara, who fought next to him for the cause and lost her son as well as one of her hands in the battles. She also nursed the wounded on the field. It is said that whenever anyone complained to Muhammad of illness, he pointed to Umm Omara's house, for she could certainly cure them. "God did not send any illness," the Prophet said, "unless he has sent a medicine for it." Like Jews, Muslims believe that God is the ultimate healer. Muhammad is often called *tabib*, physician, for prophets are considered physicians of the soul.

As in other faiths, some Muslims believe that relics can heal. The water Muhammad washed with was reused as a medicine filled with his *baraqa*, his power of blessing. The Prophet's spit was considered a healing agent, for he once soothed Ali's sore eyes by rubbing them with his saliva. To dream of the Prophet can be a cure, and certain prayers will help relieve illness.

Mystics and saints could heal, through various means, including practical ones. The mystic Nafisa healed an arthritic girl and created an effective eye salve. Eye ailments were common in the Middle East. Indeed, Muslim physicians were far advanced in ophthalmology, developing ways of operating on cataracts and other achievements.

Women, naturally, were midwives, and also performed other medical procedures for women.[24] Unfortunately, it is thus far been nearly impossible to discover how many women were in fact trained as physicians during any of the golden eras of Islam. As happened later in Europe, medicine was commandeered by men. As thirst for knowledge increased in Abbasid Baghdad, in Damascus and al-Andalus, and ancient Greek medical texts were translated and utilized, men began to dominate the field. Nonetheless, an Indo-Muslim woman of the Mughal period, Rusa, quite likely a physician, translated a medical text into Arabic on the treatment of women through the Indian science of Ayurveda, the oldest existing system of medical practice.

"Science lights the road to Paradise," the Prophet said. "Take knowledge even from an unbeliever. The ink of the scholar is more holy than the blood of the martyr."

While we have descriptions of women participating in sporting games and outings to gardens, lakes, or rivers, where they could cut loose in fresh air without interference, as time marched toward a growing middle class—and economic development which coincided with more extreme seclusion—harem life became increasingly sedentary and hard on women's mental and physical health. Restricted movement and curtailed freedom had deleterious effects on the well-being of harem women.

Whether by men or women, Muslims made incredible advances in medicine, while Europeans still struggled through the Middle Ages. The philosopher Abu Ali al-Husayn ibn Abd Allah ibn Sina (358 A.H./980 C.E. to 415 A.H./1037 C.E.), known in the West by his Latin name, Avicenna, having studied medicine in his native Bukhoro (in what is now Uzbekistan) wrote more than a hundred books, including the *Kitab ash-Shifa*, "Book of Healing," an anthology of essays on Aristotelian logic, metaphysics, psychology, the natural sciences, and other subjects. His crowning achievement was the *Canon of Medicine*, long the preeminent textbook in the Middle East and Europe. It is significant for its classification and summary of medical and pharmaceutical material. Among other things, Ibn Sina recognized the contagious nature of such diseases as tuberculosis and observed that certain diseases can be spread by water and soil.

But he was not alone among groundbreaking Muslim physicians. There were those who found ways of treating smallpox and other deadly diseases. In the tenth century C.E., Islamic doctors were performing remarkably sophisticated surgeries, which they helped develop, including cranial and vascular operations, amputations, abdominal and cancer surgeries.

And they were the first to use anesthetics—usually opium mixed with wine to increase its potency. Pharmacologists throughout the Muslim world developed drugs and even set up drugstores, pharmacies where prescriptions could be filled and that were carefully regulated. The doctors themselves often prepared their own compounds. Women not only aided in the process—as attested to in a few miniatures—they undoubtedly added significantly to the knowledge.

The first hospitals in the world were developed beginning with the Abbasid Dynasty, funded by women. They included outpatient facilities and dispensaries, special quarters for the mentally ill, separate wards to treat different diseases, and surgical theaters. Hygiene and hygienic procedures saved hundreds of lives. There can be no doubt that while they are obscured and obscure, women were involved heavily in medicine, through traditional healing arts that helped inform the healing sciences, in herbalism leading to pharmacology, and perhaps in the practice of medicine as actual physicians, alone or beside their fathers and husbands.

In 1922, the first Turkish woman opened her practice in Istanbul. In 1937, the first Iraqi woman received her degree in medicine. They and others are surely the product of an invisible lineage.

Nana Asmau

Nana Asmau was born in 1171 A.H./1793 C.E., the daughter of Uthman dan Fodio, a member of the Fulani people of northern Nigeria. Dan Fodio was a reformer, a religious and political adviser to the Hausa kings, and was critical in his writings of their negligent aristocracy, which preyed upon the poor. He called for a new state based on Islamic practices, urging Hausa and Fulani alike to become morally pure. Dan Fodio was sent into exile, but his following increased and at last they went to war, conquering lands as far east as Bornu and establishing a sultanate in 1189 A.H./1811 C.E. based on the teachings of the Qur'an. Nana's childhood was spent at war and she was eighteen when the victory came. She lived her life in service to women and died in 1243 A.H./1865 C.E.

The Hausa chief orders Uthman dan Fodio out of his home. He will not go alone, he tells the chief, there will be others. Without hesitation, the whole village packs their goods, their livestock, their cooking pots, their bed mats, their books, their children, and calling this their *hijra*, they follow Uthman from place to place, hundreds of miles, living under trees and in huts made of branches, hungry, yet fighting bravely against the corpulent and brutal Hausa. Many die and Nana, young as she is, treats the wounded, brings comfort to them as she can, all the while remembering the women who followed the Prophet into Medina.

"O God," she writes—for her father has given all his children, boys and girls, a good education—"cause Muslims to be united in friendships and follow the *Shari'a*. Give them courage to fight this *jihad*. Bless herdsmen with good pastures. Let townspeople be healthy. Give us strong horses, strong donkeys, and mules. Give us fat cattle, goats, sheep, and camels. May the dangerous empty lands be prosperous settlements for the benefit of Muslims."

Her father fights. Her brother fights. More and more true believers join his cause and move into the enemy lands, straight into the face of peril. Thousands are killed and yet they move on, into the city of Sokoto, where God finally grants them years of prosperity.

Nana looks around and realizes there can be no true success, no victory, until wounds are healed. The deep, everlasting lesions of war. The widows. The orphans. The disabled. The sick. The poor. These must be cared for if there is to be peace. Women fill the camps. Slaves with their children. Heathens who dance to drums and sacrifice animals, possessed by spirits. Nana determines to free them of this *bori* magic. She sets them to gainful work, to spinning thread, cleaning cotton, grinding grain. She tells them they must live modestly and be God-fearing. They call Nana Chief of All Women.

Uthman dies and Nana's brother Bello, her best friend and teacher, takes his place. He chooses a husband for Nana. Gidado is much older, like her brother, but kindly, too, and set to the same purpose. Nana and Bello and Gidado are a threesome, determined to make the fighting count, to make the victory sweet.

Nana gives Gidado five sons. She prays God to lead them to Truth. She writes nine books with Gidado and books of her own poetry. Bello dies. She weeps in anguish:

> O God, I turn restlessly in grief,
> alone in the wilderness,
> like an orphan,
> pitiful and weak.

Gidado encourages her to make the loss count for something, something even more than she has already accomplished. Her village is a center of learning, where women gather around her to learn reading and writing, religion and proper worship, how to apply the law, how to be judges.

Now she sends her trusted friends to other villages to bring her the most promising women, Fulani, Sulubawa, Hausa. "Bring women who are ignorant of their religion to me and I will teach them to become scholars of Qur'an, to write poetry and to be teachers of women."

They come on donkeys and on foot. They sing and bring alms. They come through the bush and across the mountains and over the desert and none ever attack them, but protect them, for they are on their way to Nana Asmau.

IX

Poets

"Enjoy life!
Who cares what
people say?"

The Qur'an—at first committed to memory and scrawled on palm leaves or stones—was poetry as it had never been experienced in Arabia, exquisite and lyrical, cadences and vocabulary tuned in such a way as to make it seem undeniably, as Muhammad claimed, the verse of God, offering immediate knowledge of God.

No translation from its original classical Arabic can truly do the Qur'an justice. The magnificence not only of its message but its rhythms and textures, its poetic quality, convinced millions, as nothing else, of Muhammad's truth.

We close with poetry, for it has near magical authority, and is perhaps the foremost artistic expression for the women and men of Islam. In pre-Islamic Arabia, as elsewhere across the globe, the poet was possessed by forces that brought into being verses of such power as to engender passionate love, soften the hearts of tyrants, arouse sedition, stop hostile armies in their tracks.

Everywhere in the Arabian peninsula, women and men recited verses aloud, inspired, they believed by djinn. Until Islam, with its dedication to knowledge and the book—reading and writing—poetry was spoken or sung, as is still common in nonliterate cultures. The poems of the *jahiliyah* were meant to be chanted to simple musical accompaniment, a custom that continued into the Islamic era. The great epics were also told in verse, often with music.

In his 1930 *Ancient Arabian Poetry*, Charles James Lyall wrote, "When there appeared a poet in a family...the other tribes round about would gather together to that family and wish them joy in their good luck. Feasts would be got ready, the women of the tribes would join together in bands, playing upon their lutes, as they were wont to do at bridals...for a poet was a defence to the honor of them all, a

weapon to ward off insult from their good name, and a means of per-
petuating their glorious deeds and of establishing their fame forever."

The Prophet's relationship to poets was ambivalent. He was
attacked by poets as he spread his message, and such was their influence that one of Muhammad's few acts of vengeance was to put
those wordsmiths to death who had harmed him.

Some men buy diverting talk
to lead astray from the way of God...
Those there await a humbling chastisement.[1]

This was not a strike against poetry, but against the poet who
was hammering against Islam with blistering satires. After the *hijra*,
when the Prophet became a *sayyid* in Medina, he had his own official poet, whom he instructed to denounce the enemy. "Pour out the
raid against them, for by God, your poetry is more potent than the
falling of arrows in the darkness of dawn." And there were poets
within his own family: his uncle and protector Abu Talib, who
although he never converted to Islam, struck back at the Quraysh
with ardent verse defending Muhammad's message and his right to
have it; Aisha and Ali were dedicated versifiers.

It is told that Muhammad was riding one day with some friends
when he asked one of them to recite the poetry of Umayya. A hundred lines were recited for him, and Muhammad said at the finish,
"Well done!...The poetry is good, and we do not see any harm in a
beautiful melody."

A *Hadith* records the Prophet saying: "Truly there is enchant-
ment in eloquence, and truly, there is wisdom in poetry."

"Teach your children poetry which will sweeten their tongue,"
Aisha instructed.

Before and since the coming of Islam, women have practiced
the art. Women of all classes, slaves and ruling elite alike, recited or
wrote poetry. Those slaves trained by great masters for the entertainment of sultans and caliphs were worth fortunes and could earn massive rewards for their skills. The Abbasids so loved poetry, it's said that

the caliph Ma'mun spent two hours a day cleaning his teeth while listening to recitations.

Like Khayzuran, Zubaydah, and multitudes more, women of the aristocracy, upper classes, and intellectual families wrote to amuse their friends, curse their enemies or curry favor, to express their sincerest feelings or even record the histories of their times. Across the centuries, other women adopted the art, many anonymous, never to be recognized, but following a calling that continues to echo with exceptional resonance among the women of the Islamic world today.[2]

Slave or free, the names of women poets were listed in page after page of the biographies across centuries and geography, starting with the first Muslim woman poet, al-Khansa, whose fame began long before her conversion. Many others of that early period have disappeared, but some such as Laila bint Lukaiz, who died in the fifth century C.E., before the coming of Islam, continue to be known and appreciated, though their work remains merely in fragments.

A slave singer Fadl, celebrated during the Abbasid period as "the most gifted poet of her time," brought men and women together in her home to present their work and hold contests, which may have resembled the "slams" popular among young poets today in the West.[3] The literary salon has continued in Muslim women's homes ever since. In eighteenth- and nineteenth-century Egypt, women assembled into poetry guilds. Women of the Ottoman Empire were obsessed with poetry: even Khurrem, whose skills at written Turkish seemed to be slow to come, wrote lyrics of longing to her husband Suleyman the Magnificent.

There is no end to the variations and diversities. Elegies and lamentations were the primary genre for women in the early period, not unlike the poetry of the "wailing women" of Ireland upon which much Irish poetry is built. In the seventh century of the Common Era, Arab poet Layla al-Akhyaliyya was famous for her funeral odes, as well as for her invective. She was triumphant in competitions, where poets vied with sarcasm and diatribes. Female poets of the era oftentimes directed invectives against their husbands in public, hardly a sign of meek passivity. Improvisation was—and is—an especially admired and difficult skill, requiring a quick imagination and sharp wit. Women were particularly noted for it.

Their poetry could wither an enemy, and as we've seen, across the fields of battle, women hurled chanted abuse at one another on behalf of their warriors, vying in words as well as in armed combat.

A seventeenth-century Safavid Iranian poet, Nihani, whose father was a grand amir of Shah Sulayman and who was engaged by the shah's mother, is remembered for writing a quatrain which she hung at the Isfahan bazaar, proclaiming that she would marry the man who could produce an appropriate reply to her verses. She was a beauty and had many suitors, but none was able to meet the poetic challenge.

There were myriad methods, from acrostics to puzzle poems. There were myriad genres, besides the elegies at which they excelled, including a type of poetry in which women described the thoughts stirred by the birth of a daughter:

> She's a credit to me. She washes my hair.
> She raises the mantle that's fallen from my head.
> She will look splendid in a gown of Yemeni cloth.
> I will marry her to a nobleman for a great dowry.

In the *jahiliyah*, the Time of Ignorance, women wrote of their agony at the prospect that their newborn girls might be buried alive.

> Is she not a pearl in her soft silken gown?
> But the prettiest gown is a burial shroud.

A later body of work was developed by noble ladies who lost their husbands before the marriage was consummated. The degenerate Abbasid caliph Amin's virgin widow Lubabah was one of these. In the third Islamic century, the male poet and scholar Utbi assembled a collection of poetry by women whose love had turned to hate.

Turkish poets dedicated much of their artistic genius to the polishing of tiny poems, which would, as one sultan said, "be worth more than all the epics." The Turkish *gazel* form has been likened to the English sonnet, although more intricate, contrasted to a flower whose petals are constantly overlapping, coming full circle to end where they began.

Vulgarity was not out of the question: a story goes that Harun al-Rashid visited Zubaydah to complain that her secretary had written "blue" verses, which he quoted to her. Zubaydah immediately countered with a recital of even coarser poetry, which she attributed to Harun's secretary, but which she'd composed on the spot so as not be outdone.

(Zubaydah, longing for Harun who had retreated to the Syrian port city of Raqqah having tired of Baghdad, once held one of her many poetry contests offering a prize—a gem worth 800,000 dirhams—to the poet whose verses could make her husband homesick and return to the city where she was happiest. She also created a *diwan*, an anthology, of bitter verses on the death of her son, Amin.)

There are genres in Persian and Urdu literature called *marthiya*, or dirge, devoted to the martyrs of Kerbela, where Muhammad's grandson and the family of Ali were done in by Mu'awiya and the Umayyads.

There were mystics writing spiritual verse, of whom Rabi'a al-Adawiyya of Basra is easily the most famous for her poetry to the Beloved. Sufi poetry is probably the best known in the West.

Poems about sensual love were pretty much a constant. It's said that the second Rightly Guided caliph Umar, on one of his nightly policings through Medina, overheard a woman lamenting from her rooftop for her husband:

Without my beloved to play with,
I cannot sleep through this long, black night.
But for fear of Allah, the only God,
Our bed would shake with love.

Sympathetic to such a plight, Umar sent to the field and brought her man back from the wars of conquest.

For poems of love few could match the women of Islamic Spain, who enjoyed considerable freedom—more than their sisters to the east—as well the delights of a flourishing synthesis of cultural styles at their disposal. Three of the most renowned were Wallada bint al-Mustakfi, Hafsa bint al-Hajj, and Naz'hun, who in eleventh-century Granada wrote candid love poems, extolling lusciously memorable nights.

Most of Wallada's work is unfortunately lost. She was the daughter of the Cordoban caliph, al-Mustakfi, an ineffectual ruler, overthrown in 1031 C.E., then killed. Wallada lived in a relaxed time for women, when many went about with faces unveiled, hair uncovered, eyes allured with kohl. Wallada was a charmer, and independent, refusing ever to be married. She exchanged vivid love poems with the illustrious ibn Zaydun, but eventually threw him over for another...and another...and another, for it was said that "poets perished to partake of her sweetness" and that "she stole hearts and restored old men to their youth."

A smitten biographer of the time testified that "her poetry and elegance were of the most perfect form, sophisticated presence of mind paired with passionately beautiful expression. She was beautiful to look upon and of a noble nature. It was pleasing to go to her and whoever left her felt refreshed and renewed. Her circle at Cordova was a gathering of the best minds, a race course for the proud stallions of poetry and prose." However, she was a source of gossip for her "unconcern and poems of sensuous openness."

It was the fashion to embroider verses upon one's sleeves. Wallada's right sleeve carried the words: "By God, I am fit for great things. I go my way armed with pride." On her left were written: "To my lover I offer the curve of my cheek, and my kiss to whoever desires it."

Her father's death left her with enormous wealth. She moved into a villa near Cordova, and continued her literary salon until she died probably in 469 A.H./1091 C.E.

European scholars visited Islamic Spain to study philosophy, mathematics, astronomy, and medicine, as well as poetic forms, which became the medieval romances and poetry of courtly love. Music and poetry, as we've seen, amalgamated from time immemorial, and came together in Spain via Arabia with the troubadours.

In addition to their frank odes to lovers, the purity of their language, their knowledge of the art of poetry, their elegance, charm, and sagacity, the women of al-Andalus were also prominent as calligraphers, an art which for many Muslims is considered sacramental, with flowing patterns, intricate geometry, and energy that articulates visually the gift of language, of which poetry is the zenith.

The development of calligraphy into art started with the need to record the Qur'an, to make the script worthy of divine revelation.[4] Papermaking also fulfilled the spiritual requirement to manufacture editions of the Qur'an and *Hadith*—which could be distributed widely—and simply to read and write, to acquire knowledge, as the Prophet had commanded.

Conquering Muslims were the first to bring paper west from Central Asia, where it had traveled from its place of origin, China, to Samarqand. In *Paper Before Print*, Jonathan Bloom tells us that while paper's first journey took five centuries, within two centuries after the Muslims encountered it, there were paper factories in Spain.

> Just as the swift spread of Islam was unprecedented in human history, so the introduction of paper and paper-making across the Islamic lands in the ninth and tenth centuries was a remarkable historical and technological achievement that transformed society in its wake.
>
> The Arabs...called paper *qirtas*, a word [which appears in the Qur'an and which] they had originally used for papyrus, papyrus rolls, and even parchment....Perhaps the most common Arabic word for paper, however was *waraq*, meaning "leaf," probably from the expression *waraq qirtas*, "a leaf or sheet of paper." From this usage in turn derive the words *warraq*—the common term for stationer, papermaker, paper merchant, and by extension, copyist—and *wiraqa*, "papermaking," as well as many modern compound expressions referring to paper money, lottery tickets, commercial papers, banknotes and the like.

With the introduction of paper, women (and men) could produce *diwans* of their work, and they did so enthusiastically. Paper allowed for freer expression of the calligrapher's art, as well as books with illustrations, another major art form in the Islamic world. The refinement of calligraphy is said to have formally begun with Abu Ali Muhammad ibn Muqlah (d. 318 A.H./940 C.E.), who laid the basis on strict mathematical principles. Yet, although she receives little formal credit, Thana, a slave woman of the Abbasid caliph al-Mansur's court, who was in service to his sons' tutor, was instrumental in calligraphy's artistic evolution and was considered to have written matchless original scripts. Calligraphers were patronized by rulers and their styles handed down from master to pupil. There are significant numbers of women calligraphers whose names are immortalized in manuscripts of the Qur'an and other texts. In the fifth century A.H., the Traditionist Fatima bint al-Hassan—in addition to being known for her devoutness and the high quality of the *Hadith* she gathered—was celebrated for her mastery of calligraphy. Shuhda bint al-Ibari, the tenth-century Traditionist, was known as "Shuhda the Writer," for her outstanding calligraphy.

Umm Hani Maryam (778 A.H./1376 C.E. to 871 A.H./1466 C.E.), an Egyptian *Hadith* scholar, was famed for her mastery of calligraphy, as well as her command of Arabic (she learned the Qur'an by heart as a child) and her poetry. She pursued an intense education in the great college at Cairo, acquiring all the Islamic sciences of theology, law, history, and grammar.

While women are a favorite subject in the exquisite miniature paintings that appear throughout the Islamic world—and which illuminate epics, show scenes of daily life or portray important folk—few if any women are known to have painted them.[5] Studies of women as artists and subjects have so far been extremely limited and are only now in their formative stages.[6]

"If our objective is to learn about women in Ottoman society, then the most productive place to look is at the manuscripts that describe the life of the court or other aspects of the Ottoman world," Nancy Micklewright says. "It goes almost without saying that there is virtually no indication that women artists were either present at the court, or members of the [court atelier]. Painting and drawing were not among the accomplishments required for women of the elite, and we have no real evidence of women artists until late in the nineteenth century....So it is only as subjects that women have any place at all within traditional Ottoman painting."[7]

Although women do not appear to have been active in the field of miniature painting for illustrated books, that does not mean they weren't. It's difficult to imagine that they did not draw and paint to exercise natural gifts. Women in the harems, with time and talent scratching at their hearts, must have given way to the necessity of art making as they did to writing poetry. The art of calligraphy—the movement of the hand that is like painting—in many ways would discharge some of this need, but it would not satisfy a driving desire for figurative art.[8]

Shahzad Sultanum (d. 940 A.H./1562 C.E.), a daughter of the Safavid Shah Ismai'l, was a distinguished calligrapher and probably a painter. During a twenty-one year imprisonment, Zeb-un-Nissa, eldest daughter of seventeenth-century Mughal emperor Aurangzeb, wrote poetry, perfected her calligraphy, and painted.

The study of poetry in Islam is exacting and abundant and can't begin to be made here. Neither can the following selections begin to touch on the fullness of the poetry of Islamic women. An anthology of verses written by Muslim women poets from the beginning, the ancient lamentations, love lyrics, quatrains, songs, and other forms, including the verses of aristocratic women, saints, slaves and scholars, would as Schimmel suggests "show how actively involved with poetry Muslim women of all nationalities were and continue to be."[9]

The literature is so vast, it would be a life's vocation.

Al-Khansa

A contemporary of the Prophet, al-Khansa—Tumadir bint Amru al-Harith bint al-Sharid—was born during the jahiliyya *and visited Mecca every year to offer her verses in the Poet's Market, where they were judged by the greatest poets of the day, and where she held her own against the men. At one of these competitions, a rival told her he had never seen a better woman poet. "Don't you want to say I'm the best poet, male or female?" she replied. She sang her laments to music. Aisha and Umar disapproved of the poetry she wrote before Islam, but al-Khansa said that many were elegies to her two brothers, expressing her grief that they had died without knowledge of Islam and her hope that they would find their ways to Paradise. Muhammad liked her poetry and defended it. Al-Khansa was a nickname meaning "pug-nosed." She died some years after the Prophet, though her dates are unknown. She was alive in 15 A.H./637 C.E., when her four sons were slain in the Battle of Qadisiyah and Umar, then caliph, wrote to congratulate her on her heroism and awarded her a pension.*

from *Lament for a Brother*

What have we done to you, Death?
That you treat us so, always another catch?
One day a warrior,

412

The next a head of state.
Charmed by the loyal,
You choose the best:
Iniquitous, nonegalitarian Death.

I would not complain
If you were just
But you take the worthy
Leaving fools for us.

Maisuna

Maisuna was from the Calab tribe in the Yemen, known for the purity of its dialect and the numbers of poets it produced. She was married to the first Umayyad caliph, Mu'awiya—son of Abu Sufyan and Hind bint Utba, who took the caliphate in 39 A.H./661 C.E.—and was installed in the pomp and splendor of Damascus, where he made his capital. Maisuna hated the stifling court and longed for the simple life of the desert. These stanzas are her famous "song" of yearning for that old life, which, when by herself, she recited. One day, Mu'awiya overheard her and was angry and offended by his wife's sentiments. As punishment, he banished her from the court and she immediately returned to her tribe, taking her infant son Yazid. She did not revisit Damascus until Mu'awiya died and Yazid ascended the throne. Maisuna's dates are unknown.

The Song of Maisuna

A russet pelt of camel's hair,
(Spirits light and eye serene)
Is dearer to me by far
Than all the trappings of a queen.

Humble tent and mumbling breeze
Through its walls

414

My fancy please
Better than splendid halls.

The colts that fly
And frolic by the litter's side,
Are dearer in my eye
Than decorated mules in all their pride.

The watchdog's voice that bays in fear
When a stranger flicks his coat
Sounds sweeter in Maisuna's ear
Than a golden trumpet's note.

A rustic youth innocent of art,
Son of my kindred, poor but free,
Will ever to Maisuna's heart
Be dearer, pampered fool, than thee.

Laila al-Akhyaliyyah

A member of a noble family in what is now Iraq, Laila al-Akhyaliyya was married to a man named Sawwar, but many of her poems were laments for Tauba ibn Humayyar, who may have been her lover, and who died an outlaw. It's said she shrugged off with blithe wit the Umayyad authorities who criticized her for her defense of Tauba—of whom she wrote, "he was honey/no, I see a beehive in his likeness." She died ca. 82 A.H./704 C.E.

(untitled)

We are those who came early—dawn
—attacking steadily on Nukhail's Day.
We destroyed the Malik al Jahjaha
forever. We stirred up mourners for him.
We left no joy for the stragglers,
not camps, nor dripping blood.
We are Banu Khuwailid without compare.

The battle neither lies nor trifles.

(untitled)

The curve of grouse watering in a flock…
Nearing the pool in all haste.

416

They stay, intoxicated, at the spring as if
They were drinkers dependent on Persian lords:
As if they took a little drink and hurried to
Take it away between Shibak and Tandib,
Night in the desert and morning as guests.

There, at brood spots among a hungry flock,
They press to belly and breast their wings
And hover a little at their favorite pool.
Then they slow the beating wings so as to end
Wings at sides, shoulder to shoulder.

So they hear the chicks' sounds and cries
And give them back a low echo.
They bend to the naked heads as if they
Were boys' balls made of rabbitskin.
When the dark leaves, they give them
A drink of the nearby (never empty) pool.

The name of harshness is theirs. The chicks
Make an uproar not understood.

Hafsa bint al-Hajj

She has been called the most illustrious woman poet of Islamic Spain. Hafsa bint al-Hajj was born ca. 513 A.H./1135 C.E., in an increasingly puritanical era, as Berber dynasties took control of the Spanish city-states. Most of Hafsa's poetry was addressed to and about her lover Abu Ja'far ibn Sai'd. When he was executed for his involvement in a plot, Hafsa would wear only black, mourned him in her poems, then stopped writing poetry altogether. She moved to Marrakech, where she lived out her life teaching the Almohad princesses and gaining a reputation as the greatest woman educator of her time. She died in 568 A.H./1190 C.E.

(excerpts, *untitled*)

Shall I visit you or will you visit me? My heart
Always tilts to what you wish.
My lips are spring of sweetness, unalloyed,
My hair a cooling shade for you.
I'd hoped you'd grow thirsty in the midday heat
When siesta hour would bring me to your couch.
So hurry, dear, with your reply:
Haughtiness would not be fitting!

If he is not a star, my eyes would not
Be filled with darkness when I'm away from him.
Greetings upon his beauty, from one who is grieved,
Deprived of his joy and of his pleasure!

Mihri Khatun

Sometimes called the Sappho of Turkish poetry, fifteenth-century Mihri Khatun never married, unlike her contemporary Zeyneb Khatun, who gave up poetry at marriage. Yet Mihri wrote many gazels inspired by love and her many affairs. In some of her poetry she mentions Alexander, a reference to her male lover Yskender. She was much influenced by the most famous male poet of her era, Necati Beg, who resented her and having no use for women poets, piled angry criticism on her and tried to destroy her career. His indignation may be explained by the fact that Mihri Khatun received much more money from the sultan, Bayezid II. She died in 884 A.H./1506 C.E.

Gazels (*untitled*)

I hoped that you would prove a kind friend;
Who would have thought you'd be such a fierce tyrant?

You who are the freshly opened rose of Paradise,
How can it be fitting you love every thorn and thistle?

I don't curse you, but I do pray to God
That you in turn may love a pitiless tyrant like yourself.

And now I'm in such a fix that, cursing, I say,
"May your fortune and portion be as dark as mine!"

A woman talks like a chattering bird?
What polecat dribbled *that* from's pen?
I'd rather hear one woman's word
Than blather from a thousand men.

Zeb-un-Nissa

The eldest daughter of Mughal emperor Aurangzeb (brother of the Sufi mystic Jahanara and son of Mumtaz Mahal), Zeb-un-Nissa was born in 1016 A.H./1638 C.E. Her mother was a famous Persian beauty, Dilras Banu. Zen-un-Nissa reportedly had a liaison with a Mughal nobleman named Agil Khan, whom she met often at her own gardens in Lahore. She was imprisoned on an island by her father for the last twenty-one years of her life for the "crime" of corresponding with her brother Akbar, who had, as did most of his siblings, rebelled against Aurangzeb, a reactionary bent on depleting the dynasty's already waning fortunes. Zeb-un-Nissa wrote in Persian under the pen name of Makhfi', often tongue-in-cheek. She died in 1080 A.H./1702 C.E.

Song of Princess Zeb-un-Nissa in Praise of her Own Beauty

When from my cheek I lift my veil,
The roses, envious, turn pale,
And from their hearts, bereaved, in pain,
Send forth their fragrance like a wail.

Or if perchance one perfumed tress
Is lowered to the wind's caress,

The honeyed hyacinths complain,
And languish in a sweet distress.

Then, when I pause, relax among
My lovely groves, a modest throng
Of nightingales awaken, strain
Their birdlight souls to silver song.

(Addressing the Waterfall at Shalimar Gardens)

O waterfall, why lament?
What grief wrinkles your face?
What pain, that all night
You strike your head on the rocks and cry?

Leyla Hanym

Leyla Hanym's marriage lasted one week. The Turkish poet is reputed to have been bisexual, many of her love poems presumably addressed to women. She was liberated by Ottoman standards and scandalized the moral majority with her verses. Hanym was physically plain, so that she was nicknamed "The Nightingale" for her poetic voice. She was renowned for her extemporaneous compositions and wrote poems on passing events. Some translations were published in Vienna periodicals. She died in 1225 A.H./1847 C.E.

(untitled)

Drink your fill in my rose garden.
Who cares what people say?
Enjoy life!
Who cares what people say?
Does my cruel love
see my tears as dewdrops?
She's all smiles like a blooming rose.
Who cares what people say?
I am your lover and your loyal slave,
until the Day of Doom.
Who cares what people say?
My rival's chasing you,
so come lie next to me.

No?
Well, then — so much for you.
Who cares what people say?
Leyla, bask in the pleasure of your moon-faced lover.
Enjoy life!
Who cares what people say?

The Five Pillars of Islam

Muhammad had no intention of starting a new religion. He wanted only to call his people to God and teach them of Allah's forgiveness, to lead more fulfilling and virtuous lives and to help those in need. The Prophet's message was that God's power and knowledge are infinite, that He is good, that He hates oppression and injustice. Muhammad taught that God requires submission, trust, and truthfulness from humankind and that on the Day of Judgment, every person's sins and good deeds will be balanced. The weight of wrongdoing versus right living determines whether she or he will be sent to Paradise or Hell.

The closeness of God to each individual means that He can be approached directly without an intermediary. Thus there is no priesthood in Islam, though there are holy men and women, clerics, prayer leaders, scholars, and lawgivers. And while the Prophet disdained the veneration of saints, they have naturally appeared, apparently an irresistible phenomenon for people in religions worldwide.

The famous Five Pillars of Islam—the *rukn*—are specific duties Muslims on the right path must perform. The testimony of faith, prayer, almsgiving, fasting, and pilgrimage are set forth in the Qur'an and more specifically detailed in *Hadith*.

Shahada, testimony, is the First Pillar, the profession of faith: "*La ilaha illa Allah; Muhammad rasul Allah,*" "There is no god but God and Muhammad is the Messenger of God." Here is the essence of Islam, repeated every day by all devout Muslims worldwide. It is the melodious call to prayer made five times a day by the *muezzin.*

427

Salat, prayer, the Second Pillar, is more accurately interpreted as "praise," and it must be performed regularly and at frequent intervals, for those who extol God and do good deeds will enter Paradise, with each *salat* absolving one of the minor sins. Every woman and man of sound mind and body is required to pray five times a day, at sunset (the beginning of the Muslim day), in the evening, at dawn, at noon, and at mid-afternoon. Praying privately is perfectly acceptable, and women for reasons of modesty often do so, or they pray with one another. Praying with others in the mosque is most preferable. In some cultures, women pray in public standing behind the men, sometimes behind a curtain. But in other cultures, they stand side by side.

The worshiper must be in a state of ritual purity and make ablutions by washing face, hands, and arms up to the elbow, rubbing water on the head, and washing or rubbing the feet. Where water, in thirsty lands, is not available, sand or clean earth will do. Prayers are made barefoot on a special rug or mat to maintain cleanliness. The prayer must be performed solemnly, without drama or false humility or undue emotion.[1]

Whatever the language or country of the worshiper, he or she performs *salat* in Arabic and follows a set form, though it is permitted to use variations of Quranic texts. The worshiper bows several times toward Mecca, kneels, and prostrates himself or herself with face and hands on the ground, repeating devotional phrases such as *Allahu Akbar,* God is most great, and reciting the opening verse of the Qur'an:[2]

> *Praise be to God,*
> *Cherisher and Sustainer of the Worlds.*
> *Most Gracious, Most Merciful,*
> *Master of the Day of Doom.*
> *You only we serve; to You alone we pray for succor.*
> *Guide us in the straight path,*
> *the path of those whom You have blessed,*
> *nor of those against whom You are wrathful,*
> *nor of those who have gone astray.*[3]

At the end, the worshiper rises and pronounces the testimony of faith, then turns to the others and says, "Peace be upon you and the mercy of God."

Zakat, almsgiving, is the Third Pillar, one of the principal duties of every Muslim. Charity is imposed by the Qur'an. Almsgiving is divided into the *zakat,* which is obligatory, and *sadaqa,* which is voluntary. *Zakat* prescribes a system of fixed taxes in money or kind on people's possession. In early times, *zakat* was collected by the state; in some traditional Muslim countries today it takes the place of income tax. And traditionally, everywhere, Muslims are openhanded with street beggars and on feast days give generously to the poor. Ostentatious waste, pride, and haughtiness are condemned.

Sawm, fasting, is the Fourth Pillar. It dictates that once a year for a period of one month, Muslims are required to abstain from food, drink, smoking, and sexual relations during the hours of daylight. Children, pregnant women, the sick, and travelers may delay fasting, or pay alms for each day the fast is broken. It is grueling and rigorous, for daily life must go on. It tests self-denial, it forces the rich to taste the plight of the poor and equalizes all stratas of society.

The fast takes place during Ramadan, the ninth month of the Islamic calendar, when Muhammad received the first Revelation. The Islamic year is lunar, ten to eleven days shorter than the solar year, so that the months move gradually through the seasons. The fast is a trial during the short winter days, but when it falls in summer, especially in countries where heat can be unbearable at best, Ramadan is a severe hardship. During Ramadan, Muslims reflect on mortality, reminded that, regardless of worldly circumstances, all are equal before God. It is a month of serious devotion.

For all its tough exertion, Ramadan is paradoxically one of the happiest and most cheerful seasons of the Muslim year. In the evenings, special foods are served, friends and families feast into the night. The mosques are brightly lit and full. There are festivities in the streets, sometimes with fairs, where children stay up until all hours riding swings and merry-go-rounds and adults gather in cafés or shops. As the month draws to a close, everyone scans the sky for the appearance of a new moon marking the fast's end. Today, radio and television frequently broadcast the news, but traditionally, the sighting of the new moon was conveyed by the blast of a cannon, the signal for the start of *Id al-fitr*, the Feast of Breaking the Fast, which lasts three days or more. Gifts are given to children, everyone wears new clothes, and alms are distributed.[4]

Hajj, pilgrimage, is the Fifth Pillar. Each adult Muslim of either sex is enjoined by the Qur'an to make the pilgrimage to Mecca at least once in a lifetime if possible.

> *And proclaim the Pilgrimage among men and women.*
> *They will come to you on foot and mounted on every kind of camel,*
> *lean on account of journeys through deep and*
> *distant mountain highways.*[5]

The sick, the insane, and women without husbands or male relatives who do not wish to travel alone are exempted. While today most people arrive by air or ship and the Saudi Arabian government has created a huge infrastructure for the *hajj*, the voyage once could take six months or a year overland in large caravans and was terribly risky. Many pilgrims died of adversity or disease. Thanks largely to the philanthropy of women, pilgrims were provided with leaders and troops for protection, money, and food. They endowed places of shelter and water cisterns along the roads for pilgrims of all classes from all over the Islamic world—Turkey and eastern Europe, North Africa, Sudan, Iran, Samarqand, or India—who assembled in caravans at such gathering points as Damascus, Cairo, and Baghdad.

There are two kinds of pilgrimages, the *umrah*, or lesser pilgrimage, which can be made at any time of the year and is voluntary, and the *hajj*, to be made during the twelfth month, *Dhu al-hajjah*. Some Muslims save their pennies for a lifetime (or earn money as they journey) in order to make the *hajj*.[6]

One who has made the *hajj* is thereafter entitled to be called *hajji* and is held in great respect. The rites are thought to have been taught to Adam by the archangel Jibril and that Ibrahim also performed them. Pilgrims circulate the veiled Ka'aba seven times and this *tawwaf*—like other rites of the *hajj*—is based on those performed by Muhammad during his Farewell Pilgrimage. The Black Stone, *al-Hajar al-aswad*, which each pilgrim kisses or touches, is embedded in the side of the building and is believed by Muslims to have descended from Heaven as the symbol of the covenant made by God and Adam and his progeny. The stone is worn smooth by the attentions of millions of pilgrims, and is today banded by a silver collar.

Having performed the *tawwaf*, the pilgrim runs seven times between the two hills of Safa and Marwah and drinks from the holy well of Zamzam, commemorating the frantic search by Hagar for water to give her son, Ismai'l. Eight days after these rituals, pilgrims head to the Plain of Arafat, to the Hill of Arafat, where they memorialize and hear the Prophet's last sermon, in which he called for peace and harmony among the faithful.

Pilgrims may not enter Mecca until ritually purified and non-Muslims may not enter at all. Throughout the *hajj*, pilgrims may not cut their hair, trim their nails, wear jewelry or perfume, or indulge in sexual intercourse. With the completion of the Feast of the Sacrifice, at the closing of the *hajj*, hair is cut, nails clipped, the ritual dress, *ihram*, is discarded for ordinary clothing (and the *ihram* saved to use as a burial shroud). Another circuit is made around the Ka'aba for closure.

Pilgrims then like to visit Medina—Madinah—although this is not part of the formal pilgrimage, but an opportunity to see Islam's most important historical sites and to visit the tomb of the Prophet and those of his family and Companions.

Notes

Introduction

1. Holy Qur'an, *Surah* CXII, "Sincere Religion."
2. *The Hadj: An American Muslim's Pilgrimage to Mecca.*
3. Holy Qur'an, *Surah* XLI, "Distinguished."
4. Holy Qur'an, *Surah* II, "The Cow."

Chapter I: In the Beginning: Women of the Prophetate

1. Holy Qur'an, *Surah* XIX, "Mary."
2. *Angels: Messengers of God*, a lovely and classic, if too brief, study of "angelography" in religions and cultures throughout time, was written in 1980, long before the "angel craze."
3. Holy Qur'an, *Surah* II, "The Cow."
4. In *Women and Gender in Islam: Historical Roots of a Modern Debate*, Leila Ahmed writes that pre-Islamic Arabs also practiced polyandry, but I have found few, fragmented references to support this. Nevertheless, I see no particular reason to doubt it, since relatively little is actually known.
5. Many European artists have depicted Jesus as an attractive blond man, with no signs of his Semitic origins. Believers everywhere must be able to identify with their spiritual leaders. (Thus we also have, for example, the "black" virgins of Africa or Mexico's indigenous Virgin of Guadalupe.)
6. Ali's description of Muhammad is found in the *Kitab shama'il al-Mustafa* of Abu Isa at-Tirmidhi (d. 892 C.E.). In his eighteenth-century *The History of the Decline and Fall of the Roman Empire*, Edward Gibbon describes Muhammad as

distinguished by the beauty of his person....Before he spoke the orator engaged on his side the affections of a public and private audience. They applauded his commanding presence, his majestic aspect, his piercing eye, his gracious smile, his flowing beard, his countenance that painted every sensation of the soul, and his gestures that enforced each expression of the tongue....His memory was capacious and retentive; his wit easy and social; his imagination sublime; his judgment clear, rapid and decisive. He possessed the courage of both thought and action; and, although his designs might gradually expand with his success, the first idea which he entertained of his divine mission bears the stamp of an original and superior genius.

7. The Persian expression used for Abu Bakr is *yar-i ghar*, "friend of the cave," which indicates the closest possible friendship between two men. In some traditions, it was in the cave that the Prophet taught Abu Bakr the secrets of silent remembrance of God, *dhikr-i khafi*.

8. Holy Qur'an, *Surah* XVII, "The Night Journey."

9. Hind is thus rendered as a harridan by the inimitable Irene Papas in what turns out to be an enjoyable 1977 film—with a few mistakes—about the history of Islam's beginnings, popularly called *The Message*, directed by Moustapha Akkad, filmed in Saudi Arabia. Anthony Quinn plays Muhammad's uncle, the mighty Hamza ibn Abu Talib. The Prophet, his wives, and the four Rightly Guided caliphs are never seen in the movie, as is appropriate to Islamic laws, lest such imagery lead to idolatry.

10. Pamela Nice writes in "Morocco: Aisha Amidst the Cybercafes" (*Aljadid: A Review and Record of Arab Culture and Arts*, Vol. 8, No. 39, Spring 2002) that feminism is "alive and well...at Mohammed V University in Rabat...[academics] are doing exciting work on traditional folktales by or about women. These scholars are applying feminist analysis to folktales that are being transcribed for the first time."

11. According to Minou Reeves in *Female Warriors of Allah*, twentieth-century Shi'a reformer Ali Shariati, "chief mentor and ideo-

logue of the [1979] Islamic Revolution" in Iran, advocated that "only in original Islam…was there true emancipation for women" and accused his own sex of distorting the egalitarian ideals of original Islam by treating women as inferior. Shariati wrote that "We have made our women slaves instead of creating the best possible conditions in which they could develop as human beings. We are Moslems, and Islam prescribes study for men and women alike; yet we have not allowed our women to study….We have practiced polygamy, we have locked our women away at home and have only allowed them to enter the mosque so that they could hear tales of martyrdom…from the mouths of fanatical mullahs," and so on. He presented an alternative model for the new Iranian woman that rejected Western feminist ideals, which he called the Legacy of Fatima, and in which, Reeves writes, "the identical value that Shariati attributes to both Ali and Fatima in his writings almost implies a dual male-female leadership."

12. *Angels: Messengers of the Gods*
13. The custom, though frowned upon, continues even in so-called developed nations.
14. Richard Burton's popular late nineteenth-century translation of *The Thousand and One Nights*, or *Arabian Nights*, in which the British adventurer often gave vent to his own sexual fantasies, exploited the stories to thrill generations of repressed Victorians and fuel their notions of Islamic cultures as promiscuous and licentious. The original tales were indeed often sensual, but in *Imperial Fictions: Europe's Myths of the Orient*, Rana Kabbani notes that although the British adventurer had spent decades in North Africa and the Middle and Near East, his

> ideas about Eastern women never gained in depth….[He] always retained his age's polarized view of women. They were either sexual beings who were whorish, or caring companions in the home, untinged by sexual ardor. Burton's fascination with the *Arabian Nights* was greatly enhanced by the fact that they upheld his own views on women, race and class….Such representations of women were in keeping with the general

Victorian prejudice. All women were inferior to men; Eastern women were doubly inferior, being women *and* Easterners… an even more conspicuous commodity than their Western sisters…goods of empire…there to be used sexually, and if it could be suggested that they were inherently licentious, then they could be exploited with no qualms whatsoever. Thus the *Arabian Nights* helped perpetuate the Victorian notion of promiscuous Eastern women, and Burton's translation in particular gave added substance to the myth. His footnotes and addenda articulated for the West the "carnal" nature of native women.

15. *Ideals and Realities in Islam.*
16. Holy Qur'an, *Surah* LXVI, "The Forbidding."
17. Holy Qur'an, *Surah* XXXIII, "The Confederates."
18. Ibid.
19. Holy Qur'an, *Surah* CV, "The Elephant."
20. Holy Qur'an, *Surah* XCVI, "The Blood-Clot."
21. Holy Qur'an, *Surah* XCIII, "The Forenoon."
22. Holy Qur'an, *Surah* VI, "Cattle."
23. Holy Qur'an, *Surah* XXVI, "The Poets."
24. Holy Qur'an, *Surah* LXX, "The Stairways."
25. Holy Qur'an, *Surah* XXV, "Salvation."
26. Holy Qur'an, *Surah* XX, "Ta Ha."
27. Holy Qur'an, *Surah* II, "The Cow."
28. Ibid.
29. Holy Qur'an, *Surah* XXXIX, "The Companies."
30. Holy Qur'an, *Surah* LX, "The Woman Tested."
31. Holy Qur'an, *Surah* XVI, "The Bee."
32. Holy Qur'an, *Surah* XVII, "The Night Journey."
33. Holy Qur'an, *Surah* XLIX, "Apartments."
34. Holy Qur'an, *Surah* V, "The Table."
35. Holy Qur'an, *Surah* VI, "Cattle."
36. Holy Qur'an, *Surah* XXXIII, "The Confederates."
37. Ibid.
38. Ibid.
39. Holy Qur'an, *Surah* XXIV, "Light."

40. Holy Qur'an, *Surah* IV, "Women."
41. Holy Qur'an, *Surah* XXXIII, "The Confederates."

Chapter II: Scholars of the *Hadith*

1. Holy Qur'an, *Surah* XXXIII, "The Confederates."
2. *Ideals and Realities in Islam.*
3. Hundreds of women studied and taught the *Sahih* of al-Bukhari, apparently overlooking his determined misogyny, whereby he wrote, for example, that "women are naturally, morally, and religiously defective," made unclean by menstruation, the enemies of men who distract them from the righteous path, intellectually, as well as physically inferior. Ahmad ibn Hanbal, founder of the Hanbali School of Law, wrote that "prayers should be interrupted if dogs, donkeys, or women pass too closely by the place of prayer."

Chapter III: Ascetics, Saints, and Mystics

1. Holy Qur'an, *Surah* II, "The Cow."
2. *My Soul Is a Woman.*
3. Ibid.
4. Ibid.
5. *Rabi'a the Mystic and her Fellow Saints in Islam.*
6. It is not my intention to debate Muslim feminism. It is not my place to judge from my particular cultural vantage point. However, I do wish to leave open possibilities that might help Western feminists avoid that pitfall.
7. *Rabi'a the Mystic and her Fellow Saints in Islam.*
8. The production of rain has a special place and prayers for rain are counted as official, while Muhammad is said to be the first to have pronounced an effective prayer for rain.
9. *Rabi'a the Mystic and her Fellow Saints in Islam.*
10. It was this cloak preserved in Kandahar that the notorious Afghan Taliban leader, Mullah Omar, forcibly borrowed (with a Kalashnikov pointed at the caretaker's head), then exploited to declare himself Commander of the Faithful and thus raise him-

self to power. Videos document the frenzy with which Mullah Omar drew followers from war-weary Afghan peasants as he preached from a rooftop, waving the sacred garment. Needless to say, for most Muslims, this was extreme sacrilege.

11. Holy Qur'an, *Surah* II, "The Cow."

Chapter IV: Warriors and Amazons

1. *Ideals and Realities of Islam.*
2. Tragically, most of the Islamic world was ultimately to be dominated. By the seventeenth century C.E., European hegemony was stretching around the globe, eventually oppressing, enslaving, and humiliating the native Muslim peoples (and others) of the Middle East, Southeast Asia, India, Africa, and elsewhere, while czarist Russia moved into the Caucasus, Central Asia, and Siberia. The kinds of prejudice and misconceptions we hold today about Muslims can be traced expressly to the racism and cultural and religious bigotry of the superpower of the hour, whether British, French, or Russian—and after World War II, the United States. In European literature, painting, scholarship, and journalism, Muslims have been misrepresented to satisfy imperialist ambitions, aesthetic fancies, or erotic fantasies, and stereotyped as dissolute, abusive of women, backward, stealthy, vicious. The Orientalist gaze we train on Islam and its cultures is, of course, colored by our own cultural and religious points of view and our own social neuroses. "Dante consigns Muhammad, with his body split from the head down to the waist, to the twenty-eighth sphere of the Inferno, and shows him tearing apart his severed breast with his own hands, because he is the chief among the damned souls who have brought schism into religion," Tor Andrae notes in *Muhammad: The Man and His Faith*. "To the medieval mind [Muhammad's] claim to deliver a Divine revelation which was to supersede Christianity could only be regarded as an impious fraud. Even today Muhammad is primarily 'the false Prophet' in the eyes of a more naïve Christian polemic."
3. Holy Qur'an, *Surah* II, "The Cow."

4. Ibid.
5. Ibid.
6. This is, of course, a generalized summary of a long, complex, and brutal period. I highly recommend Karen Armstrong's absorbing, readable, and enlightening *Holy War: The Crusades and Their Impact on Today's World.*
7. Potential enemies had to be demonized in order to recruit sympathy and bodies for the crusaders' cause. In any conflict, the first rule is to distort and dehumanize the enemy. The anonymous *Song of Roland*, born of battles between al-Andalus and France, features "depiction of warfare with the Muslim enemy," Mariá Rosa Menocal writes in *The Ornament of the World*, "in a mythological and even fantastic fashion." It transforms Islam into virtual devil worship. Misinformation about Muslims is evident in Arthurian legend with its "dark Saracens"—"black knights," such as those who challenge Perceval, the pure and innocent Grail seeker, and who are portrayed as devilish adversaries of God's Good. (Jews also dominated Western bigotry.) The Elizabethan stage routinely featured villainous Turks, Moors, Blackamoors, and Jews. The eighteenth-century French writer and philosopher Voltaire, a leader of the Enlightenment, having himself created a rather wicked Muhammad in his tragedy *Mahomet*, went on later in *Essai sur les moeurs*, to address European misrepresentations of Islam thus:

> We have imputed to the Qur'an a great number of foolish things which it never contained. It was chiefly against the Turks, who happened to be Mohammedans, that our priests wrote so many books. They have no great difficulty ranging our women on their side. They persuade them that Muhammad regarded them as merely intelligent animals, and that by the laws of Islam they were all slaves, having no property in this world nor any share in the Paradise of the next. The falsehood of all this is evident; yet it has all been believed.
>
> It was not until Vatican Council II of the 1960s that the Roman Catholic Church acknowledged Islam as a related

monotheistic religion and "urge[d] all to forget the past and to strive sincerely for mutual understanding. On behalf of all mankind, let them make common cause of safeguarding and fostering social justice, moral values, peace and freedom."

Still, the deep wounds remain unhealed and will so long as economic interests of the West and corrupt leadership in many Islamic countries prevail.

8. *Jews, Christians and Muslims.*
9. Cheerleaders at American sports events today have the same function and the same effect.
10. During the country's recent two-decade war, the Malalai Girls' School in Afghanistan disintegrated only to reappear in exile in Islamabad and Peshawar, Pakistan, then reconstituted in the capital city of Kabul in 2002. The Revolutionary Association of the Women of Afghanistan runs the Malalai Hospital for refugee women and children in Quetta, Pakistan. The spirit of Malalai lived on in Afghan women—young, old, and middle-aged—in the 1990s, when they took up arms to defend their villages, their daughters, and themselves against Taliban storm troopers. And it is said that during the Taliban reign of terror, women sometimes carried knives and kitchen implements under their burqas.
11. *The Women of Turkey and their Folk-Lore,* which covers the territories of the Ottoman Empire in 1891.
12. The Kharijites' extremely pious and puritanical beliefs—and acceptance of only a literal translation of the Qur'an—greatly influenced the present-day hyperorthodox Wahhabi movement, founded in the eighteenth century, which dominates Saudi Arabia. The Kharijites developed their own laws and collections of *Hadith.* Today, many Kharijites are called Ibadites and number around 500,000 in North and East Africa, Oman, and Zanzibar.
13. *Private Life of an Eastern King.*
14. Ibid.
15. Blacker, Valentine, *Memoirs of the Operations of the British Army in India, during the Mahratta War of 1817, 1818 & 1819,* 2 vols. (London: Black, Kingsbury, Parbury & Allen, 1821).

16. Jones, David E., *Women Warriors: A History* (Dulles, Virginia: Brassey's, 1997).
17. *The Forgotten Queens of Islam.*
18. Ibid.
19. In Moroccan legend, Aisha Kandisha is a beautiful enchantress and voracious djinn with the power to bewitch both women and men. A contemporary underground Moroccan trance band, Aisha Kandisha's Jarring Effects, is named for her.
20. *The Women of Turkey and their Folk-Lore.* Of the tomes of European travelers to the East, Lucy Garnett's 1891 two-volume work stands out as particularly unbiased, an evenhanded collection of customs and the tales told by women of diverse Muslim cultures of the Ottoman Empire.
21. Ibid.

Chapter V: Rebels and Concubines

1. Holy Qur'an, *Surah* V, "The Table."
2. Holy Qur'an, *Surah* XXIV, "Light."
3. Ibid.
4. Holy Qur'an, *Surah* IV, "Women."
5. Ibid.
6. Holy Qur'an, *Surah* II, "The Cow."
7. Ibid.
8. In his 1986 book, *Colonial Harem*, Malek Alloula collected, arranged, and annotated picture postcards of Algerian women produced and sent by the French during the first three decades of the twentieth century. These staged pictures (and their captions) are stunning examples of Western and colonialist distortions of non-European societies via colonial morality, and reminiscent of the photographer Edward Curtis's insidious fabrications of Native Americans.
9. *Two Queens of Baghdad.*
10. Ibid.
11. It's crucial to keep events, actions, and attitudes of the distant past in perspective. Even where human nature may not neces-

sarily have changed, societies have. Modern Muslims despise the practice of slavery yet understand its continued existence after the advent of Islam in the context of the early *umma*. But why did the religious authorities, so vigilant about Islam and knowing the Prophet disparaged it, not protest slavery, especially as it increased to such a degree? It's a question that is also asked of any Christian slaving society, including the newfound United States, so solicitous of liberty for white males. It is about politics and economics, which ultimately overpower spiritual directives and humanist values. Sadly, there are still pockets of slavery among Muslims today, notably in the Gulf states, but a billion-dollar trade which exploits women as unwilling sex workers also thrives in non-Muslim cultures from Asia to Eastern Europe and the Americas. While trafficking in people has gone on for millennia, today's trade relationships and global capitalism are preventing crackdowns. Victims are primarily women and children, used for sex and cheap labor.

Chapter VI: Musicians and Dancers

1. Music has always been a crucial art form among Muslims and female singers continue to be especially acclaimed and admired, celebrities with superstar status. With the advent of radio, recordings, and television, new opportunities arose for them. Umm Kulthum was the twentieth-century's most famous singer, a cultural icon and national symbol, who sang traditional as well as contemporary works. Her career lasted fifty years until her death in 1973. She was born in Egypt in 1904, a woman of peasant origins, whose father dressed her as a boy to sing in public. In 1934, she began singing on Egyptian Radio, concerts broadcast live on Thursdays, which became known as "Umm Kulthum Night," and it was said that life in the Arab world stopped while she sang. When she died, her funeral was described as larger than that of President Gamal Abdel Nasser.

2. In *The Arabic Role in Medieval Literary History*, María Rosa Menocal writes:

[The] academic conceptual banishment of the Arab from medieval Europe was to have extraordinary power. While versions of the Arabist theory were to be brought up again and again, it would not be reinstituted as part of the mainstream of philological thought. The sporadic suggestions of Arabic influence on this or that aspect of medieval European literature or on salient features of its lexicon, such as *trobar*, were largely ignored, were dismissed as unworthy of serious consideration, or at best were subjected to unusually heated and vitriolic criticism. The proponents of such ideas, predominantly Arabists, were dismissed as individuals who simply had an ax to grind rather than a conceivably legitimate contribution to make and who, in any case, were not knowledgeable in the field of European literature.

3. In Arabic, the male storyteller is a *rawi* or *hakawati*, who tells stories in cafés.

4. In *Imperial Fictions*, Kabbani says that *The Arabian Nights* "were originally recounted to an all male audience desiring bawdy entertainment...purposefully crude...pandered to the prejudices of uneducated men who listened to them being narrated....They reflected a certain mode of apprehending women prevalent in the repressively patriarchal societies of which they were a product."

5. Despite controversies over Richard Burton's translation of *The Book of the Thousand and One Nights*, Mernissi lauds and recommends it in several of her own books, including *Dreams of Trespass*. She notes, however, that the "Burton translation can be confusing at times with its archaic language."

6. In a personal correspondence with the author, Umm Ahmad, a physician in Gaza, wrote,

> as for dancers, you will likely not find any for your book, at least not one considered as representative of being Muslima. Dancing among women in Islam is only among women—unless for one's husband. Anything outside of that is outside of Islam. I would think that inclusion of

even that area itself in the book would spark a lot of unwanted controversy. Personally, I would not consider a woman "great" because she is a famous dancer—it is more something to be ashamed of, in Muslim circles. It is one thing to be known for dancing skills among your own circle of women, quite another to be what is called a *junkiya* (in both Islamic and Arabic circles they are on the same level of prostitutes). It would be a shame to see such a woman among the pages of the truly inspiring Muslim women of the past.

Umm Ahmad's intense feelings about the issue are meaningful and not unusual in contemporary Islam but attitudes vary. One cannot walk across any bridge in Cairo on any evening without observing weddings lining the banks of the Nile and everyone dancing. Those watching the celebrations from above dance on the sidewalks—usually men. There are rules—sometimes breached—that while men and women might be dancing in one another's vicinity, even visible to one another, they are not dancing together.

7. Holy Qur'an, *Surah* XXXV, "The Angels."
8. Holy Qur'an, *Surah* VII, "The Battlements."
9. Holy Qur'an, *Surah* XXXI, "Lokman."
10. In a personal conversation with Afghan musician and scholar, Wahid Omar.
11. *The History of Arabian Music.*
12. Ibid.
13. Ibid.
14. For examples of the diversity of Sufi dance, Gabrielle Roth's 1995 documentary *Hidden Egypt*, is fascinating, as is a somewhat obscure French production from the 1970s called *Les Soufis d'Afghanistan*, made by Arnaud Desjardins and Mohammed Ali Raonaq.
15. With so little thorough documentation of dancing in Islam, Buonaventura has certainly given it a good try. Unfortunately, her book is dotted with historical inaccuracies. It is a lovely, pleasurable book to look at, and to her credit, Buonaventura,

herself a dancer, attempts to offer the reader a clear picture of dance in the Arab world and its roots, and how Arabic dance was exported to the West and inspired Western dancing.

16. "*A Trade Like Any Other.*" Van Nieuwkerk's is a rare book of scholarship that speaks to the lives, attitudes, and prestige—or lack of it—among contemporary performers in Egypt.

17. *The Complete Letters of Lady Mary Wortley Montagu*, Vol. 1.

18. *The City of the Sultans and Domestic Manners of the Turks.* In reviewing this chapter, dancer and lay dance historian Shireen Malik noted casually that the dances described by Pardoe recall early flamenco, before the introduction of flamenco's fancy footwork.

19. *The Women of Turkey and their Folk-Lore.*

20. Meyda Yegenoglu offers a necessary corrective to Said in her book *Colonial Fantasies: Towards a Feminist Reading for Orientalism,* arguing that the Orient is invariably represented as feminine, secretive, secluded, subordinated, and exotic, merely waiting to be penetrated by the paragons of Western progress. "Unveiling and thereby modernizing the woman of the Orient," Yegenoglu writes, "signified the transformation of the Orient itself."

Chapter VII: Rulers, Regents, Queen Mothers, and Philanthropists

1. "Armed Women Retainers in the Zenanas of the Indo-Muslim Rulers: The Case of Bibi Fatima," in *Women in the Medieval Islamic World.*

2. *The Imperial Harem.*

3. Pitiably, when the Ottoman Empire finally dissolved in the early twentieth century, discarded eunuchs made a few feeble and failed attempts at forming unions. No one wanted them or wanted to be reminded of what they'd stood for.

4. *Two Queens of Baghdad.*

5. *Muhammad; A Biography of the Prophet.*

6. Dunn, Ross E., *The Adventures of Ibn Battuta, A Muslim Traveler of the 14th Century.*

7. *The Imperial Harem.*
8. *The Forgotten Queens of Islam.*
9. Mernissi and others have written of how numerous women sharing one man were often lonely in romance. Other scholars assume that harem members found fulfillment in lesbian affairs as well as in flirtations and love affairs with eunuchs.
10. *Two Queens of Baghdad.*
11. Mernissi's *The Forgotten Queens of Islam* carefully breaks down how a woman could not, but sometimes did, receive legitimate titles of rulership. With some exceptions, she writes primarily of women in the Arab world, but the conventions, based on religious interpretation, apply to almost any Islamic woman who would be queen.
12. The Begam of Bhopal's memoir was printed in an extremely limited edition in India and is so thoroughly out of print, I was only able to find fragments of it in a few old British accounts. That these rulers had male names before their titles of *begam* — princess — such as Sikander (Alexander), gives me pause, but I could not locate an explanation, nor am I knowledgeable enough of the place, period, or customs to decipher the discrepancy.
13. *The Forgotten Queens of Islam.*
14. Numerous women carried the title of "al-Hurra." In her meticulous descriptions of noble designations, their etymologies, and political import, in *The Forgotten Queens of Islam*, Mernissi explains that "*hurr* is what distinguishes a person from being a slave, from being inferior."
15. *Two Queens of Baghdad.*
16. "Women in Safavid Iran: The Evidence of European Travelers," in *Women in the Medieval Islamic World.*
17. Wiebke Walther provides a romp through Muslim women's history in *Woman in Islam*, where, with other entertaining details, she gives vivid pictures of wedding ceremonies.
18. *Two Queens of Baghdad.*
19. Holy Qur'an, *Surah* II, "The Cow."
20. *My Soul Is a Woman.*

21. *The Women of Turkey and their Folk-lore.*
22. *The Private Life of an Eastern King.*
23. *The Forgotten Queens of Islam.*
24. Holy Qur'an, *Surah* XXVII, "The Ant."

Chapter VIII: Tradeswomen and Learned Ladies

1. In *Ideals and Realities of Islam,* Nasr notes that this lack of distinction between the spiritual and temporal, the sacred and profane, makes Islam a religion of Unity, which "also manifests itself in the reality of the arts and sciences."
2. Sales were frequently of inherited land or buildings made to their brothers below market price. From an article by Ronald C. Jennings, "Women in Early Seventeenth Century Ottoman Judicial Records," *Journal of the Economic and Social History of the Orient* 18 (1975).
3. From an article by Abraham Marcus, "Men, Women and Property," *Journal of the Economic and Social History of the Orient* 26 (1983).
4. Fay, Mary Ann, "Women and *Waqf,*" in *Women and the Ottoman Empire.*
5. Ibid.
6. Hambly, Gavin R. G., "Armed Women Retainers in the Zenanas of Indo-Muslim Rulers: The Case of Bibi Fatima," from *Women in the Medieval Islamic World.*
7. *The Women of Turkey and their Folk-Lore.*
8. Al-Hasan, Idris Salim, and Neil McHugh, "Sitt Nasra bint Adlan: A Sudanese Noblewoman in History and Tradition," *Women in the Medieval Islamic World.*
9. From an essay, "Mainstreaming Middle East Gender Research: Promise or Pitfall?" *Middle East Studies Association Bulletin,* Vol. 35, Number 1, Summer 2001.
10. Marsot, Afaf Lutfi al-Sayyid, "Revolutionary Gentlewomen in Egypt," from *Women in the Muslim World.*
11. Khoury, Dina Rizk, "Slippers at the Entrance or Behind Closed Doors," from *Women in the Ottoman Empire.*

12. Sorainen, Elina, "The Women Potters of Ancient Kalpourkan: Maintainers of Ancient Tradition," in *The Arts Paper: A Journal of the Boulder Arts Commission*, Vol. 3, Issue 1, February/March 2002.

13. Holy Qur'an, *Surah* XXXIII, "The Confederates"

14. For a further and fascinating in-depth discussion, the reader is referred to Fatima Mernissi's *The Veil and the Male Elite: A Feminist Interpretation of Women's Rights in Islam,* as well as to other books listed in the bibliography.

15. Echoing the words of the Prophet, Qasim Amin, a nineteenth-century Egyptian lawyer, called for the education of women in a book titled *Liberation of the Woman.* "It is not possible to raise successful men if their mothers are not capable of preparing them for success. This is the noble profession that civilization has placed in the hands of the woman of our generation. She undertakes this heavy burden in all the civilized countries where we see her giving birth to children and moulding them into men." Sounding for all the world like a Victorian gentleman, Amin's intentions were nevertheless in service of liberality and justice, and he seemed to use whatever argument necessary to convince a male-dominated society. However, like many of the colonized, he was boxed in by European frames of reference, which undermined his position to nationalists, who were outraged by what they considered alien and enemy values.

16. Aspiring poets often spent time among the desert tribes in order to refine their knowledge of pure Arabic.

17. In *Women in Islamic Biographical Collections,* Ruth Roded notes that modern biographical dictionaries pattern themselves after the Western Who's Who. "The numbers and proportions of women in these modern collections are greater than those in the traditional dictionaries that directly preceded them, but there are fewer than are found in some of the classical works." A list in 1951 in Syria includes women engaged in education, philanthropy, literature, and medicine—each category with fewer than ten—plus two lawyers and a military heroine. "Most women were identified with prominent men...but some mothers from

noted families are cited." A 1967 Who's Who in the Arab World featured women in literature and the arts, government and diplomacy, some royal women, including a princess-diplomat and a queen-industrialist. Two decades later, the lists of women in the Who's Who doubled, with entries for the first woman ambassador, the first of ministerial rank, the first female radio broadcaster, women in international civil service, as well as those in education, literature and the arts, medicine, and so on.

18. Hundreds of studies exist about women's education throughout the Muslim world. This book cannot begin to disseminate that material, but it is well worth pursuing, for these studies can enlighten our knowledge about Islam and help in comparing ways in which women worldwide have struggled for the right not only to learn but to practice their skills openly and professionally.

19. Annette Beveridge's edition of *Humayan-nama* offers the Persian original and an English translation, as well as an important introduction, detailed notes, and a biographical glossary.

20. *Two Queens of Baghdad.*

21. According to Fanny Davis in *The Ottoman Lady: 1718 to 1918,* "Halil Halit, a Turk who wrote his autobiography at the turn of the twentieth century, reports that his mother could read but not write. There was, he says, an old superstition to the effect that learning to write turned women into witches. A more frequently encountered excuse was that the ability to write tempted them to write love letters."

22. A spelling text, *Qaeda-e-Baghdadi* (The Baghdad Method) was fairly universally employed (and is still used today) in *kuttabs* and *madrassas,* Quranic schools, where mullahs do the teaching.

23. *The Ottoman Lady.*

24. Among the services performed by midwives in some regions of the Middle East were female circumcisions. This highly controversial procedure is too often labeled a *Muslim* practice, though it has nothing to do with the religion and is a *cultural* practice in a limited number of societies.

Chapter IX: Poets

1. Holy Qur'an, *Surah* XXVI, "Lokman."
2. A marvelous recent book, *The Poetry of Arab Women: A Contemporary Anthology*, edited by Nathalie Handal, gathers eighty-three women poets from the first quarter of the twentieth century to the present, showing the scope and range of women's poetic work and providing context for it in an introductory essay describing the rich lineage from which these modern women have come.
3. Poetry competitions—today sometimes called "slams" in the United States—have been known worldwide for millennia. The ancient Celts indulged in such contests and even today, in Irish pubs or in public establishments in Iceland, poets gather to render spontaneous verse, each one-upping the other. In Taos, New Mexico, there is an annual "heavyweight championship," featuring renowed experimental poets. The final "round" is judged for the poets' ability to improvise.
4. Arabic calligraphy continues to expand and diversify as an art form. The highly stylized, postmodern work of contemporary practitioners such as Palestinian Nihad Dukan is evidence of the form's endless flexibility.
5. Contemporary artist Shazia Sikander, now based in the United States, studied miniature painting in her native Pakistan, where it is still taught to girls and boys. She has brought this demanding classical training into a dazzling, edgy, contemporary style with modern themes. Sikander's work may be best known to general audiences from her appearance on the 2001 PBS documentary, "Art 21."
6. Wiebke Walther's 1981 *Women in Islam: From Medieval to Modern Times*—a gorgeous coffeetable tome—is the only book-length work that touches on the subject through its illustrations. Scattered articles, such as Nancy Micklewright's excellent "'Musicians and Dancing Girls': Images of Women in Ottoman Miniature Painting," in *Women in the Ottoman Empire* or the entire spring 1993 issue of Asian Art, have explored the subject.

In her *My Soul Is a Woman,* Schimmel—who in her books frequently calls on scholars to realize certain ideas—suggests that a comprehensive book about past Muslim women artists, representations of women in Islamic art, and women who patronized the arts is long overdue.

7. "'Musicians and Dancing Girls': Images of Women in Ottoman Miniature Painting."
8. Islam, like Judaism, prohibits the representation of living beings. The rule, however, was quickly ignored as Islam spread, taking under its wing cultures, such as the Persian, that already had long traditions of figurative depictions. Portraits of the Prophet or any saint cannot be legitimately produced, though there are quite a few Turkish, Persian, and Indian miniatures that show Muhammad and his family. As late as the fourteenth century C.E., portraits show them unveiled, but subsequently they were usually veiled. But this is considered heresy—idolatry, *shirk.*
9. *My Soul is a Woman.*

The Five Pillars of Islam

1. In his 1954 book, *Islam,* Alfred Guillaume writes, "Apart from the testimony to Muhammad being the apostle of God, there is nothing in the official worship of Islam in which a Christian could not join, and one who understands the words of praise and adoration is tempted to do so. A Christian who, like the writer, goes from a visit to the Church of the Holy Sepulchre [in Jerusalem] with its warring, noisy, competitive sects to the peace and demotion of the Great Mosque of Jerusalem cannot help but be saddened and chastened to find in the one what he was looking for in the other."
2. Some religious scholars compare *Surah* I of the Qur'an, "The Opening," to the Lord's Prayer in Christianity, for it testifies to faith and beseeches mercy and is the core of faith.
3. Holy Qur'an, *Surah* I, "The Opening."
4. In recent years, children's books have been published in the United States for Muslim and non-Muslim youngsters that

describe Ramadan. Among the titles are *Ramadan,* by Suhaib Hamid Ghazi, illustrated by Omar Rayyan (Holiday House, 1996) and *Majid Fasts for Ramadan,* by Mary Matthews, illustrated by E.B. Lewis (Clarion Books, 1996). These are charming and informative for adults as well as children.

5. Holy Qur'an, *Surah* XXII, "The Pilgrimage."

6. The written experiences of *hajjis* throughout the centuries are anthologized in Michael Wolfe's *One Thousand Roads to Mecca.* Wolfe's own pilgrimage in the early 1990s, at the brink of the Gulf War, described in *The Hadj: An American Muslim's Pilgrimage to Mecca,* makes for captivating, educative, and enlightening reading. Wolfe's language and imagery are gorgeous and accessible. Read alongside *Mecca the Blessed, Medina the Radiant: The Two Holiest Cities of Islam,* with photos by Ali Kazuyoshi Nomachi and text by Sayyed Hossein Nasr, the non-Muslim can enjoy a nearly complete, if virtual experience.

Glossary of Terms
(All terms are Arabic, unless otherwise specified)

Abu: father of (see **kunya**)

Adhan: the call to prayer

Allah: God, used by all Muslims and Arabic-speaking Christians

Allahu Akbar: "God is great"

Amir: commander, official

Ayat: a verse of the Qur'an

Azrail: Angel of Death

Badiyah: desert—also a woman's name

Banu or **bani:** clan or tribe

Baraqa: blessing, grace, power of blessing

Basha (Turkish, also **Pasha** or **Bey**): Ottoman title, equivalent to "Lord"

Beg: prince (Indo-Muslim)

Begam: princess (Indo-Muslim)

Bint: daughter of (e.g., Fatima **bint** Muhammad)

Caliph: successor to the Prophet

Dajjal: false prophet

Dar al-Islam: the realm of Islam; those regions in the world where Muslims are the majority

Da'ud: David

Dhikr: among Sufis, continual invocation and repetition of the various names of God.

Dhimma: protected minority, i.e., Jews and Christians

Dinar: monetary unit

Dirham: monetary unit

452

Djinn (also **jin, jinni**): in pre-Islam, supernatural beings (probably animistic gods), thought to haunt the landscape, usually mischievous, but sometimes evil. They were retained in the Qur'an, as a separate creation

Du'a: nonproscribed prayer or supplication

Faqr: spiritual poverty, the renunciation of materialism

Fitna: creating disorder where there should be peace

al-Fitra: innate disposition toward virtue; the opposite of the Christian concept of original sin

Gazel: Turkish poetic form, resembling a sonnet

Ghazal: love song

Ghazu: raid for booty

Ghulam: Turkish slave commander

Gul: (Persian) rose

Hadith (**ahadith**): discourse, any reliable report of the Prophet Muhammad's sayings or doings

Hafiza: one who knows the Qur'an by heart

Hajj: annual pilgrimage to Mecca, required once in a lifetime for any who are able

Hanif: monotheist, but neither Christian nor Jewish

al-Hamdulillah: "thanks be to God"

Hanim: (Turkish) lady

Haram: sacred or inviolable space, sanctuary

Haramlek: the area in a house reserved for women, entered by men only with permission of the women

Haroun: Aaron

Haseki: (Turkish) sultan's favorite concubine

Hawdaj: litter or hut atop a camel

Hijab: veil, curtain

Hijaz: the province, western Saudi Arabia, bordering the Red Sea, where Mecca and Medina, the principal holy cities of Islam, are located

Hijra: Hegira, emigration or flight to Medina in 622 C.E.

Ibn: son of (Muhammad **ibn** Abdallah)

Id al-Fitr: feast celebrating the end of the month-long fast of Ramadan

Idda: obligatory waiting period, before women are allowed to enter a new marriage

Ihram: white ritual dress—today made of terry cloth—worn by *hajj* pilgrims

Ijtihad: legal decision-making

Imam: prayer leader

Inshallah: "God willing"

Iqra: recite

Isa: Jesus

Islam: surrender to God

Isra': Muhammad's Night Journey

Jahiliyah: The Time of Ignorance (before Islam)

Jarya (plural, **jawari**): concubine

Jibril: angel Gabriel

Jihad: exertion

Ka'aba: stone shrine in Mecca, toward which Muslims pray

Kafir: non-Muslim, unbeliever

Kahin: ecstatic prophets or soothsayers of pre-Islamic Arabia

Karamat: wonders or saintly miracles

Khalil Allah: friend of God

Khirqa-i-sharif: (also **burda**) noble cloak of the Prophet

Khutba: Friday prayers

Kiswah: clothing covering the Ka'aba

Kunya: honorific whereby a woman or man rather than being called by their given names are called *umm* or *abu* followed by the name of the eldest child

Madrassa: theological school

Mahar: bride-price

Majnun: *djinn*-possessed madness—and inspiration—of the poet

Malahi: forbidden pleasures

Malaika: angels

Mi'raj: Muhammad's Ascension during the Night Journey

Muezzin: mosque crier who calls the faithful to prayer

Mu'jizat: evidentiary miracles

Musa: Moses

Muslim: (feminine: **muslima**) one who surrenders to God

Musnida: transmitter

Mutawali: *waqf* or endowment administrators

Nafs: soul or self

Purdah (Hindi, **screen, veil**): commonly used word for seclusion of women, practiced as well by various Hindus

Qaina (plural, **qainat**): singing girl(s)

Qibla: direction of the Ka'aba in Mecca; direction of prayer

Ramadan: annual month-long daytime fast

Rukn: the Five Pillars of Islam

Sakina—enveloping radiance, like a halo, from the Hebrew *Shekina*, "the cloud of glory indicating the presence of God"; the spirit of peace

Salaam aleikoum: "peace be upon you," universal greeting

Salamlek: part of the house where men can move freely

Salat: ritual prayer, required five times a day; one of the Five Pillars of Islam

Sawm: fasting, Fourth Pillar of Islam

Sayyid: master

Shahada: the creed: "I bear witness that there is no God but God and Muhammad is his prophet"

Shahid: martyr

Shari'a: body of laws and rules that regulate Muslim life

Sharif: descendant of the prophet Muhammad

Shaykh (feminine, **shaykah**): a person of knowledge, a guide, teacher

Shayytan: Satan

Shi'a: "partisans," a major sectarian movement of Muslims claiming Ali's right to succeed Muhammad directly and that the previous caliphs were usurpers. Shi'ites maintain that only the descendants of Ali and his wife, Fatima, Muhammad's daughter, were entitled to rule the Muslim community.

Shirk: idolatry

Suleyman: Solomon

Sultan (feminine – **sultana**): ruler

Sunna: practice and example of Muhammad, his "custom" or "example"

Sunni: branch of Islam constituting the vast majority in the world Muslim community. Sunnites refer to themselves as "people of the

sunna," meaning "middle of the road," and does not refer to the
Sunna, or "custom" of the prophet Muhammad. All Islamic groups
and sects accept the Sunna, along with the Qur'an, as binding.
Surah: a chapter of the Qur'an.
Taghbir: recitation, cantilation of the Qur'an
Tahil: chantings of the pilgrimage
Tawwaf: circumambulation of the Ka'aba
'Ulama: religious authorities
Umm: mother (see kunya)
Umma: the community of Muslims worldwide
Ummi: unlettered, nonliterate
Umrah: lesser pilgrimage
Urdubegi (Hindi): armed female retainers, and sometimes adminis-
trators for the women's quarters of Indo-Muslim rulers
Valide Sultan: (Turkish) queen mother/first lady
Vizier (also wazir): "bearer of burdens," ministerial title applied in
Muslim monarchies to high governmental officials.
Waqf: endowment for religious or charitable purposes
Yusuf: Joseph
Zakat: almsgiving, Third Pillar of Islam
Zamzam: the sacred well inside the mosque at Mecca
Zenana (Hindi): women's quarters of Indo-Muslim rulers and other
members of the ruling elite

Bibliography

Abbott, Nabia, *Aisha, The Beloved of Muhammad*, Chicago: University of Chicago Press, 1942.

———, *Studies in Arabic Literary Papyri*, Chicago: University of Chicago Press, 1972.

———, *Two Queens of Baghdad*, Chicago: University of Chicago Press, 1946.

Ahmed, Leila, *Women and Gender in Islam: Historical Roots of a Modern Debate*, New Haven: Yale University Press, 1992.

Ali, Ahmed, *al-Qur'an: A Contemporary Translation*, Princeton, N.J.: Princeton University Press, 1988.

Alloula, Malek, Myrna and Wlad Godzich, translators, *The Colonial Harem*, Minneapolis: University of Minnesota Press, 1986.

Andrae, Tor, *Mohammed, The Man and His Faith*, New York: Harper & Row, 1960.

Arberry, A. J., translator, *The Koran, Interpreted*, London: George Allen & Unwin, Ltd., 1955.

Armstrong, Karen, *Holy War: The Crusades and Their Impact on Today's World*, New York: Anchor Books, 1991.

———, *Islam: A Short History*, New York: Modern Library, 2002.

———, *Muhammad: A Biography of the Prophet*, San Francisco: HarperSanFrancisco, 1992.

Awde, Nicholas, translator and editor, *Women in Islam: An Anthology from the Qur'an and Hadiths*, Surrey, England: Curzon Press, 2000.

Beck, Lois, ed., *Women in the Muslim World*, Cambridge, Mass.: Harvard University Press, 1978.

Bloom, Jonathan M., *Paper Before Print: The History and Impact of Paper in the Islamic World*, New Haven: Yale University Press, 2001.

Buonaventura, Wendy, *Serpent of the Nile: Women and Dance in the Arab World*, New York: Interlink Books, 1994.

Bushnaq, Inea, ed., *Arab Folktales*, New York: Pantheon Books, 1986.

Corrigan, John, Frederick M., Denny, Carlos M. N. Eire, Martin S. Jaffee, *Jews, Christians, Muslims: A Comparative Introduction to Monotheistic Religions*, Upper Saddle River, N.J.: Prentice Hall, 1998.

Croutier, Alev Lytle, *Harem: The World Behind the Veil*, New York: Abbeville Press, 1989.

Davis, Fanny, *The Ottoman Lady: A Social History from 1718 to 1918*, New York: Greenwood Press, 1986.

Diner, Helen, *Mothers and Amazons: The First Feminine History of Culture*, New York: Julian Press, 1965.

Dunn, Ross E., *The Adventures of Ibn Battuta: A Muslim Traveler of the 14th Century*, Berkeley: University of California Press, 1989.

Encyclopedia of Islam, new edition, Leiden: E.J. Brill, 1960–1993.

Esposito, John L., ed., *The Oxford Encyclopedia of the Modern Islamic World*, New York: Oxford University Press, 1995.

Farmer, Henry George, *A History of Arabian Music to the XIIIth Century*, Hertford, England: Steven Austin and Sons, Ltd., 1929.

Fernea, Elizabeth Warnock, *In Search of Islamic Feminism: One Woman's Global Journey*, New York: Doubleday, 1998.

Garnett, Lucy M. J., *The Women of Turkey and their Folk-lore*, "The Jewish and Moslem Women," Vol. II, London: David Nutt, 1891.

Glubb, Sir John, *Soldiers of Fortune: The Story of the Mamlukes*, New York: Stein and Day, 1973.

Goldziher, Ignác, C. R. Barber, and S. M. Stern, translators, *Muslim Studies (Muhammedanische Studein)*, Vols. 1 & 2, New York: George Allen & Unwin, Ltd., 1971.

Guillaume, Alfred, *Islam*, Baltimore: Penguin Books, 1962.

Guindi, Fawda El, *Veil: Modesty, Privacy and Resistance*, Oxford: Berg, 1999.

Gul-Badan Begam, Annette S. Beveridge, translator, *The History of Humayan (Humayun-Nama)*, London: Royal Asiatic Society, 1902.

Halsband, R., ed., *The Complete Letters of Lady Mary Wortley Montagu*, Oxford, Clarendon Press, 1965.

Hambly, Gavin R. G., ed., *Women in the Medieval Islamic World/ Power, Patronage and Piety*, New York: St. Martin's Press, 1998.

Handal, Nathalie, ed., *The Poetry of Arab Women: A Contemporary Anthology*, New York: Interlink Books, 2001.

Harrison, Jane Ellen, *Themis: A Study of the Social Origins of the Greek Religion*, Cambridge: Cambridge University Press, 1912.

Harrow, Kenneth, ed., *The Marabout and the Muse: New Approaches to Islam in African Literature*, Portsmith, N.H.: Heinemann, 1996.

Harvey, L. P., *Islamic Spain: 1250 to 1500*, Chicago: University of Chicago Press, 1990.

Helminski, Camille Adams, ed., *Women of Sufism, A Hidden Treasure*, Boston: Shambhala Publications, 2003.

Horne, Charles F., ed., *The Sacred Books and Early Literature of the East*, New York: Parke, Austin & Lipscomb, 1917.

Ibn Doi, A. Rahman, *Hadith: An Introduction*, Ile-Ife, Nigeria: Kazi Publications, 1980.

Jurji, Edward J., ed., *The Great Religions of the Modern World: Confucianism, Taoism, Hinduism, Buddhism, Shintoism, Islam, Judaism, Eastern Orthodoxy, Roman Catholicism, Protestantism*, Princeton, N.J.: Princeton University Press, 1946.

Kabanni, Rana, *Imperial Fictions: Europe's Myths of Orient*, London: HarperCollins Publishers, 1988.

Kahf, Mohja, *Western Representations of the Muslim Woman: From Termagant to Odalisque*, Austin: University of Texas Press, 1999.

Keohane, Alan, *The Berbers of Morocco*, London: Hamish Hamilton, Ltd., 1991.

Knappert, Jan, *Islamic Legends: Histories of the Heroes, Saints, and Prophets of Islam*, Leiden: E. J. Brill, 1985.

Knighton, William, *The Private Life of an Eastern King, Together with Elihu Jan's Story, or The Private Life of an Eastern Queen*, Oxford: Oxford University Press, 1921.

Lazreg, Marnia, *The Eloquence of Silence: Algerian Women in Question*, New York: Routledge, 1994.

Lings, Martin, *Muhammad: His Life Based on the Earliest Sources*, Rochester, Vt.: Inner Traditions International, 1983.

Lyall, Charles James, *Translations of Ancient Arabian Poetry: Chiefly Pre-Islamic Poetry, with Introduction and Notes*, Westport, Conn.: Hyperion Press, 1981.

Mann, Vivian B., et al., eds., *Convivencia: Jews, Muslims, and Christians in Medieval Spain*, New York: George Braziller, 1992.

Marmon, Shaun E., ed., *Slavery in the Islamic Middle East*, Princeton, N.J.: Markus Wiener Publishers, 1999.

Medicine and Pharmacy/An Informal History: Ancient Jews and Arabs, Bloomfield, N.J.: Schering Corporation, 1957.

Menocal, María Rosa, *Shards of Love: Exile and the Origins of the Lyric*, Durham, N.C.: Duke University Press, 1994.

———, *The Ornament of the World: How Muslims, Jews, and Christians Created a Culture of Tolerance in Medieval Spain*, New York: Little, Brown and Company, 2002.

Mernissi, Fatima, *Dreams of Trespass: Tales of a Harem Girlhood*, Cambridge, Mass.: Perseus Books, 1994.

———, Lakeland, Mary Jo, translator, *The Forgotten Queens of Islam*, Minneapolis: University of Minnesota Press, 1993.

———, *Scheherazade Goes West: Different Cultures, Different Harems*, New York: Washington Square Press, 2001.

———, Lakeland, Mary Jo, translator, *Women and Islam/An Historical and Theological Enquiry*, Oxford: Basil Blackwell, 1991.

Nasr, Seyyed Hossein, *Ideals and Realities of Islam*, London: Unwin Hyman Ltd., 1966.

———, and Ali Kazuyoshi Nomachi, *Mecca the Blessed, Medina the Radiant: The Holiest Cities of Islam*, New York: Aperture, 1997.

———, *Muhammad, Man of Allah*, Chicago: KAZI Publications, 1995.

Nicholson, R. A., *The Idea of Personality in Sufism*, Cambridge, 1923.

Nurbakhsh, Javad, *Sufi Women*, London: Khaniqahi-Nimatullahi Publications, 1983.

Nykl, A. R., *Hispano-Arabic Poetry and Its Relations with the Old Provençal Troubadours*, Baltimore: J. H. Furst Company, 1946.

Parrinder, Geoffrey, *Sex in the World's Religions*, Oxford: Oxford University Press, 1980.

Peirce, Leslie P., *The Imperial Harem: Women and Sovereignty in the Ottoman Empire*, Oxford: Oxford University Press, 1993.

Pool, John J., *Woman's Influence in the East*, New Delhi: Inter-India Publications, 1892.

Rahmatallah, Maleeha, *The Women of Baghdad in the Ninth and Tenth Centuries as Revealed in the History of Baghdad of al-Hatib*, University of Pennsylvania Master of Arts thesis, published with the aid of Baghdad University, 1952.

Reeves, Minou, *Female Warriors of Allah: Women and the Islamic Revolution*, New York: E. P. Dutton, 1989.

Renard, John, *Islam and the Heroic Image: Themes in Literature and the Visual Arts*, Macon, Ga.: Mercer University Press, 1999.

———, *Responses to 101 Questions on Islam*, Mahwah, N.J., Paulist Press, 1998.

———, ed., *Windows on the House of Islam: Muslim Sources on Spirituality and Religious Life*, Berkeley: University of California Press, 1996.

Roded, Ruth, ed., *Women in Islam in the Middle East: A Reader*, London: I.B. Tauris Publishers, 1999.

———, *Women in Islamic Biographical Collections: From Ibn Sa'd to Who's Who*, Boulder: Lynne Rienner Publishers, 1994.

Rodinson, Maxime, Anne Carter, translator, *Mohammed*, New York: Pantheon, 1971.

Ruggles, D. Fairchild, ed., *Women, Patronage and Self-Representation in Islamic Societies*, Albany: State University of New York Press, 2000.

Safadi, Y. H., *Islamic Calligraphy*, London: Thames and Hudson, Ltd., 1978.

Said, Edward, *Covering Islam: How the Media and Experts Determine How We See the Rest of the World*, New York: Pantheon Books, 1981.

———, *Culture and Imperialism*, New York: Vintage Books, 1994.

————, *Orientalism*, New York: Vintage Books, 1979.

Schimmel, Annemarie, *And Muhammad Was His Messenger: The Veneration of the Prophet in Islamic Piety*, Chapel Hill, N.C.: University of North Carolina Press, 1985.

————, *Islamic Calligraphy*, Leiden: E. J. Brill, 1970.

————, *My Soul Is a Woman: The Feminine in Islam*, New York: The Continuum Publishing Co., 1999.

Schuon, Frithjof, J. Peter Hobson, translator, *Islam and the Perennial Philosophy*. Preface by S. H. Nasr. London: World of Islam Festival Publishing Co., 1976.

Shakir, M. H., translator, *The Qur'an*, Elmhurst, N.Y.: Tahrike Tarsile Qur'an, Inc., 1990.

Smith, Margaret, *Rabi'a the Mystic and her Fellow Saints in Islam: Being the Life and Teachings of Rabi'a al-'Adawiyya Al-Qaysiyya of Basra Together with Some Account of the Place of the Women Saints in Islam*, Cambridge: Cambridge University Press, 1984.

Söderblom, Nathan, *The Living God*. The Gifford Lectures. London: Oxford University Press, 1930.

Stewart, Iris J., *Sacred Woman, Sacred Dance: Awakening Spirituality Through Movement and Ritual*, Rochester, Vt.: Inner Traditions, 2000.

Thanawi, Maulana Ashraf Ali, Barbara Daly Metcalf, translator, *Bihishti Zewar (Perfecting Women)*, Berkeley: University of California Press, 1990.

Van Nieuwkerk, Karin, *"A Trade Like Any Other": Female Singers and Dancers in Egypt*, Austin: University of Texas Press, 1995.

Waddy, Charis, *Women in Muslim History*, London and New York: Longman, 1980.

Wadud-Muhsin, Amina, *Qur'an and Woman*, Kuala Lumpur: Penerbit Fajar Bakti SDN, BHD, 1992.

Walther, Wiebke, *Women in Islam*, Princeton and New York: Markus Wiener Publishing, 1993.

Wilson, Peter Lamborn, *Angels: Messengers of the Gods*, New York: Thames and Hudson, 1980.

Wolfe, Michael, ed., *One Thousand Roads to Mecca: Ten Centuries of Travelers Writing about the Muslim Pilgrimage*, New York: Grove Press, 1997.

——, *The Hadj: An American's Pilgrimage to Mecca*, New York: The Atlantic Monthly Press, 1993.

Yegenoglu, Meyda, *Colonial Fantasies: Towards a Feminist Reading of Orientalism*, Cambridge: Cambridge University Press, 1998.

Zilfi, Madeline G., ed., *Women in the Ottoman Empire: Middle Eastern Women in the Early Modern Era*, Leiden: Koninklijke Brill, 1997.

Zuhur, Sherifa, *Revealing Reveiling: Islamist Gender Ideology in Contemporary Egypt*, Albany: State University of New York Press, 1992.

Acknowledgments

There are many, many to thank:

My beloved husband, Jack Collom, for his unwavering support, patience, and love, as well as his practical help in editing my sometimes questionable prose.

My dearest godmother, Clara M. Redmond, who, though she had her doubts about this one, always gave me encouragement and the courage not to back down. I miss her.

My family—Matthew Heath and Sarah Bell, Robin Heath, Chrisopher Collom and Fotina Karavas, Joshua Lehrman and Cameron Heath—brings me such joy and laughter, and fortunately forgives me when I'm neglectful, ill-tempered, or forgetful.

My wonderful cousins, Tharwat and Karen Leggett Abouraya.

My father, who never leaves my heart and seems to sit lightly on my shoulders guiding my words and actions (the good ones). My mother, the fiery *djinn* whose memory—when I let her out of the bottle—eggs me on.

My agent, Ellen Geiger, who, speaking of risks, is willing to entertain even my most arcane and nuttiest ideas and is the angel who has kept my writing life going.

Jan-Erik Guerth, my editor at HiddenSpring, had faith in this project from the moment it was proposed a year before September 11, 2001, when few seemed interested. After the tragedy, ears perked up, and books about Islam have poured into the marketplace. Jan-Erik was keen to take chances regardless of geo-politics, fashion, or the media.

Rosemary Ahern, Gloria Bartek, Lucia Berlin, Norene Berry, Henrik Boes, Reed Bye, Mary Chandler, Susie Chandler, Nan De

Grove, Debra Denker, Linda Dettling, Janine Gastineau, Jim Geiser, Nell Geiser, J. Gluckstern, Bobbie Louise Hawkins, Nita Hill, Caroline Hinkley, Judith Hussie-Taylor, Stefan Hyner, Lucy Lippard, Tenah Johnson, Harun Omar, Soraya Omar, Sulleiman Omar, Wahid Omar, Patrick Pritchett, Sheryl Shapiro, Rickie Solinger, Karin Sturm, Betsy Tobin, Lisa Trank, John Wright, Sahar Warraq, Barbara Wilder, David Wilson, Peter Lamborn Wilson, Jane Wodening, Michael Wolfe…friends, indeed.

Sandra Simpson Wilson, whose death in May 2002 was an inexpressible blow.

Steven Blackburn, head librarian at the Hartford Seminary, without whom I'd have been paralyzed.

The scholars. To them, I again offer an apology for my loose footnotes and other scholarly gaffs. Through this book, I have come to appreciate their work as never before and because of their efforts found more pleasure than ever in research.

Annemarie Schimmel, who died in Bonn, Germany, on January 26, 2003, just as I was finishing this book. I dearly wish I could have met her, and I am, as we all should be, intensely appreciative of the all-consuming passion that brought to light so much we in the West might never know about Islam.

All women of Islam, past and present, for they are truly inspirations.

And others. My gratitude is impossible to measure. I send you blessings and prayers for peace.